Shojo Beat

# OTOMEN

Story & Art by
Aya Kanno

Volume
TWO

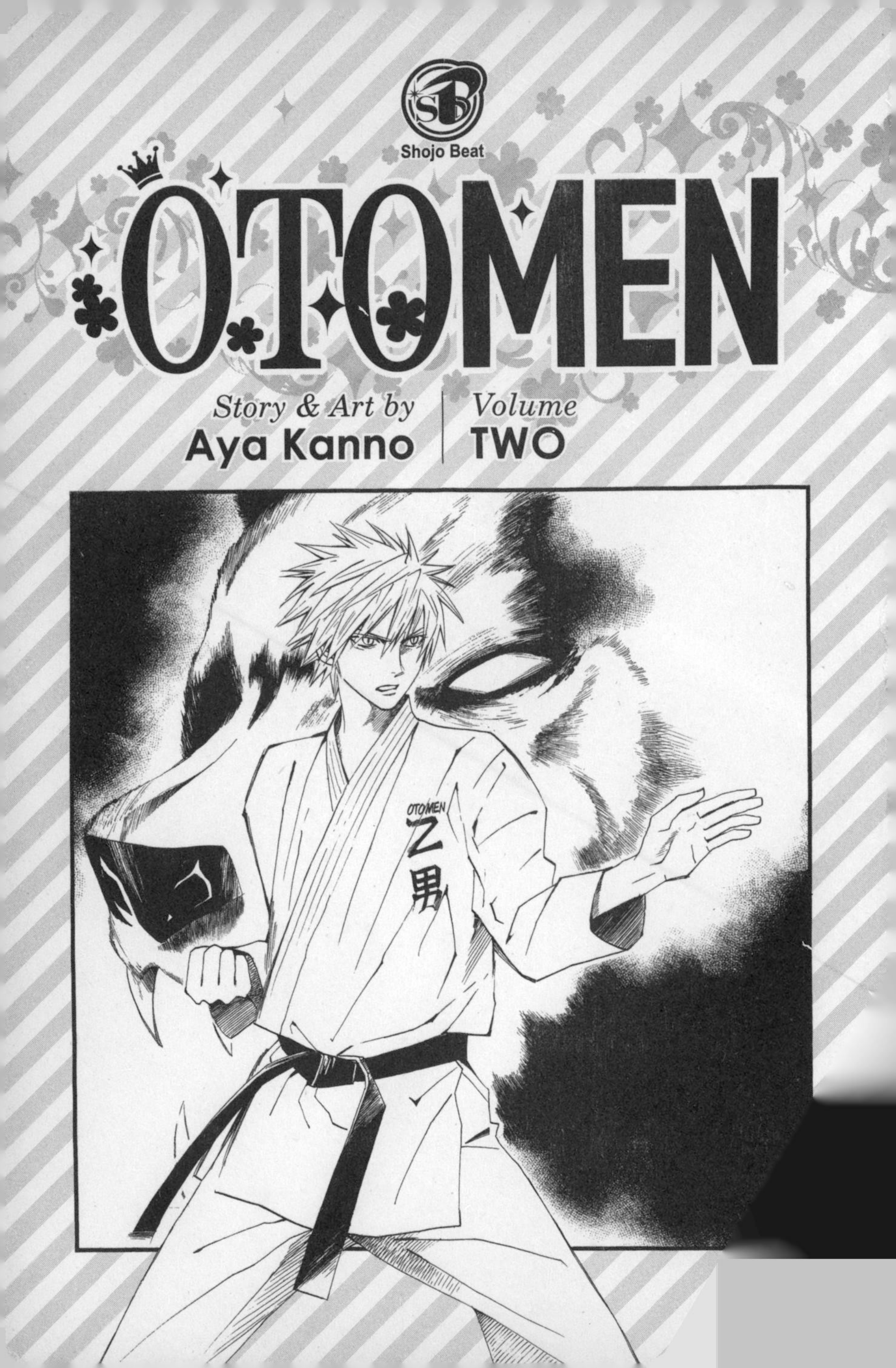
OTOMEN
乙男

# OTOMEN *volume 2* CONTENTS

OTOMEN 05

GLOSSARY 187

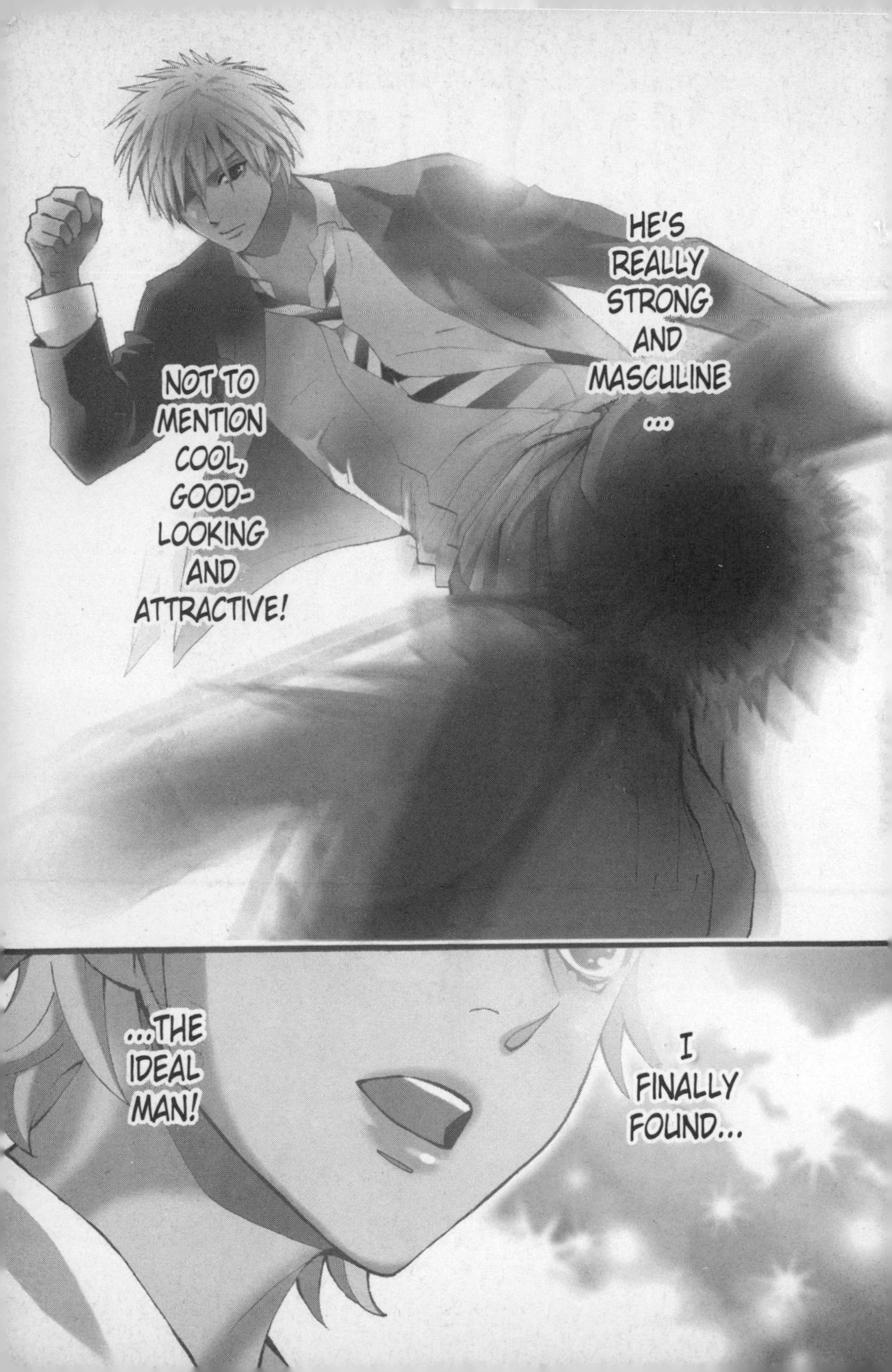
HE'S REALLY STRONG AND MASCULINE...
NOT TO MENTION COOL, GOOD-LOOKING AND ATTRACTIVE!
I FINALLY FOUND...
...THE IDEAL MAN!

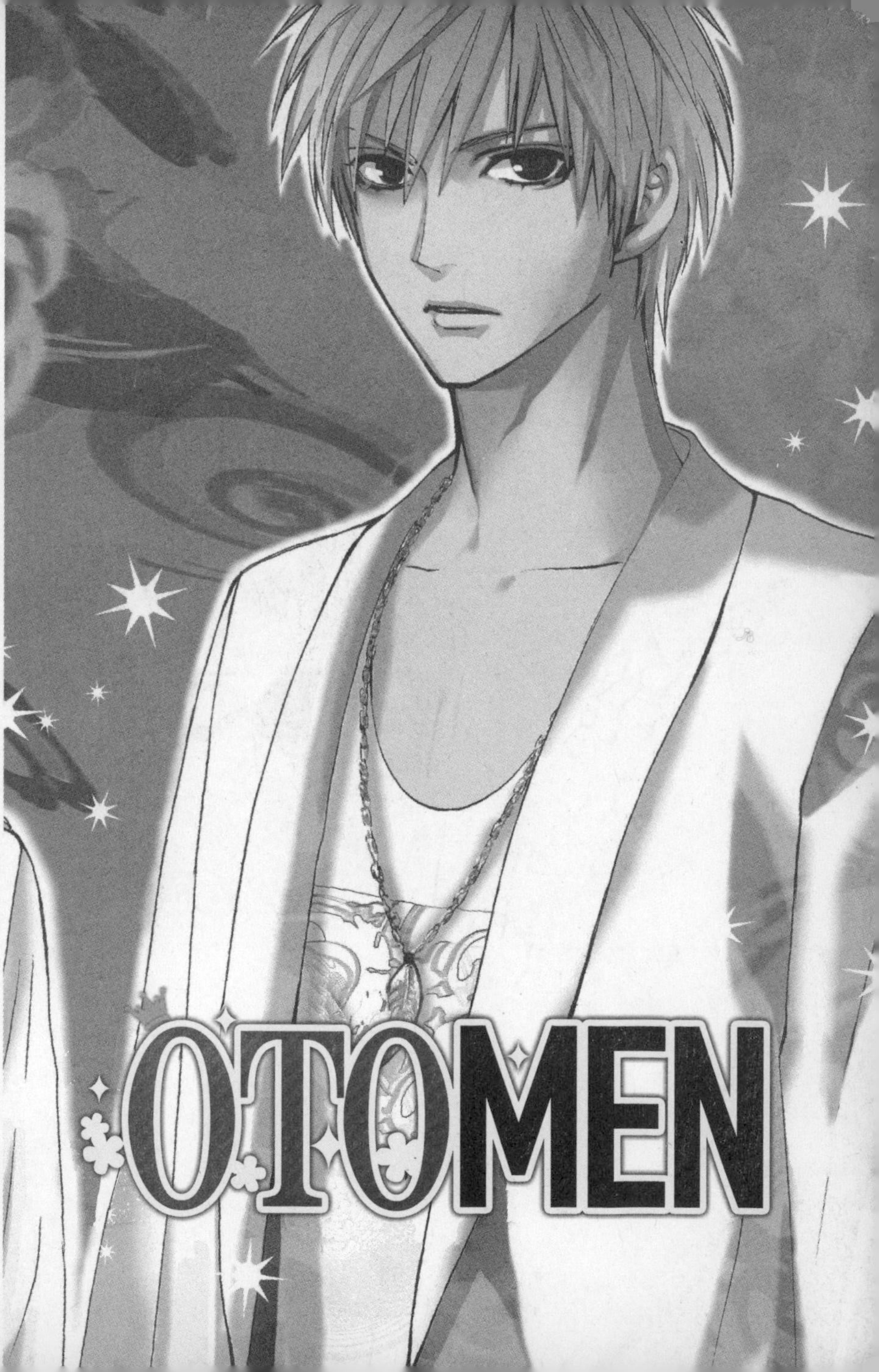
OTOMEN

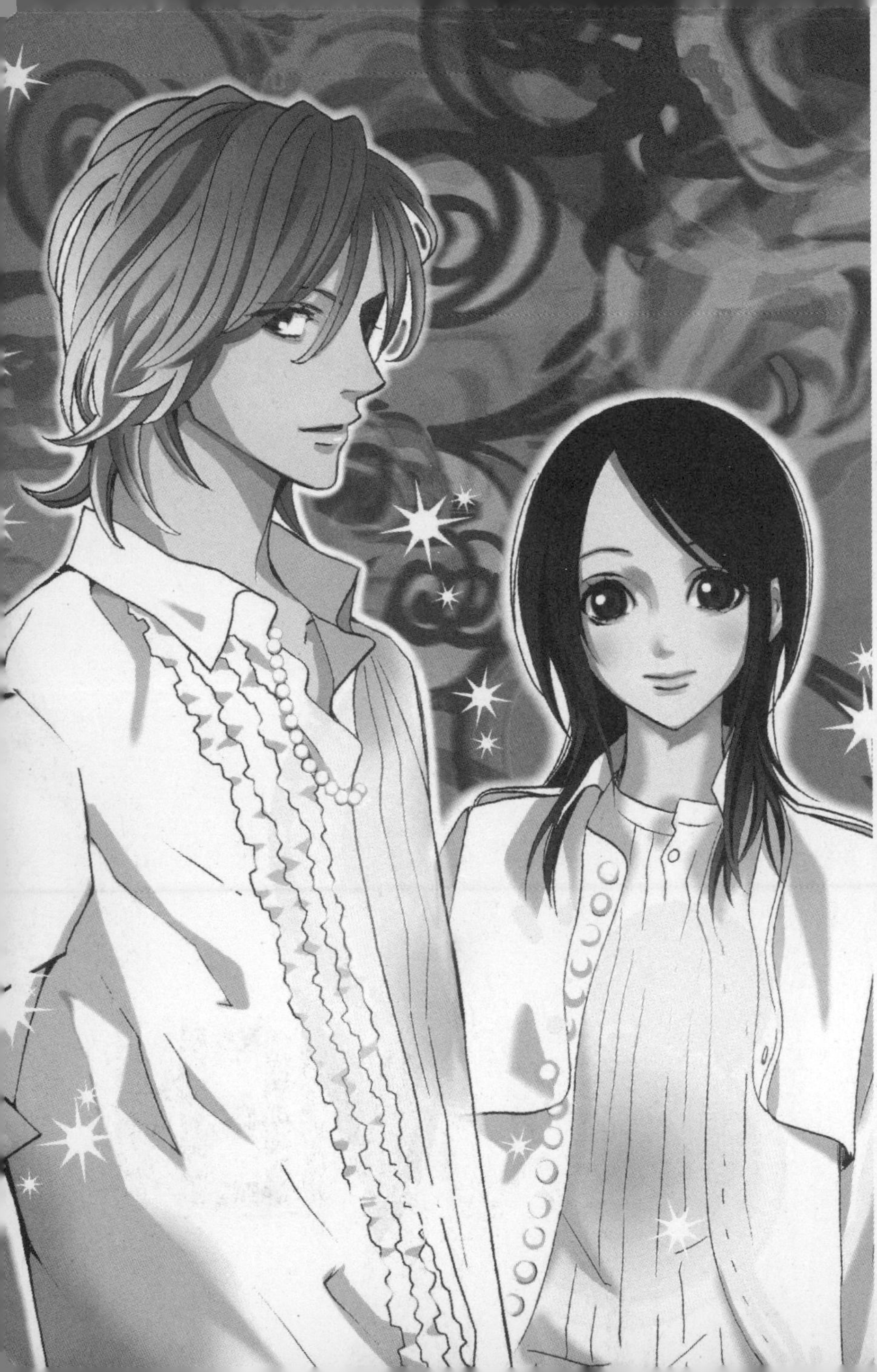

OTOMEN

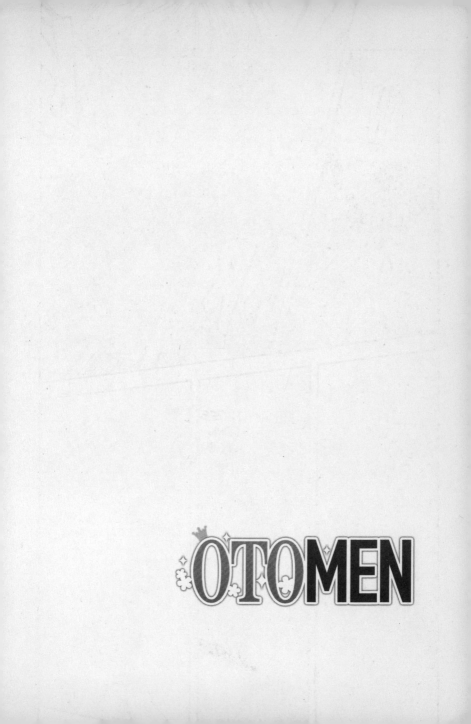

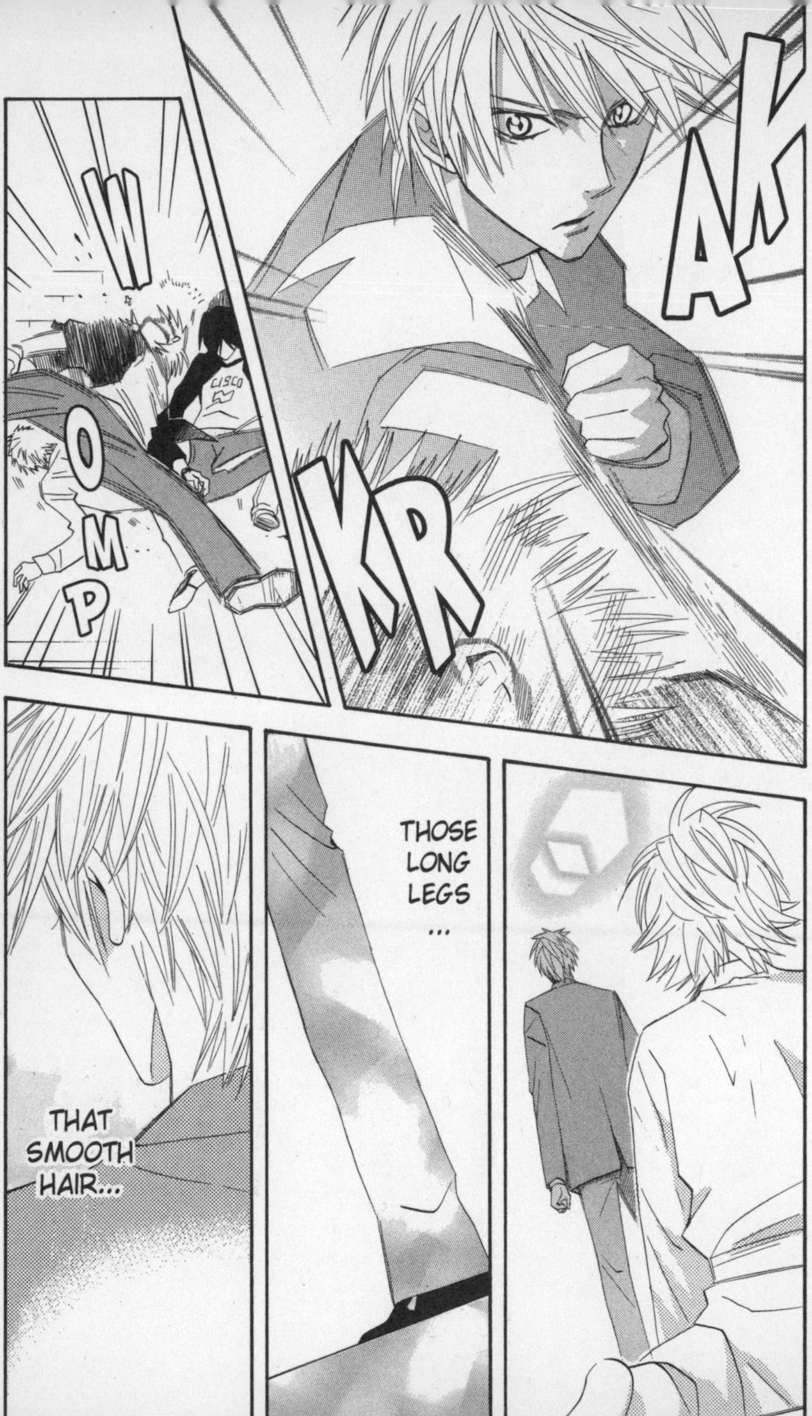
KR
AK
WOMP
CISCO
THOSE LONG LEGS ...
THAT SMOOTH HAIR...

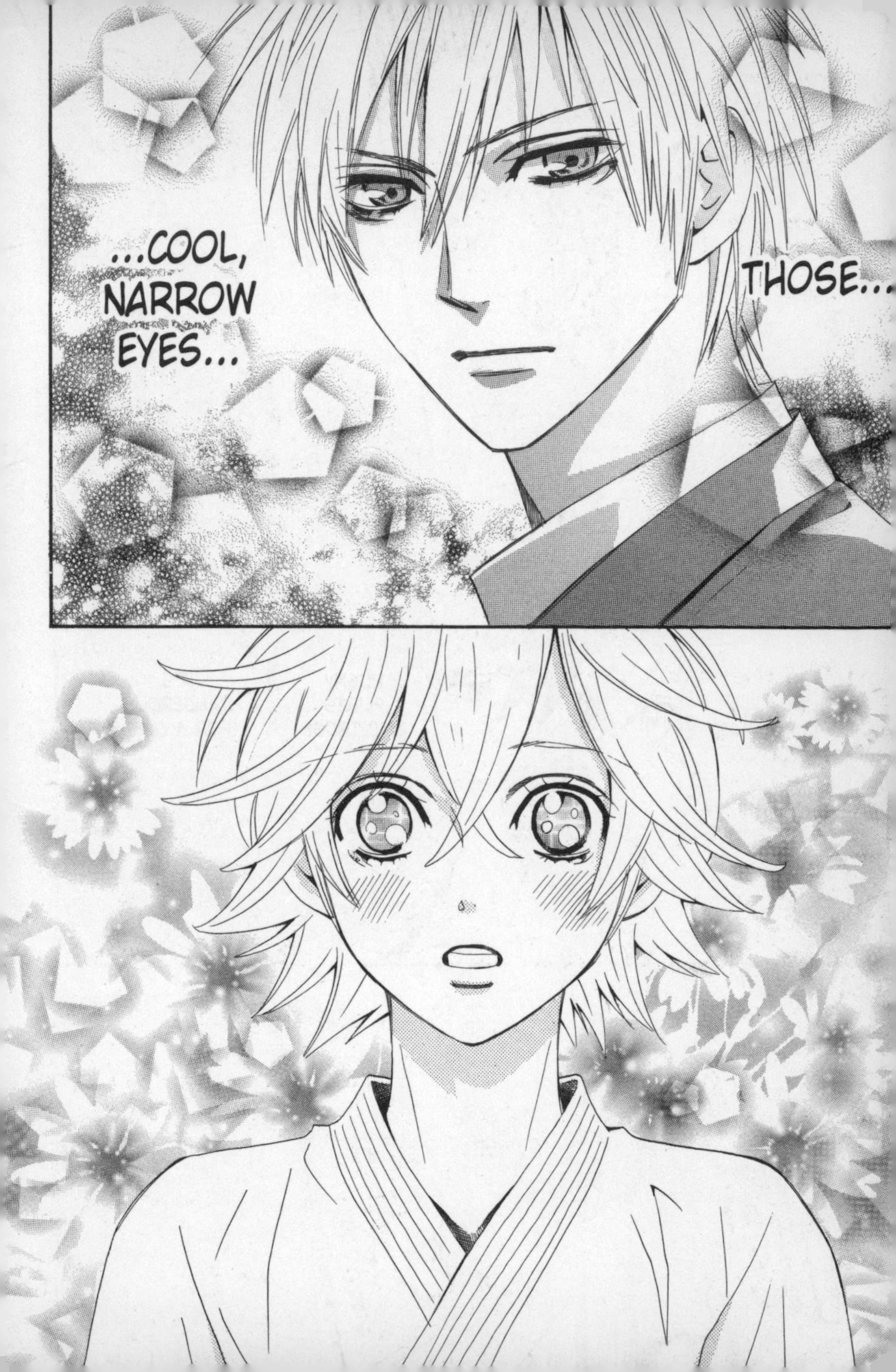
THOSE...
...COOL, NARROW EYES...

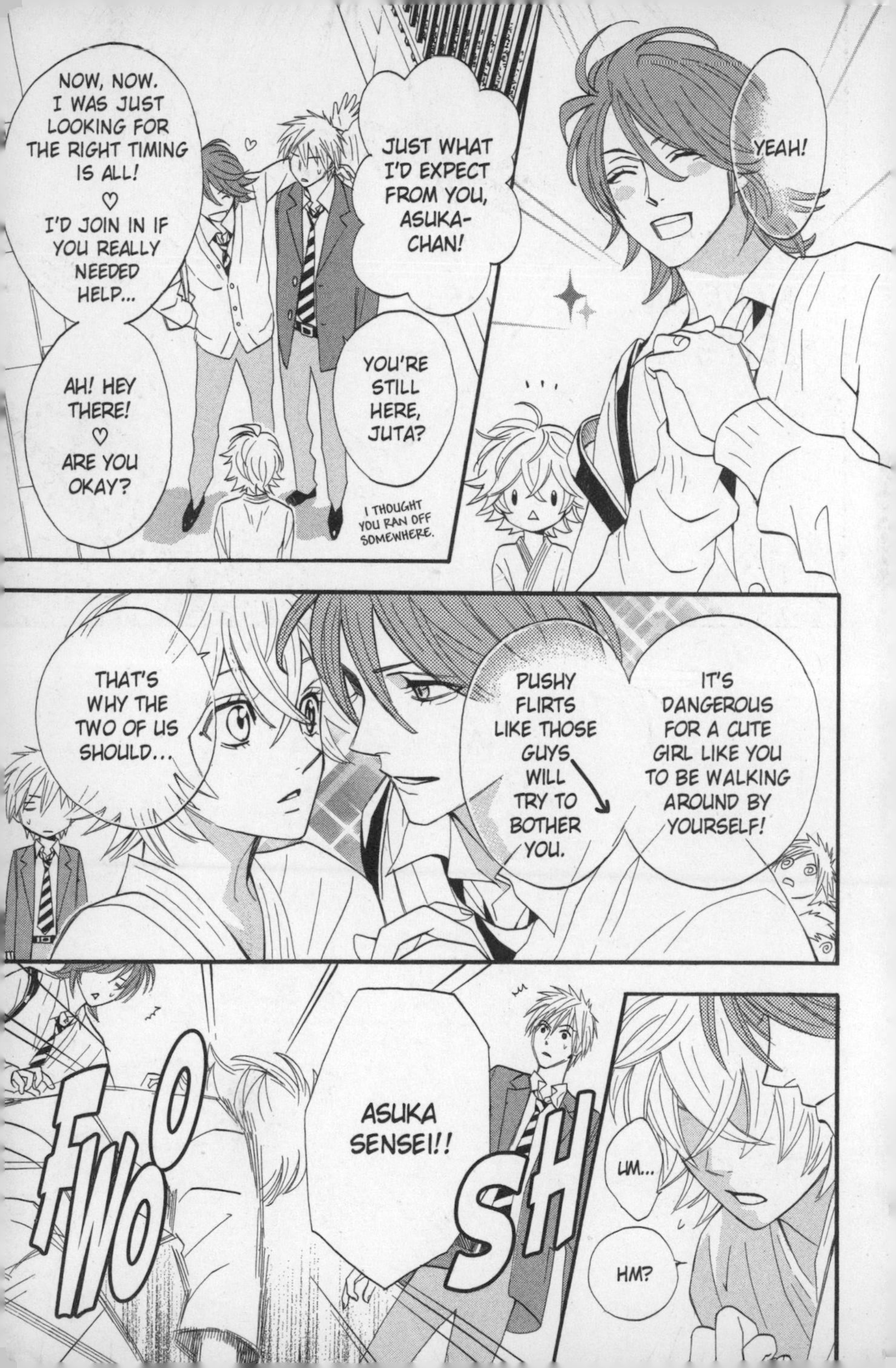
YEAH!
JUST WHAT I'D EXPECT FROM YOU, ASUKA-CHAN!
NOW, NOW. I WAS JUST LOOKING FOR THE RIGHT TIMING IS ALL! ♡ I'D JOIN IN IF YOU REALLY NEEDED HELP...
YOU'RE STILL HERE, JUTA?
I THOUGHT YOU RAN OFF SOMEWHERE.
AH! HEY THERE! ♡ ARE YOU OKAY?
IT'S DANGEROUS FOR A CUTE GIRL LIKE YOU TO BE WALKING AROUND BY YOURSELF!
PUSHY FLIRTS LIKE THOSE GUYS WILL TRY TO BOTHER YOU.
THAT'S WHY THE TWO OF US SHOULD...
UM...
HM?
ASUKA SENSEI!!
FWOOSH

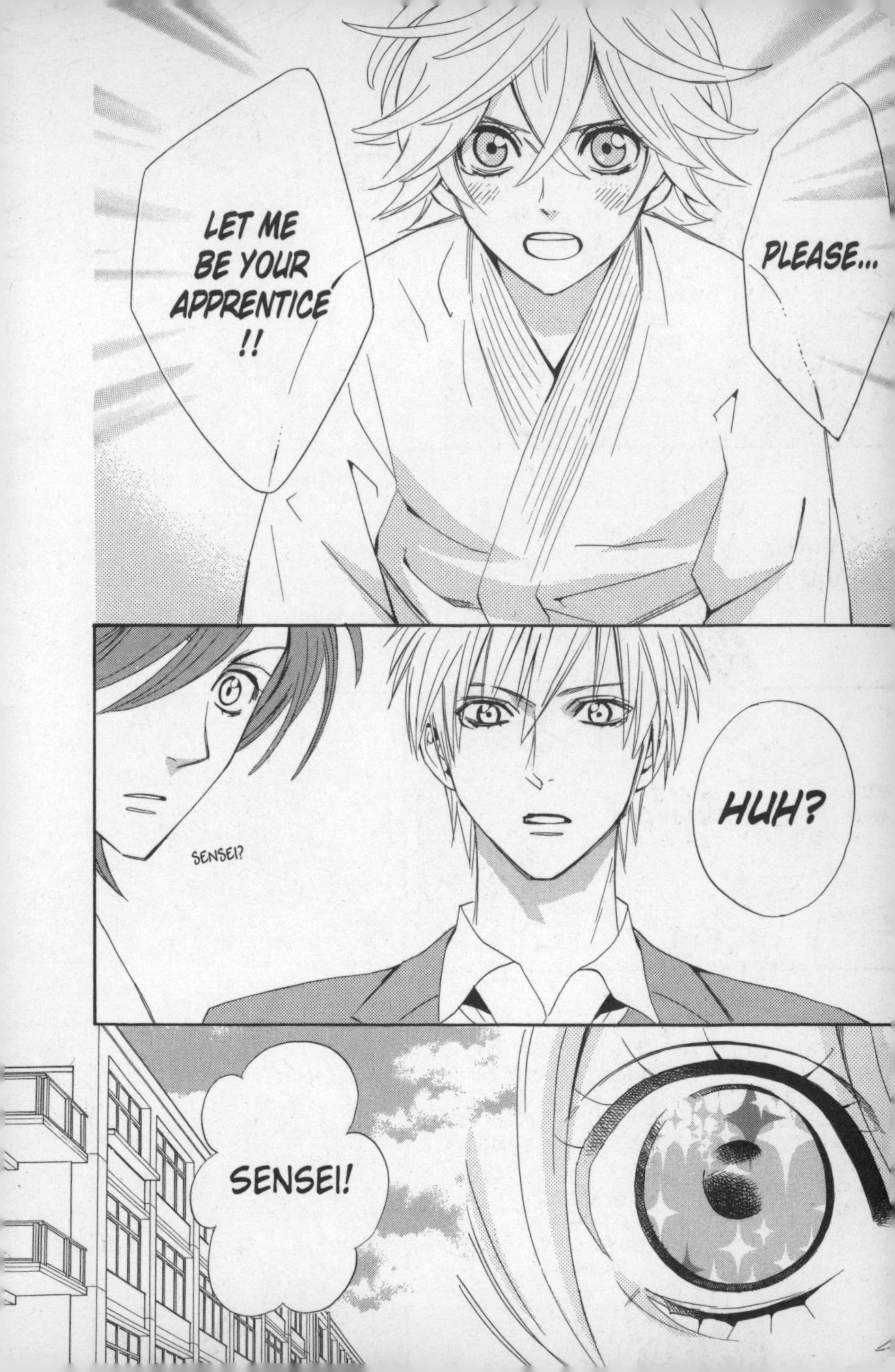
PLEASE...
LET ME BE YOUR APPRENTICE !!
HUH?
SENSEI?
SENSEI!

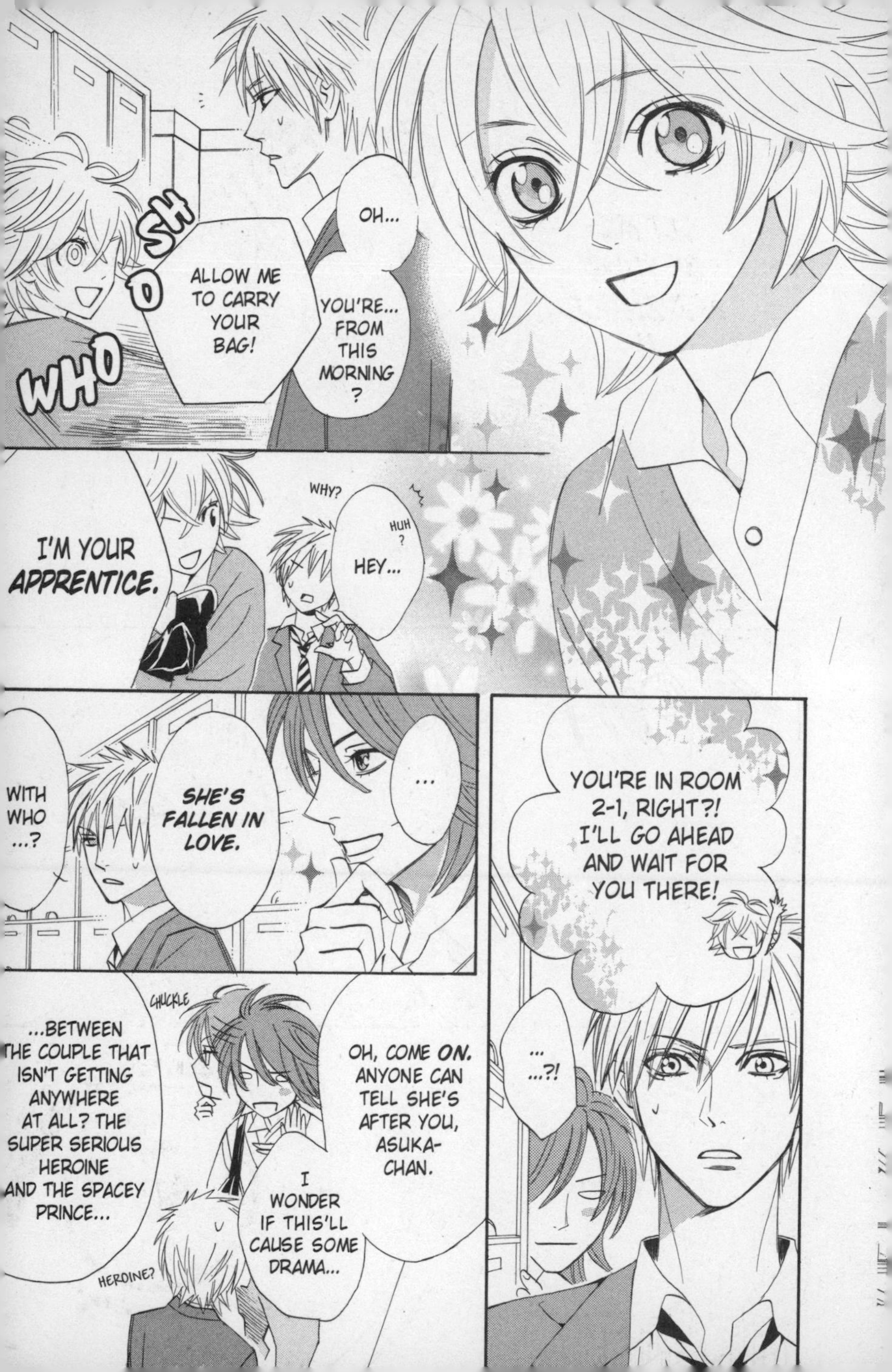
OH...
YOU'RE... FROM THIS MORNING?
ALLOW ME TO CARRY YOUR BAG!
WHOOSH
HUH?
HEY...
WHY?
I'M YOUR APPRENTICE.
YOU'RE IN ROOM 2-1, RIGHT?! I'LL GO AHEAD AND WAIT FOR YOU THERE!
... ...?!
...
SHE'S FALLEN IN LOVE.
WITH WHO ...?
OH, COME ON. ANYONE CAN TELL SHE'S AFTER YOU, ASUKA-CHAN.
CHUCKLE
...BETWEEN THE COUPLE THAT ISN'T GETTING ANYWHERE AT ALL? THE SUPER SERIOUS HEROINE AND THE SPACEY PRINCE...
I WONDER IF THIS'LL CAUSE SOME DRAMA...
HEROINE?

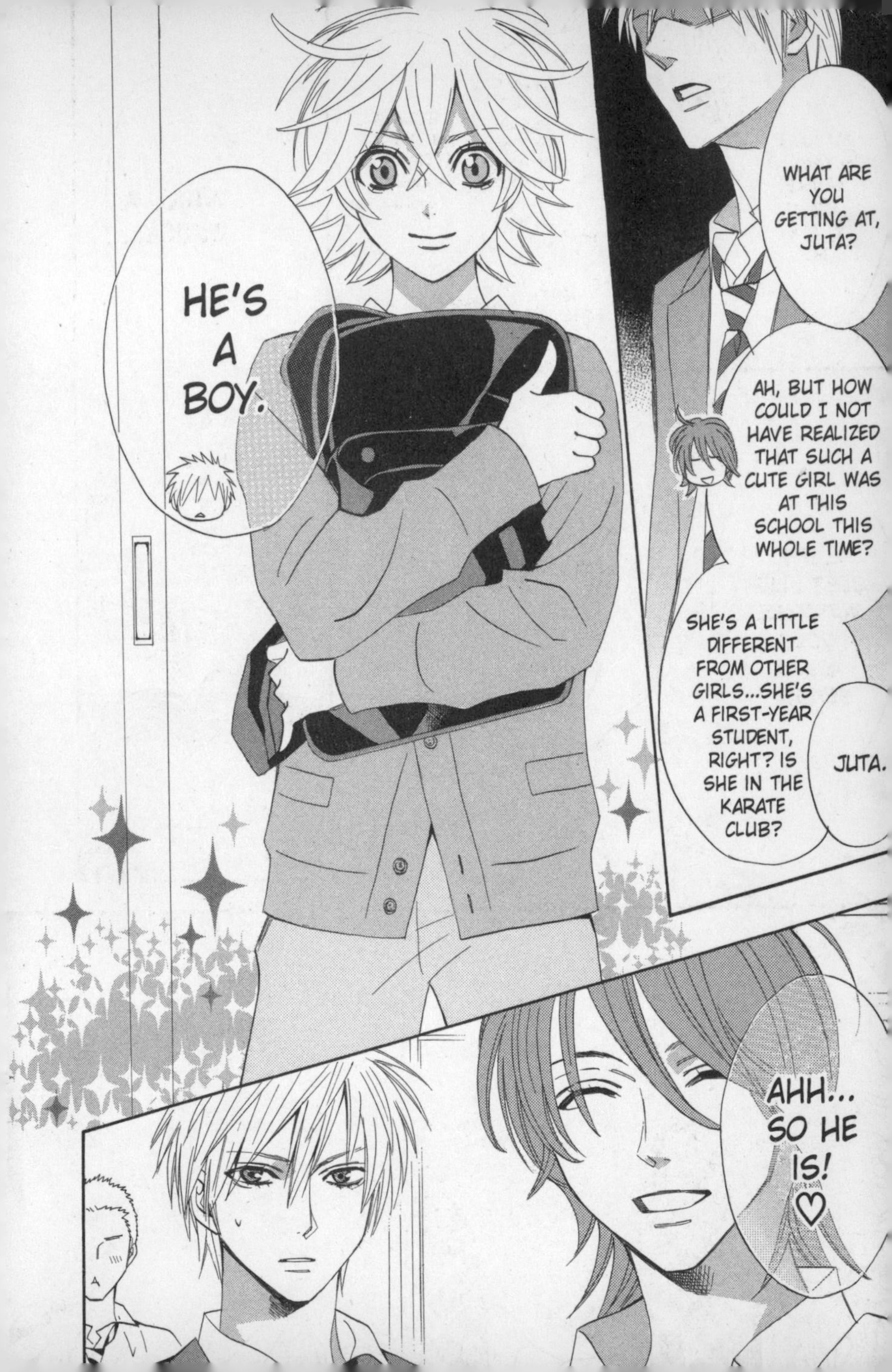
WHAT ARE YOU GETTING AT, JUTA?
AH, BUT HOW COULD I NOT HAVE REALIZED THAT SUCH A CUTE GIRL WAS AT THIS SCHOOL THIS WHOLE TIME?
SHE'S A LITTLE DIFFERENT FROM OTHER GIRLS...SHE'S A FIRST-YEAR STUDENT, RIGHT? IS SHE IN THE KARATE CLUB?
JUTA.
HE'S A BOY.
AHH... SO HE IS! ♡

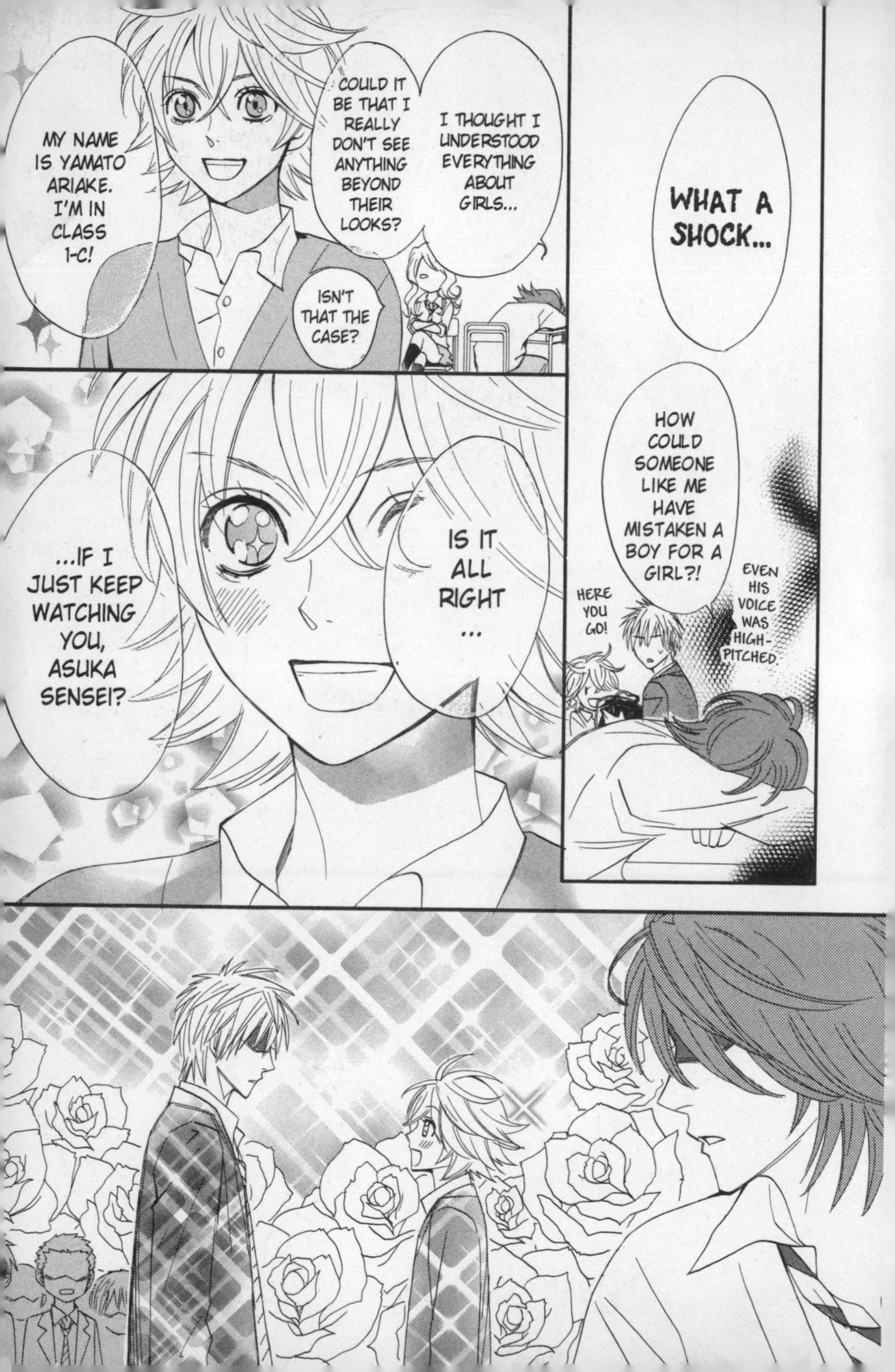
WHAT A SHOCK...
HOW COULD SOMEONE LIKE ME HAVE MISTAKEN A BOY FOR A GIRL?!
EVEN HIS VOICE WAS HIGH-PITCHED.
HERE YOU GO!
I THOUGHT I UNDERSTOOD EVERYTHING ABOUT GIRLS...
COULD IT BE THAT I REALLY DON'T SEE ANYTHING BEYOND THEIR LOOKS?
ISN'T THAT THE CASE?
MY NAME IS YAMATO ARIAKE. I'M IN CLASS 1-C!
IS IT ALL RIGHT ...
...IF I JUST KEEP WATCHING YOU, ASUKA SENSEI?

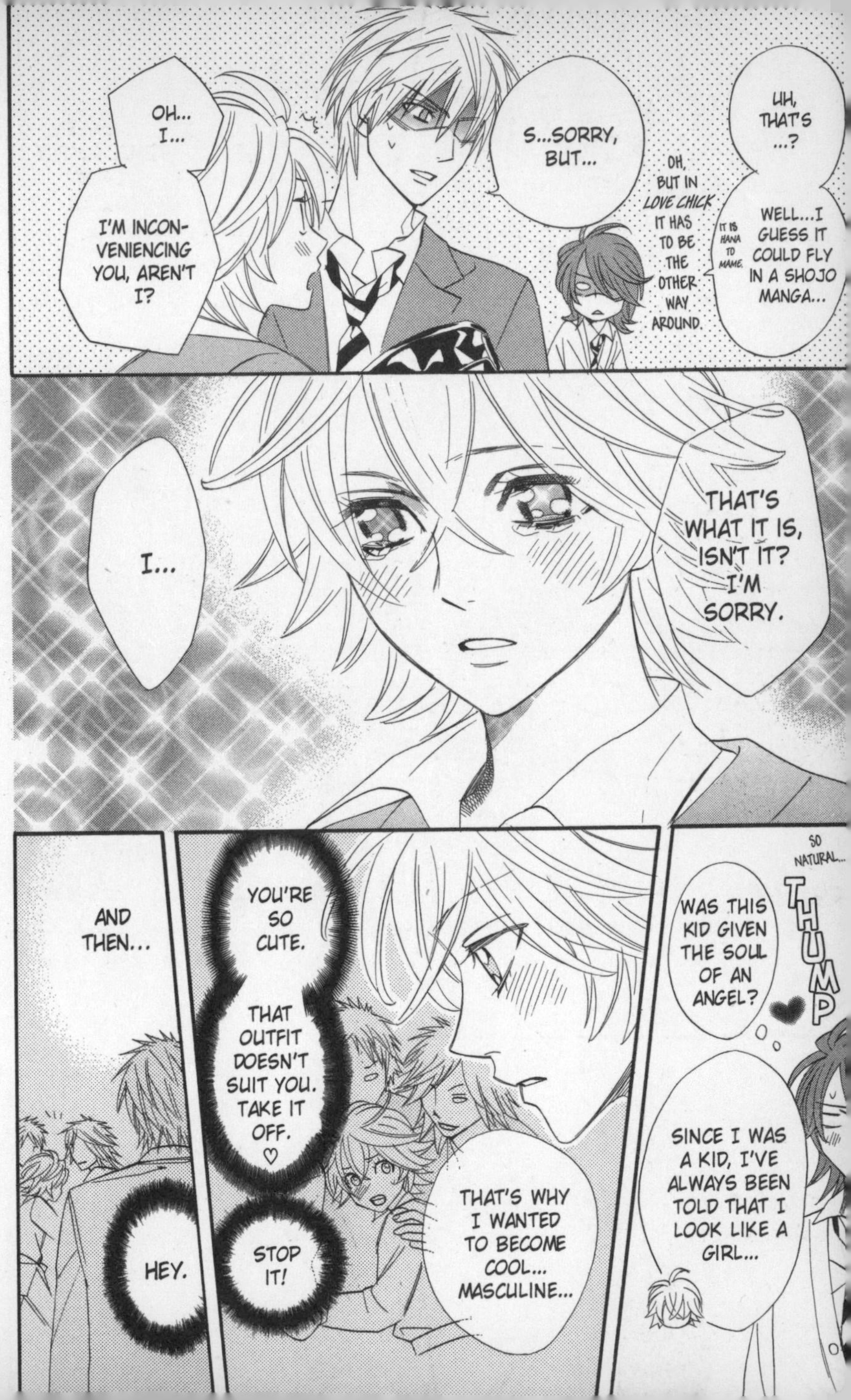
UH, THAT'S ...?
WELL...I GUESS IT COULD FLY IN A SHOJO MANGA...
IT IS HANA TO MAME.
OH, BUT IN LOVE CHICK IT HAS TO BE THE OTHER WAY AROUND.
S...SORRY, BUT...
OH... I...
I'M INCON-VENIENCING YOU, AREN'T I?
THAT'S WHAT IT IS, ISN'T IT? I'M SORRY.
I...
SO NATURAL...
THUMP
WAS THIS KID GIVEN THE SOUL OF AN ANGEL?
SINCE I WAS A KID, I'VE ALWAYS BEEN TOLD THAT I LOOK LIKE A GIRL...
THAT'S WHY I WANTED TO BECOME COOL... MASCULINE...
YOU'RE SO CUTE.
THAT OUTFIT DOESN'T SUIT YOU. TAKE IT OFF. ♡
STOP IT!
AND THEN...
HEY.

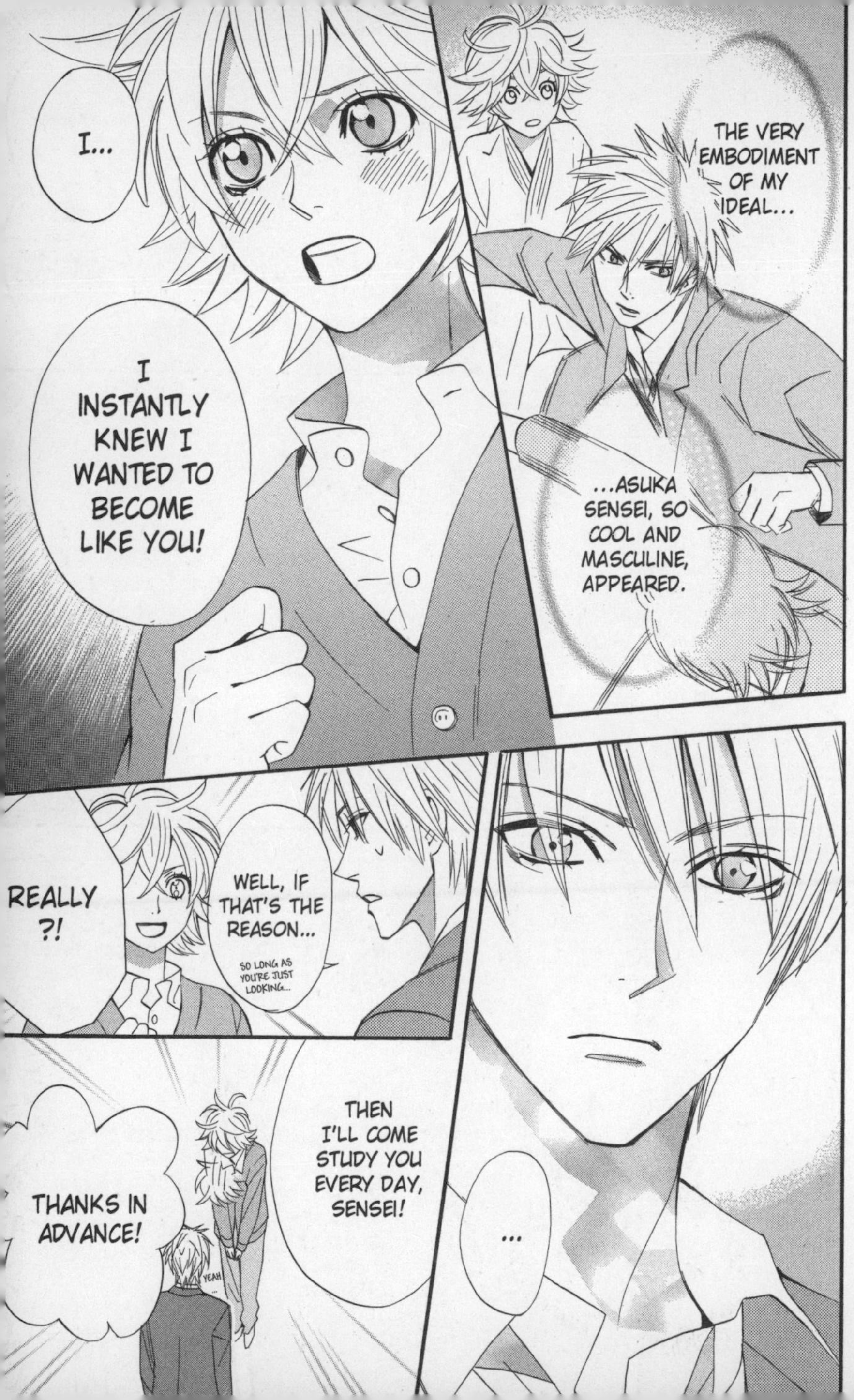
THE VERY EMBODIMENT OF MY IDEAL...
...ASUKA SENSEI, SO COOL AND MASCULINE, APPEARED.
I...
I INSTANTLY KNEW I WANTED TO BECOME LIKE YOU!
...
WELL, IF THAT'S THE REASON...
SO LONG AS YOU'RE JUST LOOKING...
REALLY ?!
THEN I'LL COME STUDY YOU EVERY DAY, SENSEI!
THANKS IN ADVANCE!
YEAH ...

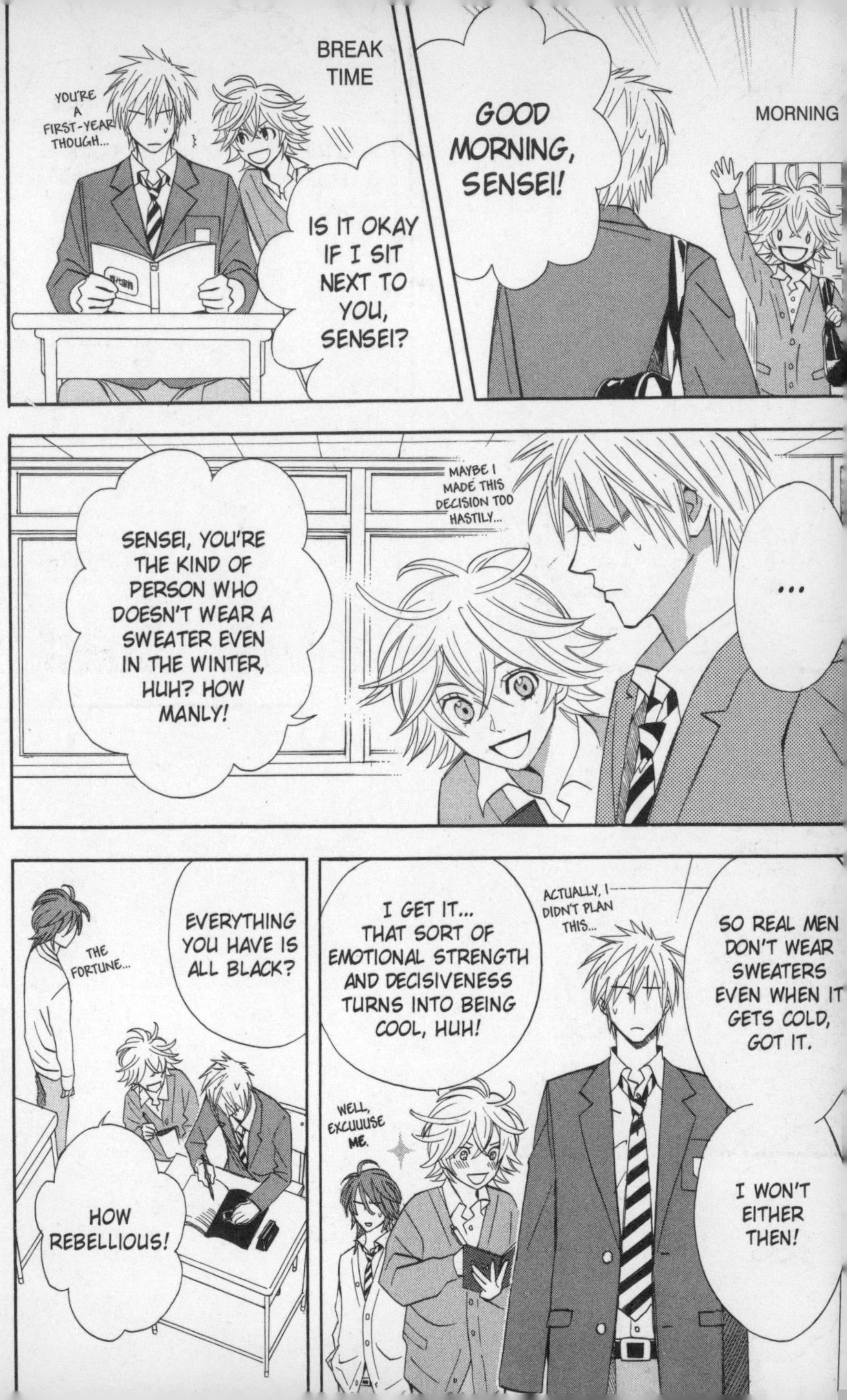
MORNING
GOOD MORNING, SENSEI!
BREAK TIME
IS IT OKAY IF I SIT NEXT TO YOU, SENSEI?
YOU'RE A FIRST-YEAR THOUGH...
...
MAYBE I MADE THIS DECISION TOO HASTILY...
SENSEI, YOU'RE THE KIND OF PERSON WHO DOESN'T WEAR A SWEATER EVEN IN THE WINTER, HUH? HOW MANLY!
SO REAL MEN DON'T WEAR SWEATERS EVEN WHEN IT GETS COLD, GOT IT.
ACTUALLY, I DIDN'T PLAN THIS...
I GET IT... THAT SORT OF EMOTIONAL STRENGTH AND DECISIVENESS TURNS INTO BEING COOL, HUH!
I WON'T EITHER THEN!
WELL, EXCUUUSE ME.
EVERYTHING YOU HAVE IS ALL BLACK?
THE FORTUNE...
HOW REBELLIOUS!

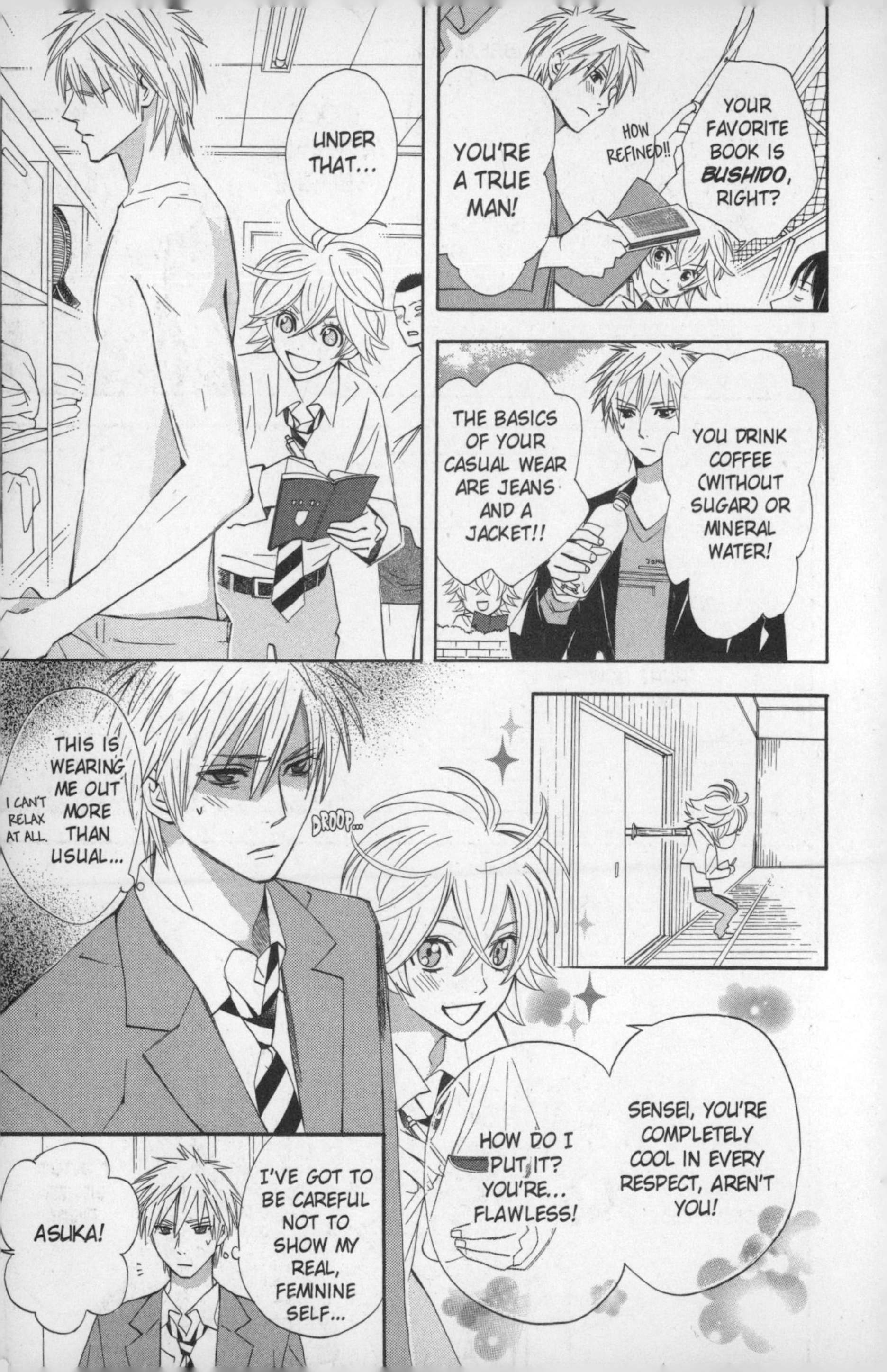
YOUR FAVORITE BOOK IS BUSHIDO, RIGHT?
HOW REFINED!!
YOU'RE A TRUE MAN!
YOU DRINK COFFEE (WITHOUT SUGAR) OR MINERAL WATER!
THE BASICS OF YOUR CASUAL WEAR ARE JEANS AND A JACKET!!
UNDER THAT...
SENSEI, YOU'RE COMPLETELY COOL IN EVERY RESPECT, AREN'T YOU!
HOW DO I PUT IT? YOU'RE... FLAWLESS!
DROOP...
THIS IS WEARING ME OUT MORE THAN USUAL...
I CAN'T RELAX AT ALL.
I'VE GOT TO BE CAREFUL NOT TO SHOW MY REAL, FEMININE SELF...
ASUKA!

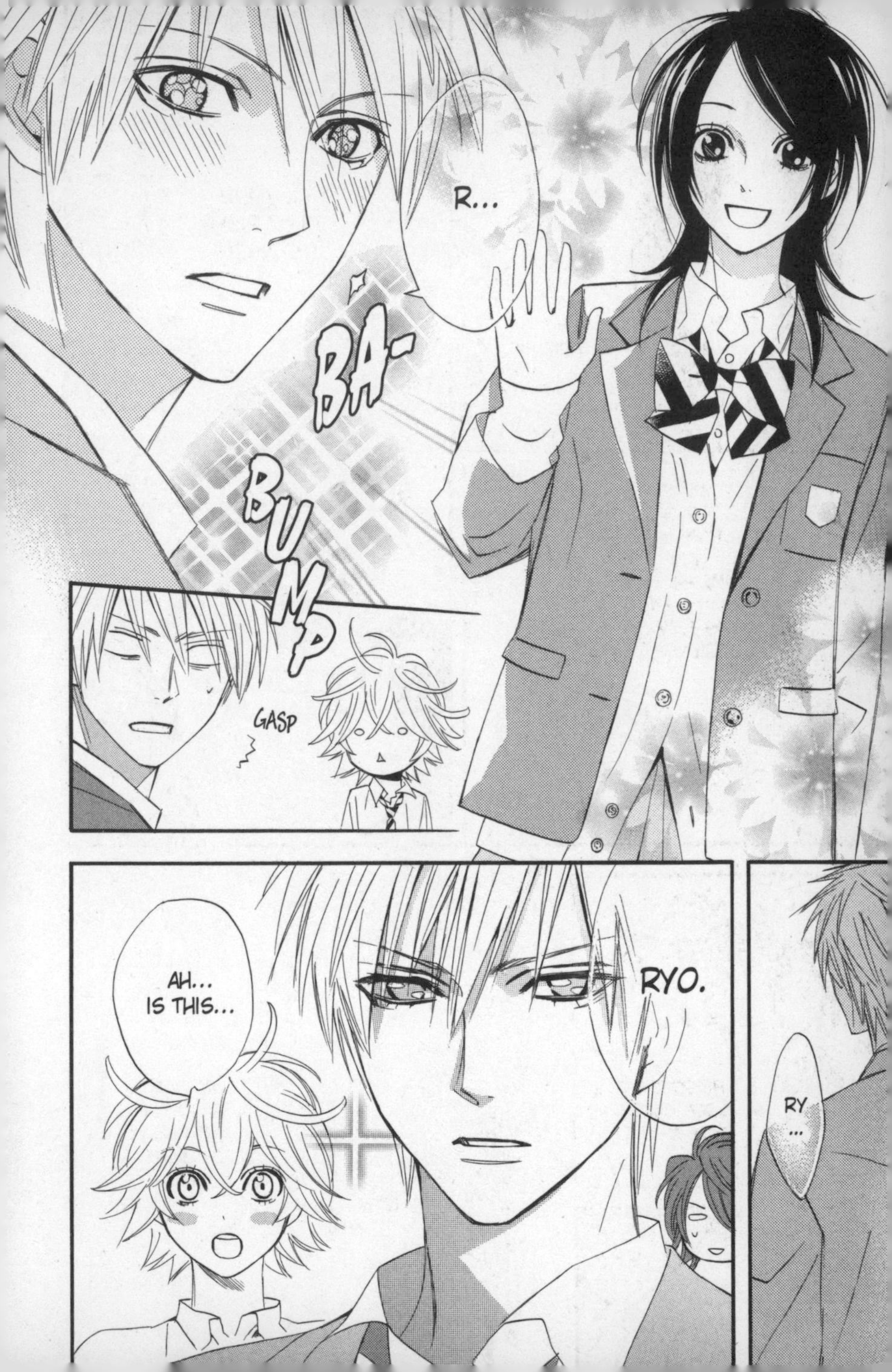
R...
BA-BUMP
GASP
RY ...
RYO.
AH... IS THIS...

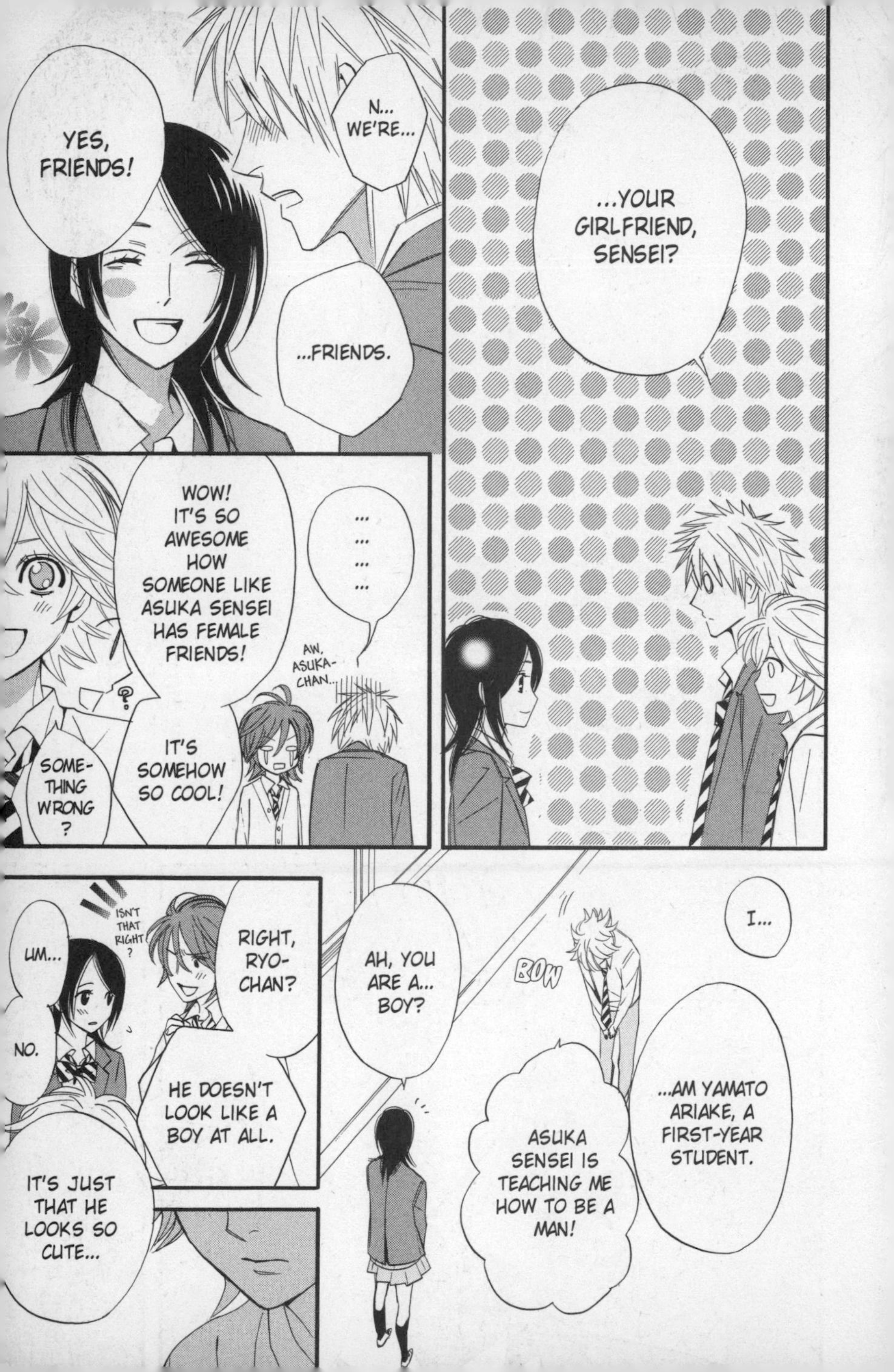

...YOUR GIRLFRIEND, SENSEI?
N... WE'RE...
YES, FRIENDS!
...FRIENDS.
...
...
...
...
AW, ASUKA-CHAN...
WOW! IT'S SO AWESOME HOW SOMEONE LIKE ASUKA SENSEI HAS FEMALE FRIENDS!
IT'S SOMEHOW SO COOL!
?
SOME-THING WRONG?
I...
BOW
...AM YAMATO ARIAKE, A FIRST-YEAR STUDENT.
ASUKA SENSEI IS TEACHING ME HOW TO BE A MAN!
AH, YOU ARE A... BOY?
RIGHT, RYO-CHAN?
ISN'T THAT RIGHT?
UM...
NO.
HE DOESN'T LOOK LIKE A BOY AT ALL.
IT'S JUST THAT HE LOOKS SO CUTE...

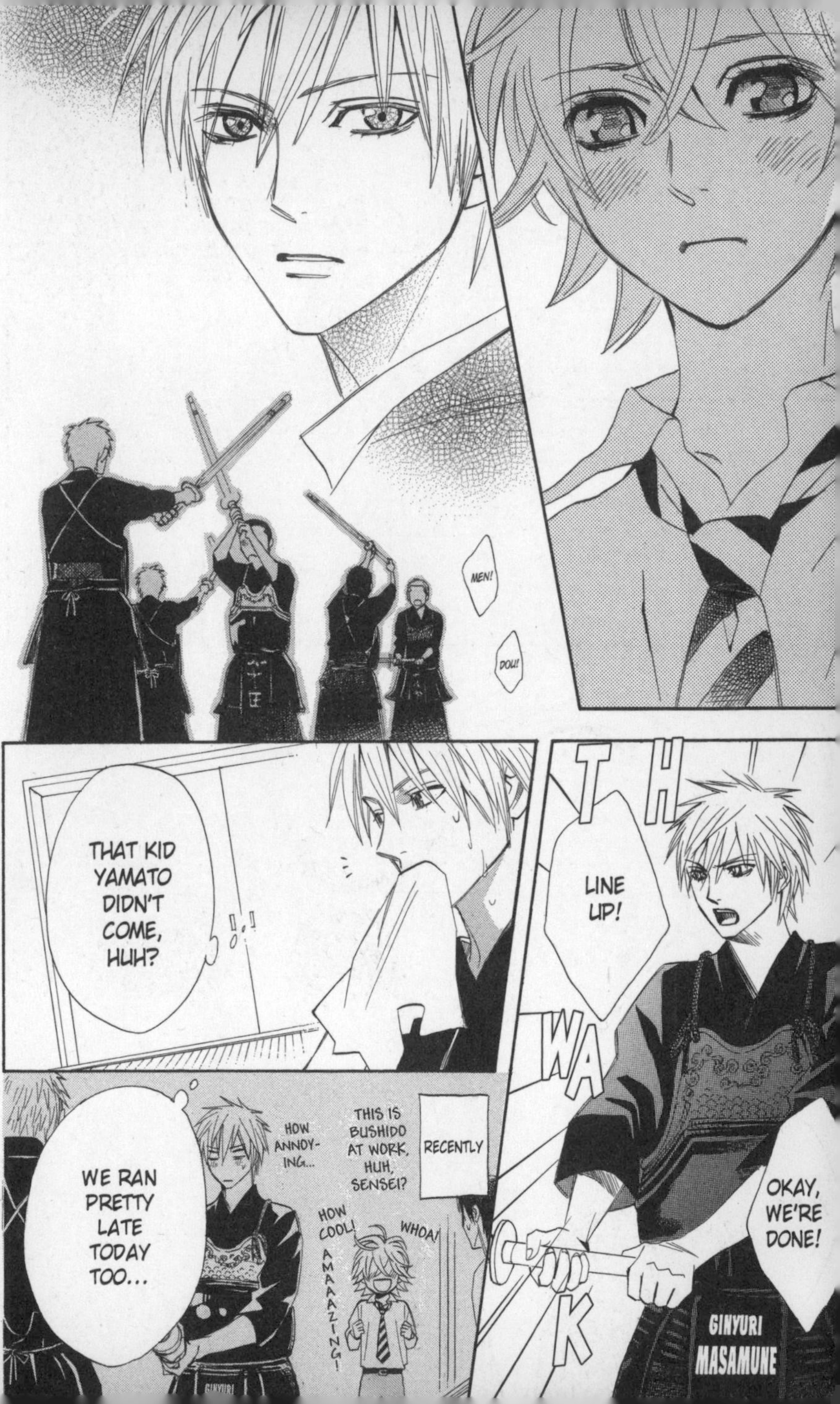
MEN!
DOU!
LINE UP!
THWAK
OKAY, WE'RE DONE!
GINYURI MASAMUNE
THAT KID YAMATO DIDN'T COME, HUH?
!!
RECENTLY
THIS IS BUSHIDO AT WORK, HUH, SENSEI?
HOW ANNOYING...
WHOA!
HOW COOL!
AMAAAZING!
WE RAN PRETTY LATE TODAY TOO...

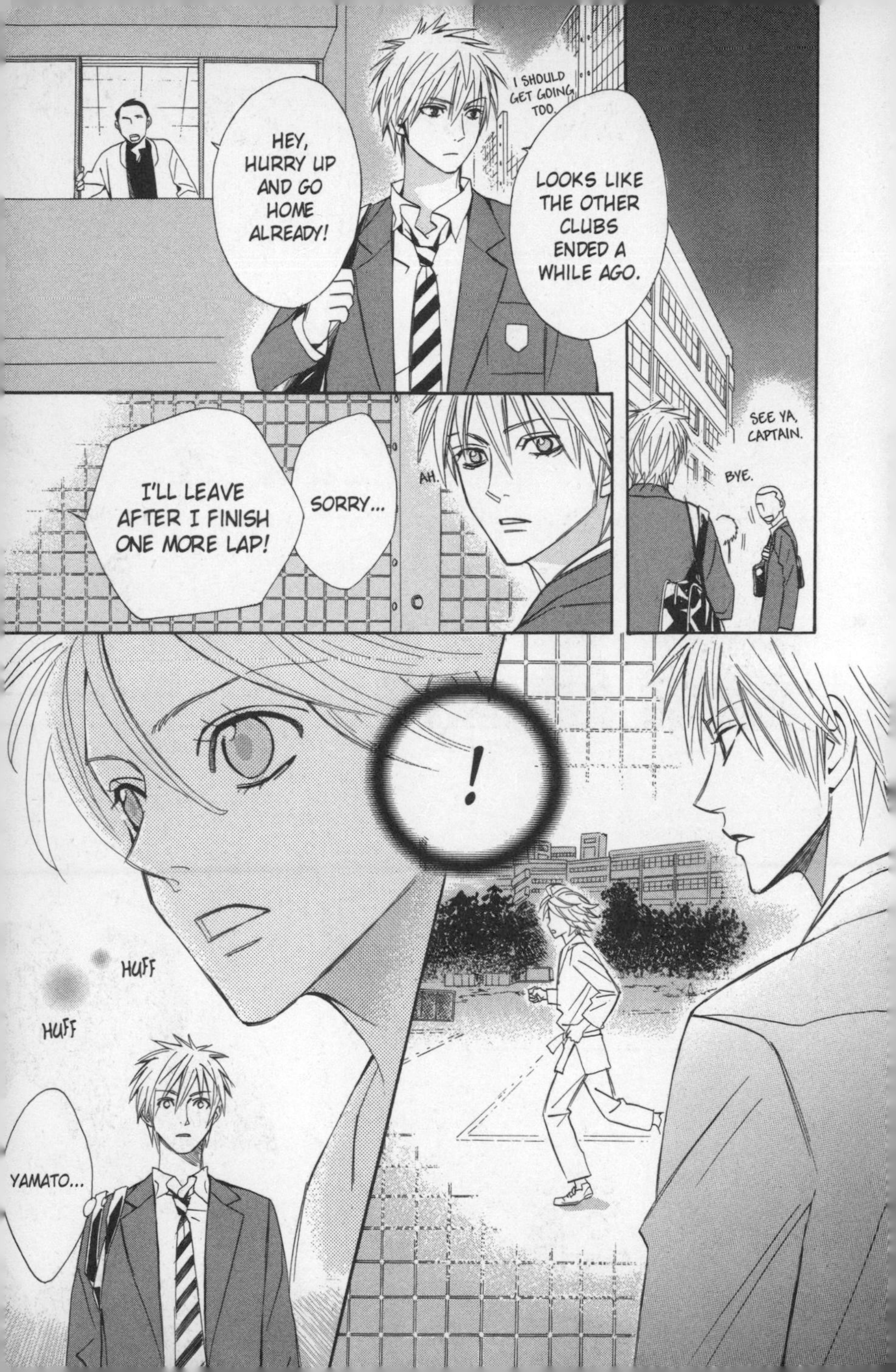
I SHOULD GET GOING TOO.
LOOKS LIKE THE OTHER CLUBS ENDED A WHILE AGO.
HEY, HURRY UP AND GO HOME ALREADY!
SEE YA, CAPTAIN.
BYE.
AH.
SORRY...
I'LL LEAVE AFTER I FINISH ONE MORE LAP!
!
HUFF
HUFF
YAMATO...

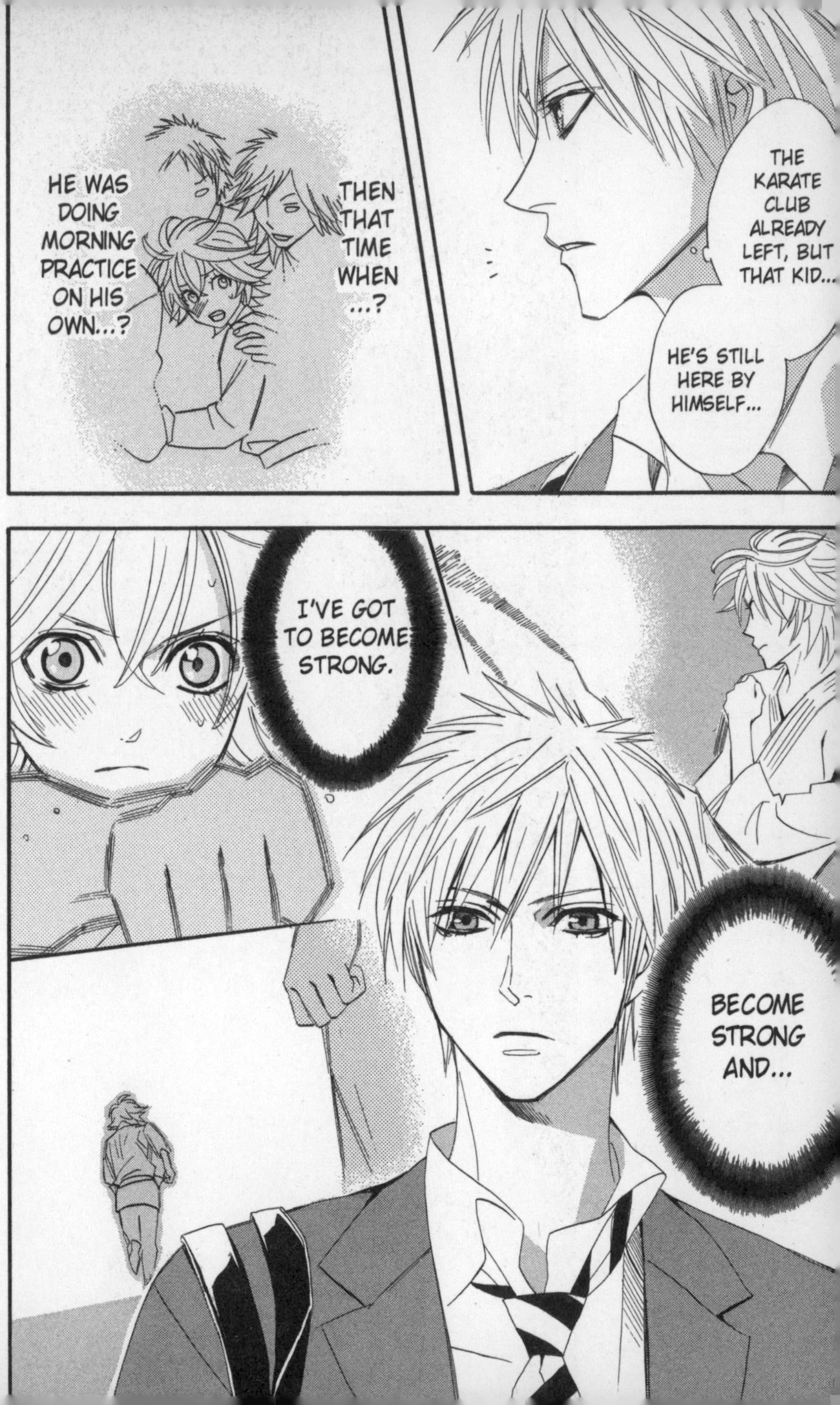
THE KARATE CLUB ALREADY LEFT, BUT THAT KID...
HE'S STILL HERE BY HIMSELF...
THEN THAT TIME WHEN ...?
HE WAS DOING MORNING PRACTICE ON HIS OWN...?
I'VE GOT TO BECOME STRONG.
BECOME STRONG AND...

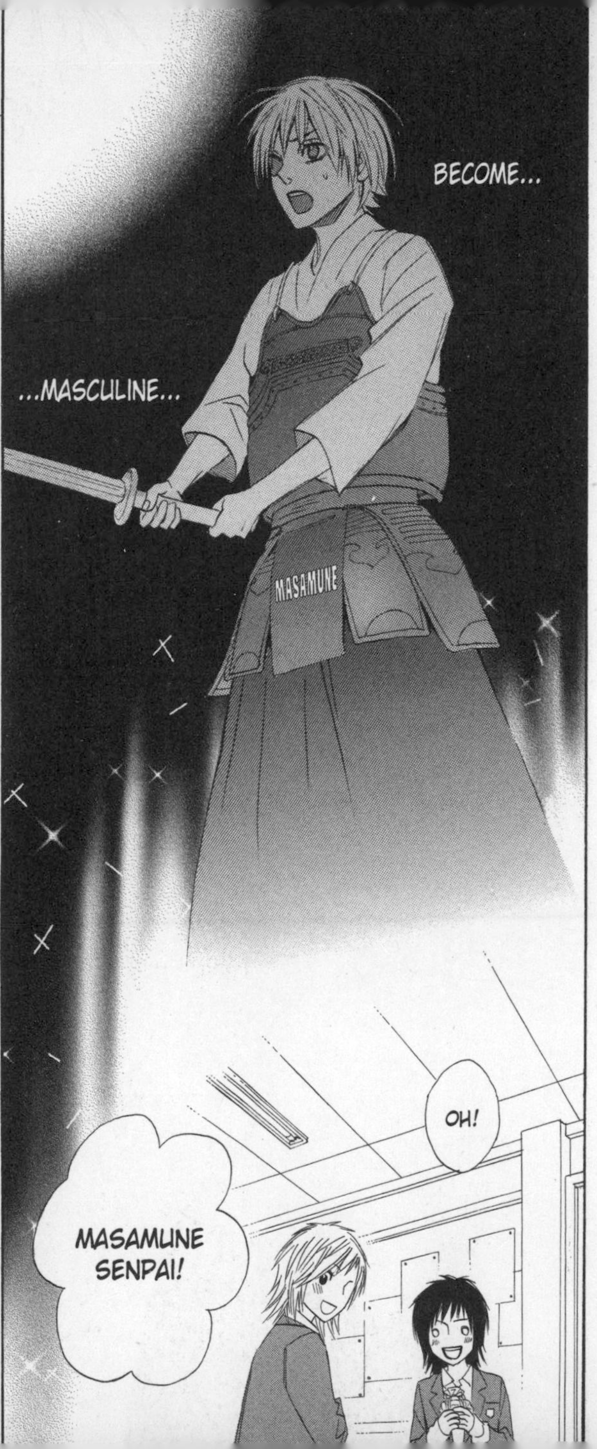
BECOME...
...MASCULINE...
MASAMUNE
OH!
MASAMUNE SENPAI!

Hello.
This is
volume 2.

Let's bring out some new characters! That's what I was thinking when I introduced Yamato Ariake here. But after this storyline, he hasn't appeared again to this day...

Yamato is somehow difficult to connect to the main story, but I inserted him in with the intention of having him be a regular character. That's why I'd like to draw him again if I get the chance.

"Yamato!"
"Sensei!"
That's all I wanted to have them do...
Or not.
Right.

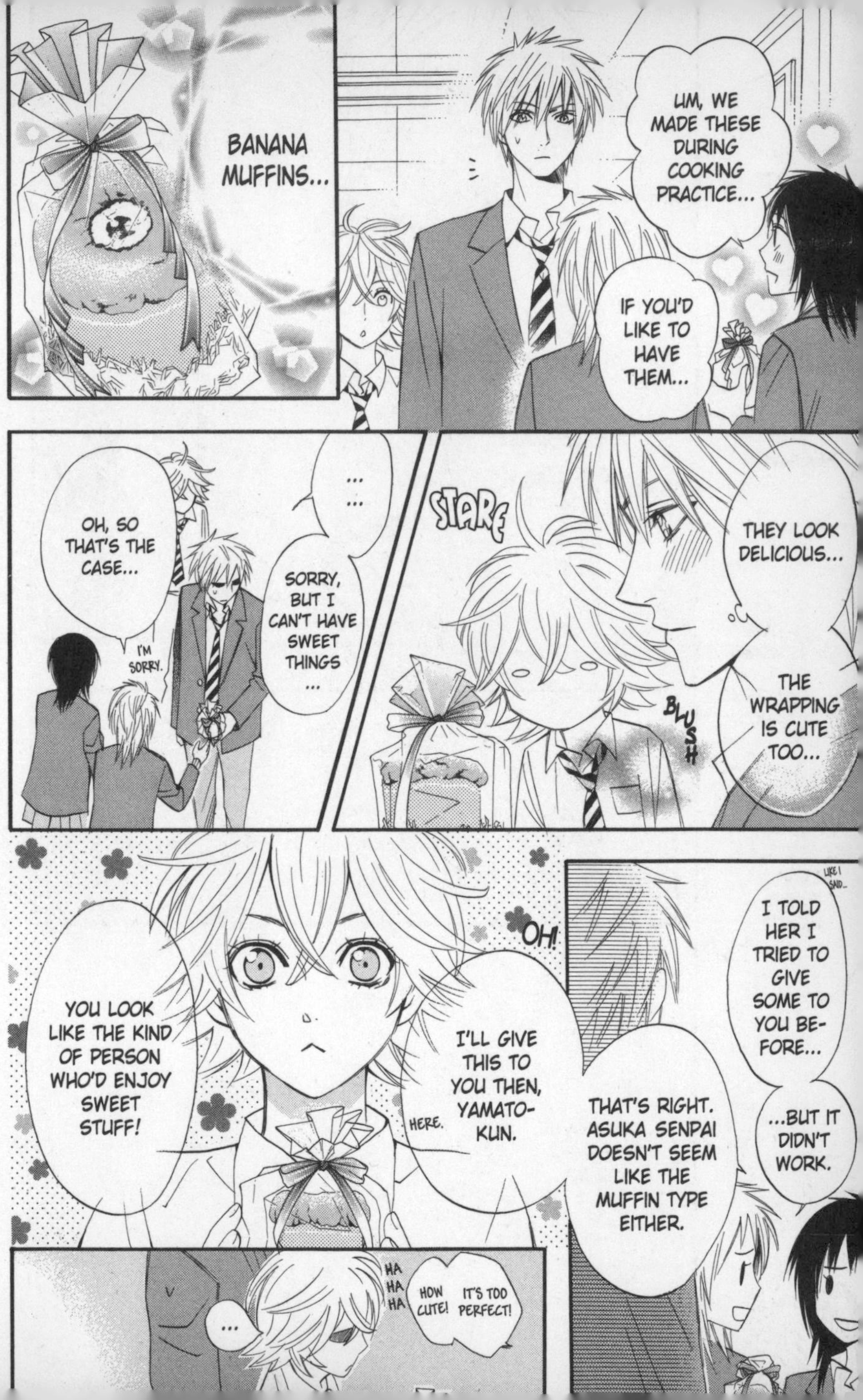
UM, WE MADE THESE DURING COOKING PRACTICE...
IF YOU'D LIKE TO HAVE THEM...
BANANA MUFFINS...
STARE
THEY LOOK DELICIOUS...
THE WRAPPING IS CUTE TOO...
BLUSH
... ...
SORRY, BUT I CAN'T HAVE SWEET THINGS ...
OH, SO THAT'S THE CASE...
I'M SORRY.
LIKE I SAID...
I TOLD HER I TRIED TO GIVE SOME TO YOU BE-FORE...
...BUT IT DIDN'T WORK.
THAT'S RIGHT. ASUKA SENPAI DOESN'T SEEM LIKE THE MUFFIN TYPE EITHER.
OH!
I'LL GIVE THIS TO YOU THEN, YAMATO-KUN.
HERE.
YOU LOOK LIKE THE KIND OF PERSON WHO'D ENJOY SWEET STUFF!
IT'S TOO PERFECT!
HOW CUTE!
HA HA HA
...

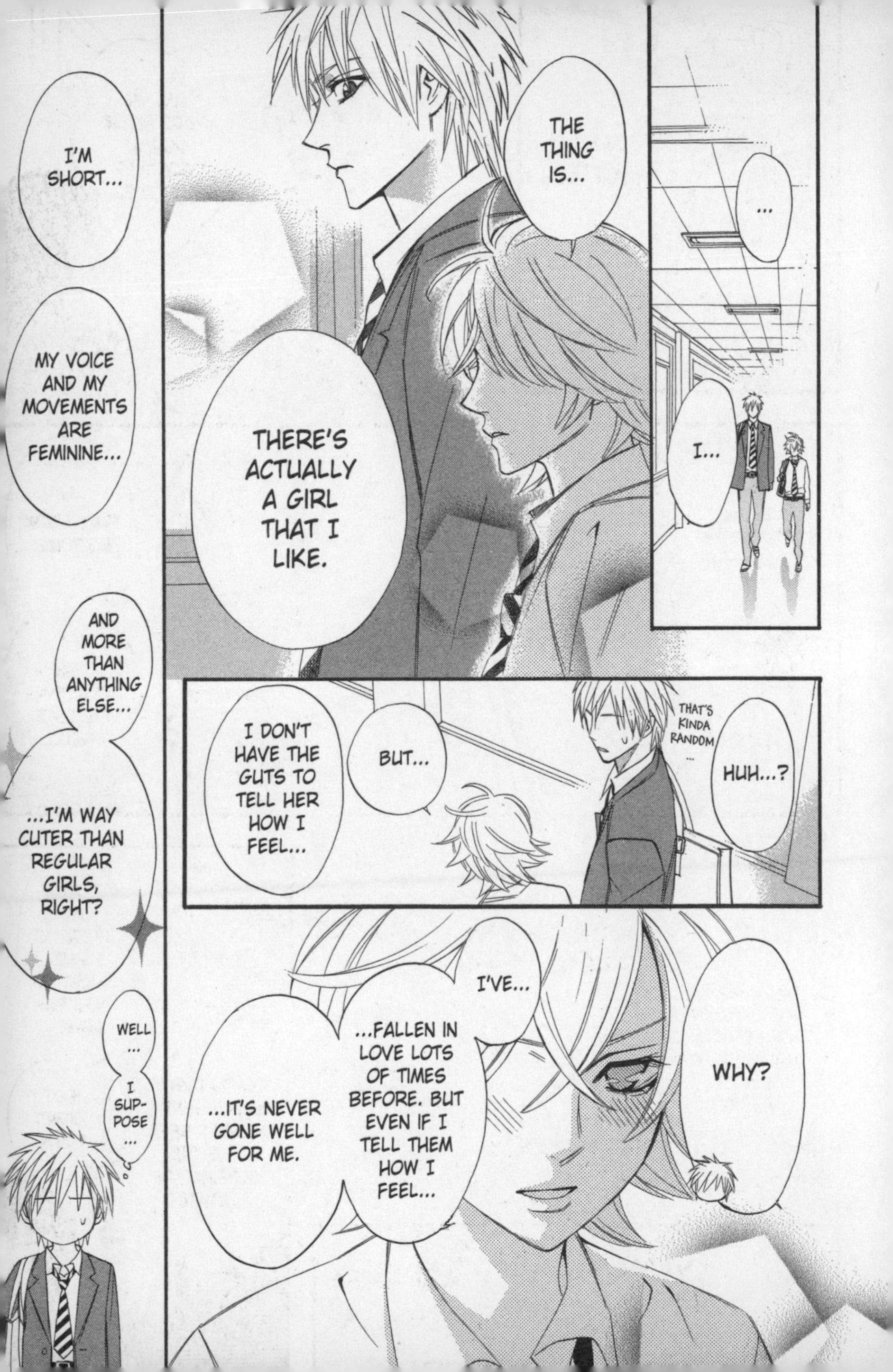
...
I...
THE THING IS...
THERE'S ACTUALLY A GIRL THAT I LIKE.
HUH...?
THAT'S KINDA RANDOM...
BUT...
I DON'T HAVE THE GUTS TO TELL HER HOW I FEEL...
WHY?
I'VE...
...FALLEN IN LOVE LOTS OF TIMES BEFORE. BUT EVEN IF I TELL THEM HOW I FEEL...
...IT'S NEVER GONE WELL FOR ME.
I'M SHORT...
MY VOICE AND MY MOVEMENTS ARE FEMININE...
AND MORE THAN ANYTHING ELSE...
...I'M WAY CUTER THAN REGULAR GIRLS, RIGHT?
WELL... I SUPPOSE...

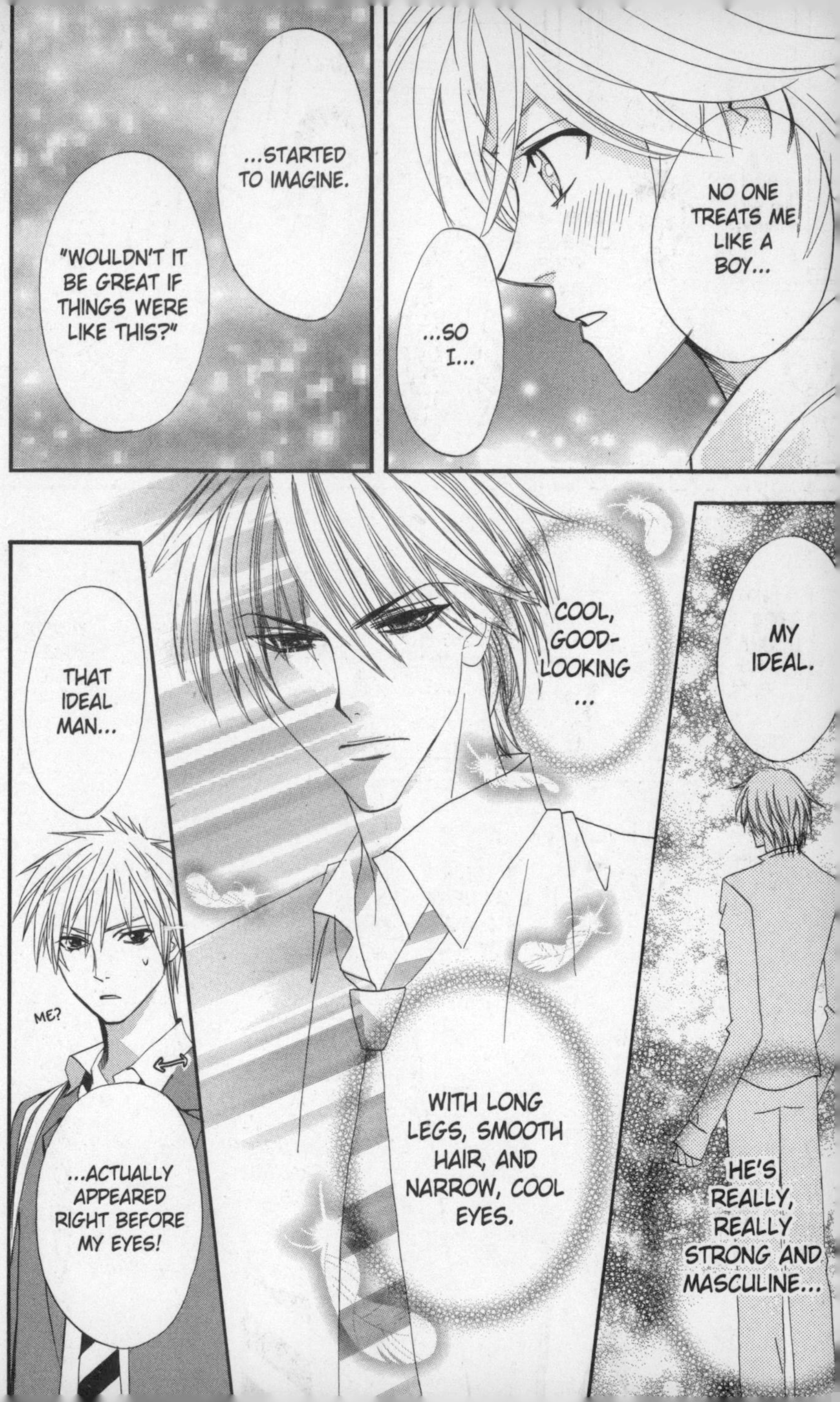
NO ONE TREATS ME LIKE A BOY...
...SO I...
...STARTED TO IMAGINE.
"WOULDN'T IT BE GREAT IF THINGS WERE LIKE THIS?"
MY IDEAL.
HE'S REALLY, REALLY STRONG AND MASCULINE...
COOL, GOOD-LOOKING ...
WITH LONG LEGS, SMOOTH HAIR, AND NARROW, COOL EYES.
THAT IDEAL MAN...
ME?
...ACTUALLY APPEARED RIGHT BEFORE MY EYES!

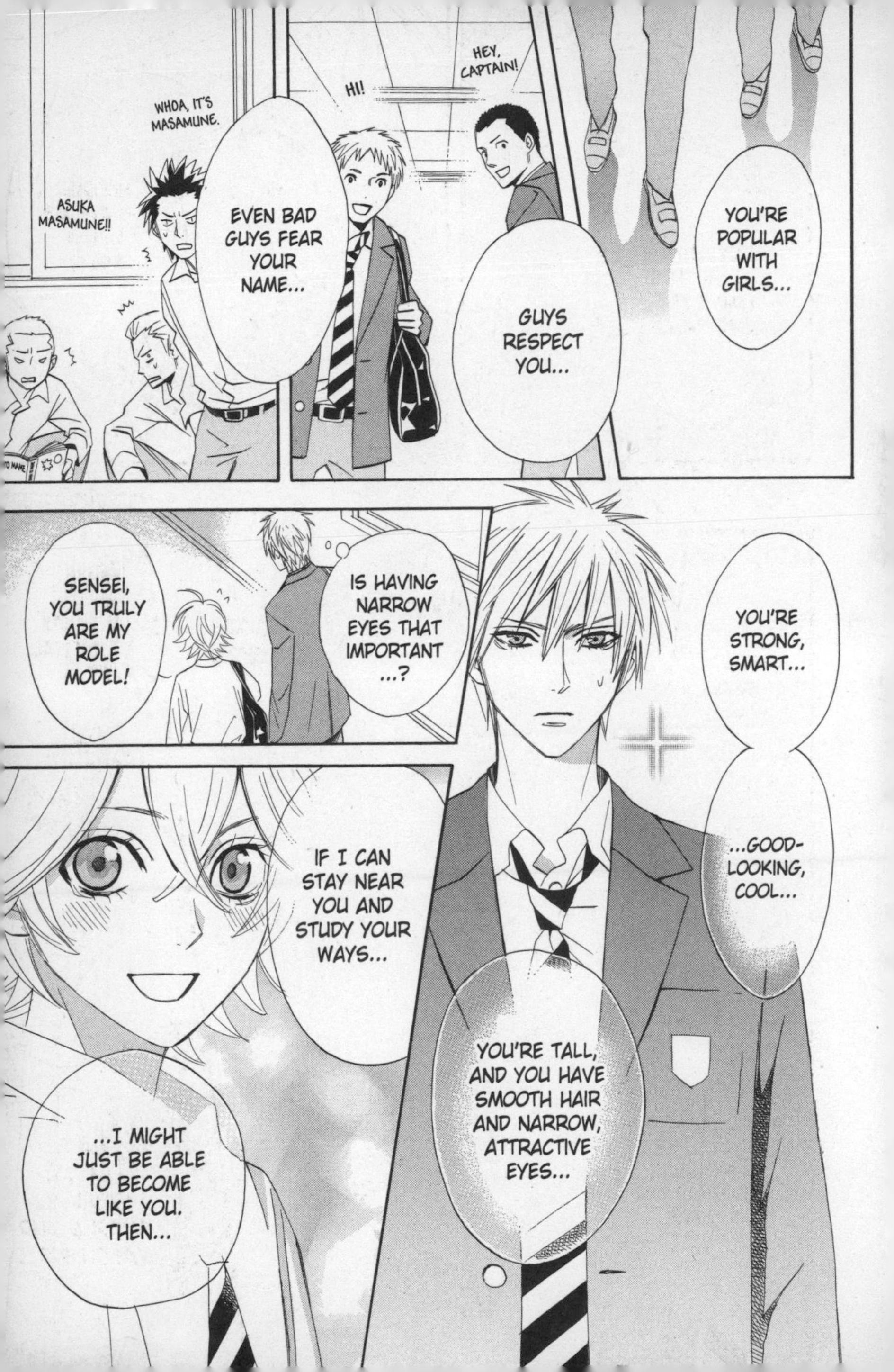
YOU'RE POPULAR WITH GIRLS...
HEY, CAPTAIN!
HI!
GUYS RESPECT YOU...
WHOA, IT'S MASAMUNE.
ASUKA MASAMUNE!!
EVEN BAD GUYS FEAR YOUR NAME...
YOU'RE STRONG, SMART...
...GOOD-LOOKING, COOL...
YOU'RE TALL, AND YOU HAVE SMOOTH HAIR AND NARROW, ATTRACTIVE EYES...
IS HAVING NARROW EYES THAT IMPORTANT ...?
SENSEI, YOU TRULY ARE MY ROLE MODEL!
IF I CAN STAY NEAR YOU AND STUDY YOUR WAYS...
...I MIGHT JUST BE ABLE TO BECOME LIKE YOU. THEN...

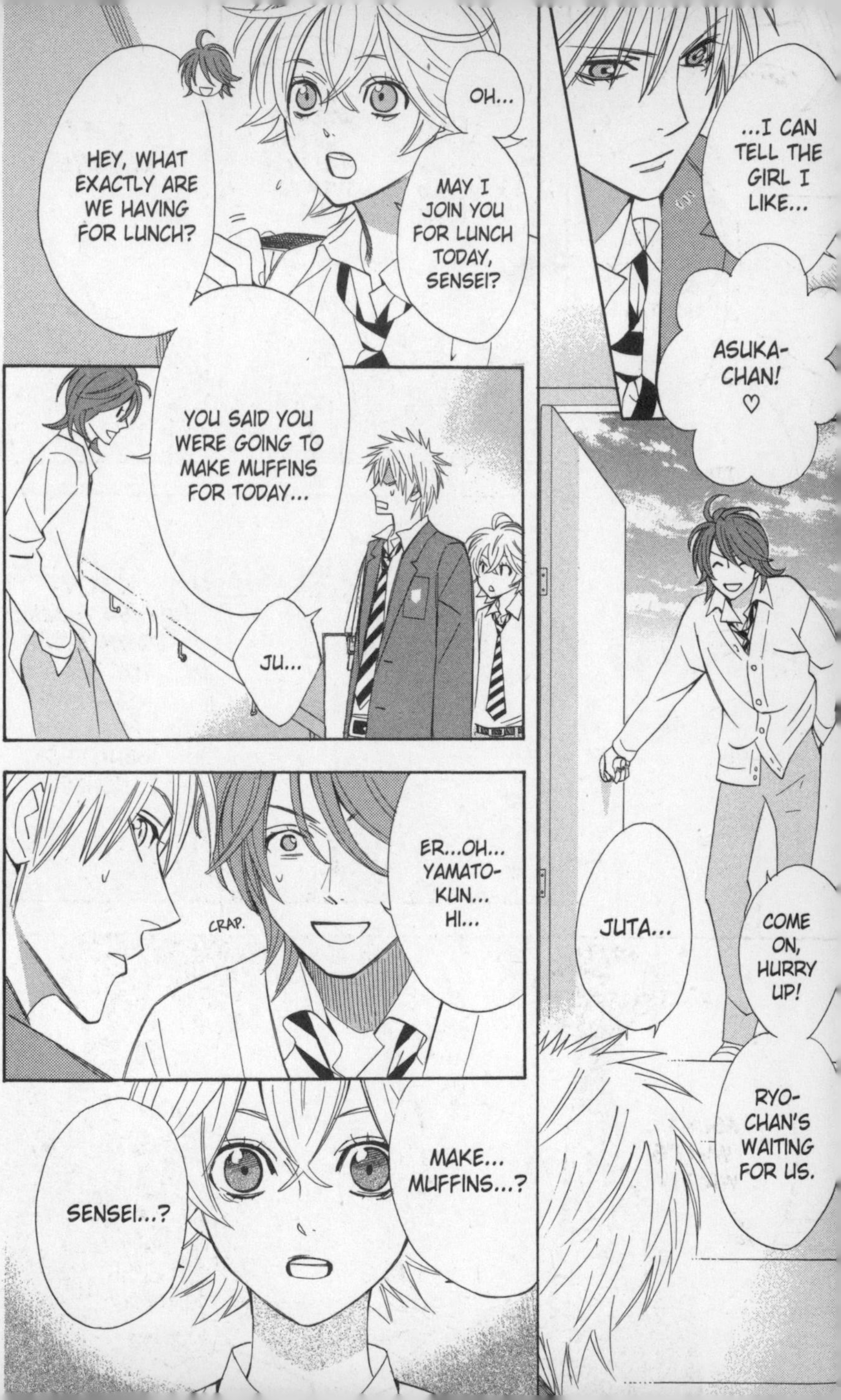
...I CAN TELL THE GIRL I LIKE...
ASUKA-CHAN! ♡
COME ON, HURRY UP!
JUTA...
RYO-CHAN'S WAITING FOR US.
OH...
MAY I JOIN YOU FOR LUNCH TODAY, SENSEI?
HEY, WHAT EXACTLY ARE WE HAVING FOR LUNCH?
YOU SAID YOU WERE GOING TO MAKE MUFFINS FOR TODAY...
JU...
ER...OH... YAMATO-KUN... HI...
CRAP.
MAKE... MUFFINS...?
SENSEI...?

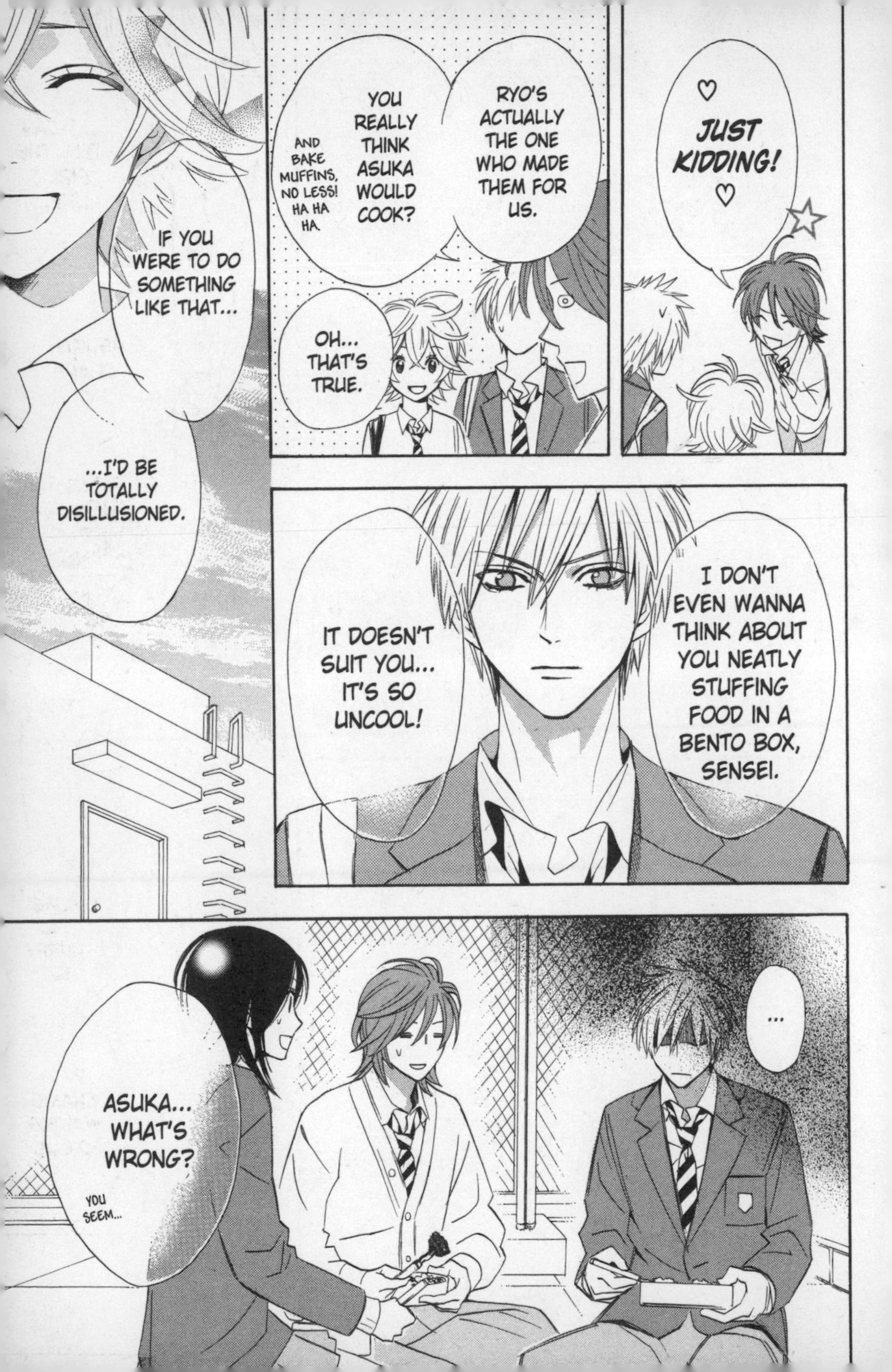
♡ JUST KIDDING! ♡
RYO'S ACTUALLY THE ONE WHO MADE THEM FOR US.
YOU REALLY THINK ASUKA WOULD COOK?
AND BAKE MUFFINS, NO LESS! HA HA HA.
OH... THAT'S TRUE.
I DON'T EVEN WANNA THINK ABOUT YOU NEATLY STUFFING FOOD IN A BENTO BOX, SENSEI.
IT DOESN'T SUIT YOU... IT'S SO UNCOOL!
IF YOU WERE TO DO SOMETHING LIKE THAT...
...I'D BE TOTALLY DISILLUSIONED.
...
ASUKA... WHAT'S WRONG?
YOU SEEM...

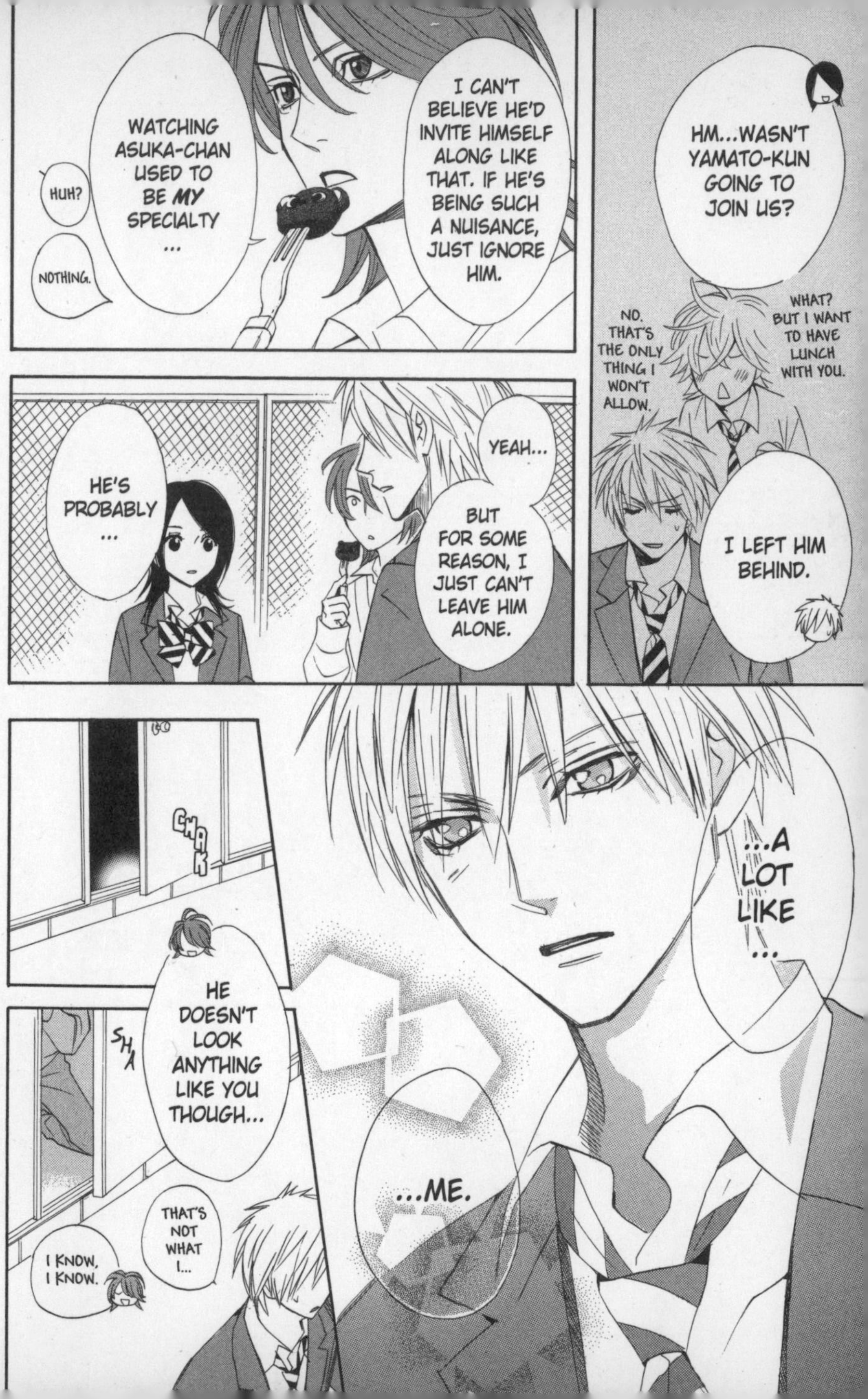
HM...WASN'T YAMATO-KUN GOING TO JOIN US?
WHAT? BUT I WANT TO HAVE LUNCH WITH YOU.
NO. THAT'S THE ONLY THING I WON'T ALLOW.
I LEFT HIM BEHIND.
I CAN'T BELIEVE HE'D INVITE HIMSELF ALONG LIKE THAT. IF HE'S BEING SUCH A NUISANCE, JUST IGNORE HIM.
WATCHING ASUKA-CHAN USED TO BE MY SPECIALTY ...
HUH?
NOTHING.
YEAH...
BUT FOR SOME REASON, I JUST CAN'T LEAVE HIM ALONE.
HE'S PROBABLY ...
...A LOT LIKE ...
...ME.
CHAK
HE DOESN'T LOOK ANYTHING LIKE YOU THOUGH...
SHA
THAT'S NOT WHAT I...
I KNOW, I KNOW.

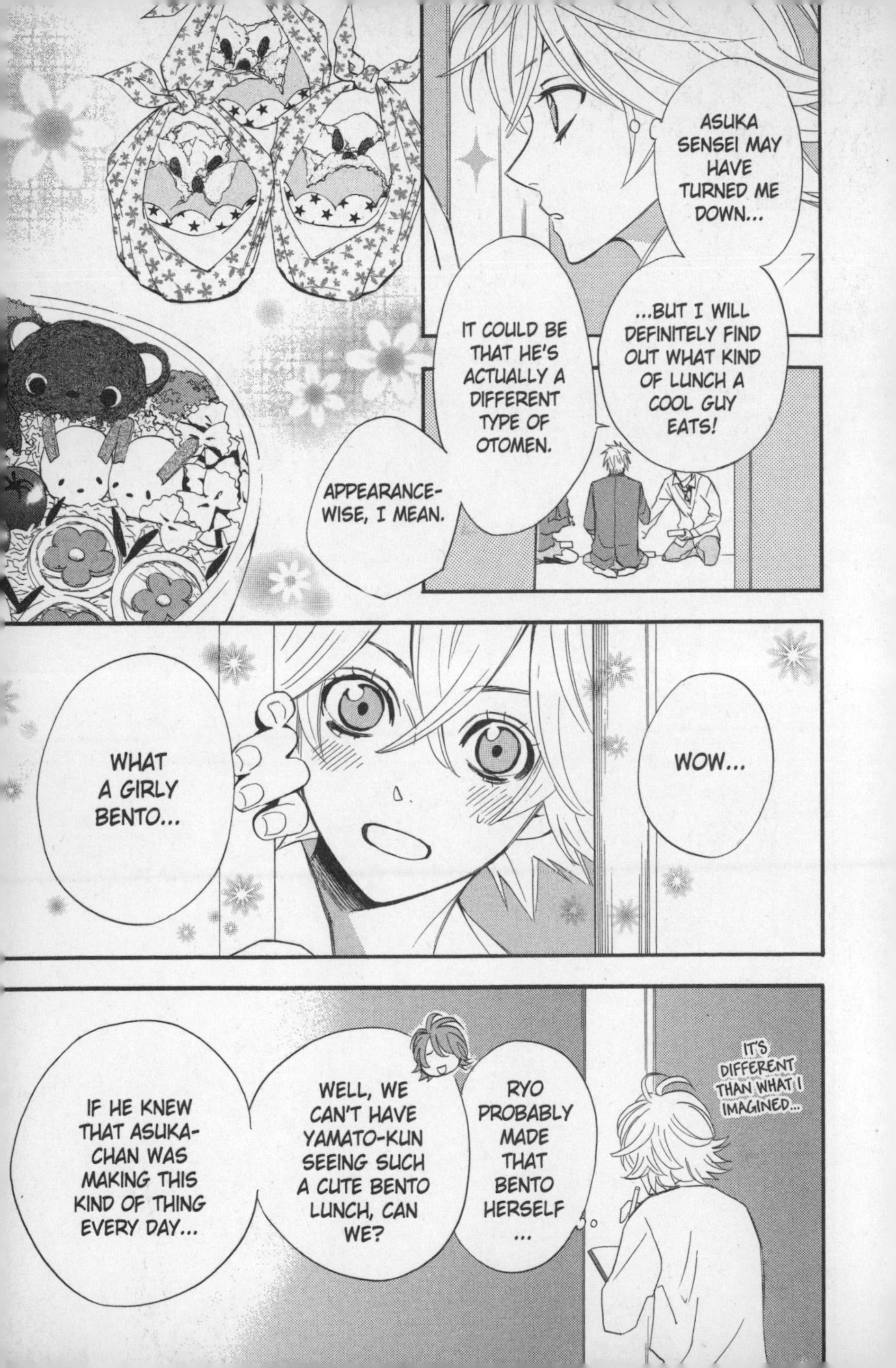
ASUKA SENSEI MAY HAVE TURNED ME DOWN...
...BUT I WILL DEFINITELY FIND OUT WHAT KIND OF LUNCH A COOL GUY EATS!
IT COULD BE THAT HE'S ACTUALLY A DIFFERENT TYPE OF OTOMEN.
APPEARANCE-WISE, I MEAN.
WOW...
WHAT A GIRLY BENTO...
IT'S DIFFERENT THAN WHAT I IMAGINED...
RYO PROBABLY MADE THAT BENTO HERSELF...
WELL, WE CAN'T HAVE YAMATO-KUN SEEING SUCH A CUTE BENTO LUNCH, CAN WE?
IF HE KNEW THAT ASUKA-CHAN WAS MAKING THIS KIND OF THING EVERY DAY...

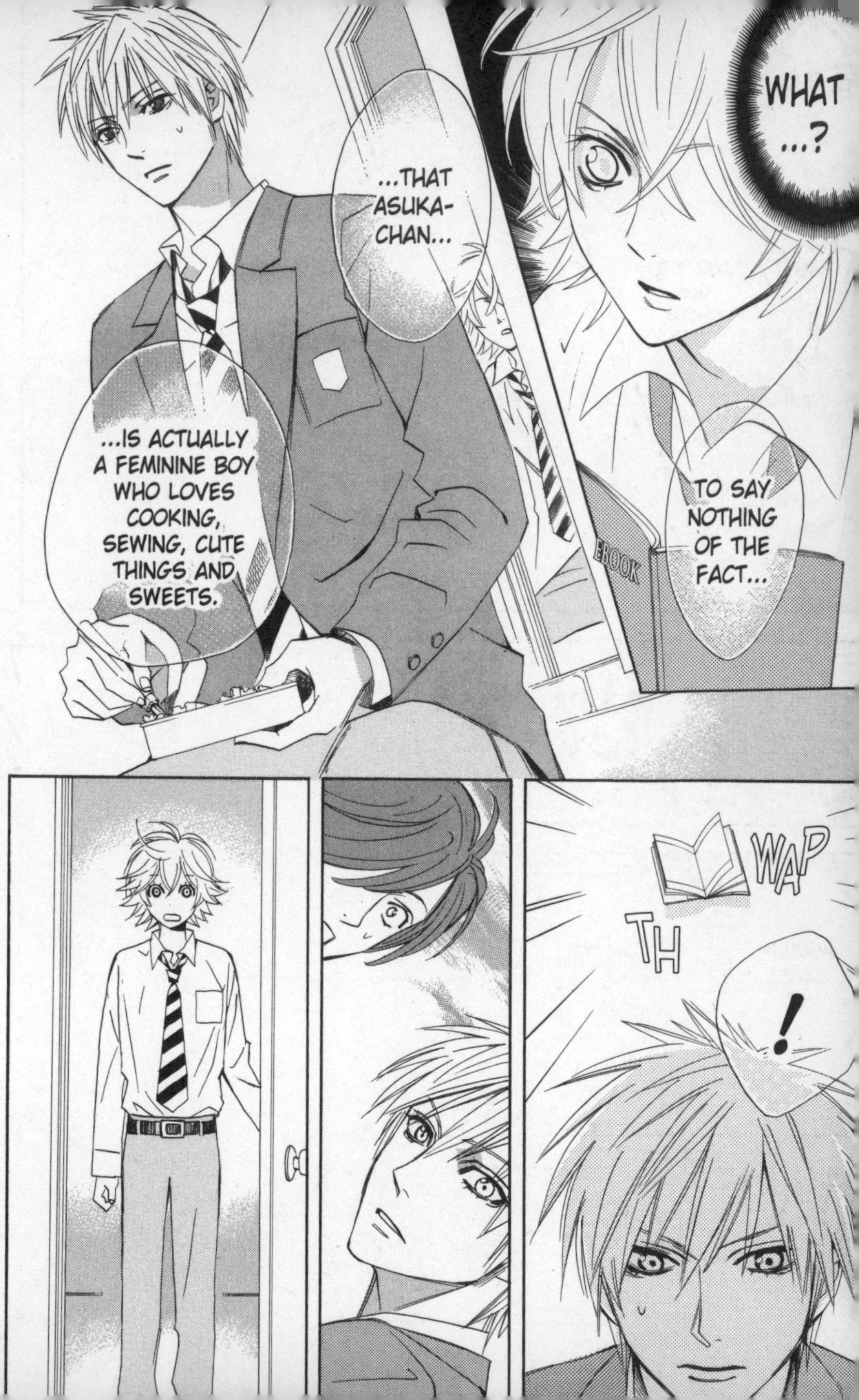
WHAT ...?
TO SAY NOTHING OF THE FACT...
EBOOK
...THAT ASUKA-CHAN...
...IS ACTUALLY A FEMININE BOY WHO LOVES COOKING, SEWING, CUTE THINGS AND SWEETS.
THWAP
!

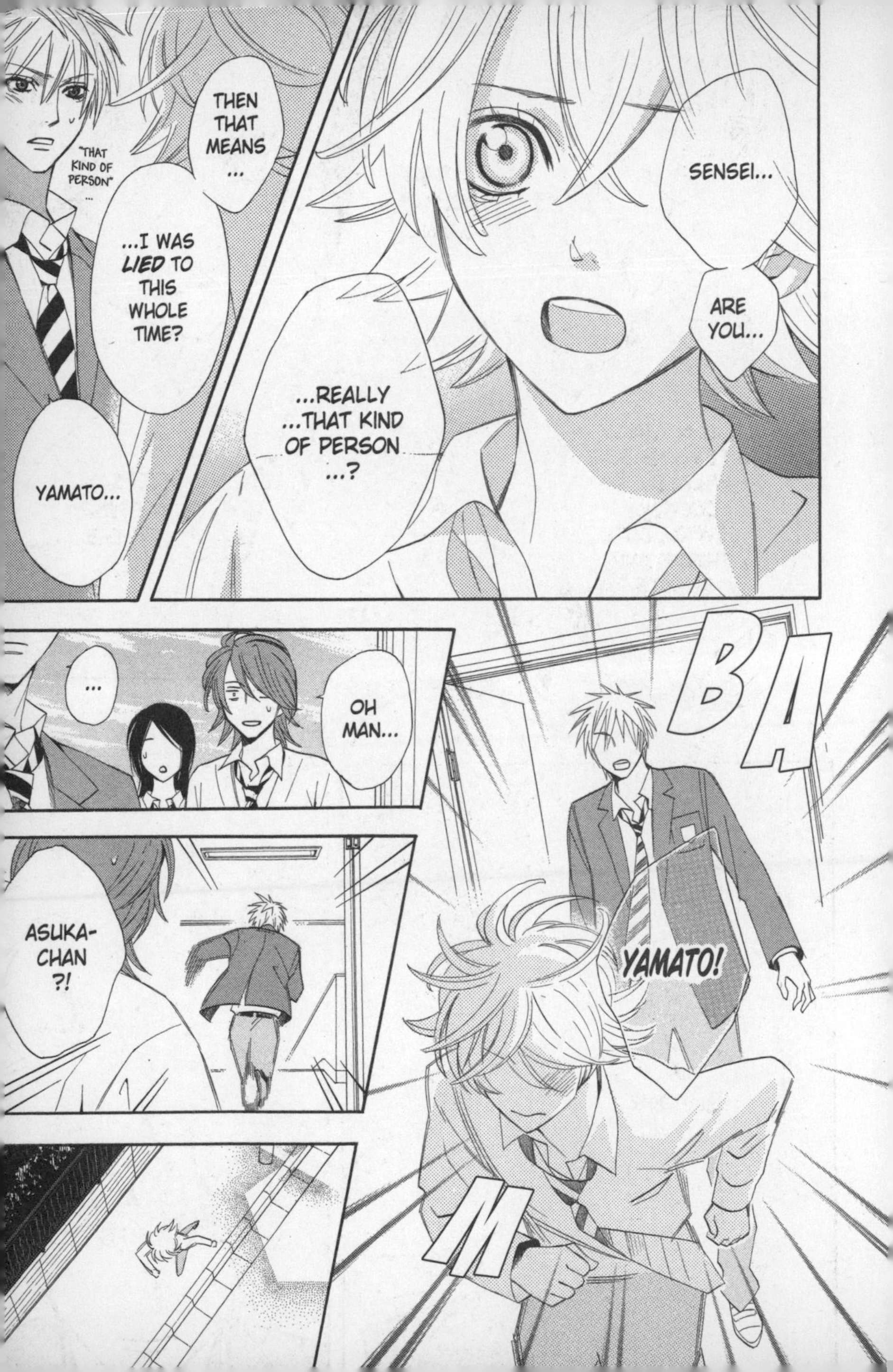
SENSEI...
ARE YOU...
...REALLY ...THAT KIND OF PERSON ...?
THEN THAT MEANS ...
"THAT KIND OF PERSON" ...
...I WAS *LIED* TO THIS WHOLE TIME?
YAMATO...
BA
YAMATO!
M
OH MAN...
...
ASUKA-CHAN ?!

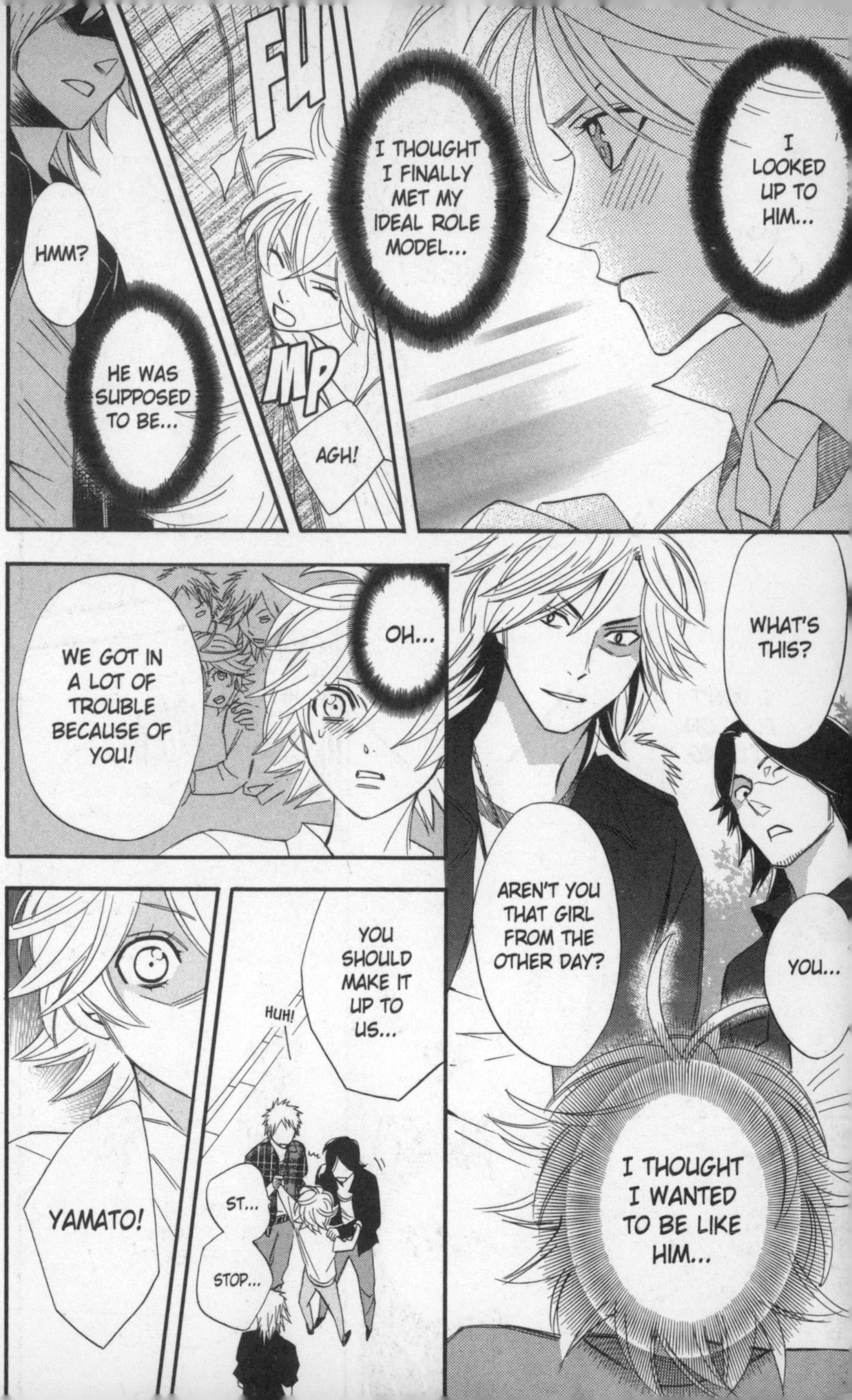
I LOOKED UP TO HIM...
I THOUGHT I FINALLY MET MY IDEAL ROLE MODEL...
FU
MP
AGH!
HMM?
HE WAS SUPPOSED TO BE...
WHAT'S THIS?
AREN'T YOU THAT GIRL FROM THE OTHER DAY?
YOU...
I THOUGHT I WANTED TO BE LIKE HIM...
OH...
WE GOT IN A LOT OF TROUBLE BECAUSE OF YOU!
YOU SHOULD MAKE IT UP TO US...
HUH!
ST...
STOP...
YAMATO!

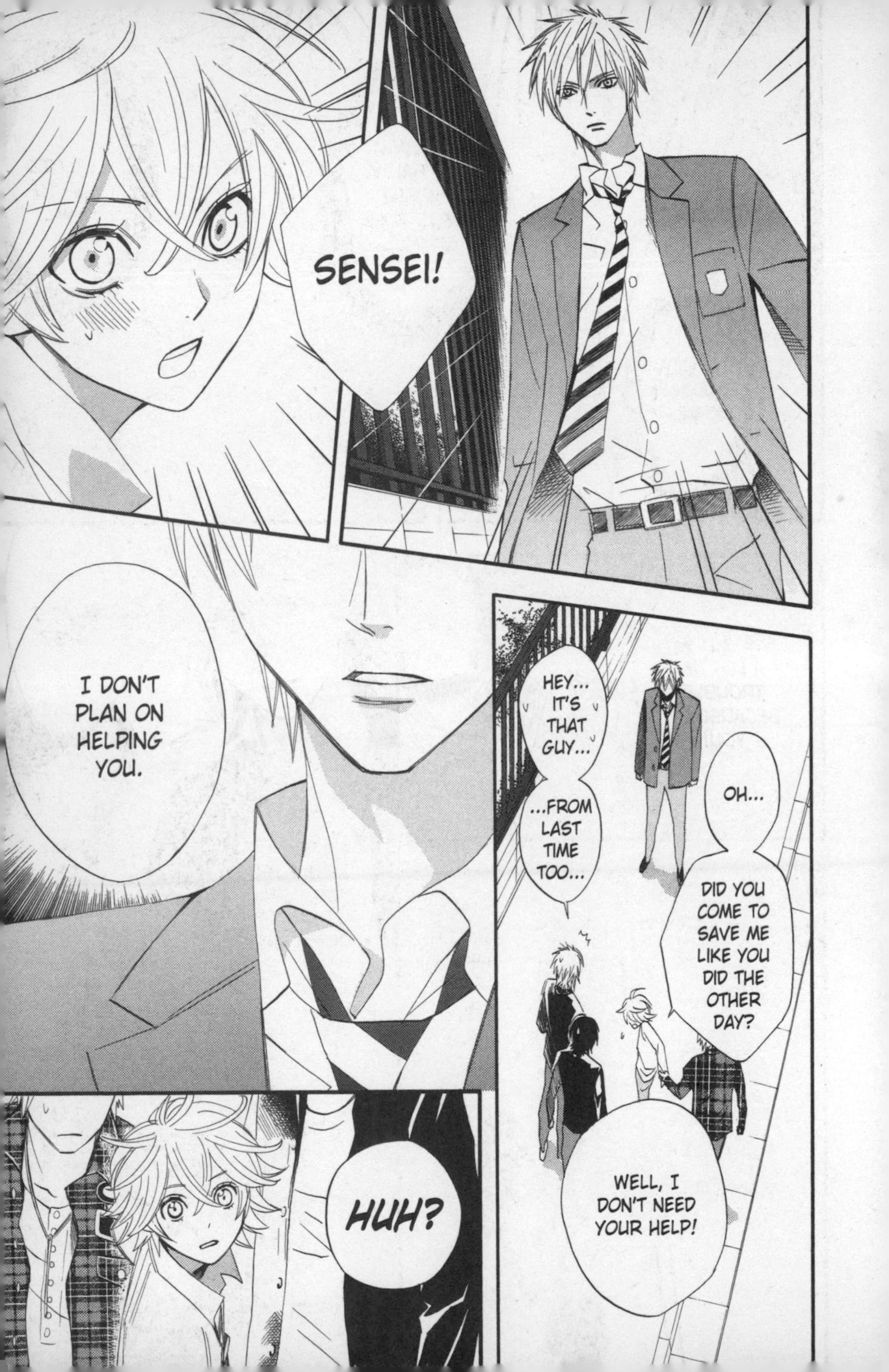
SENSEI!
HEY... IT'S THAT GUY...
...FROM LAST TIME TOO...
OH...
DID YOU COME TO SAVE ME LIKE YOU DID THE OTHER DAY?
WELL, I DON'T NEED YOUR HELP!
I DON'T PLAN ON HELPING YOU.
HUH?

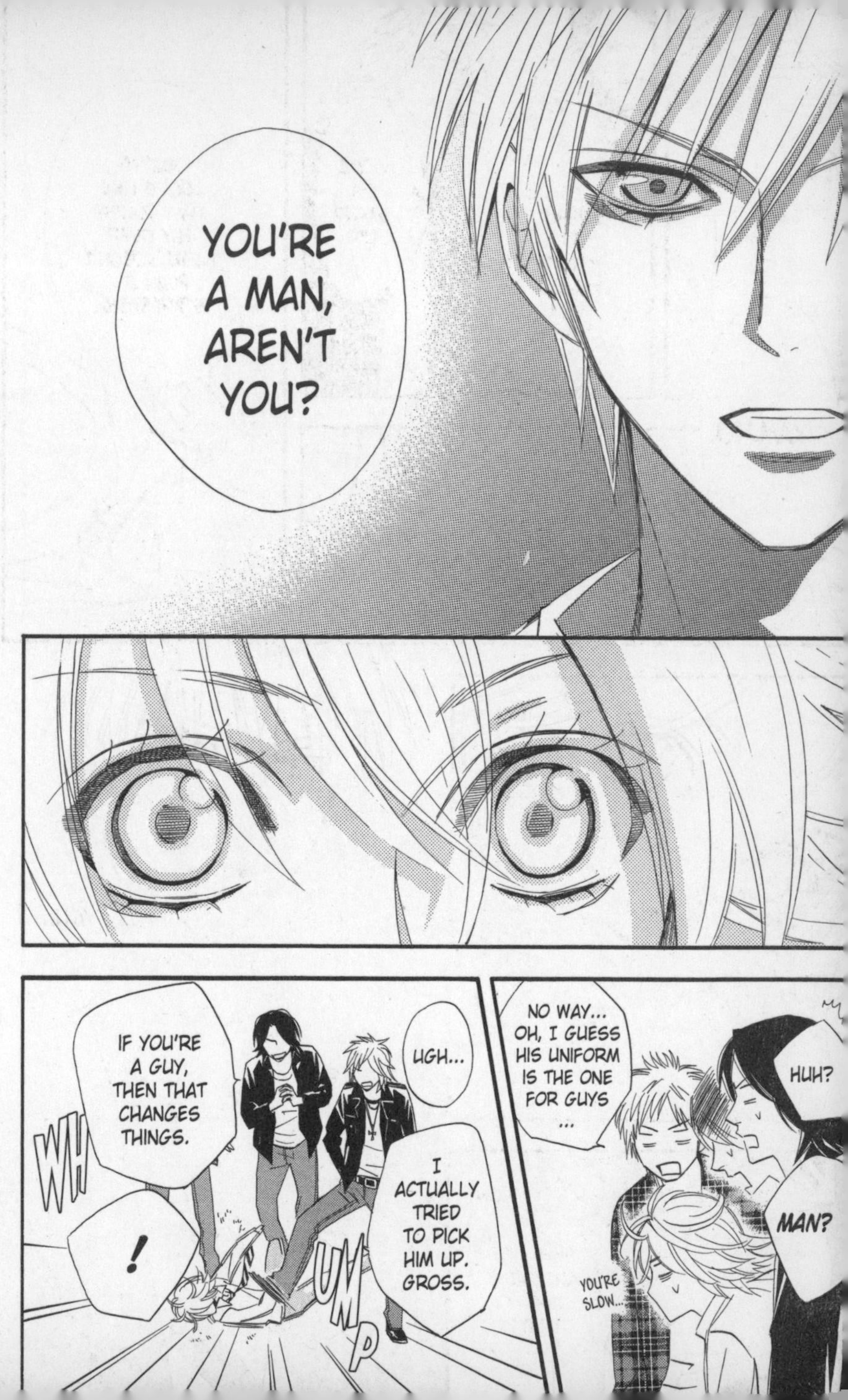
YOU'RE A MAN, AREN'T YOU?
HUH?
MAN?
NO WAY... OH, I GUESS HIS UNIFORM IS THE ONE FOR GUYS ...
YOU'RE SLOW...
UGH...
IF YOU'RE A GUY, THEN THAT CHANGES THINGS.
I ACTUALLY TRIED TO PICK HIM UP. GROSS.
!
WHUMP

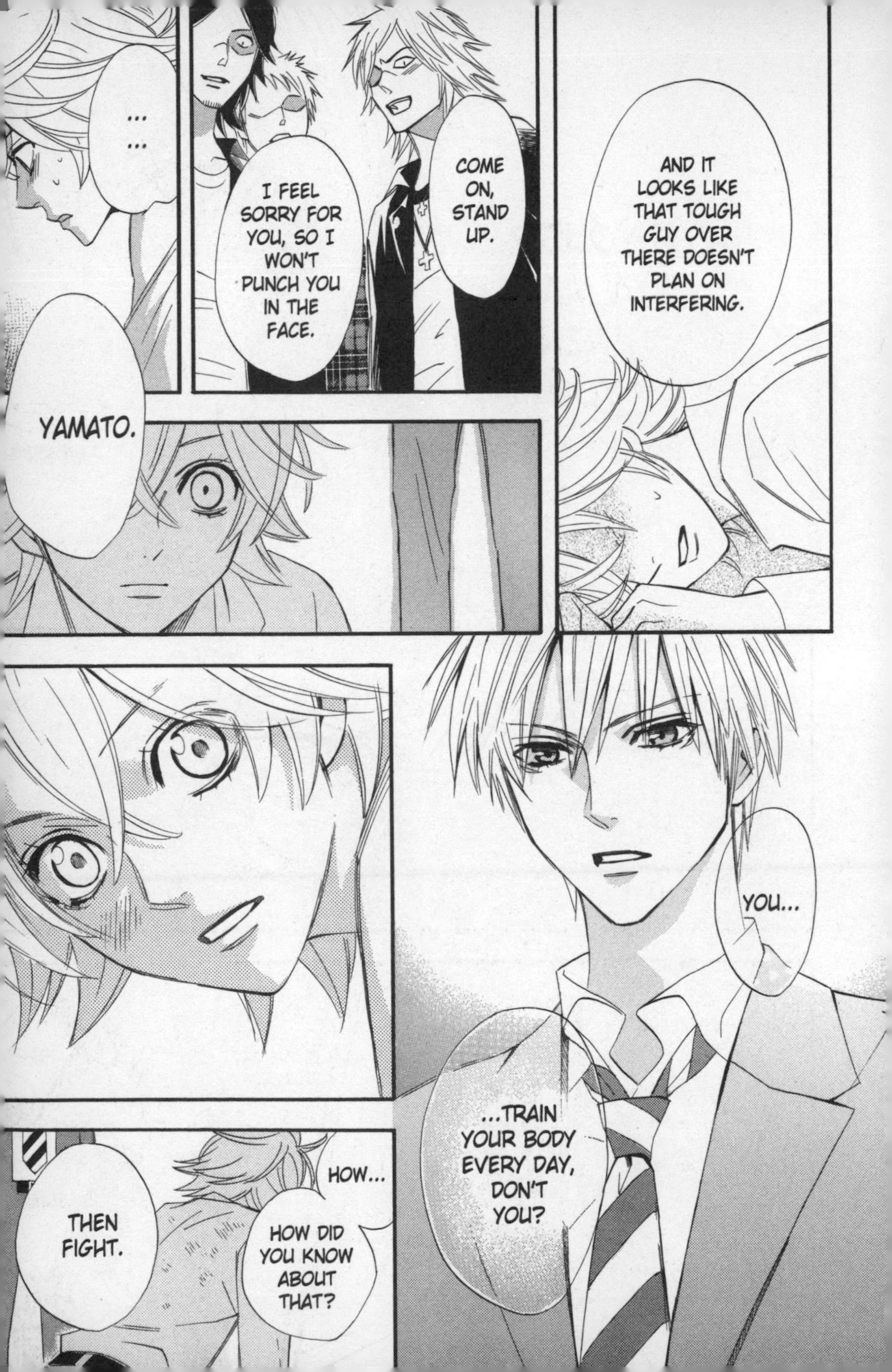
AND IT LOOKS LIKE THAT TOUGH GUY OVER THERE DOESN'T PLAN ON INTERFERING.
COME ON, STAND UP.
I FEEL SORRY FOR YOU, SO I WON'T PUNCH YOU IN THE FACE.
... ...
YAMATO.
YOU...
...TRAIN YOUR BODY EVERY DAY, DON'T YOU?
HOW...
HOW DID YOU KNOW ABOUT THAT?
THEN FIGHT.

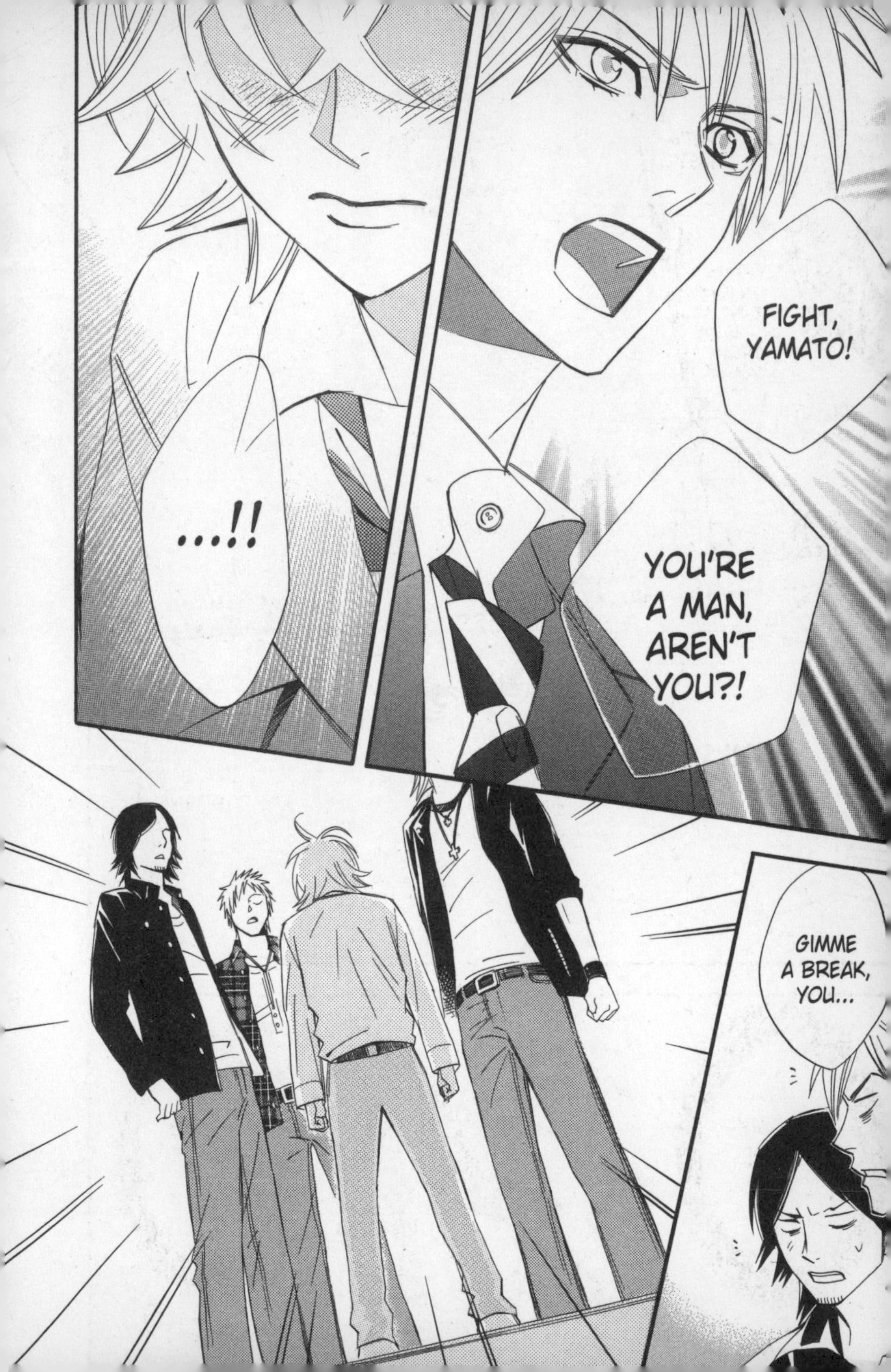
FIGHT, YAMATO!
YOU'RE A MAN, AREN'T YOU?!
...!!
GIMME A BREAK, YOU...

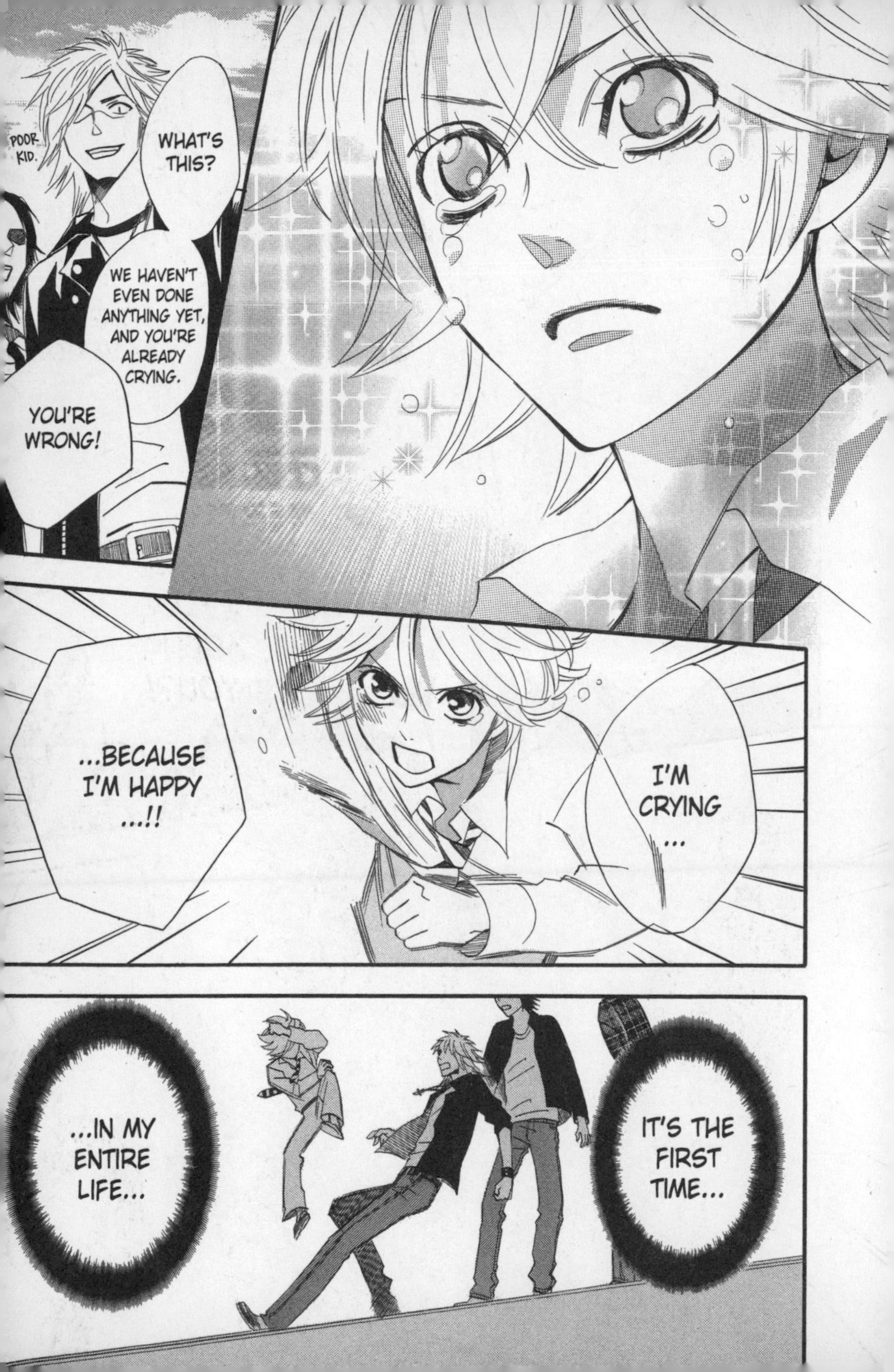
WHAT'S THIS?
POOR KID.
WE HAVEN'T EVEN DONE ANYTHING YET, AND YOU'RE ALREADY CRYING.
YOU'RE WRONG!
I'M CRYING ...
...BECAUSE I'M HAPPY ...!!
IT'S THE FIRST TIME...
...IN MY ENTIRE LIFE...

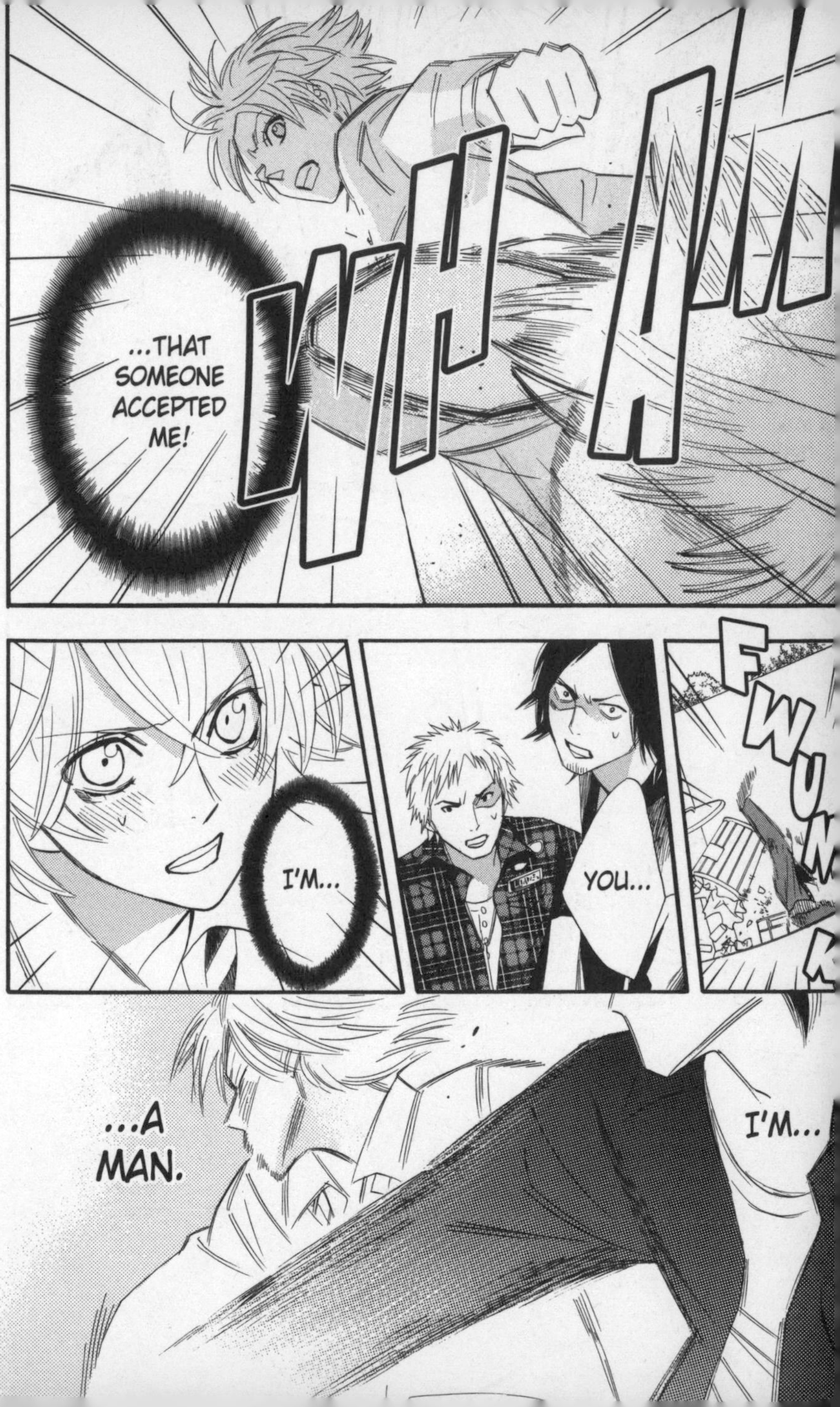
WHAM
...THAT SOMEONE ACCEPTED ME!
FWUNK
YOU...
I'M...
I'M...
...A MAN.

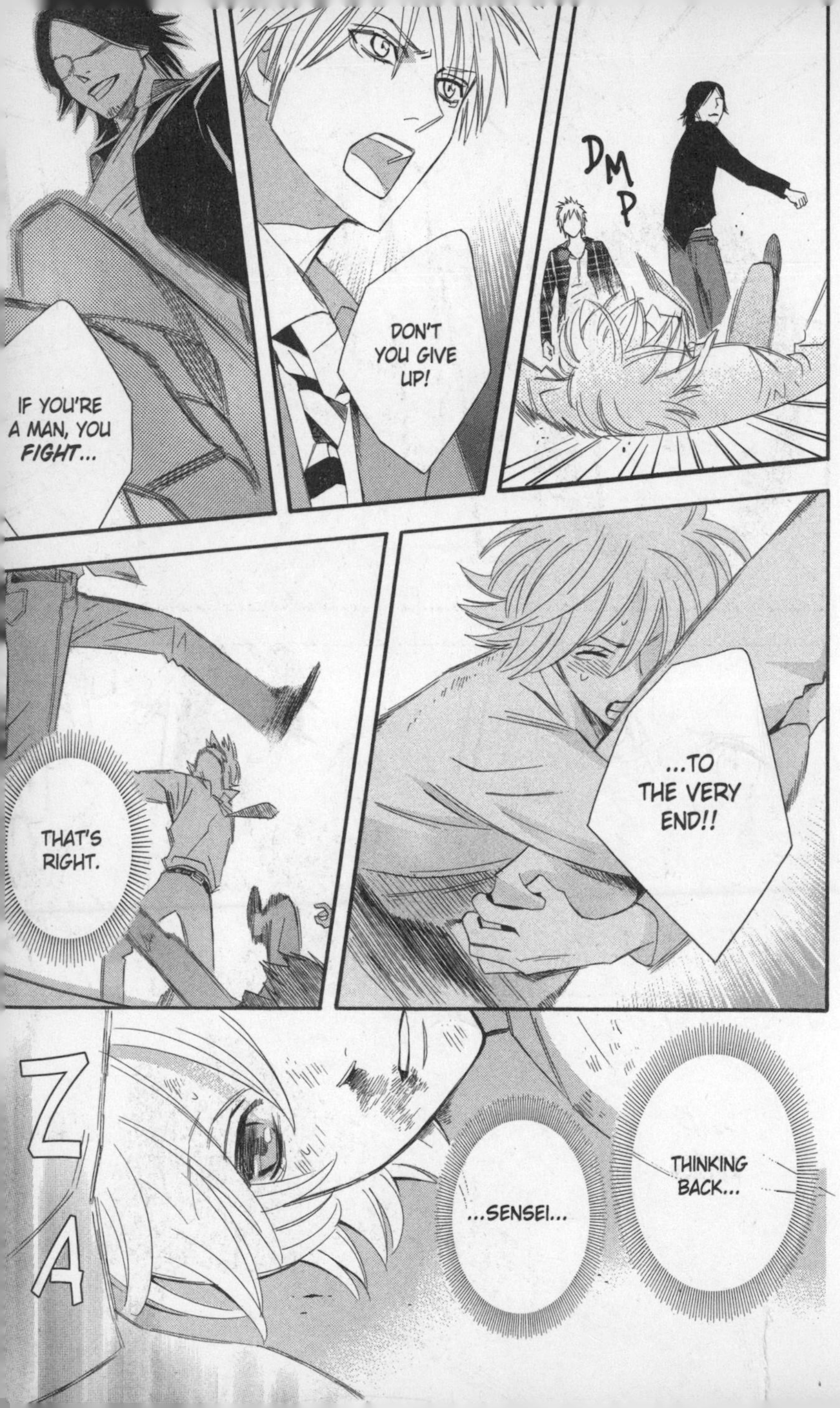
DMP
DON'T YOU GIVE UP!
IF YOU'RE A MAN, YOU FIGHT...
...TO THE VERY END!!
THAT'S RIGHT.
THINKING BACK...
...SENSEI...
ZA

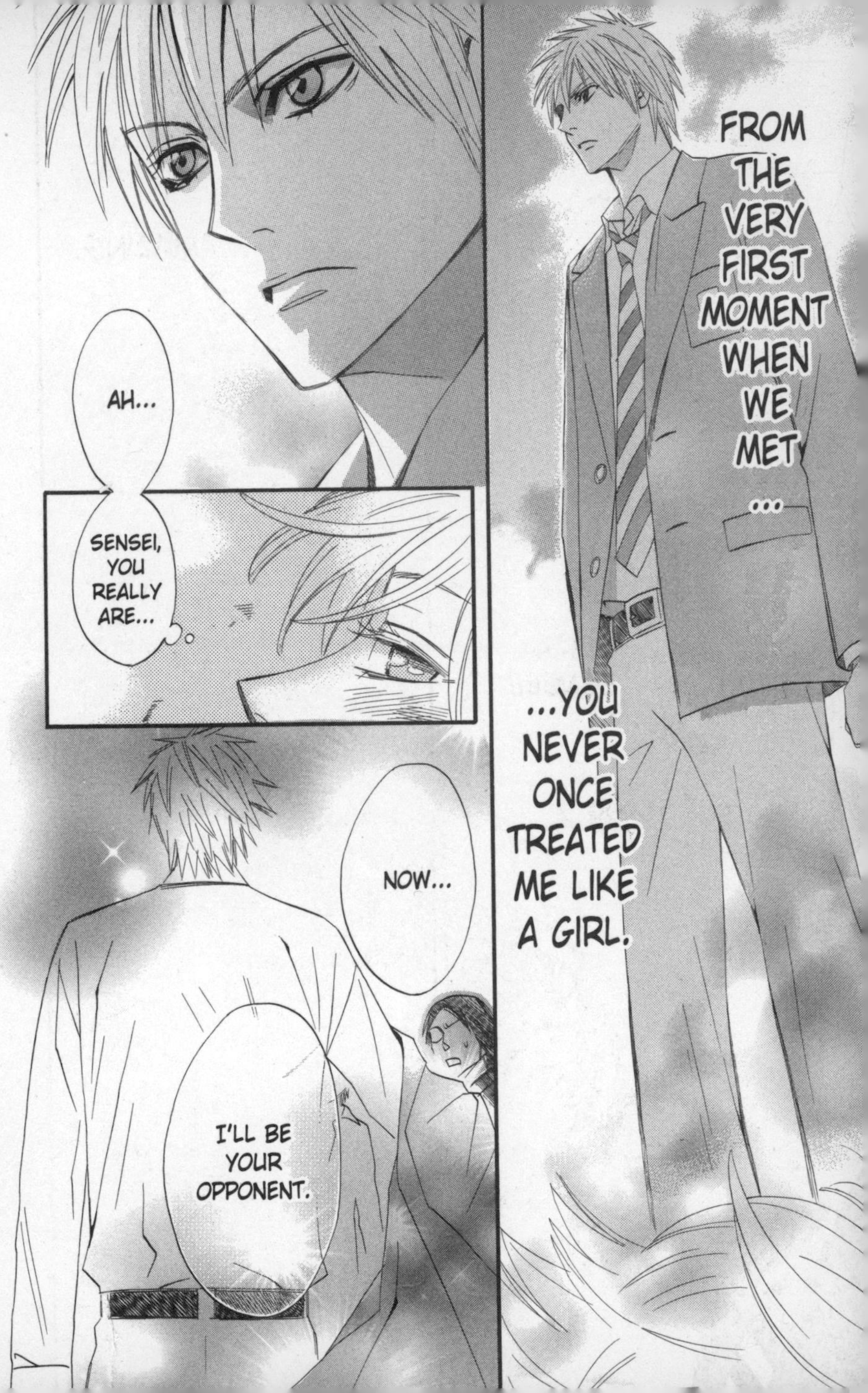
FROM THE VERY FIRST MOMENT WHEN WE MET ...
...YOU NEVER ONCE TREATED ME LIKE A GIRL.
AH...
SENSEI, YOU REALLY ARE...
NOW...
I'LL BE YOUR OPPONENT.

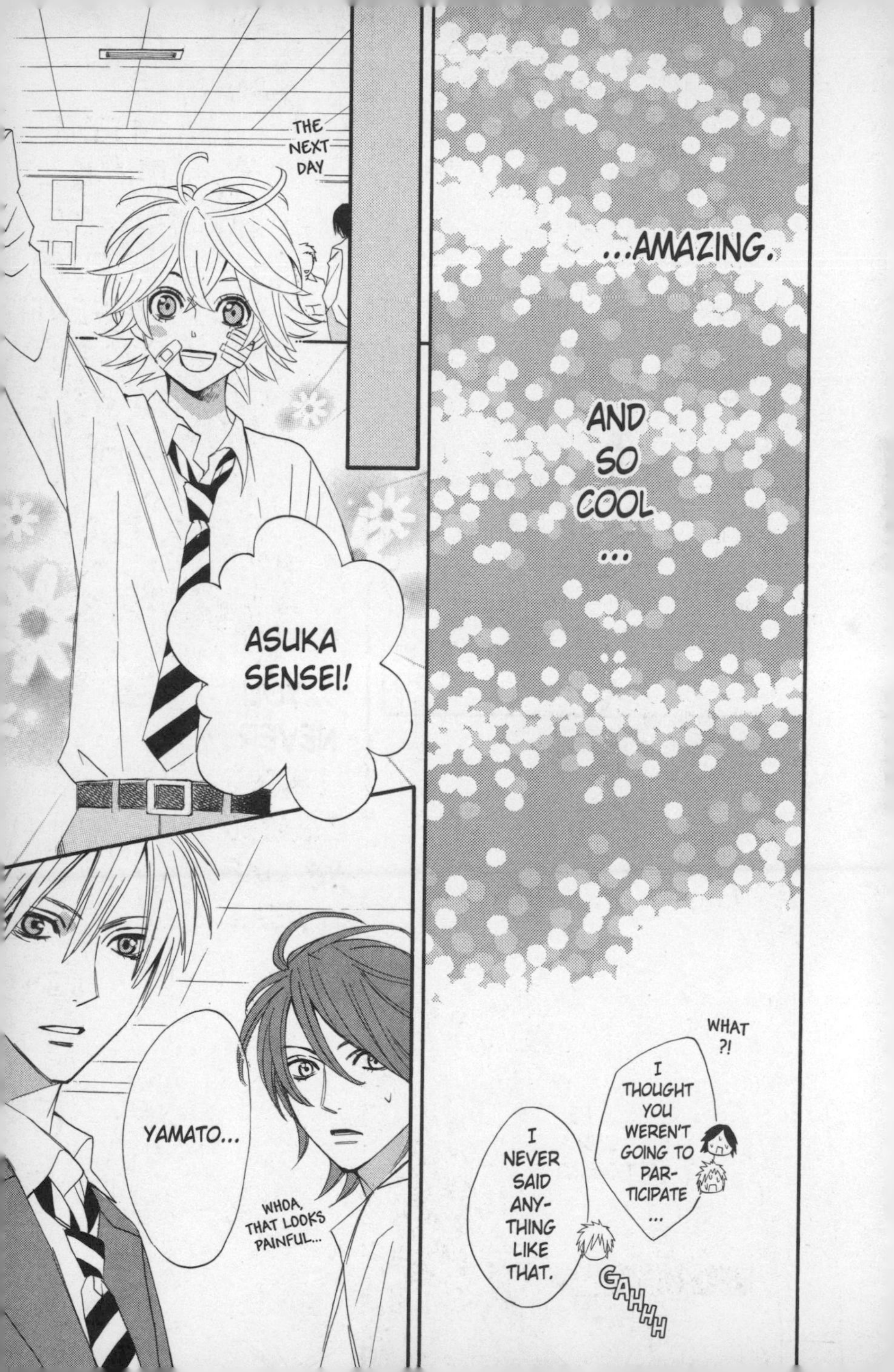
...AMAZING.
AND SO COOL ...
...
WHAT?!
I THOUGHT YOU WEREN'T GOING TO PAR-TICIPATE ...
I NEVER SAID ANY-THING LIKE THAT.
GAHHH
THE NEXT DAY
ASUKA SENSEI!
YAMATO...
WHOA, THAT LOOKS PAINFUL...

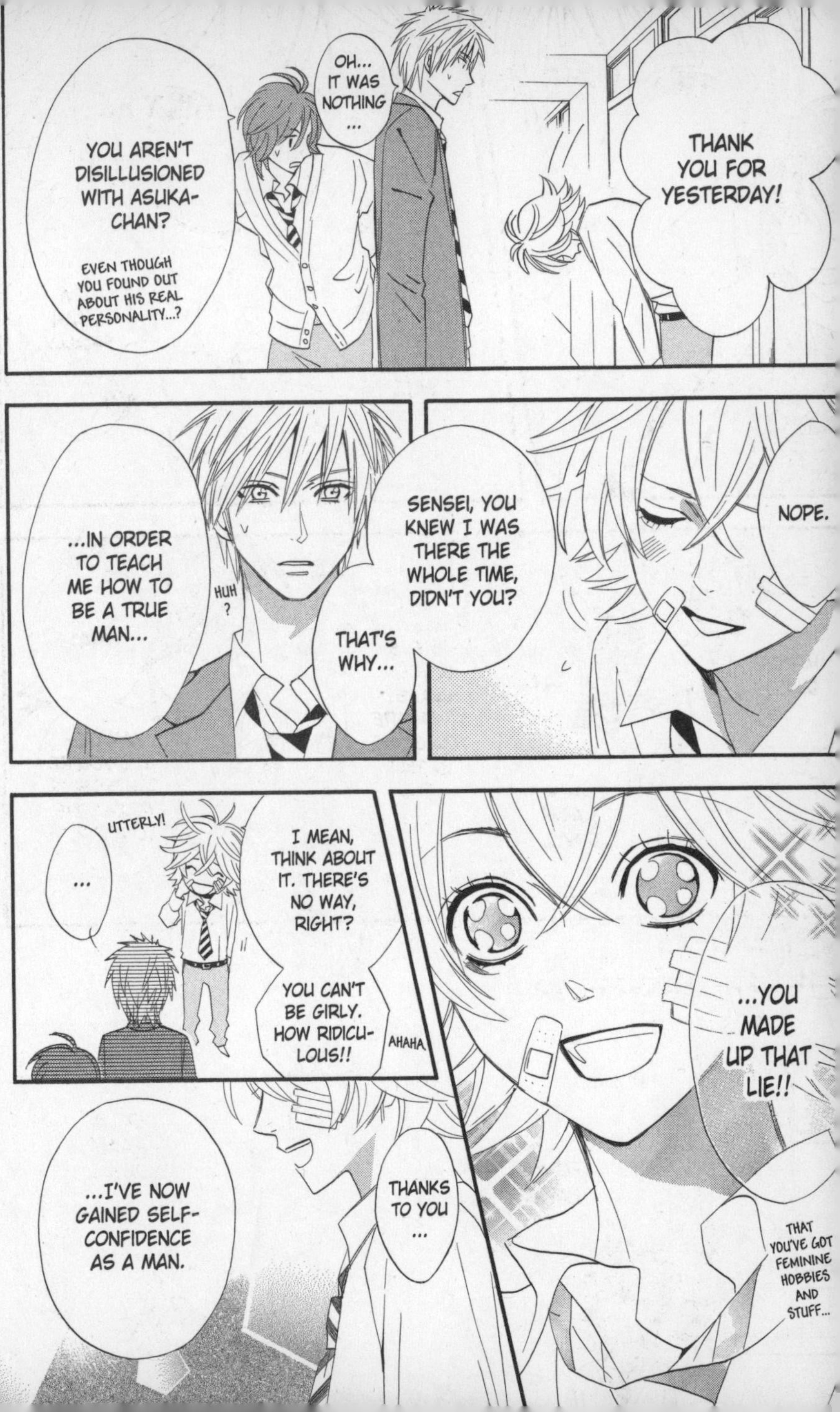
THANK YOU FOR YESTERDAY!
OH... IT WAS NOTHING ...
YOU AREN'T DISILLUSIONED WITH ASUKA-CHAN?
EVEN THOUGH YOU FOUND OUT ABOUT HIS REAL PERSONALITY...?
NOPE.
SENSEI, YOU KNEW I WAS THERE THE WHOLE TIME, DIDN'T YOU?
THAT'S WHY...
HUH ?
...IN ORDER TO TEACH ME HOW TO BE A TRUE MAN...
...YOU MADE UP THAT LIE!!
THAT YOU'VE GOT FEMININE HOBBIES AND STUFF...
I MEAN, THINK ABOUT IT. THERE'S NO WAY, RIGHT?
YOU CAN'T BE GIRLY. HOW RIDICU-LOUS!!
AHAHA
UTTERLY!
...
THANKS TO YOU ...
...I'VE NOW GAINED SELF-CONFIDENCE AS A MAN.

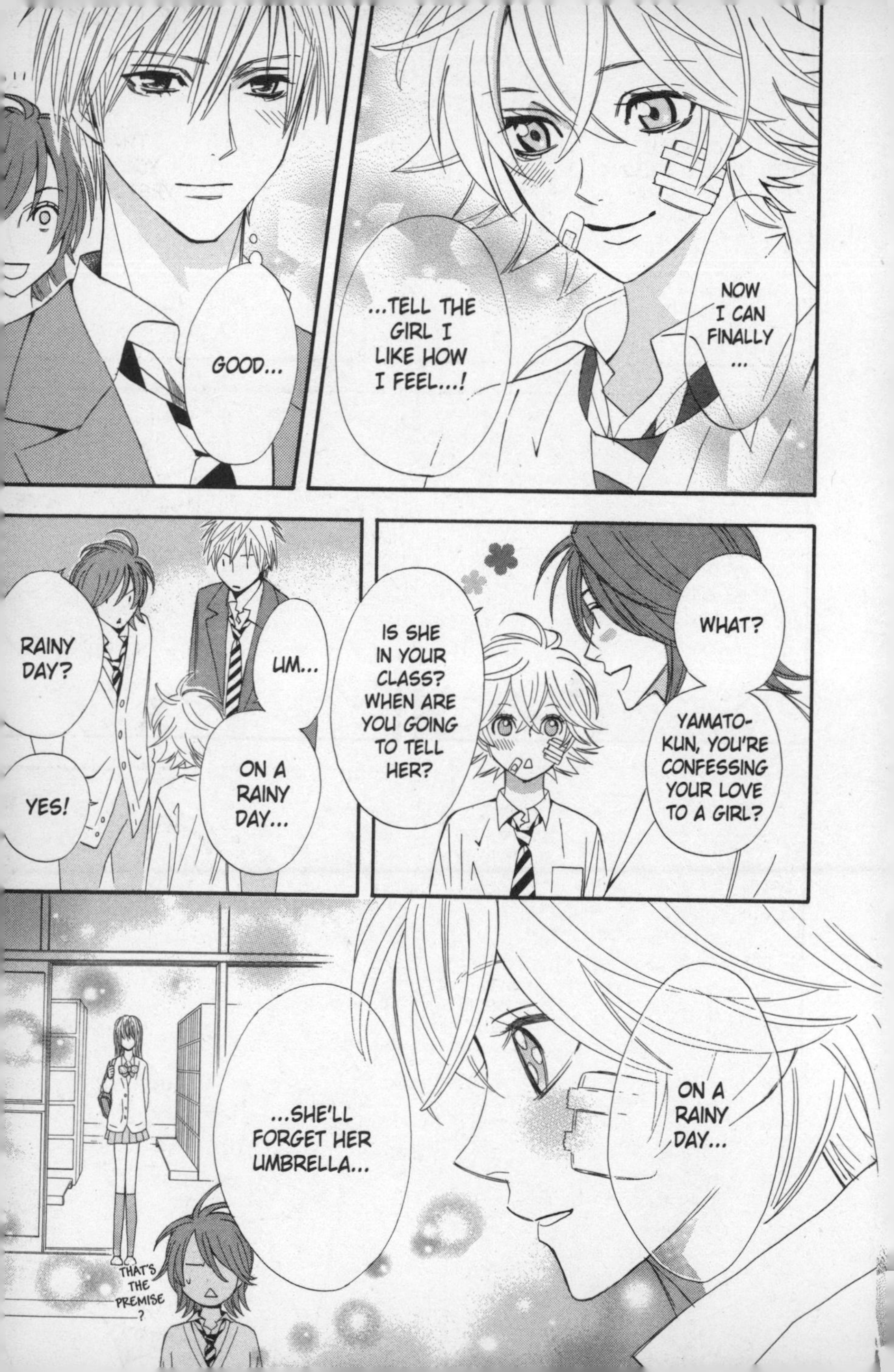
NOW I CAN FINALLY ...
...TELL THE GIRL I LIKE HOW I FEEL...!
GOOD...
WHAT?
YAMATO-KUN, YOU'RE CONFESSING YOUR LOVE TO A GIRL?
IS SHE IN YOUR CLASS? WHEN ARE YOU GOING TO TELL HER?
UM...
ON A RAINY DAY...
RAINY DAY?
YES!
ON A RAINY DAY...
...SHE'LL FORGET HER UMBRELLA...
THAT'S THE PREMISE ?

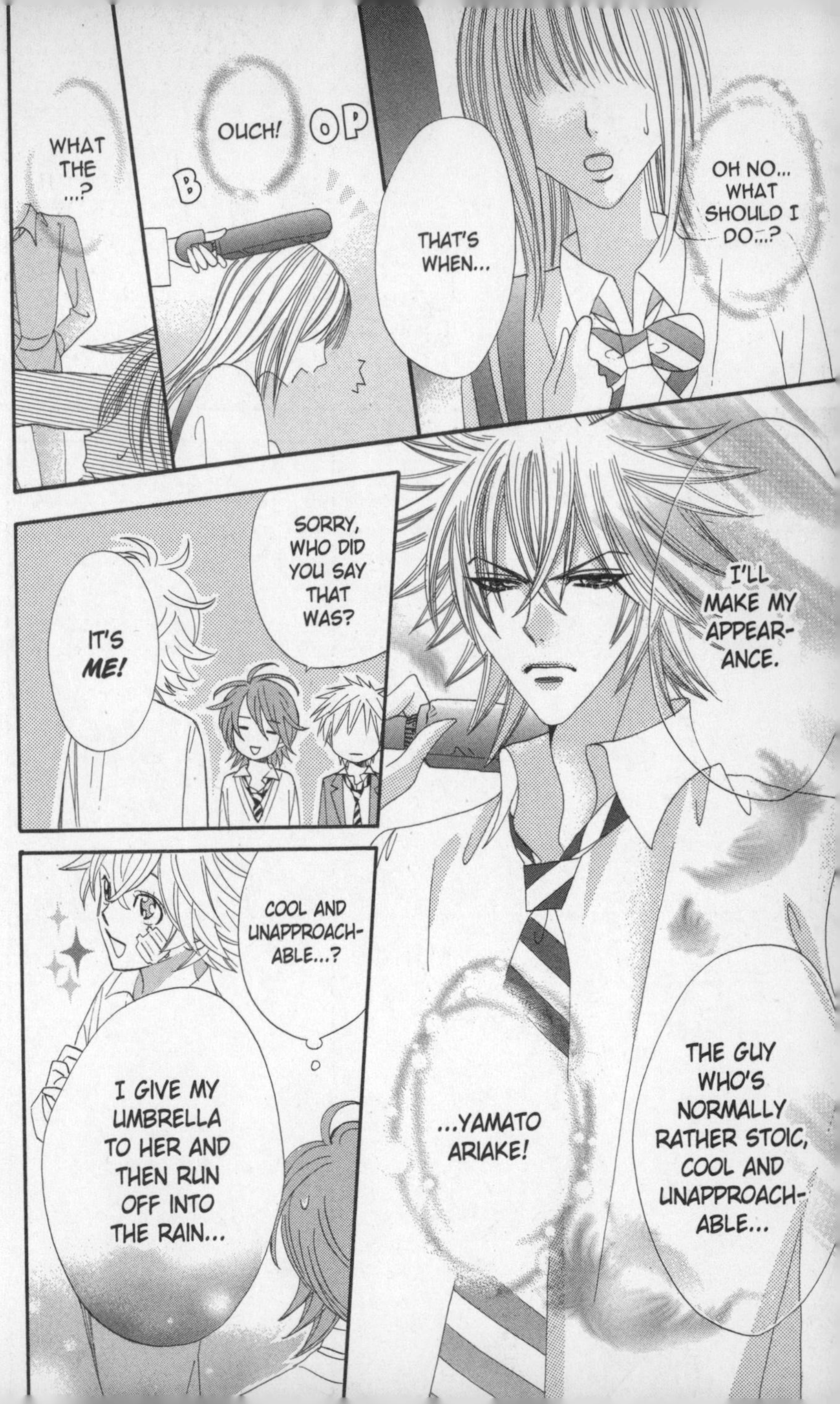
OH NO... WHAT SHOULD I DO...?
THAT'S WHEN...
OUCH!
BOP
WHAT THE ...?
I'LL MAKE MY APPEAR-ANCE.
THE GUY WHO'S NORMALLY RATHER STOIC, COOL AND UNAPPROACH-ABLE...
...YAMATO ARIAKE!
SORRY, WHO DID YOU SAY THAT WAS?
IT'S *ME!*
COOL AND UNAPPROACH-ABLE...?
I GIVE MY UMBRELLA TO HER AND THEN RUN OFF INTO THE RAIN...

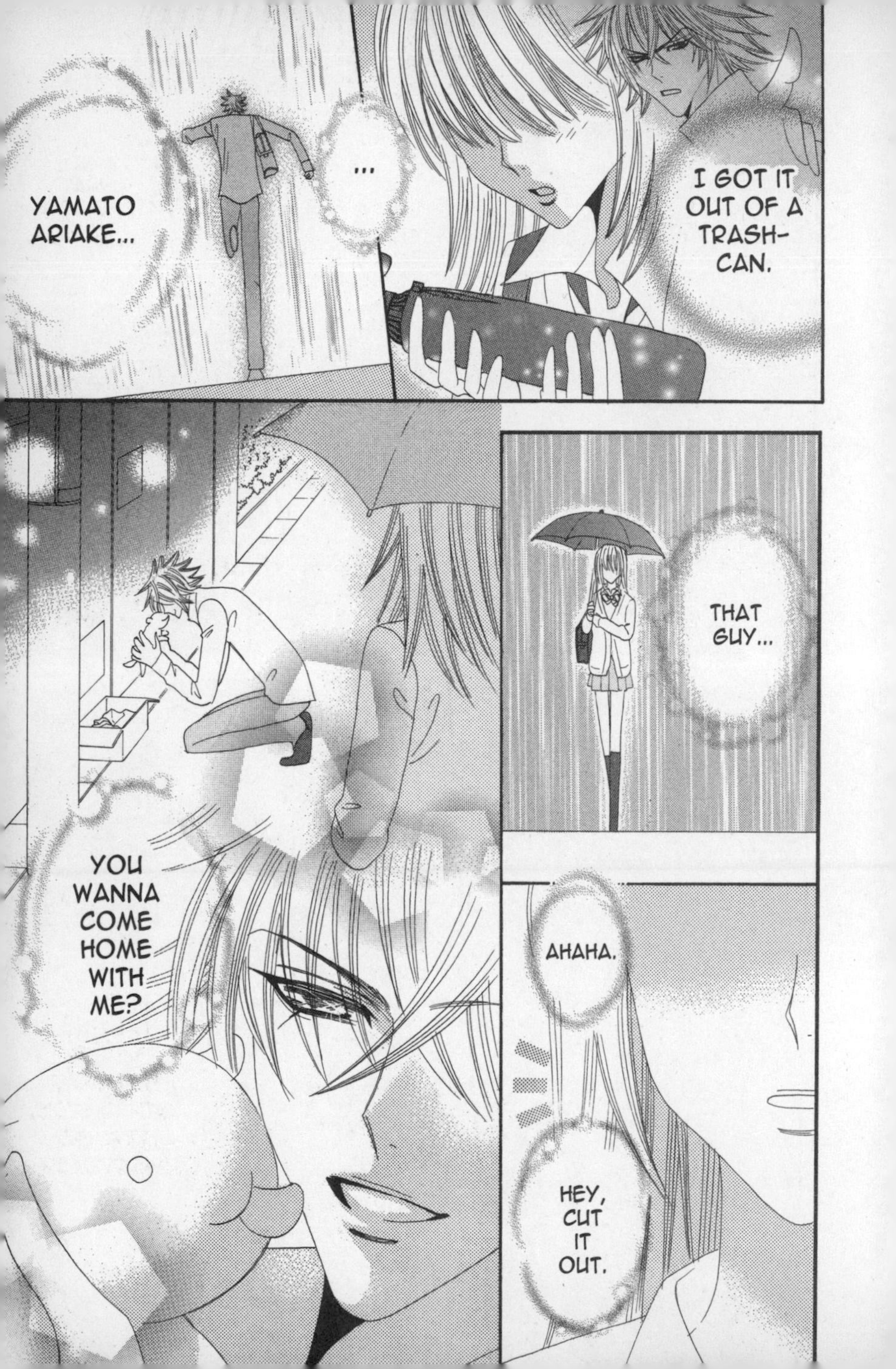
I GOT IT OUT OF A TRASH-CAN.
...
YAMATO ARIAKE...
THAT GUY...
AHAHA.
HEY, CUT IT OUT.
YOU WANNA COME HOME WITH ME?

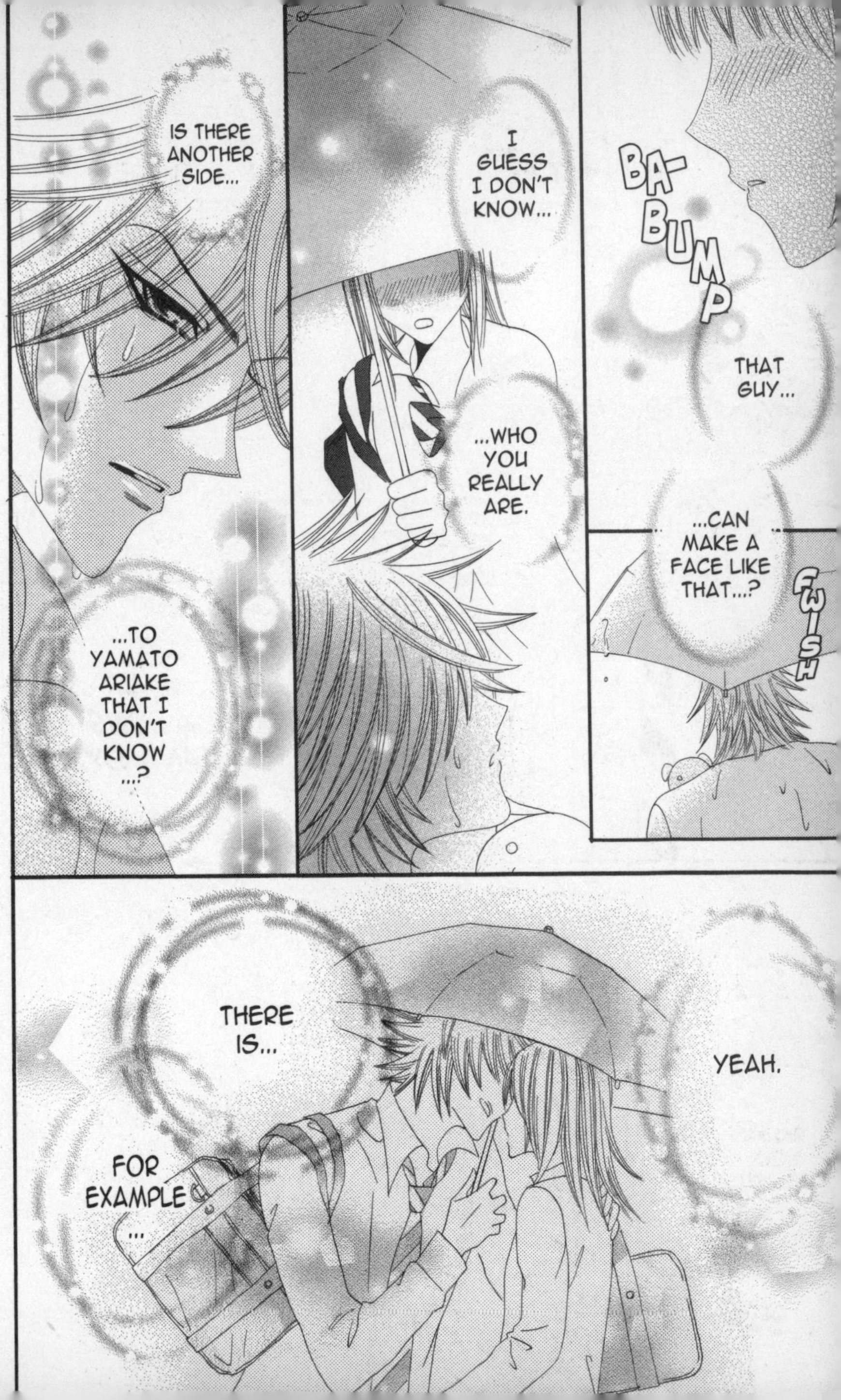
BA-BUMP
THAT GUY...
...CAN MAKE A FACE LIKE THAT...?
FWISH
I GUESS I DON'T KNOW...
...WHO YOU REALLY ARE.
IS THERE ANOTHER SIDE...
...TO YAMATO ARIAKE THAT I DON'T KNOW...?
YEAH.
THERE IS...
FOR EXAMPLE...

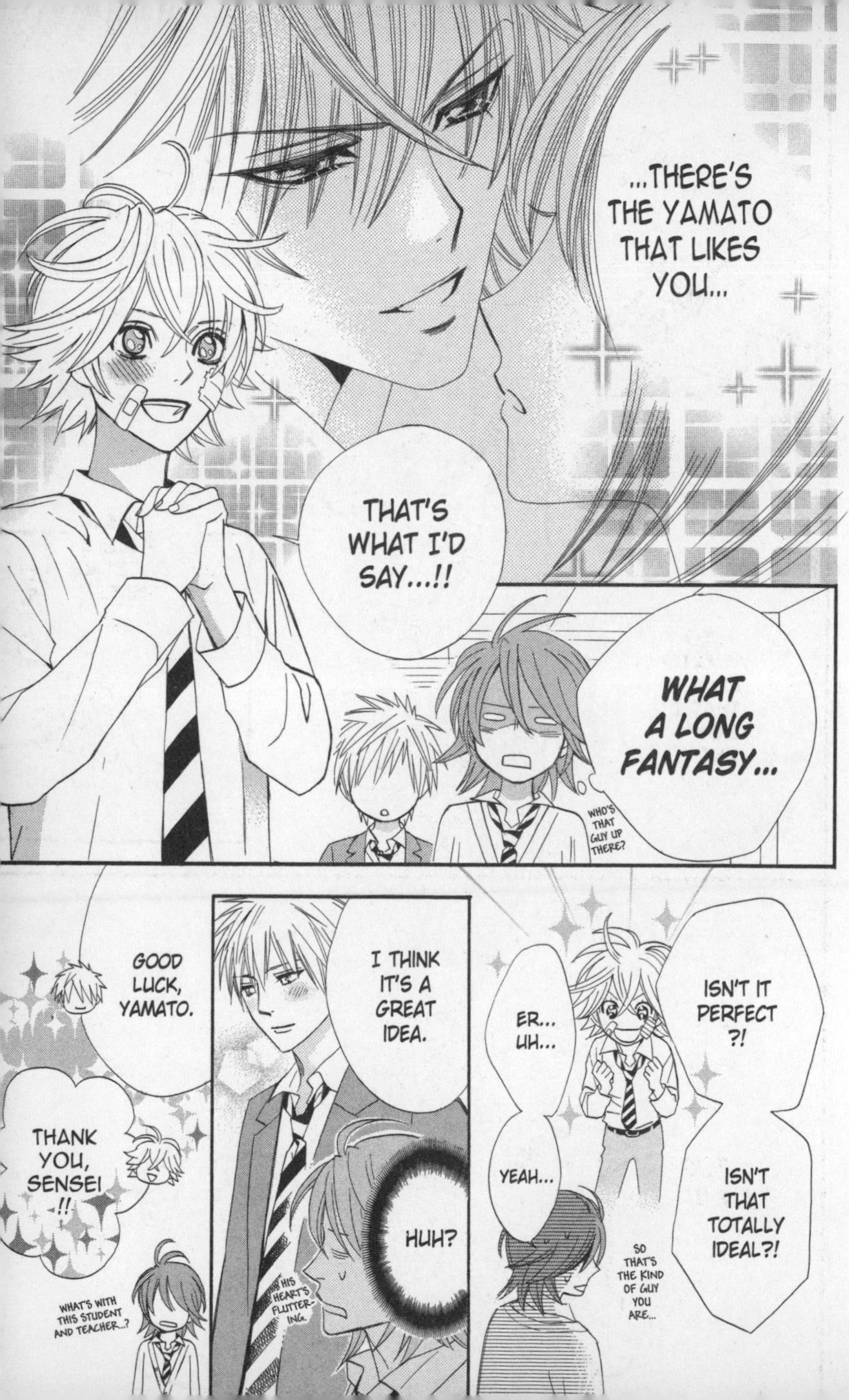
...THERE'S THE YAMATO THAT LIKES YOU...
THAT'S WHAT I'D SAY...!!
WHAT A LONG FANTASY...
WHO'S THAT GUY UP THERE?
ISN'T IT PERFECT ?!
ER... UH...
ISN'T THAT TOTALLY IDEAL?!
YEAH...
SO THAT'S THE KIND OF GUY YOU ARE...
I THINK IT'S A GREAT IDEA.
HUH?
HIS HEART'S FLUTTER-ING.
GOOD LUCK, YAMATO.
THANK YOU, SENSEI !!
WHAT'S WITH THIS STUDENT AND TEACHER...?

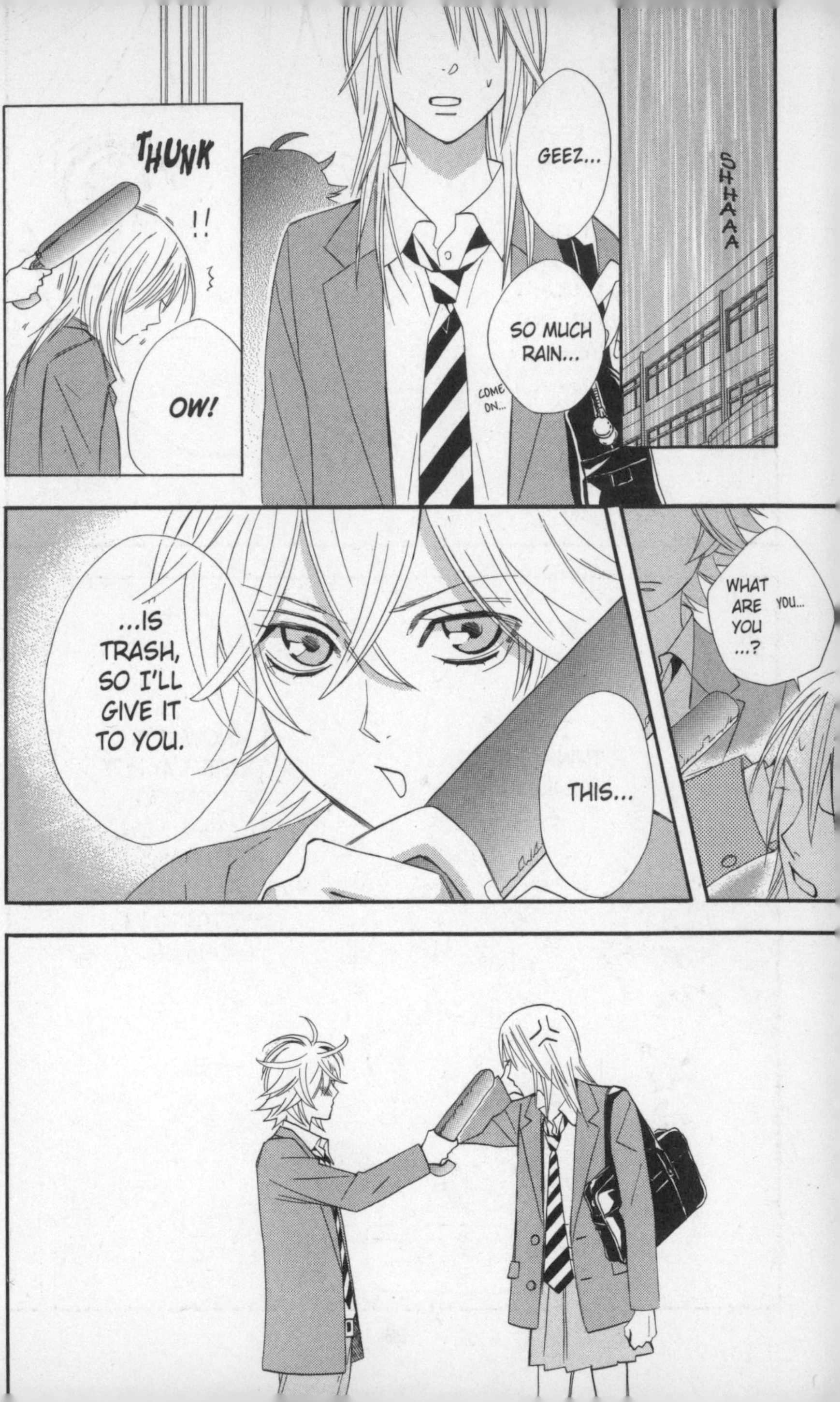
SHHAAA
GEEZ...
SO MUCH RAIN...
COME ON...
THUNK
!!
OW!
WHAT ARE YOU ...?
YOU...
THIS...
...IS TRASH, SO I'LL GIVE IT TO YOU.

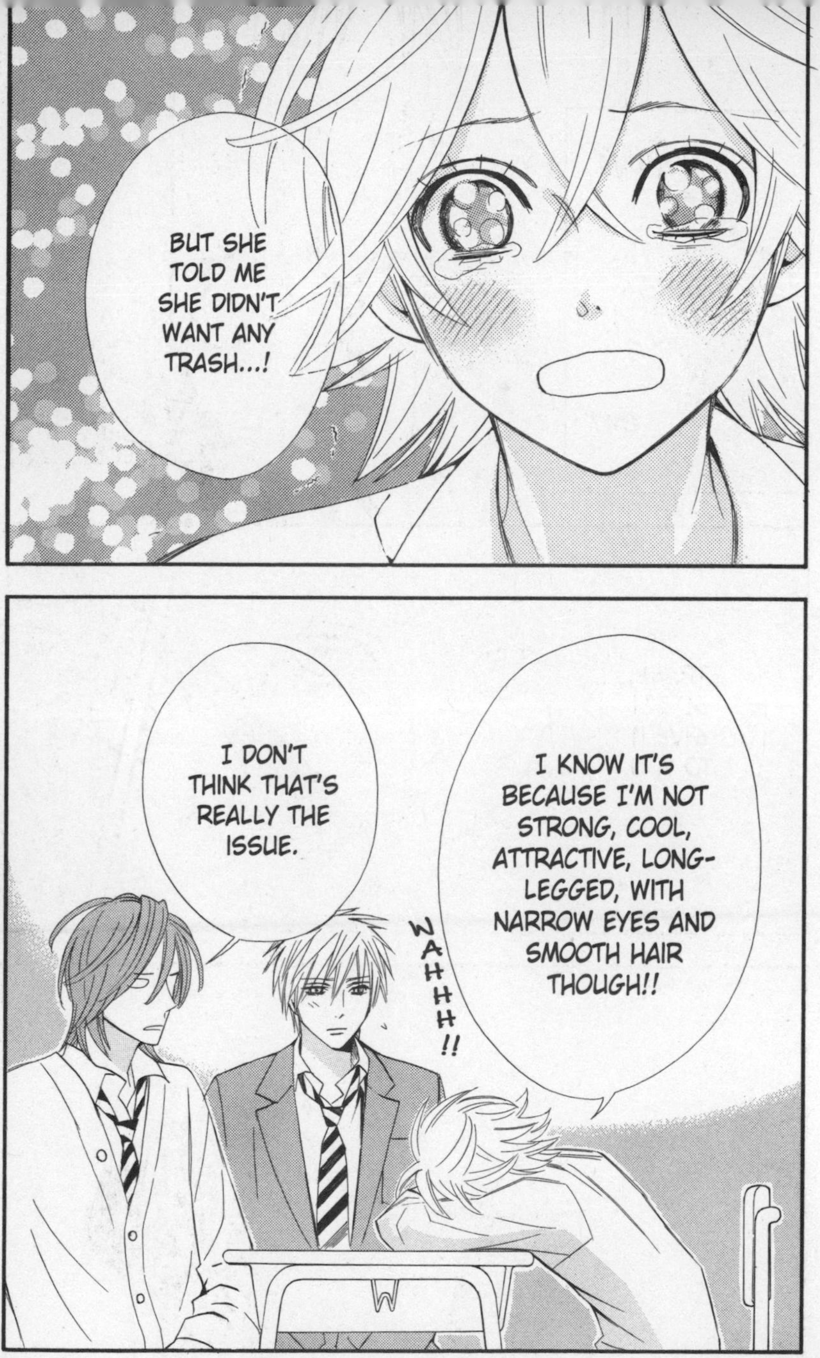
BUT SHE TOLD ME SHE DIDN'T WANT ANY TRASH...!
I KNOW IT'S BECAUSE I'M NOT STRONG, COOL, ATTRACTIVE, LONG-LEGGED, WITH NARROW EYES AND SMOOTH HAIR THOUGH!!
WAHHH!!
I DON'T THINK THAT'S REALLY THE ISSUE.

OTOMEN

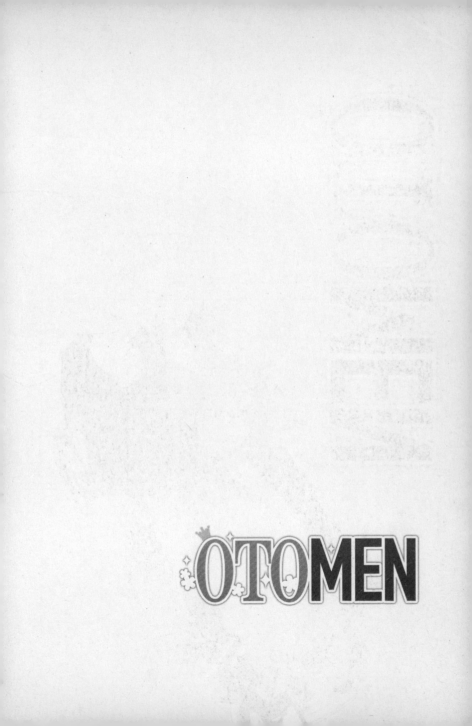

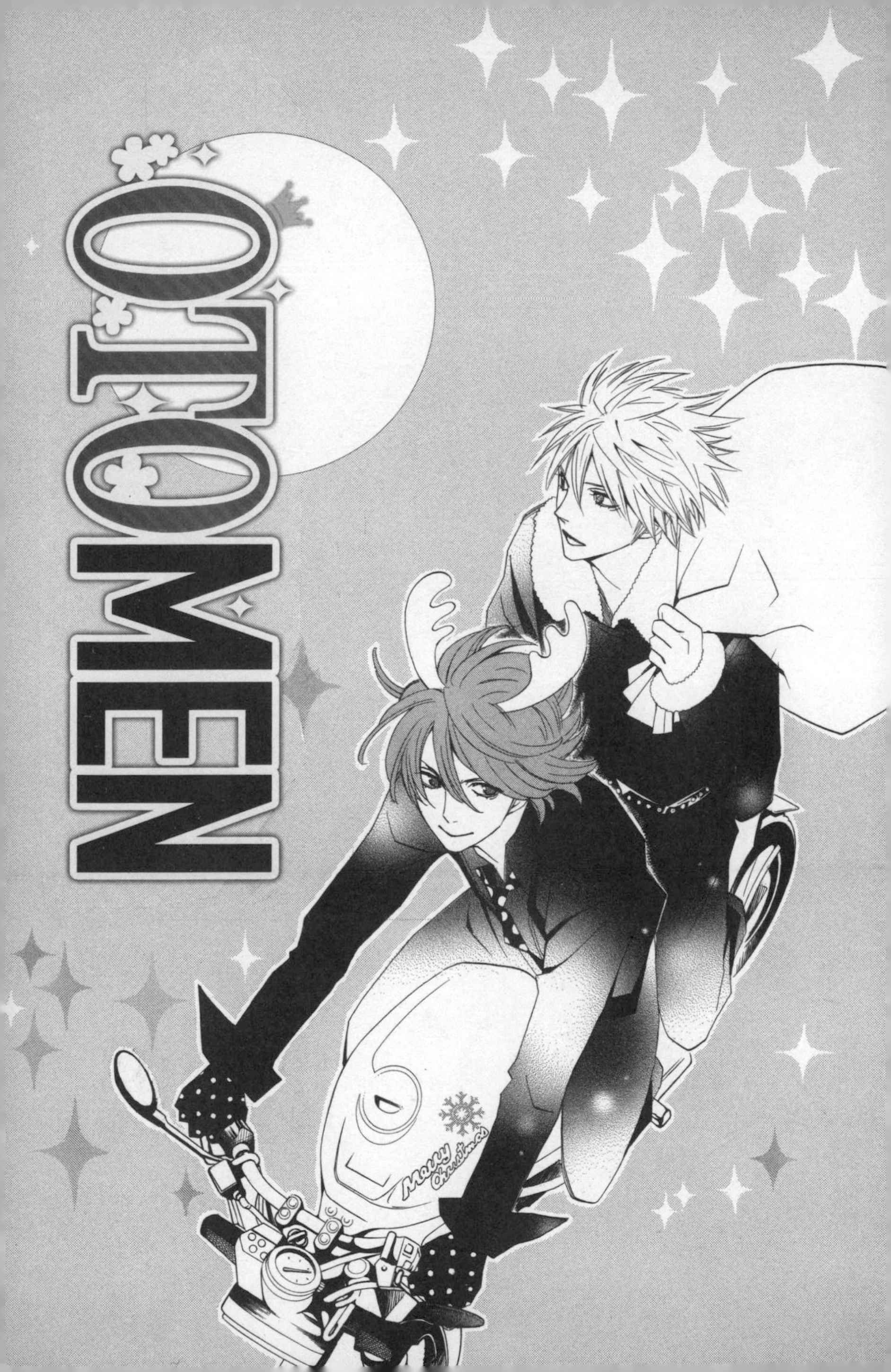
OTOMEN
Merry Christmas

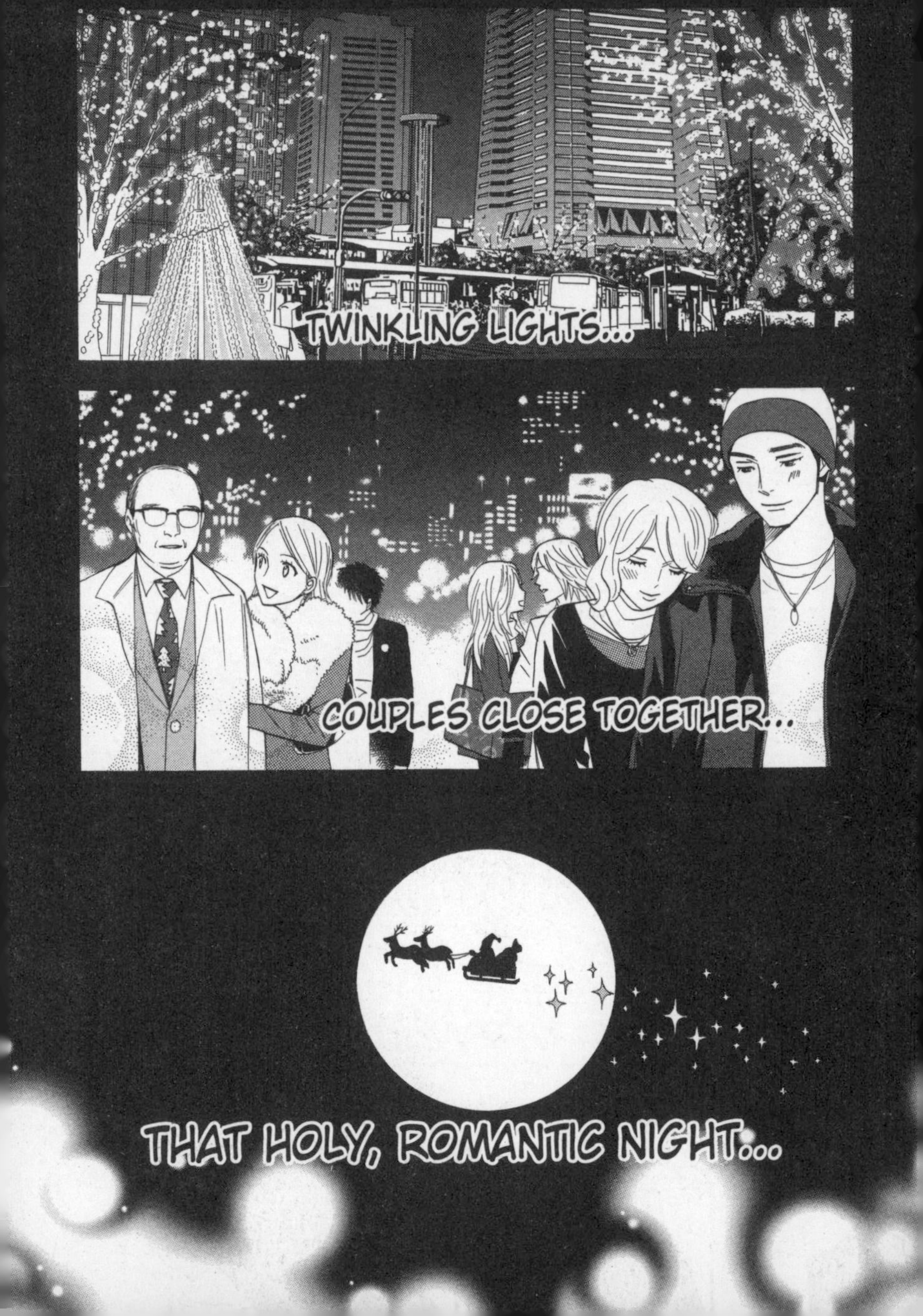
TWINKLING LIGHTS...
COUPLES CLOSE TOGETHER...
THAT HOLY, ROMANTIC NIGHT...

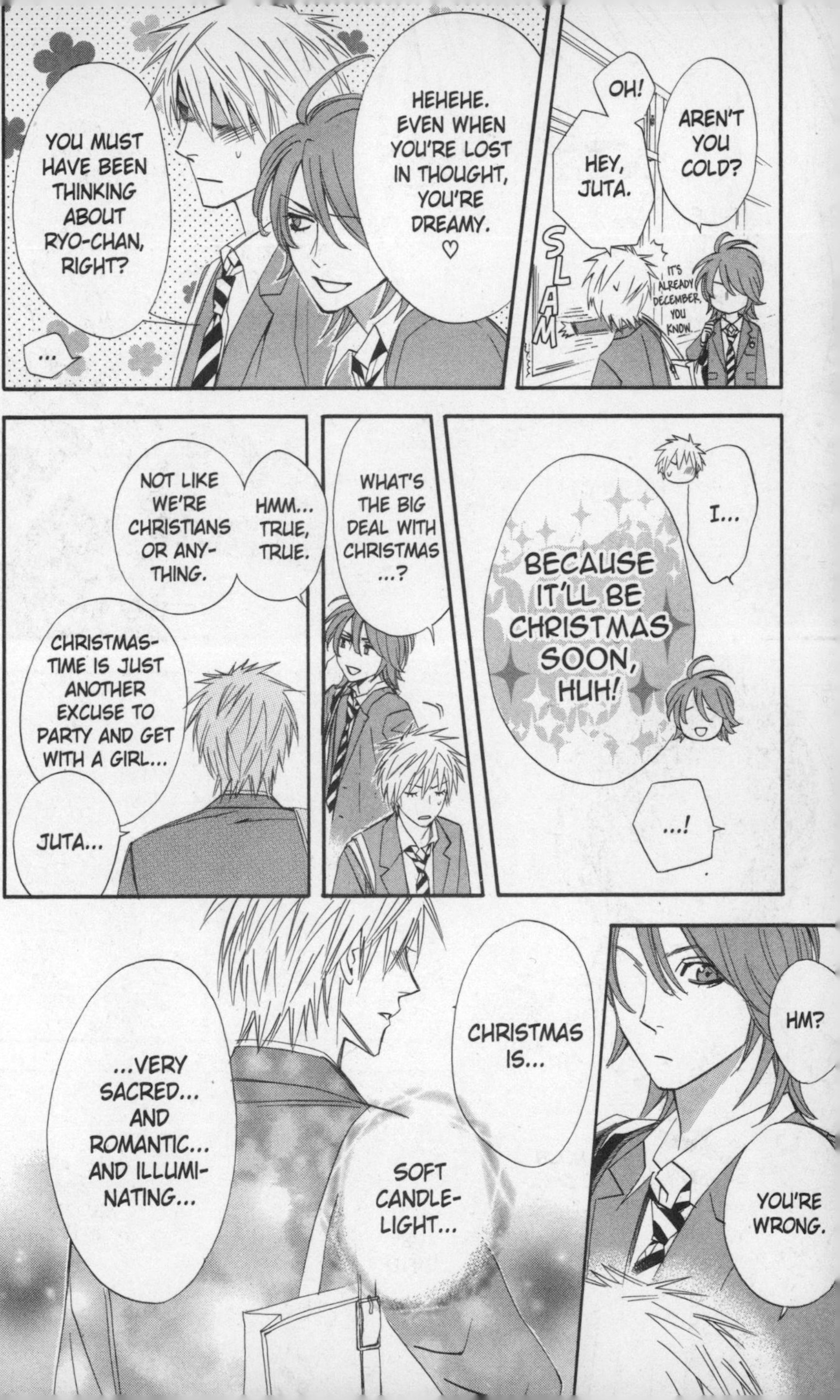
OH!
HEY, JUTA.
AREN'T YOU COLD?
SLAM
IT'S ALREADY DECEMBER, YOU KNOW.
HEHEHE. EVEN WHEN YOU'RE LOST IN THOUGHT, YOU'RE DREAMY. ♡
YOU MUST HAVE BEEN THINKING ABOUT RYO-CHAN, RIGHT?
...
I...
BECAUSE IT'LL BE CHRISTMAS SOON, HUH!
...!
WHAT'S THE BIG DEAL WITH CHRISTMAS ...?
HMM... TRUE, TRUE.
NOT LIKE WE'RE CHRISTIANS OR ANY-THING.
CHRISTMAS-TIME IS JUST ANOTHER EXCUSE TO PARTY AND GET WITH A GIRL...
JUTA...
HM?
YOU'RE WRONG.
CHRISTMAS IS...
...VERY SACRED... AND ROMANTIC... AND ILLUMI-NATING...
SOFT CANDLE-LIGHT...

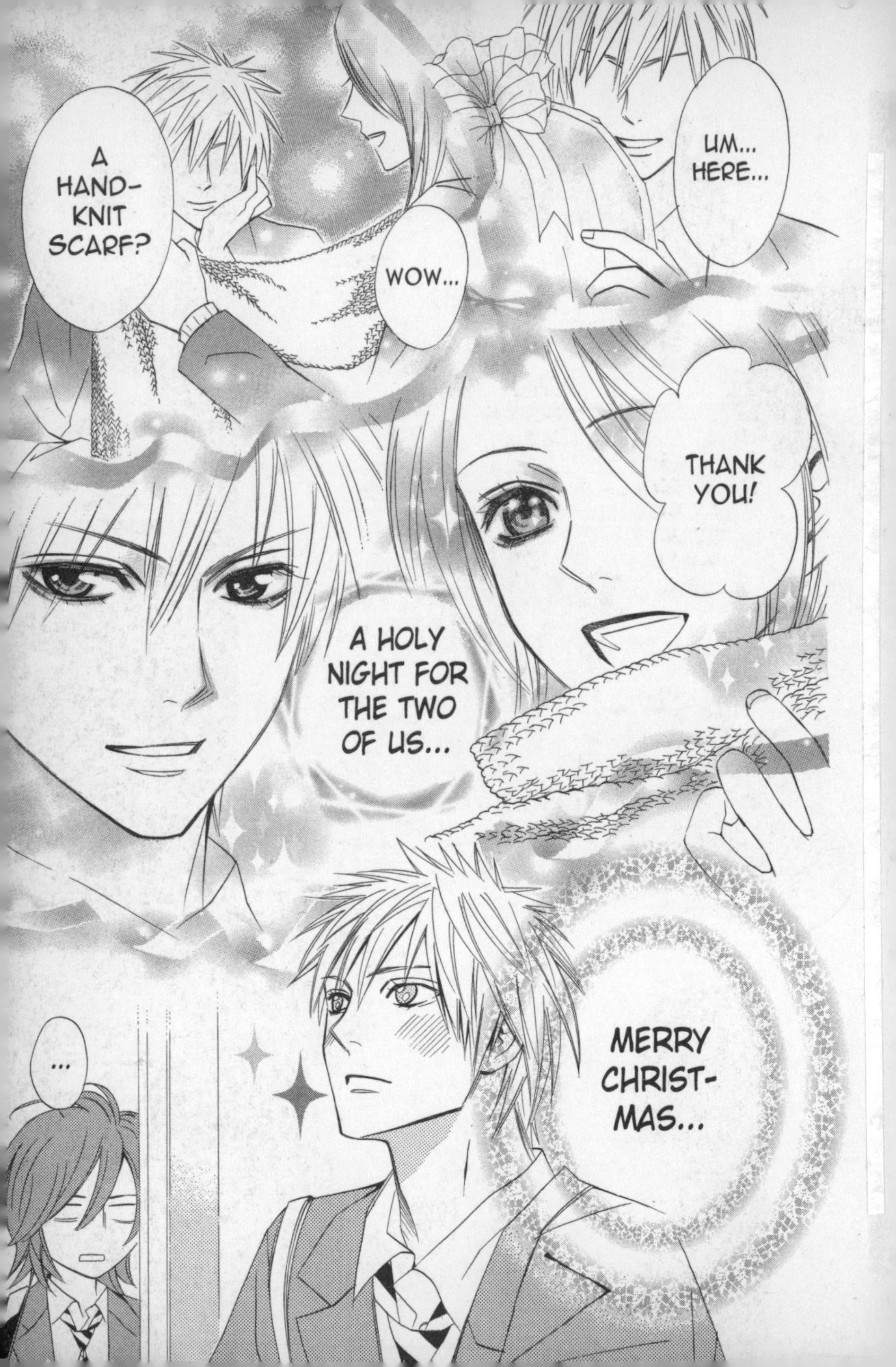
UM... HERE...
WOW...
A HAND-KNIT SCARF?
THANK YOU!
A HOLY NIGHT FOR THE TWO OF US...
MERRY CHRIST-MAS...
...

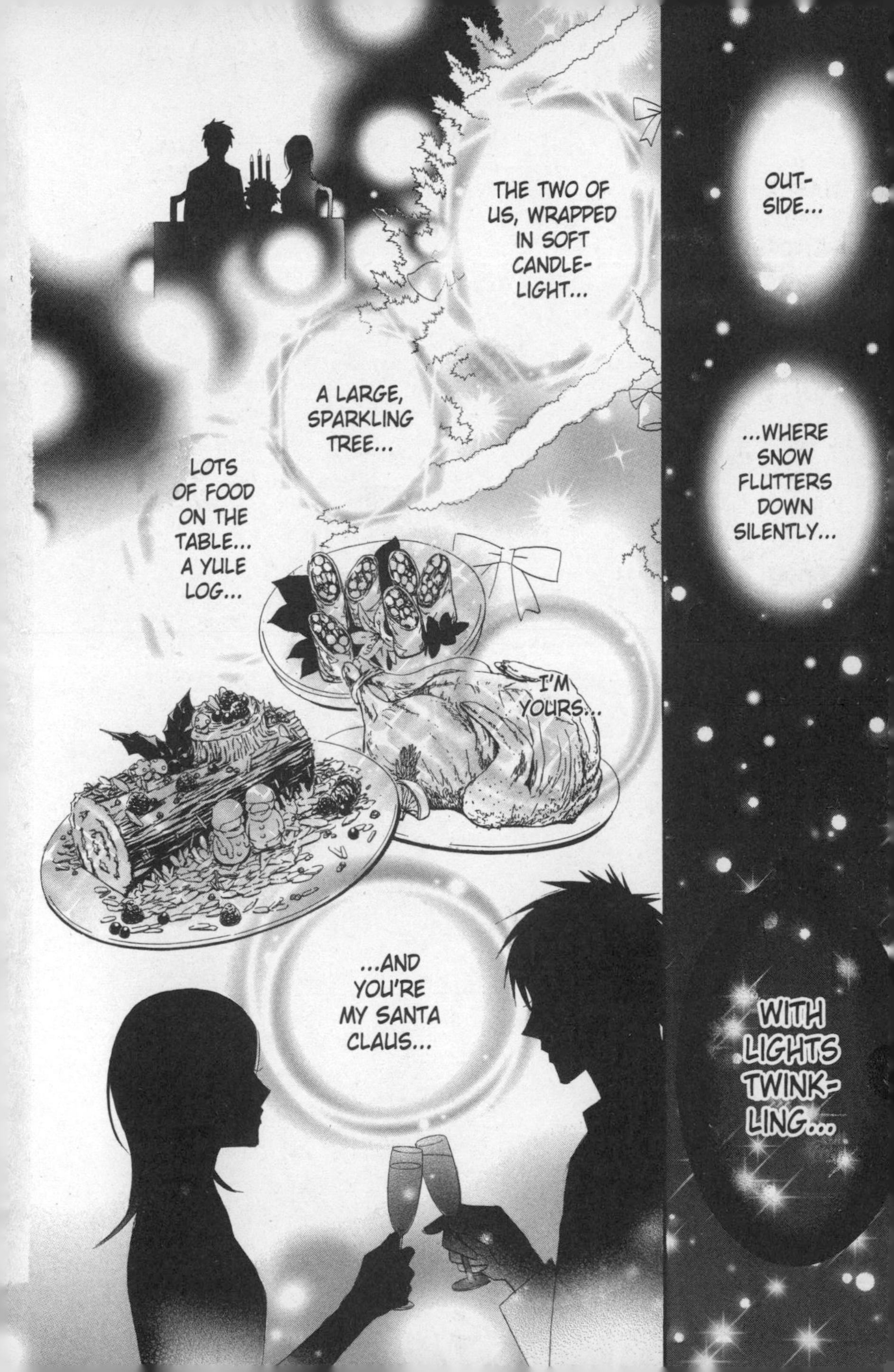
OUT-SIDE...
...WHERE SNOW FLUTTERS DOWN SILENTLY...
WITH LIGHTS TWINK-LING...
THE TWO OF US, WRAPPED IN SOFT CANDLE-LIGHT...
A LARGE, SPARKLING TREE...
LOTS OF FOOD ON THE TABLE... A YULE LOG...
I'M YOURS...
...AND YOU'RE MY SANTA CLAUS...

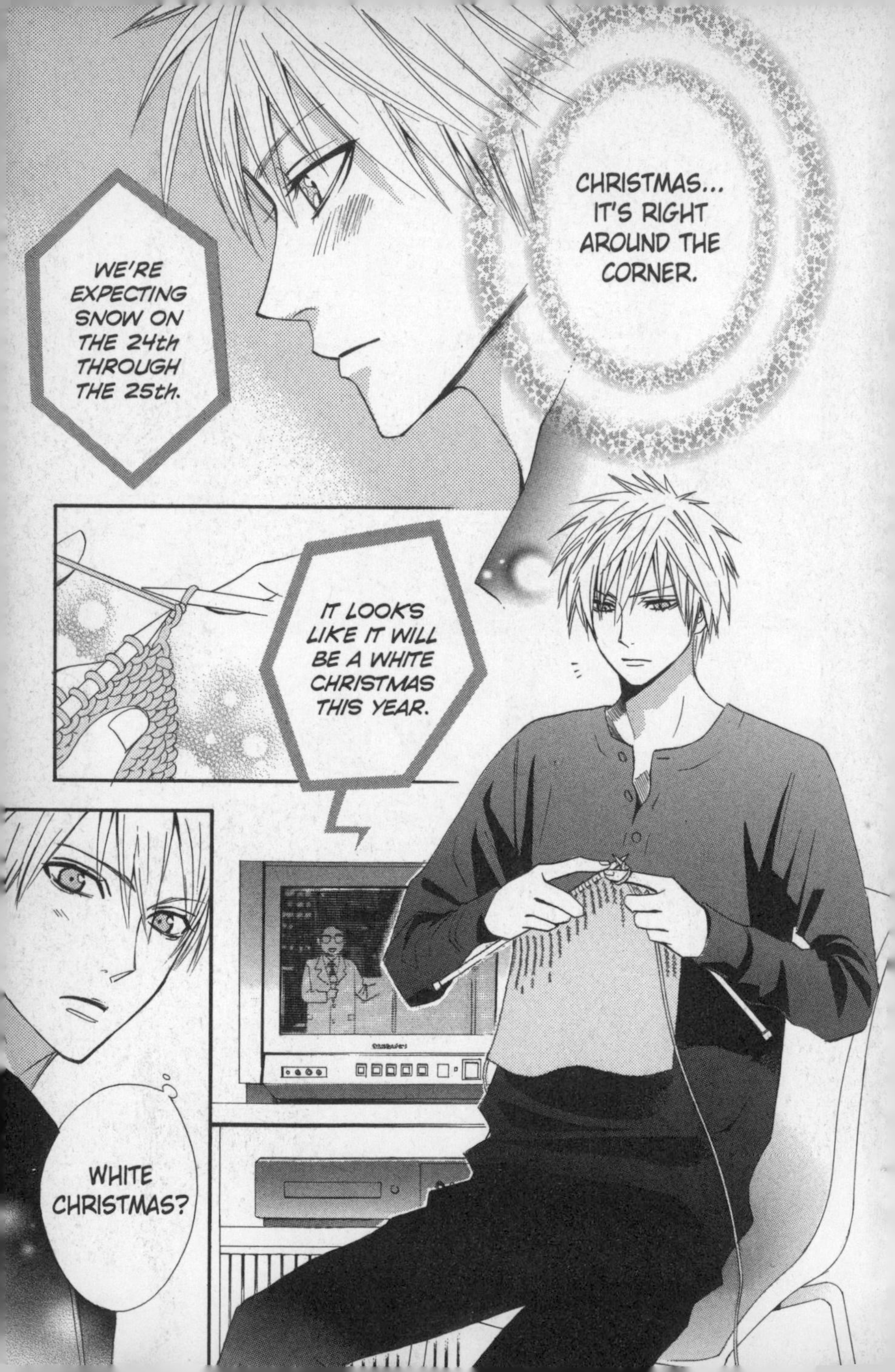
CHRISTMAS... IT'S RIGHT AROUND THE CORNER.
WE'RE EXPECTING SNOW ON THE 24th THROUGH THE 25th.
IT LOOKS LIKE IT WILL BE A WHITE CHRISTMAS THIS YEAR.
WHITE CHRISTMAS?

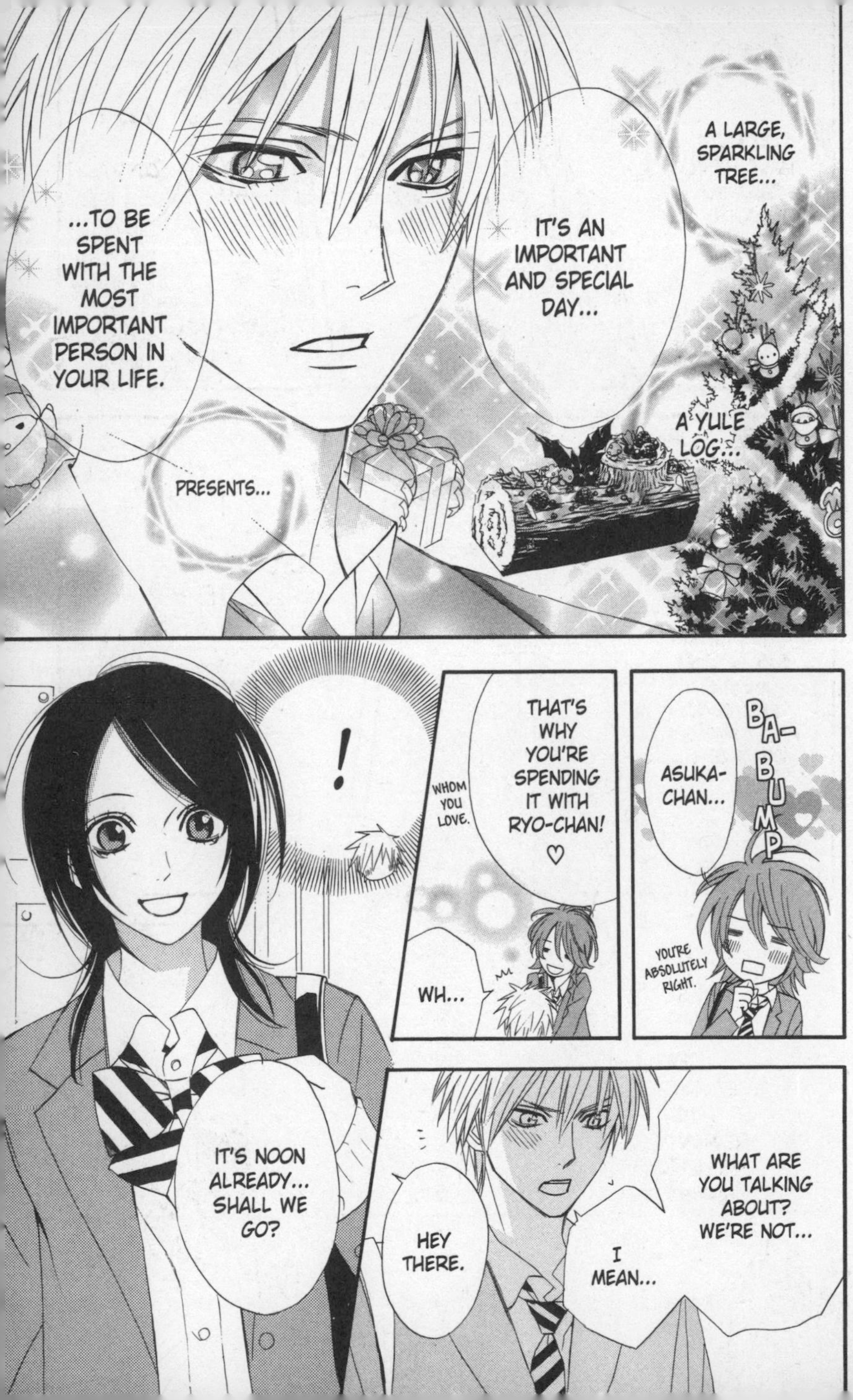
A LARGE, SPARKLING TREE...
A YULE LOG...
IT'S AN IMPORTANT AND SPECIAL DAY...
PRESENTS...
...TO BE SPENT WITH THE MOST IMPORTANT PERSON IN YOUR LIFE.
BA-BUMP
ASUKA-CHAN...
YOU'RE ABSOLUTELY RIGHT.
THAT'S WHY YOU'RE SPENDING IT WITH RYO-CHAN! ♡
WHOM YOU LOVE.
WH...
WHAT ARE YOU TALKING ABOUT? WE'RE NOT...
I MEAN...
HEY THERE.
!
IT'S NOON ALREADY... SHALL WE GO?

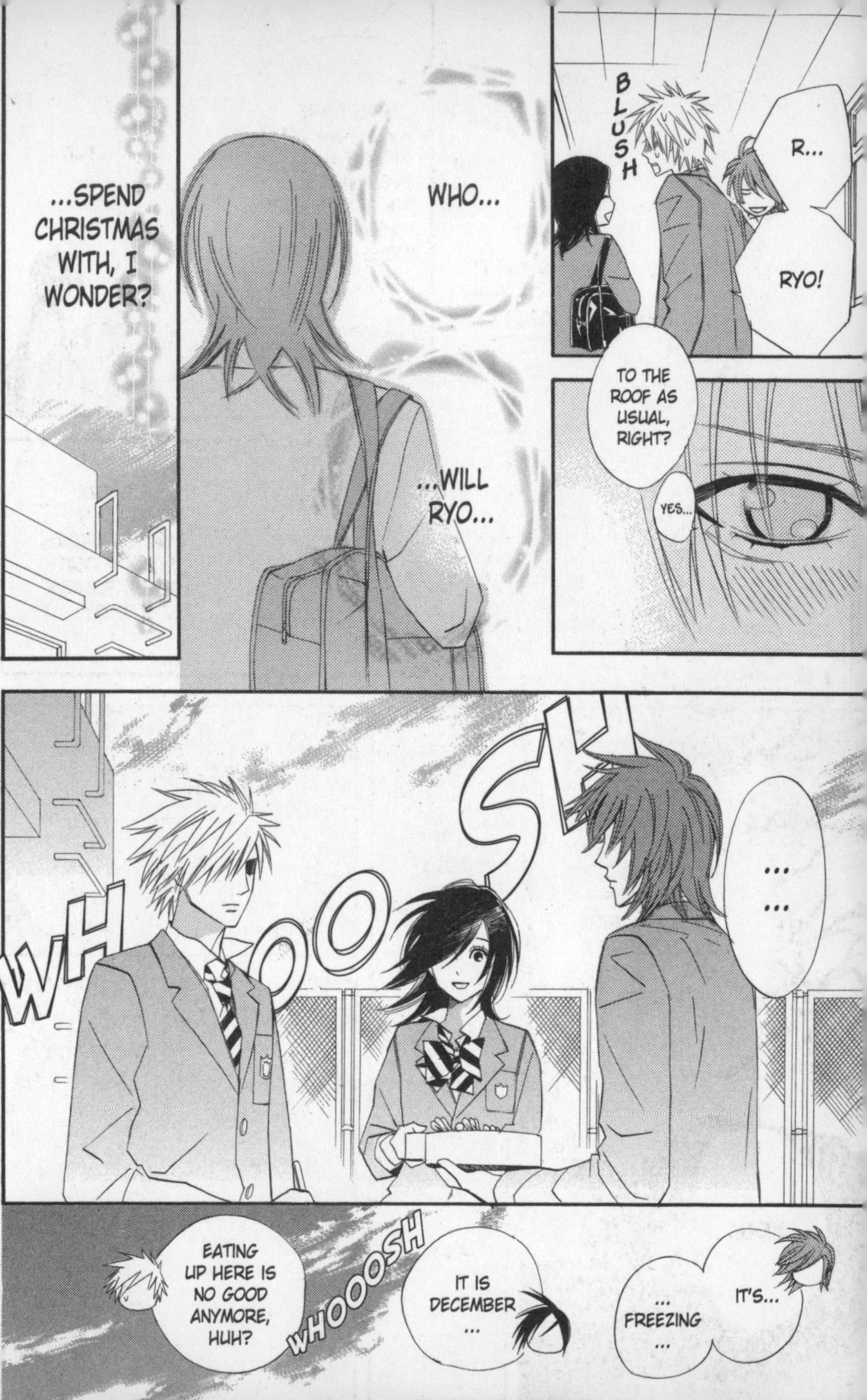
BLUSH
R...
RYO!
TO THE ROOF AS USUAL, RIGHT?
YES...
WHO...
...WILL RYO...
...SPEND CHRISTMAS WITH, I WONDER?
WHOOOSH
... ...
IT'S...
... FREEZING ...
IT IS DECEMBER ...
EATING UP HERE IS NO GOOD ANYMORE, HUH?
WHOOOSH

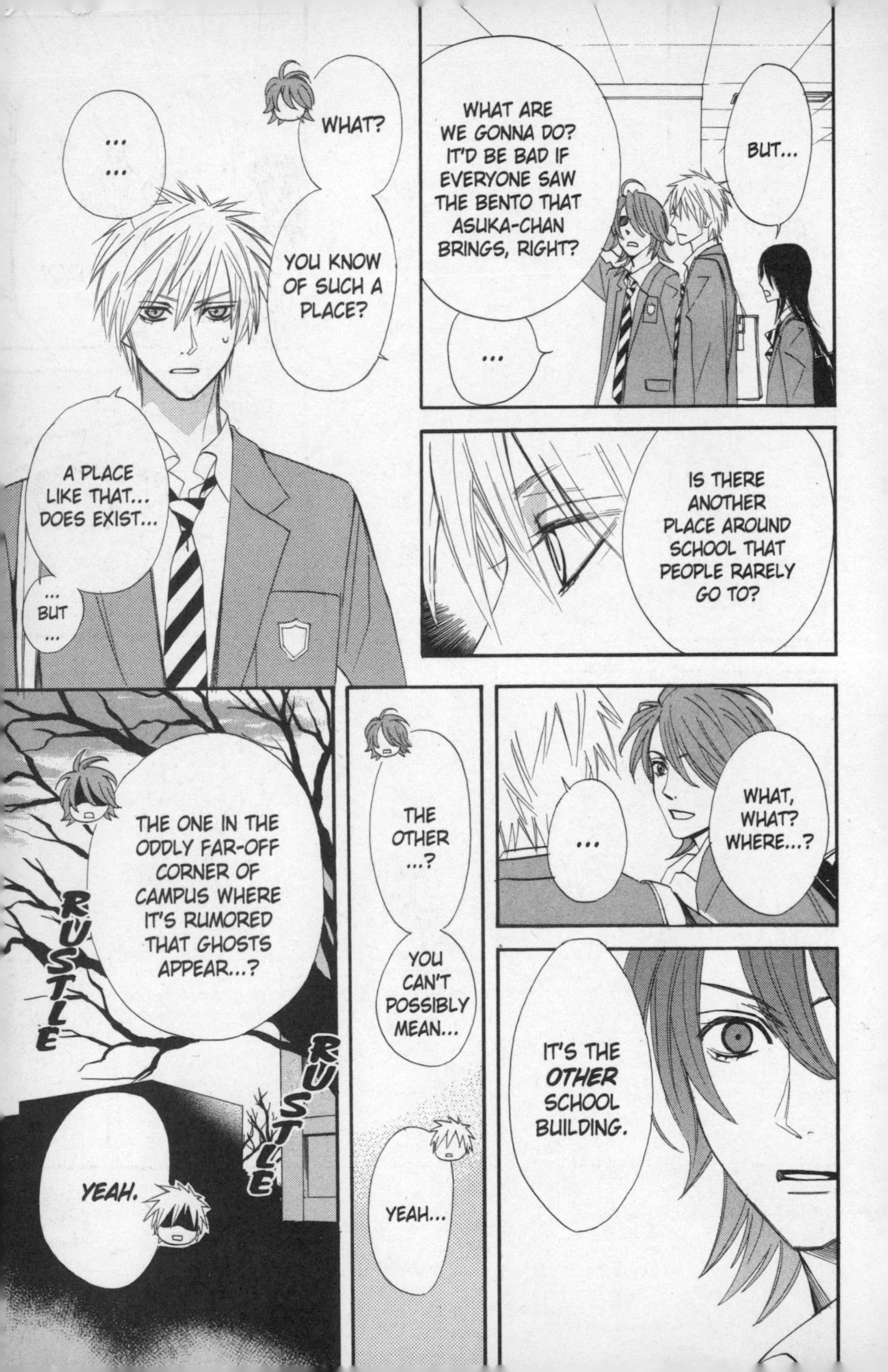
BUT...
WHAT ARE WE GONNA DO? IT'D BE BAD IF EVERYONE SAW THE BENTO THAT ASUKA-CHAN BRINGS, RIGHT?
...
IS THERE ANOTHER PLACE AROUND SCHOOL THAT PEOPLE RARELY GO TO?
WHAT?
YOU KNOW OF SUCH A PLACE?
... ...
A PLACE LIKE THAT... DOES EXIST...
... BUT ...
WHAT, WHAT? WHERE...?
...
IT'S THE *OTHER* SCHOOL BUILDING.
THE OTHER ...?
YOU CAN'T POSSIBLY MEAN...
YEAH...
THE ONE IN THE ODDLY FAR-OFF CORNER OF CAMPUS WHERE IT'S RUMORED THAT GHOSTS APPEAR...?
RUSTLE
RUSTLE
YEAH.

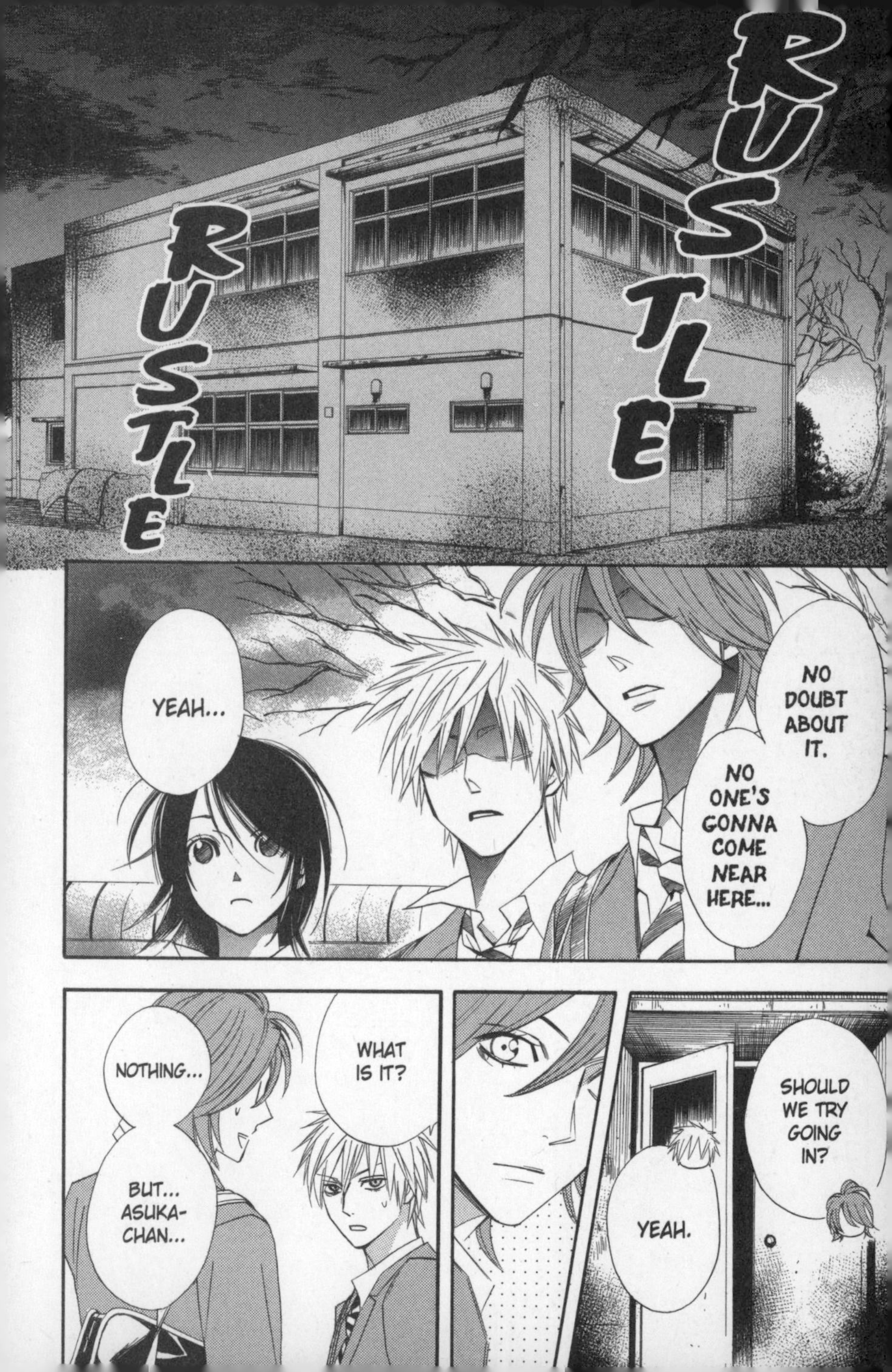
RUSTLE
RUSTLE
NO DOUBT ABOUT IT.
NO ONE'S GONNA COME NEAR HERE...
YEAH...
SHOULD WE TRY GOING IN?
YEAH.
WHAT IS IT?
NOTHING...
BUT... ASUKA-CHAN...

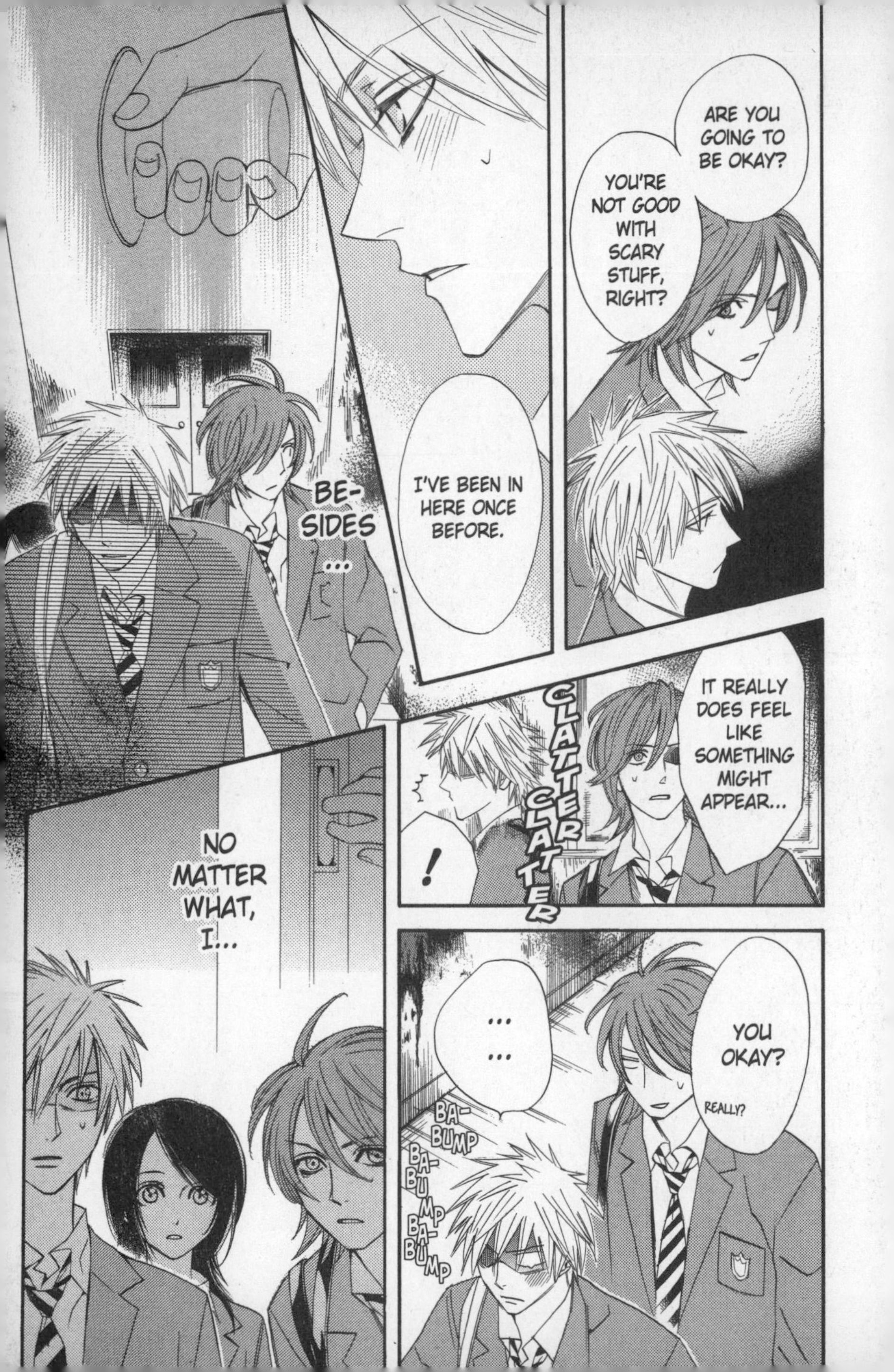
ARE YOU GOING TO BE OKAY?
YOU'RE NOT GOOD WITH SCARY STUFF, RIGHT?
I'VE BEEN IN HERE ONCE BEFORE.
BE-SIDES ...
IT REALLY DOES FEEL LIKE SOMETHING MIGHT APPEAR...
CLATTER CLATTER CLATTER
!
YOU OKAY?
REALLY?
... ...
BA-BUMP BA-BUMP BA-BUMP
NO MATTER WHAT, I...

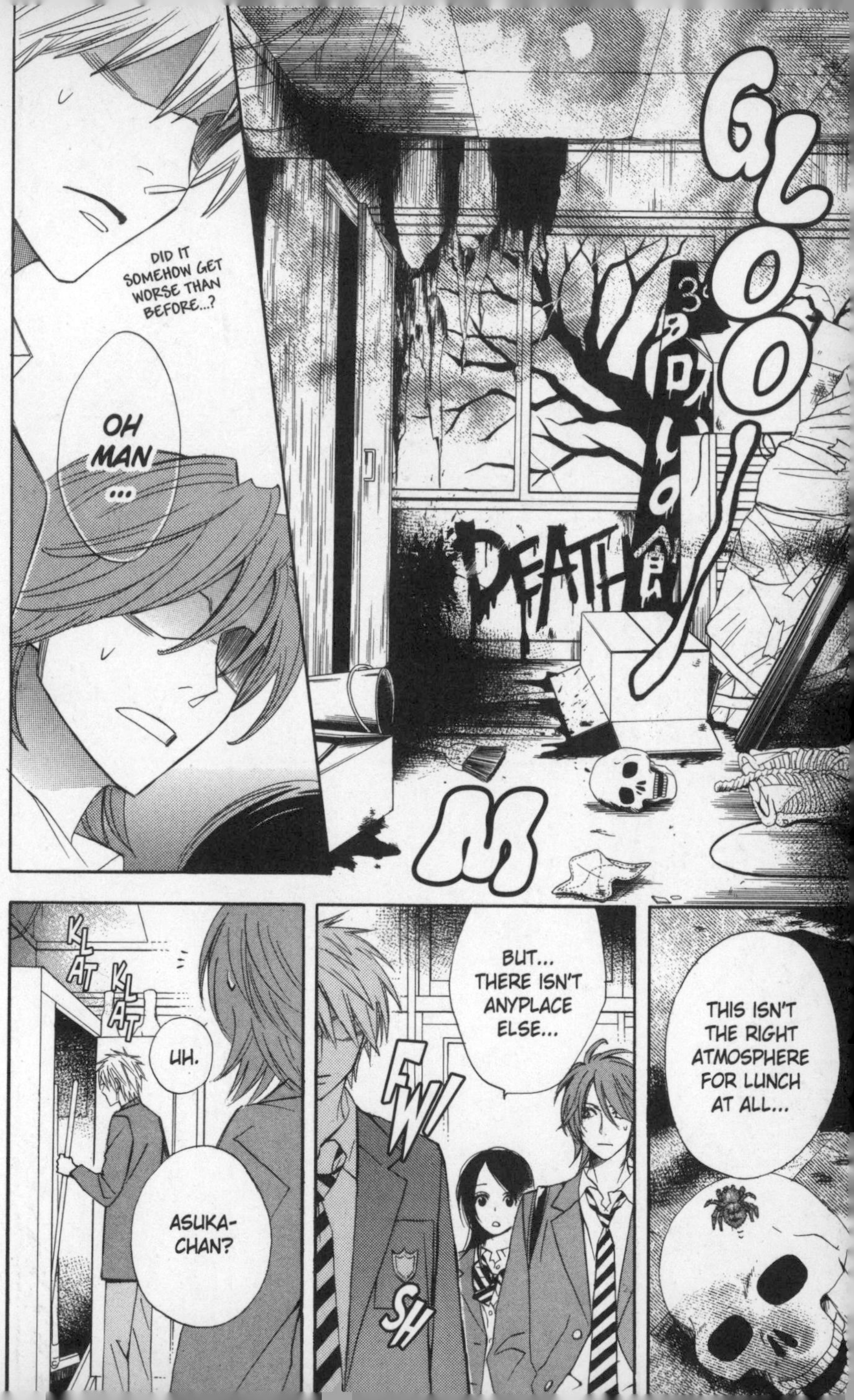
GLOOO
M
DEATH
DID IT SOMEHOW GET WORSE THAN BEFORE...?
OH MAN...
THIS ISN'T THE RIGHT ATMOSPHERE FOR LUNCH AT ALL...
BUT... THERE ISN'T ANYPLACE ELSE...
FWI
SH
KLAT KLAT
UH.
ASUKA-CHAN?

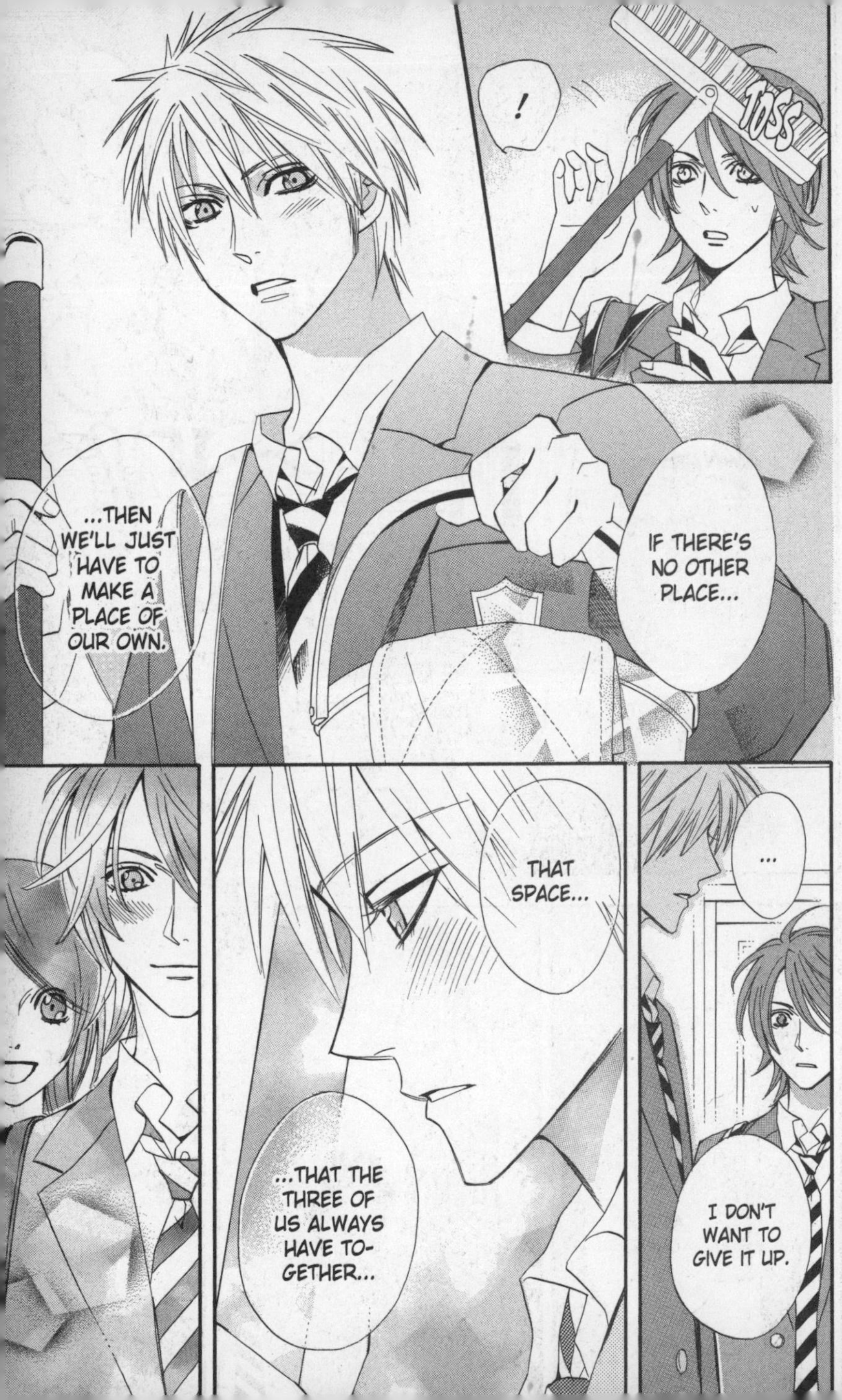
!
TOSS
IF THERE'S NO OTHER PLACE...
...THEN WE'LL JUST HAVE TO MAKE A PLACE OF OUR OWN.
...
I DON'T WANT TO GIVE IT UP.
THAT SPACE...
...THAT THE THREE OF US ALWAYS HAVE TO-GETHER...

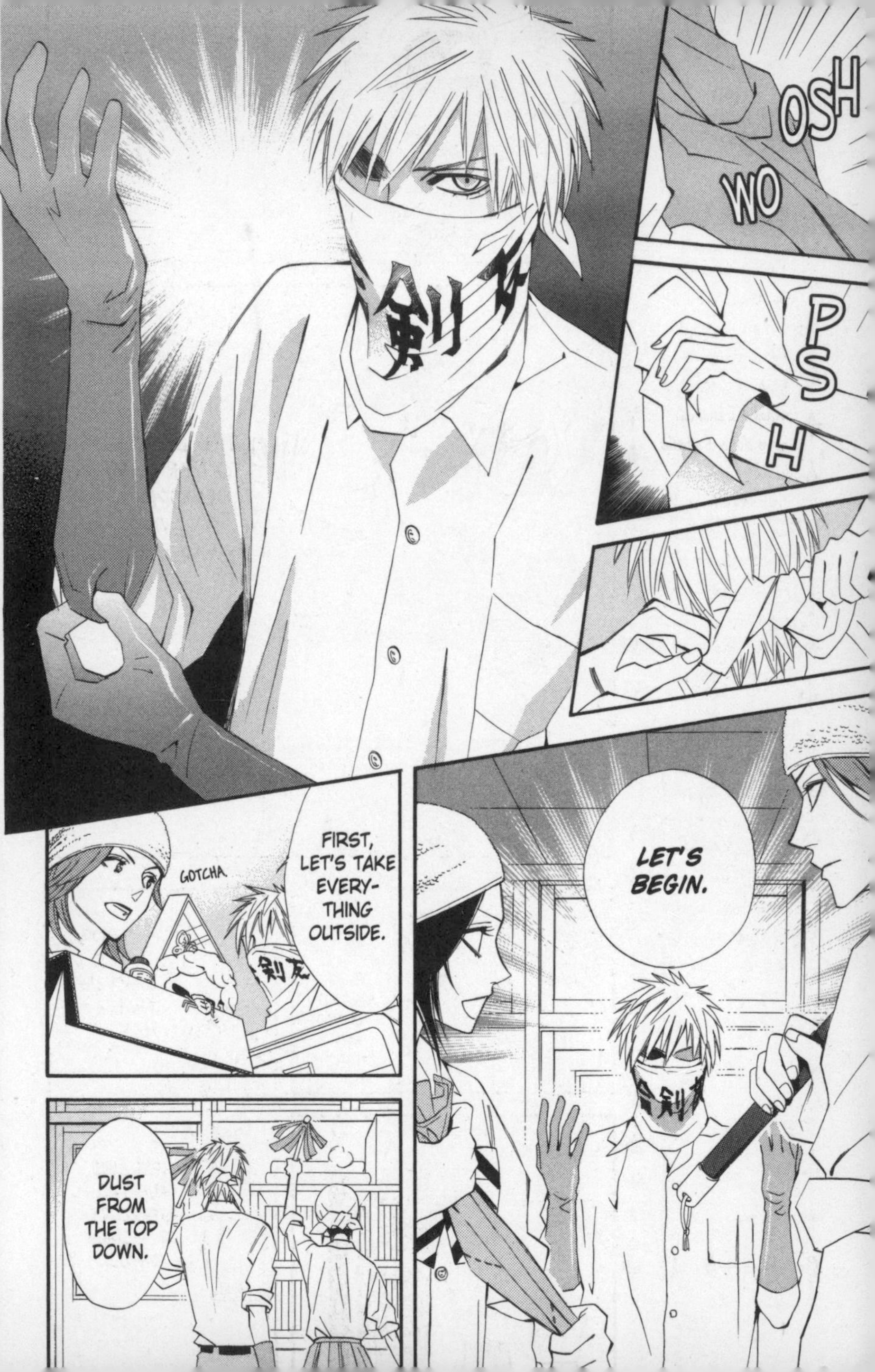
WOOSH
PSH
LET'S BEGIN.
FIRST, LET'S TAKE EVERY-THING OUTSIDE.
GOTCHA.
DUST FROM THE TOP DOWN.

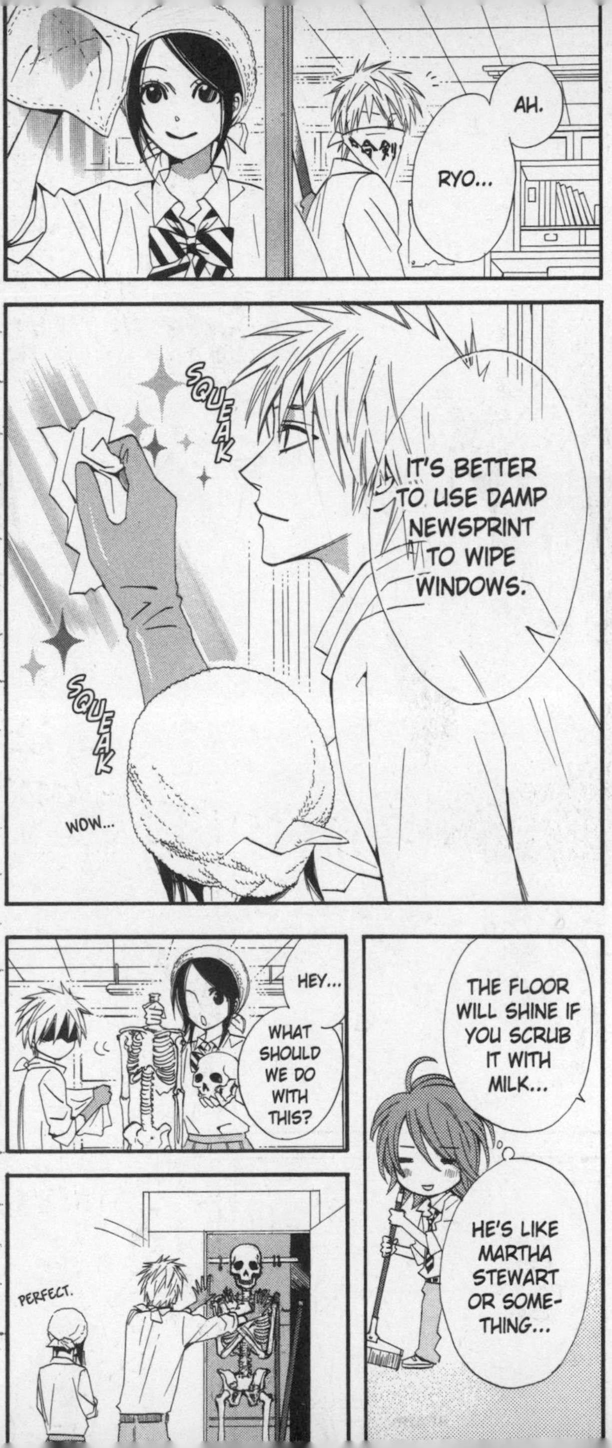
AH.
RYO...
SQUEAK
IT'S BETTER TO USE DAMP NEWSPRINT TO WIPE WINDOWS.
SQUEAK
WOW...
THE FLOOR WILL SHINE IF YOU SCRUB IT WITH MILK...
HE'S LIKE MARTHA STEWART OR SOME-THING...
HEY...
WHAT SHOULD WE DO WITH THIS?
PERFECT.

I really wanted to do a Christmas theme. After I drew this, however, I thought maybe I should have done it a little bit later instead... In this chapter, I aimed for a gentle love story without much comedic flavor, but (avalanche aside) I completely failed...

For a sort of bland chapter, the original sketches were really difficult, and I only have all sorts of painful memories about working on it. To a certain assistant, thank you very much for your help at the time...

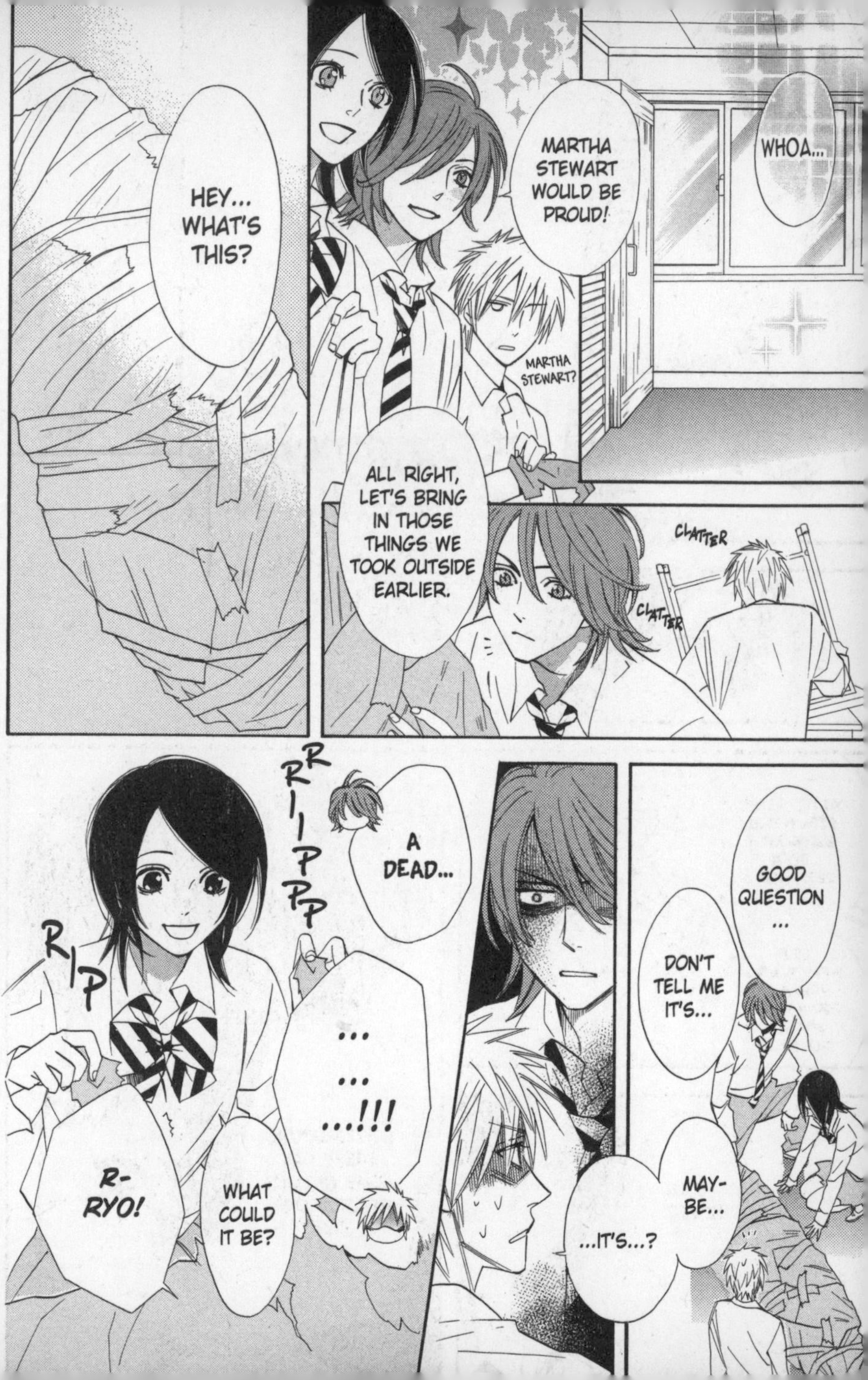
WHOA...
MARTHA STEWART WOULD BE PROUD!
MARTHA STEWART?
ALL RIGHT, LET'S BRING IN THOSE THINGS WE TOOK OUTSIDE EARLIER.
CLATTER
CLATTER
HEY... WHAT'S THIS?
GOOD QUESTION...
DON'T TELL ME IT'S...
MAY-BE...
...IT'S...?
A DEAD...
RRIPPP
...
...
...!!!
WHAT COULD IT BE?
RIP
R-RYO!

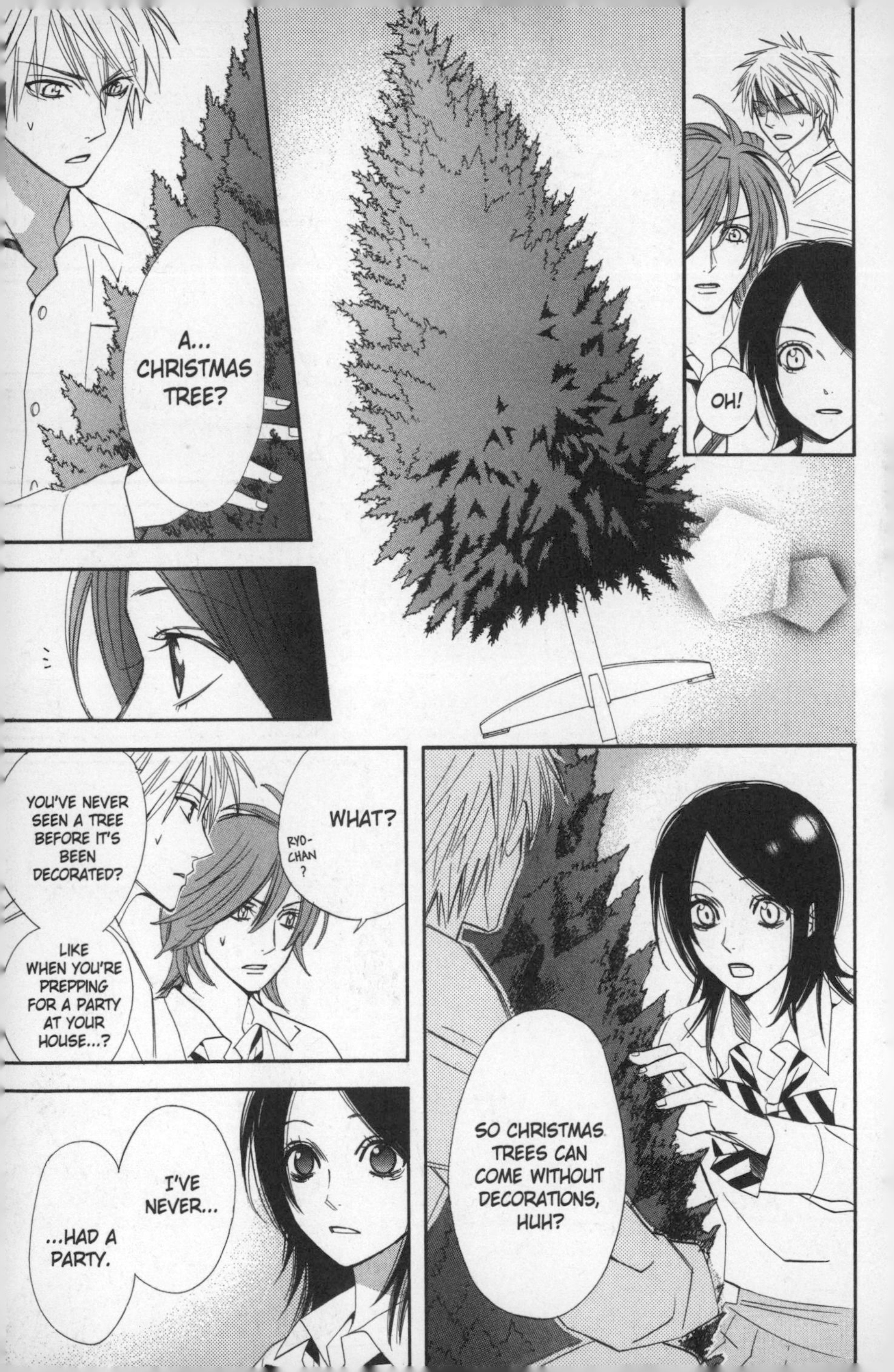
OH!
A... CHRISTMAS TREE?
SO CHRISTMAS TREES CAN COME WITHOUT DECORATIONS, HUH?
WHAT?
RYO-CHAN?
YOU'VE NEVER SEEN A TREE BEFORE IT'S BEEN DECORATED?
LIKE WHEN YOU'RE PREPPING FOR A PARTY AT YOUR HOUSE...?
I'VE NEVER...
...HAD A PARTY.

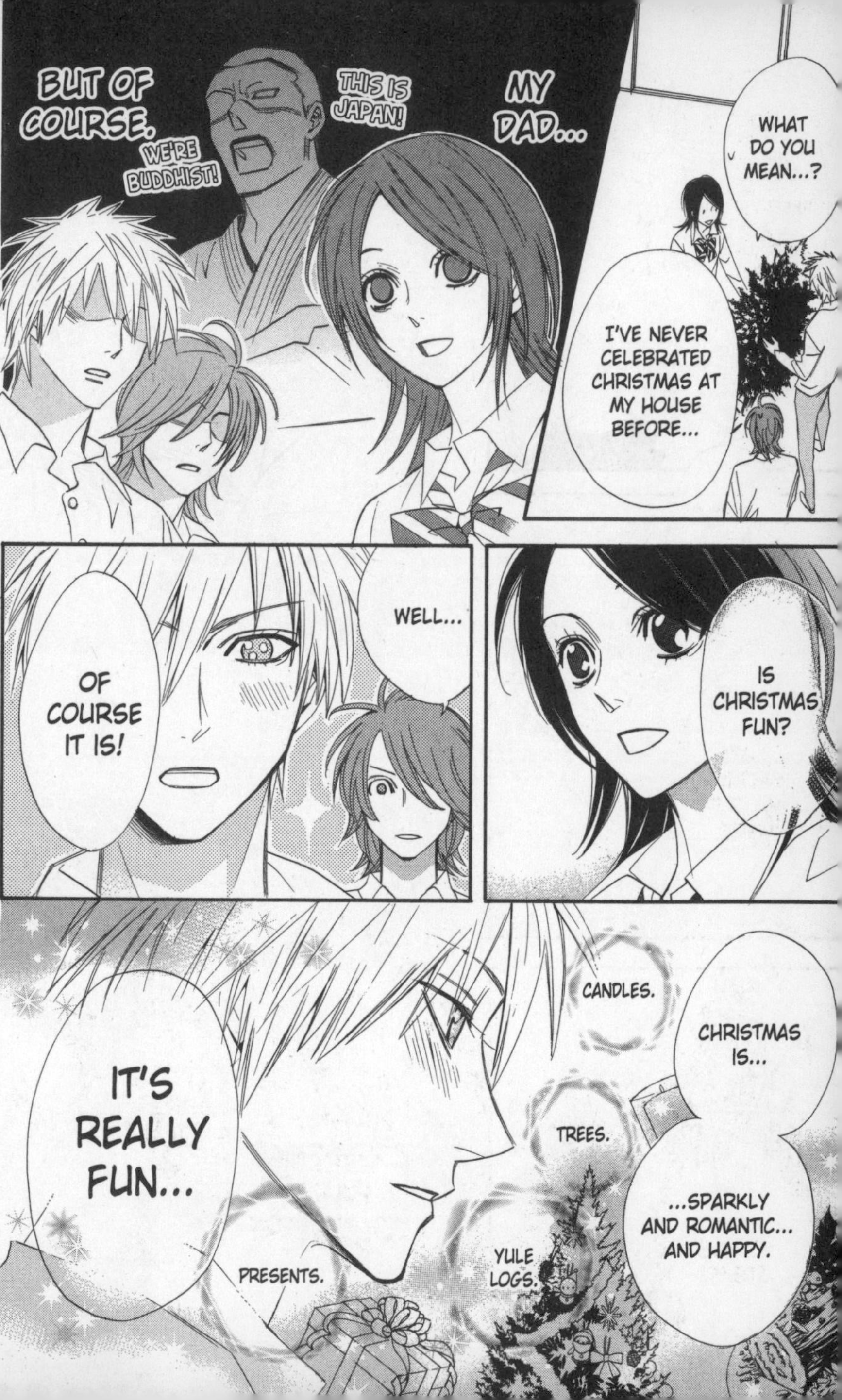
WHAT DO YOU MEAN...?
I'VE NEVER CELEBRATED CHRISTMAS AT MY HOUSE BEFORE...
MY DAD...
THIS IS JAPAN!
BUT OF COURSE.
WE'RE BUDDHIST!
IS CHRISTMAS FUN?
WELL...
OF COURSE IT IS!
CHRISTMAS IS...
CANDLES.
TREES.
...SPARKLY AND ROMANTIC... AND HAPPY.
YULE LOGS.
PRESENTS.
IT'S REALLY FUN...

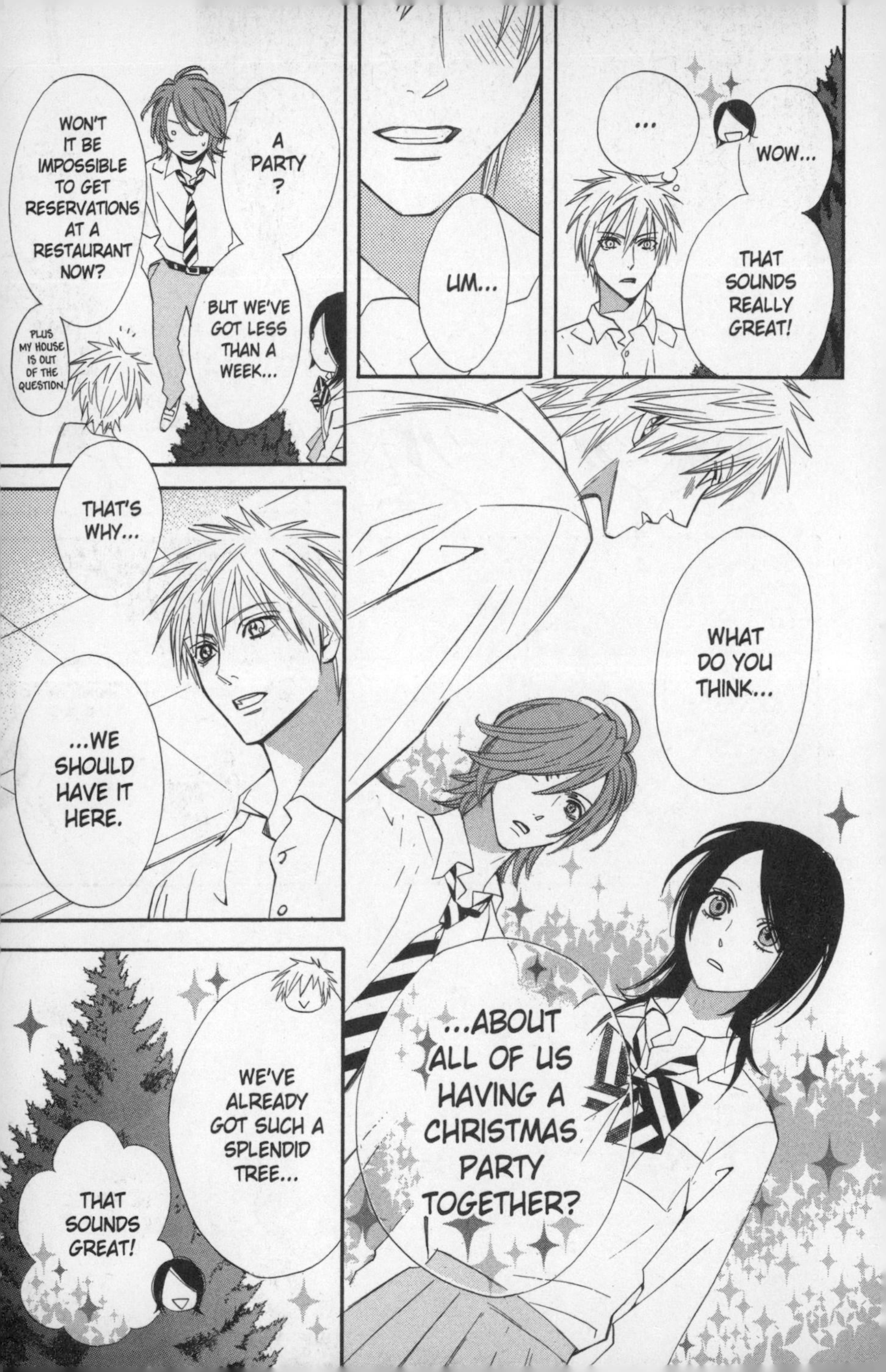
WOW... THAT SOUNDS REALLY GREAT!
...
UM...
A PARTY?
BUT WE'VE GOT LESS THAN A WEEK...
WON'T IT BE IMPOSSIBLE TO GET RESERVATIONS AT A RESTAURANT NOW?
PLUS MY HOUSE IS OUT OF THE QUESTION.
WHAT DO YOU THINK...
...ABOUT ALL OF US HAVING A CHRISTMAS PARTY TOGETHER?
THAT'S WHY...
...WE SHOULD HAVE IT HERE.
WE'VE ALREADY GOT SUCH A SPLENDID TREE...
THAT SOUNDS GREAT!

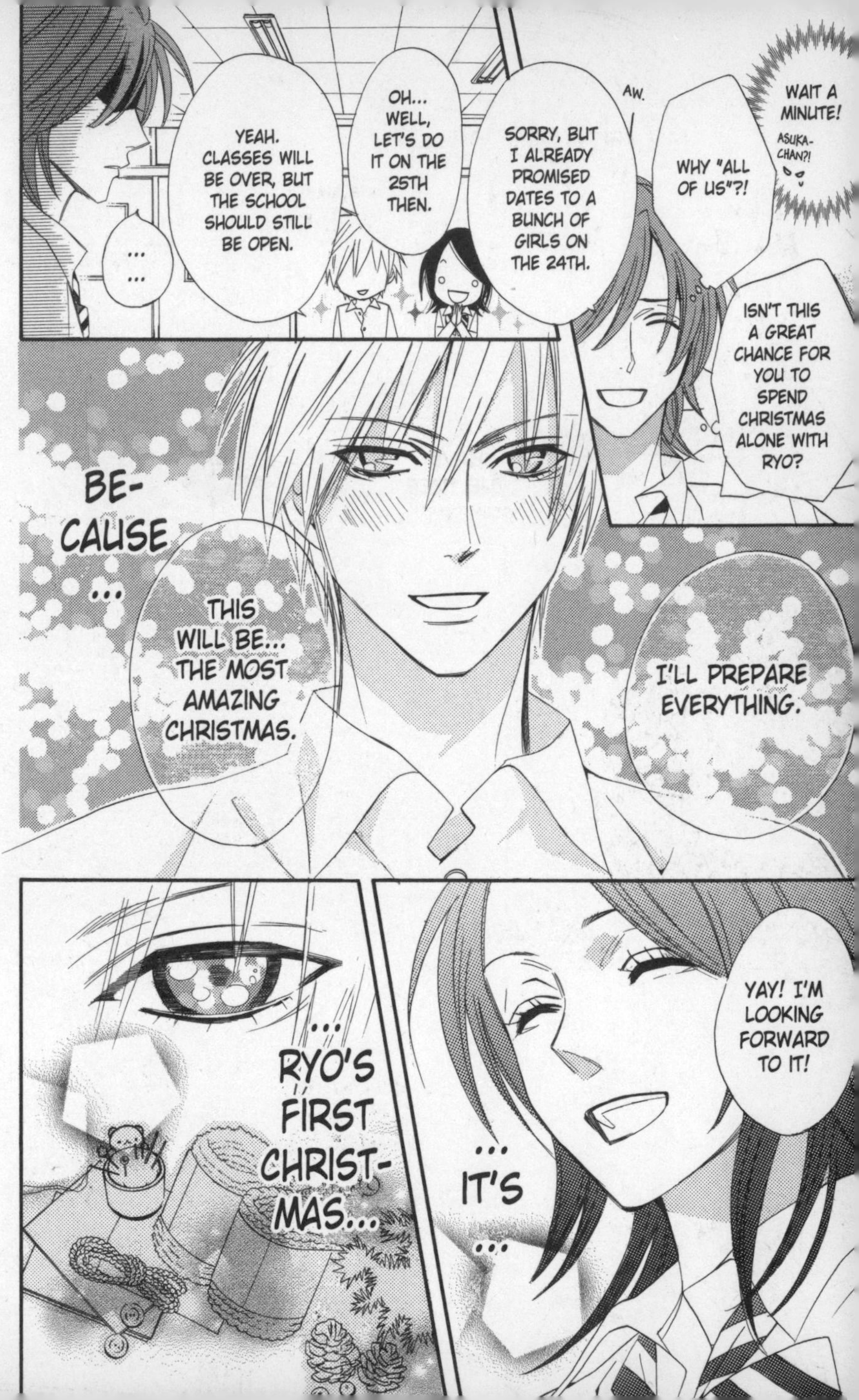
AW.
SORRY, BUT I ALREADY PROMISED DATES TO A BUNCH OF GIRLS ON THE 24TH.
OH... WELL, LET'S DO IT ON THE 25TH THEN.
YEAH. CLASSES WILL BE OVER, BUT THE SCHOOL SHOULD STILL BE OPEN.
... ...
WAIT A MINUTE!
ASUKA-CHAN?!
WHY "ALL OF US"?!
ISN'T THIS A GREAT CHANCE FOR YOU TO SPEND CHRISTMAS ALONE WITH RYO?
I'LL PREPARE EVERYTHING.
THIS WILL BE... THE MOST AMAZING CHRISTMAS.
BE-CAUSE ...
YAY! I'M LOOKING FORWARD TO IT!
... IT'S ...
... RYO'S FIRST CHRIST-MAS...

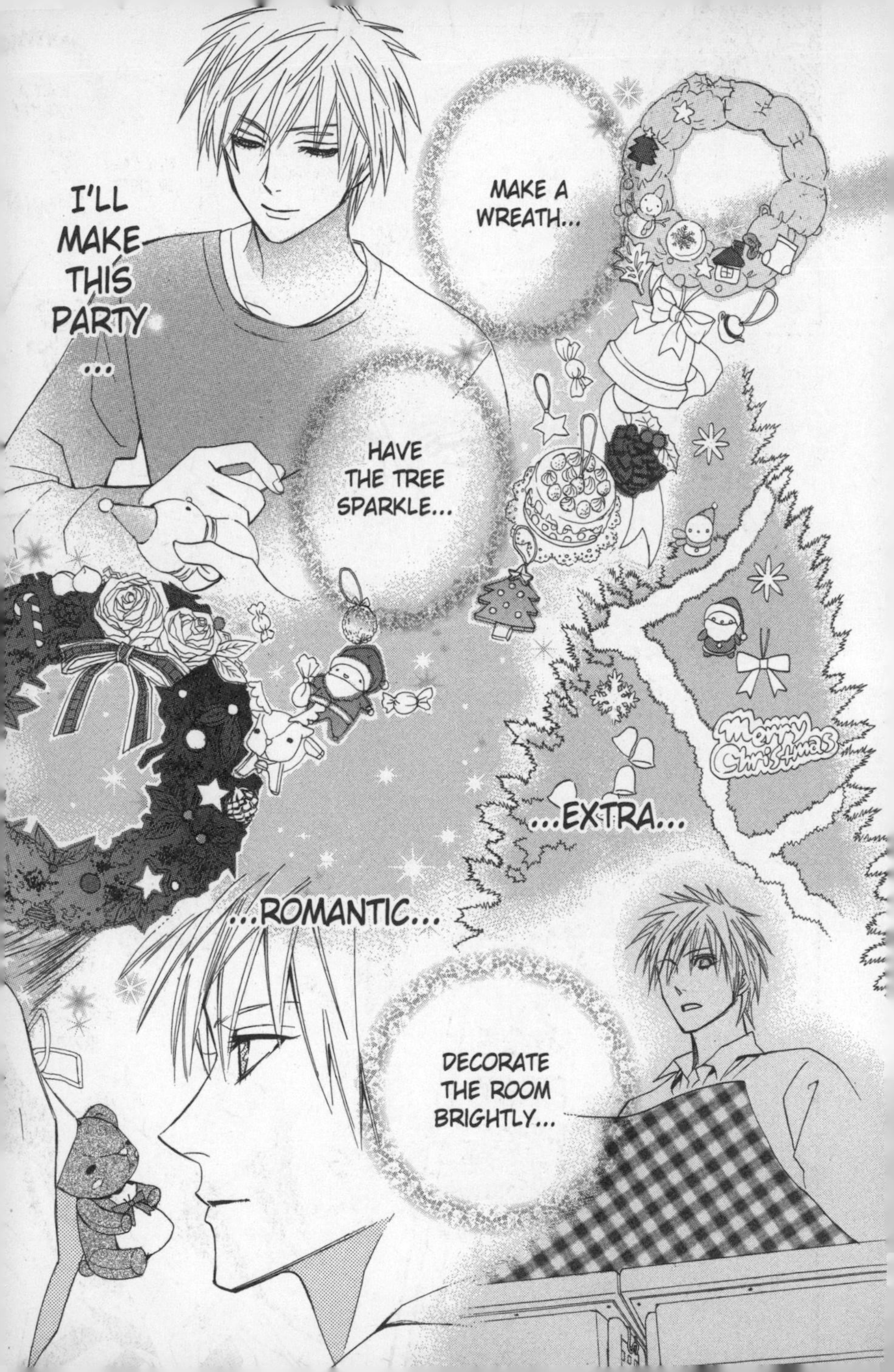
MAKE A WREATH...
I'LL MAKE THIS PARTY...
HAVE THE TREE SPARKLE...
...EXTRA...
...ROMANTIC...
DECORATE THE ROOM BRIGHTLY...
Merry Christmas

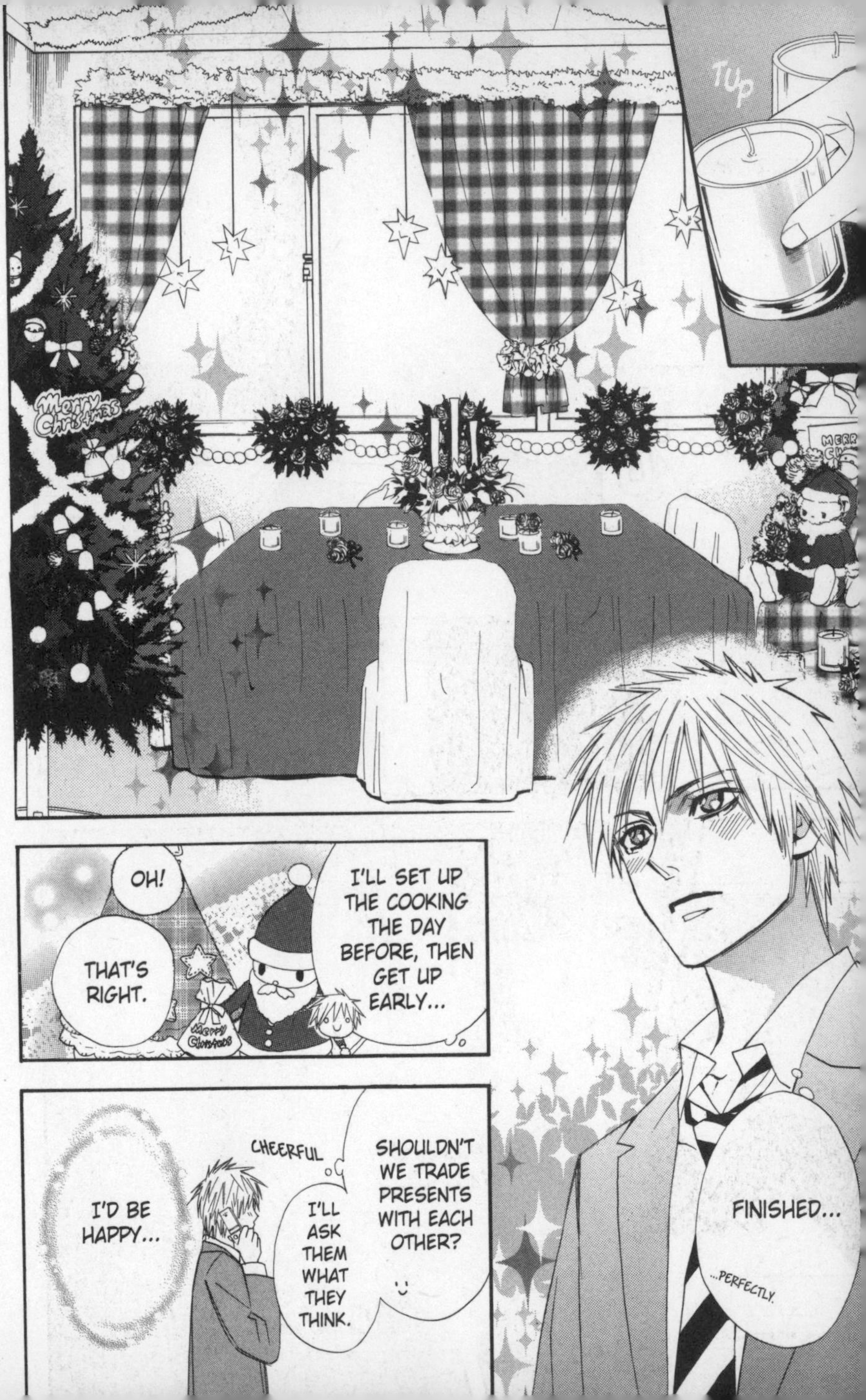
TUP
FINISHED...
...PERFECTLY.
I'LL SET UP THE COOKING THE DAY BEFORE, THEN GET UP EARLY...
OH!
THAT'S RIGHT.
SHOULDN'T WE TRADE PRESENTS WITH EACH OTHER?
I'LL ASK THEM WHAT THEY THINK.
CHEERFUL
I'D BE HAPPY...

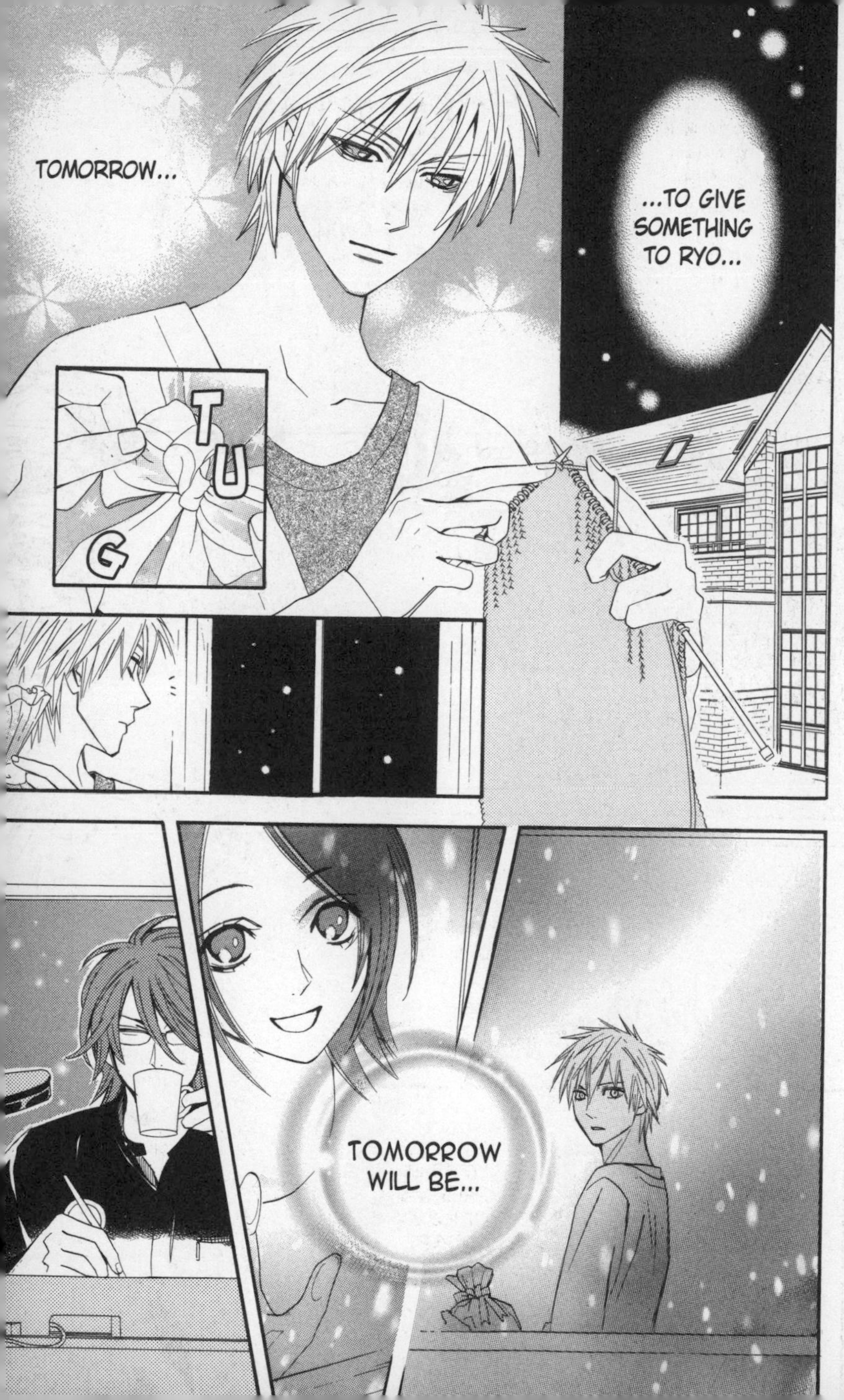
...TO GIVE SOMETHING TO RYO...
TOMORROW...
TUG
TOMORROW WILL BE...

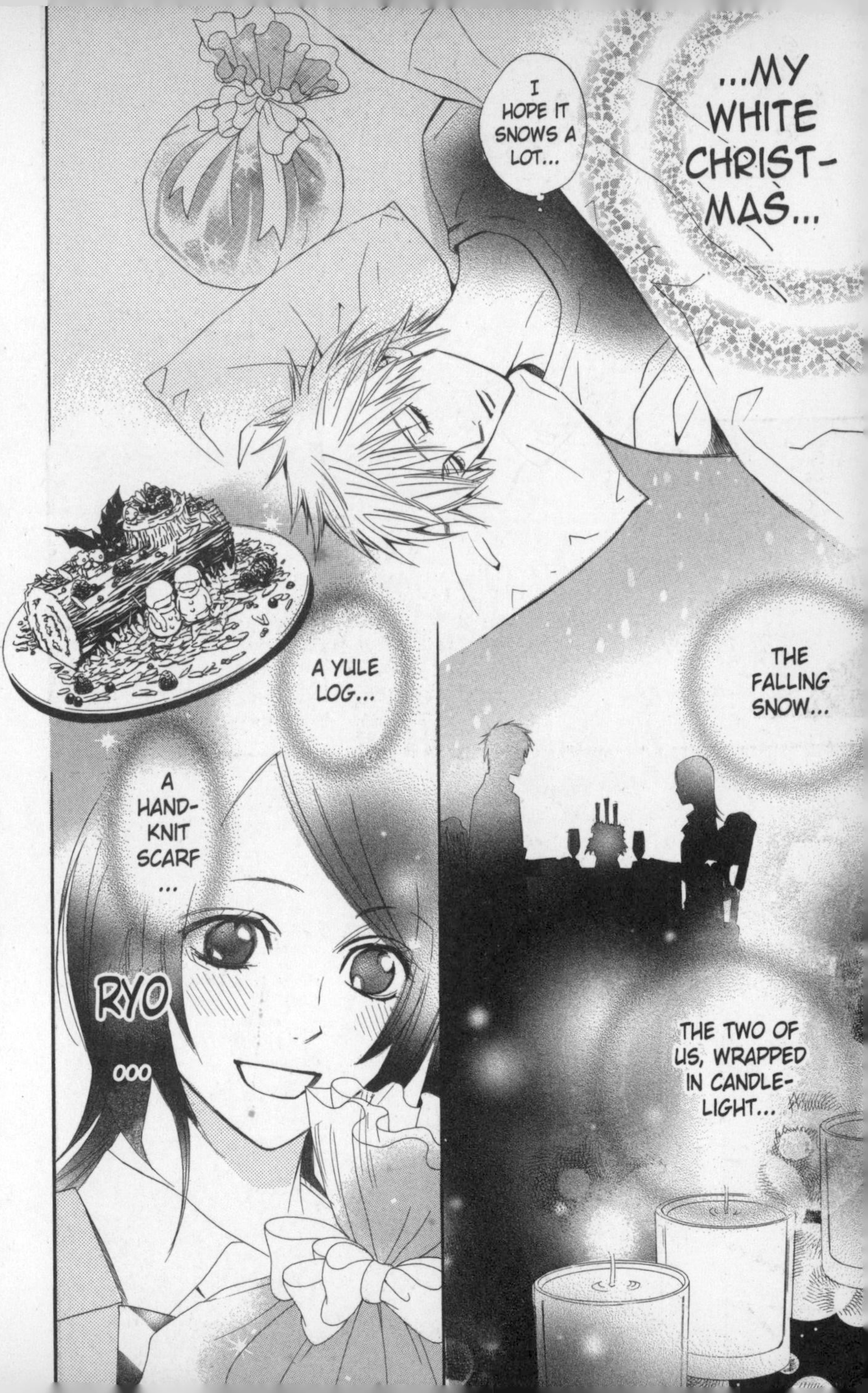
...MY WHITE CHRIST-MAS...
I HOPE IT SNOWS A LOT...
THE FALLING SNOW...
THE TWO OF US, WRAPPED IN CANDLE-LIGHT...
A YULE LOG...
A HAND-KNIT SCARF...
RYO
ooo

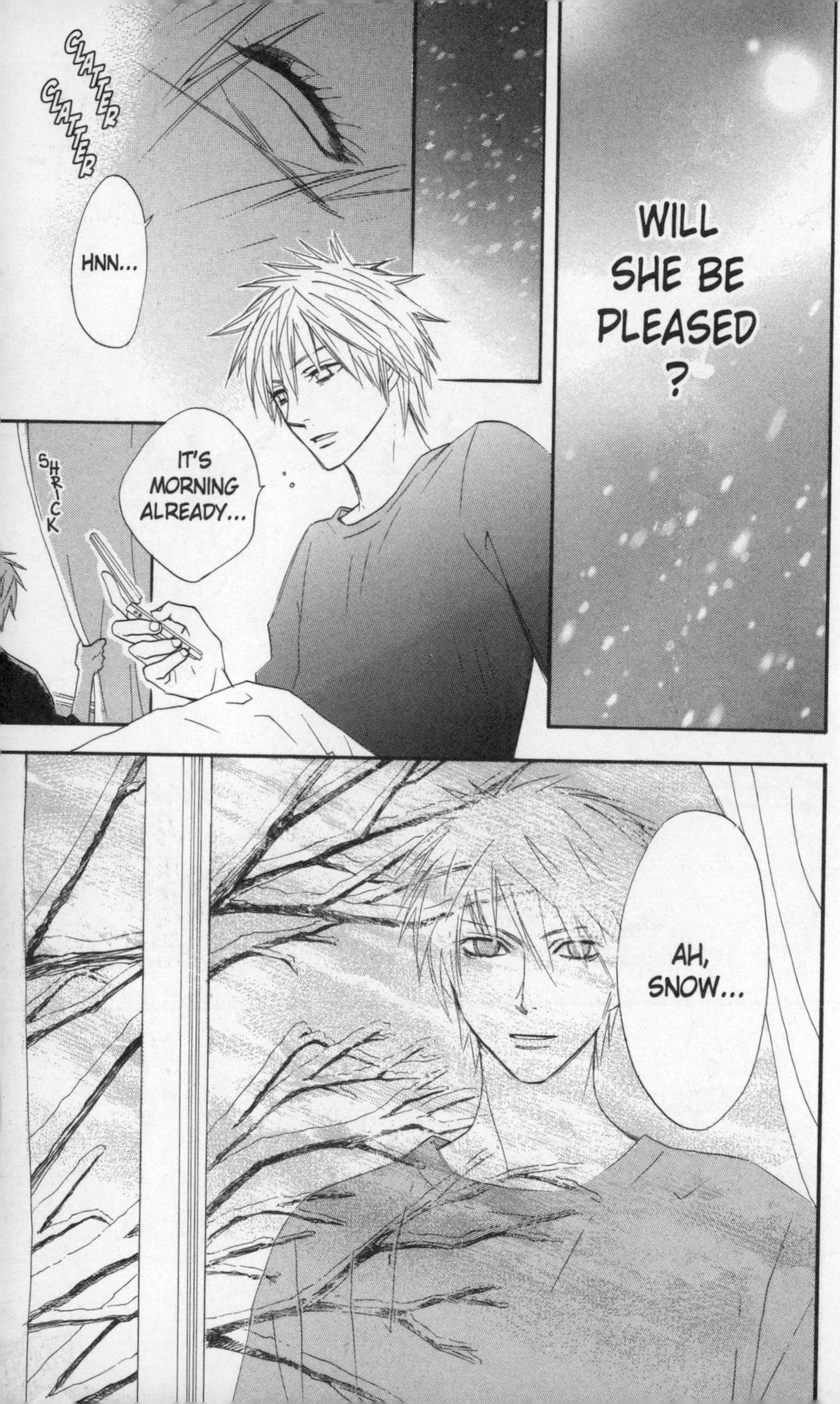
WILL SHE BE PLEASED ?
CLATTER CLATTER
HNN...
IT'S MORNING ALREADY...
SHRICK
AH, SNOW...

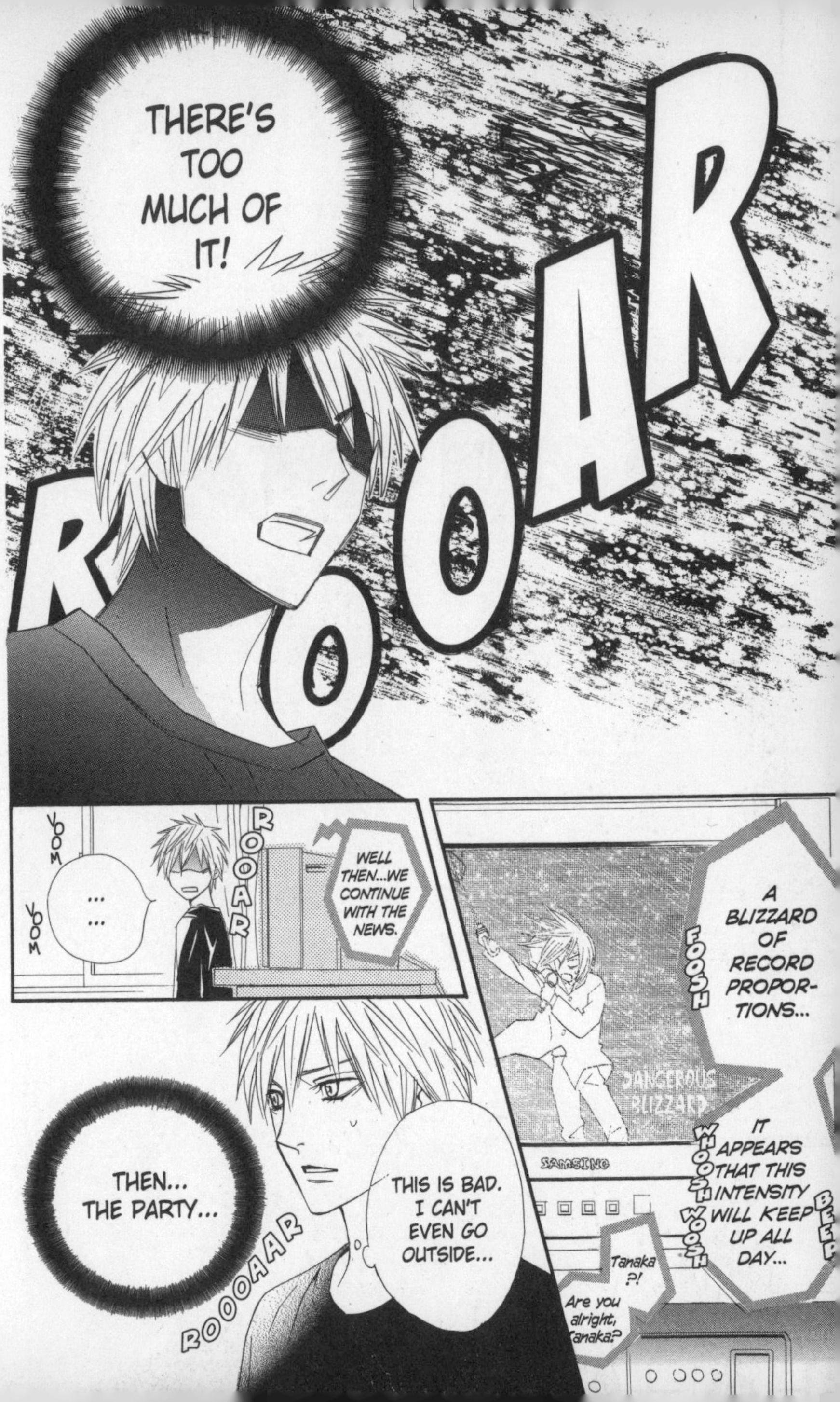
THERE'S TOO MUCH OF IT!
ROOOAR
A BLIZZARD OF RECORD PROPORTIONS...
FOOSH
DANGEROUS BLIZZARD
SAMSING
WELL THEN...WE CONTINUE WITH THE NEWS.
ROOOAR
VOOM VOOM
... ...
IT APPEARS THAT THIS INTENSITY WILL KEEP UP ALL DAY...
WHOOSH WOOSH
BEEP
Tanaka ?!
Are you alright, Tanaka?
THIS IS BAD. I CAN'T EVEN GO OUTSIDE...
THEN... THE PARTY...
ROOOAAR
ROOOAAR

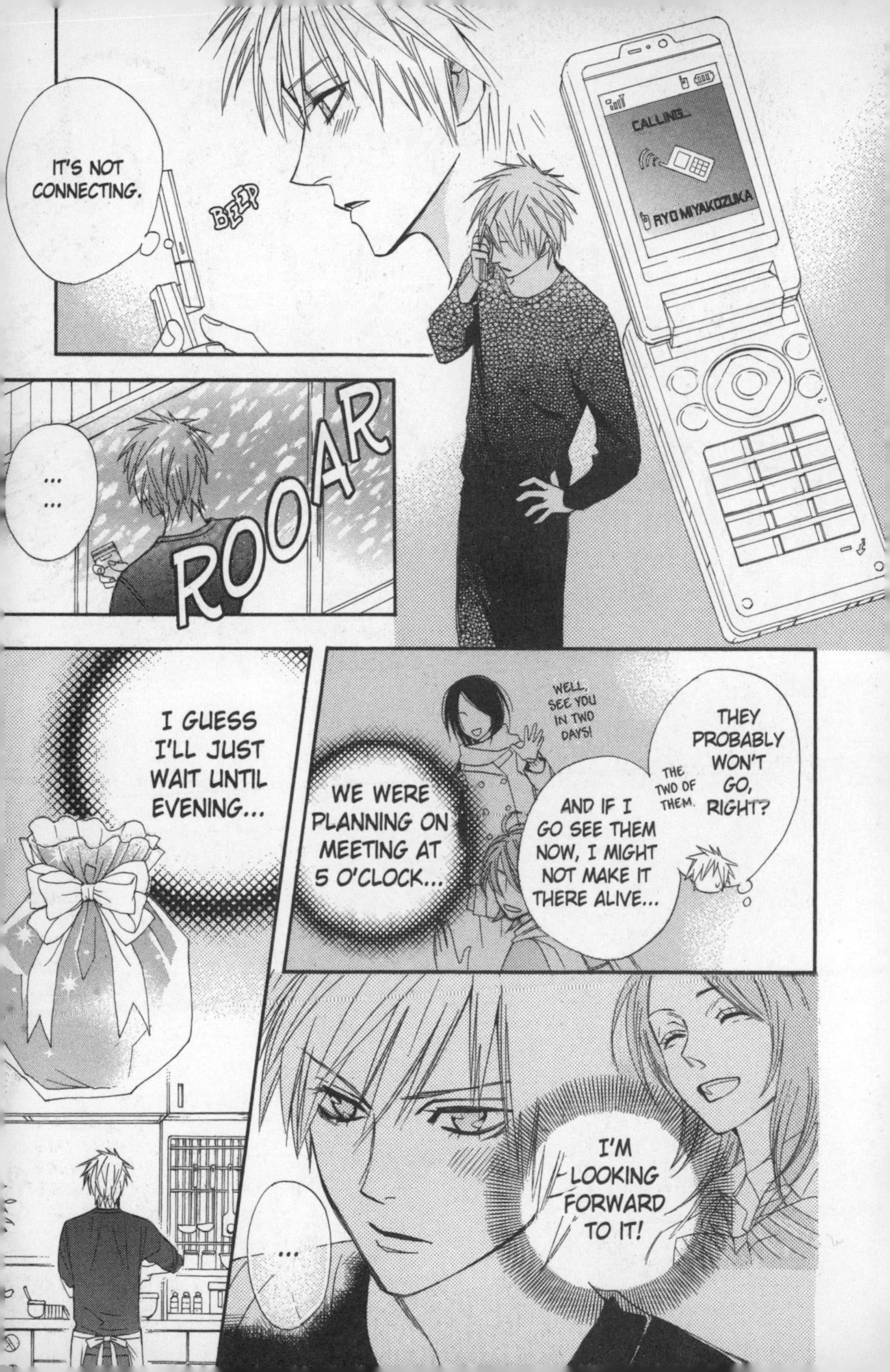
CALLING...
RYO MIYAKOZUKA
IT'S NOT CONNECTING.
BEEP
... ...
ROOAR
THEY PROBABLY WON'T GO, RIGHT?
THE TWO OF THEM.
AND IF I GO SEE THEM NOW, I MIGHT NOT MAKE IT THERE ALIVE...
WELL, SEE YOU IN TWO DAYS!
WE WERE PLANNING ON MEETING AT 5 O'CLOCK...
I GUESS I'LL JUST WAIT UNTIL EVENING...
I'M LOOKING FORWARD TO IT!
...

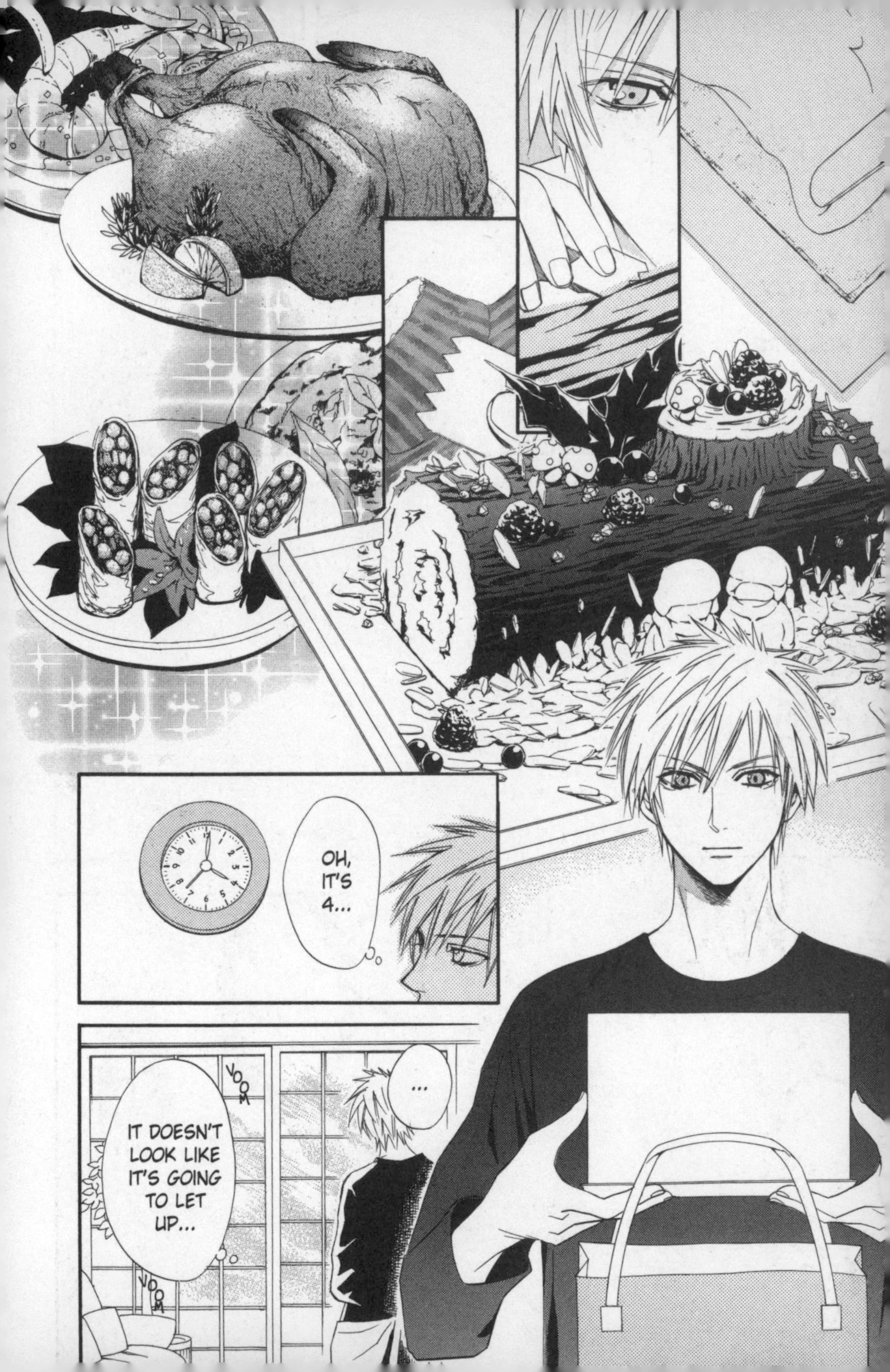
OH, IT'S 4...
...
VOOM
IT DOESN'T LOOK LIKE IT'S GOING TO LET UP...
VOOM

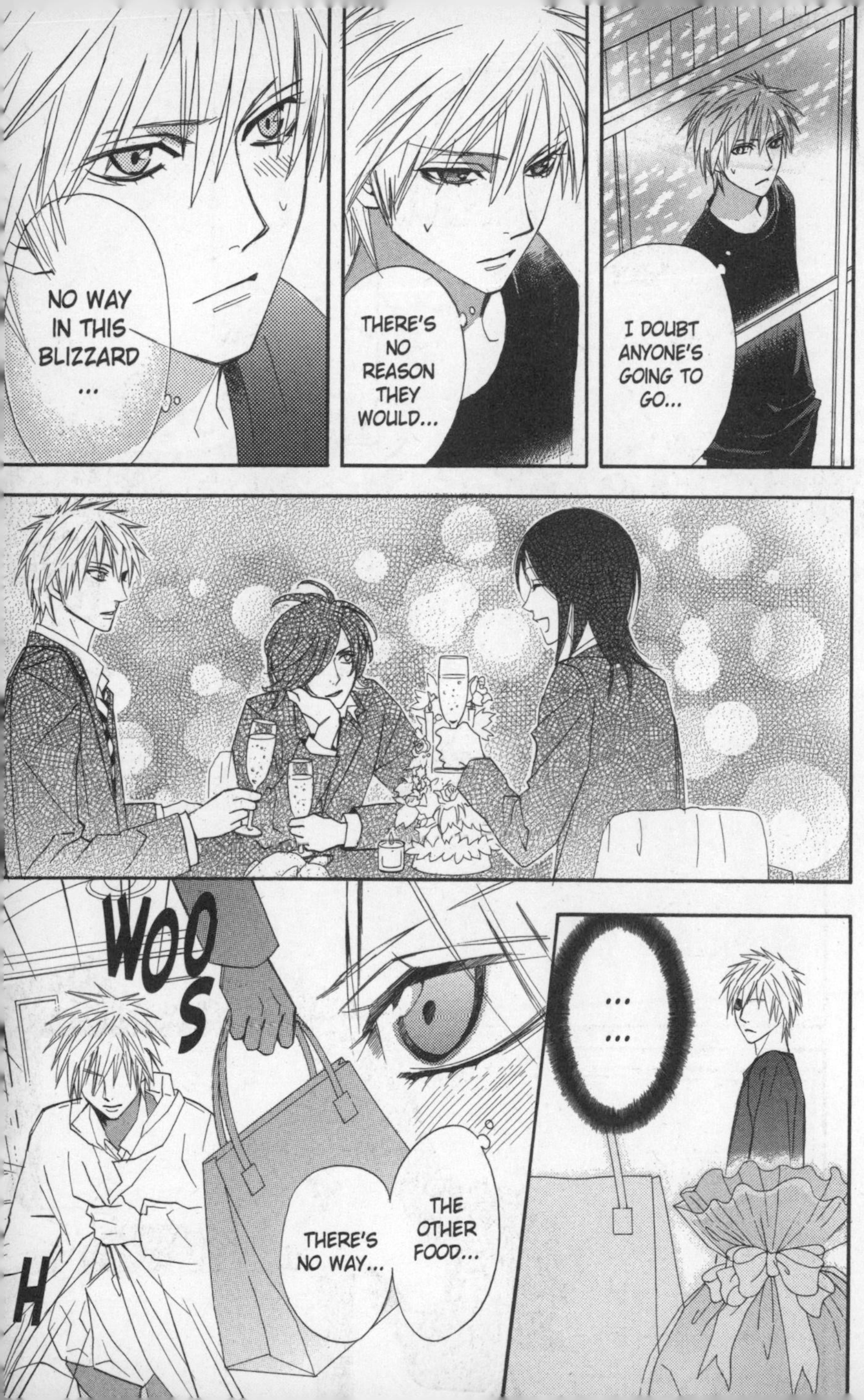
I DOUBT ANYONE'S GOING TO GO...
THERE'S NO REASON THEY WOULD...
NO WAY IN THIS BLIZZARD ...
... ...
THE OTHER FOOD...
THERE'S NO WAY...
WOOSH

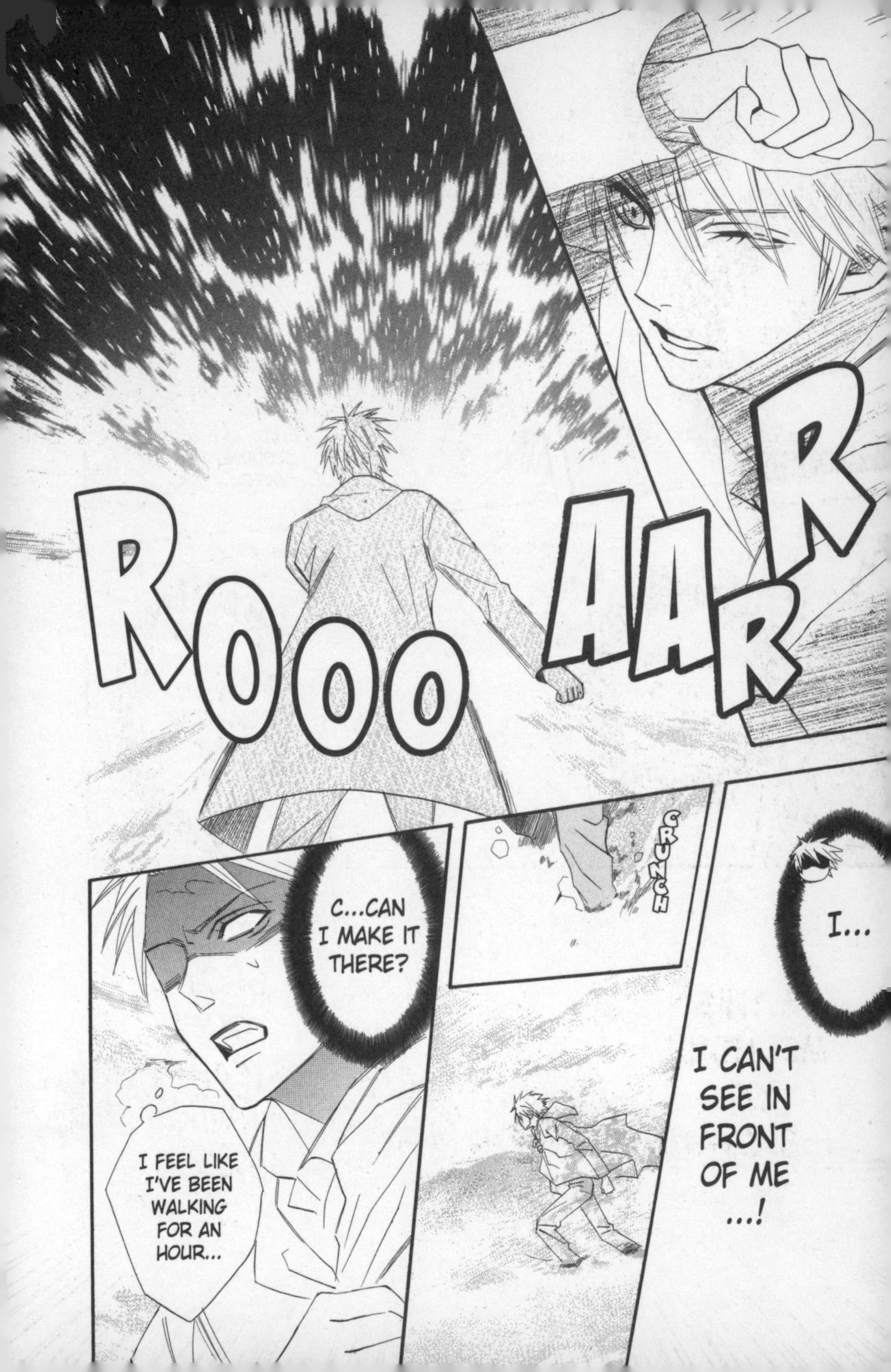
ROOOAARR
I...
I CAN'T SEE IN FRONT OF ME ...!
CRUNCH
C...CAN I MAKE IT THERE?
I FEEL LIKE I'VE BEEN WALKING FOR AN HOUR...

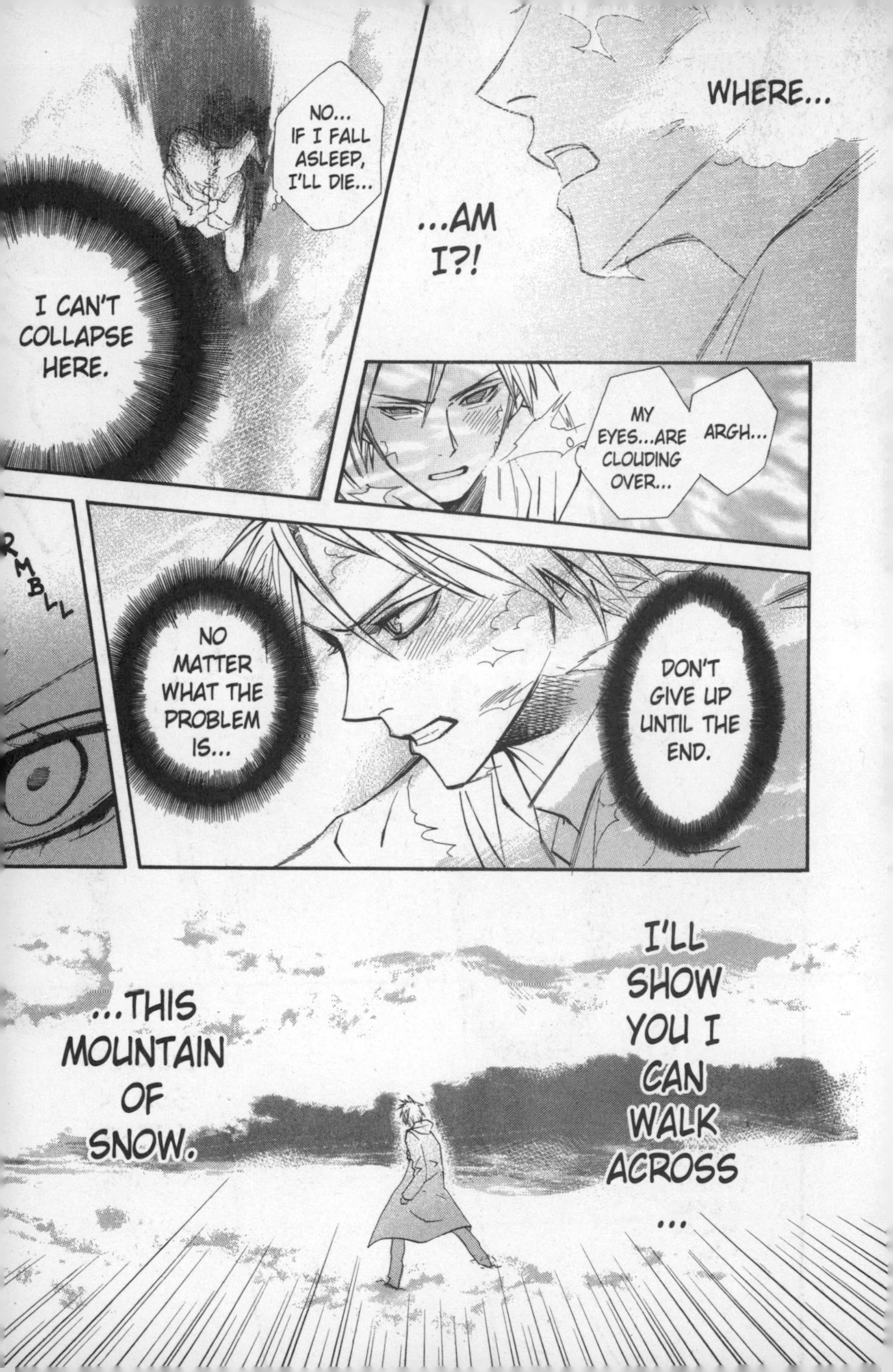
WHERE...
...AM I?!
ARGH...
MY EYES...ARE CLOUDING OVER...
NO... IF I FALL ASLEEP, I'LL DIE...
I CAN'T COLLAPSE HERE.
NO MATTER WHAT THE PROBLEM IS...
DON'T GIVE UP UNTIL THE END.
RMBLLL
I'LL SHOW YOU I CAN WALK ACROSS...
...THIS MOUNTAIN OF SNOW.

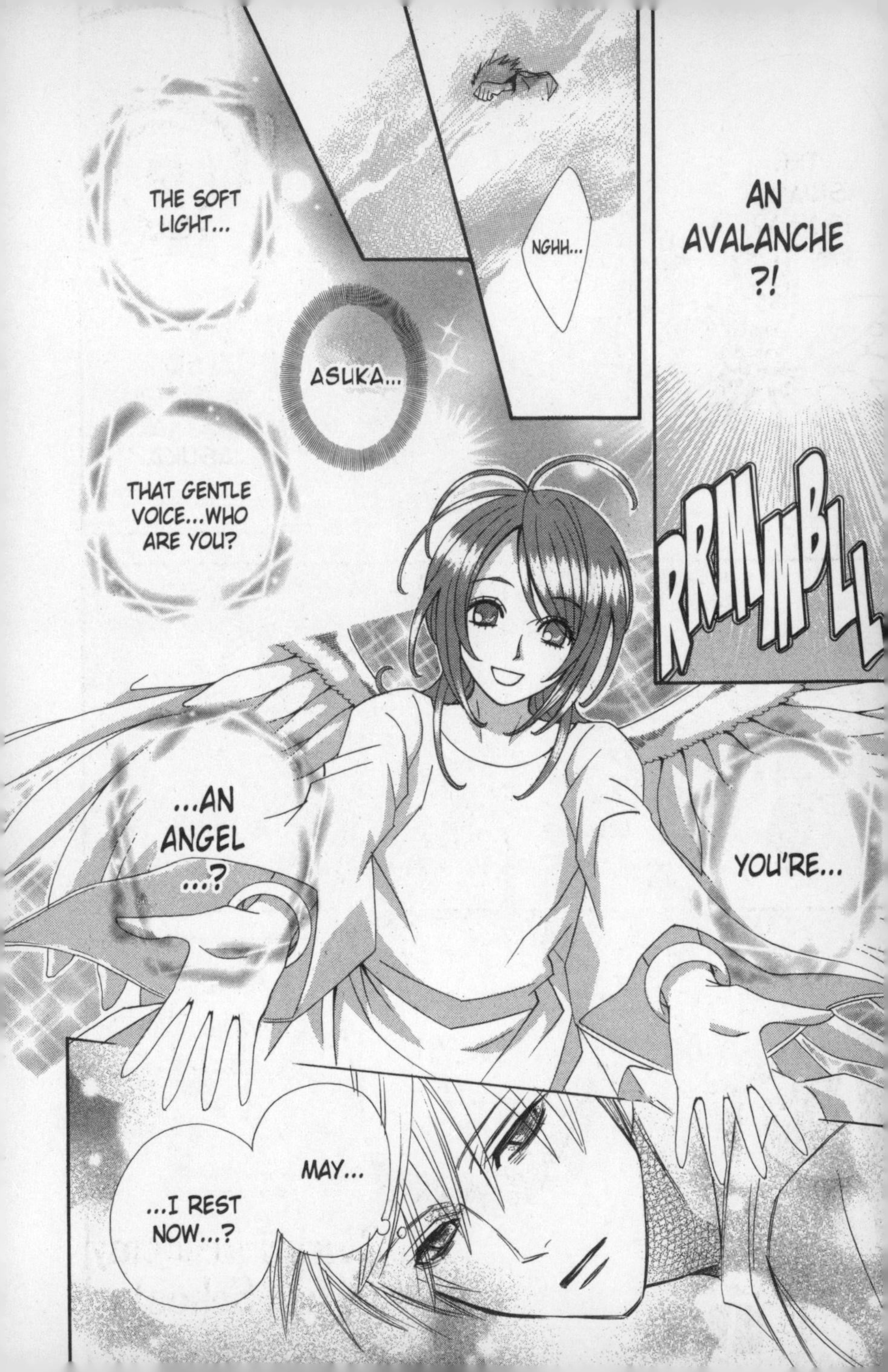
AN AVALANCHE ?!
RRMMBLL
NGHH...
THE SOFT LIGHT...
ASUKA...
THAT GENTLE VOICE...WHO ARE YOU?
YOU'RE...
...AN ANGEL ...?
MAY...
...I REST NOW...?

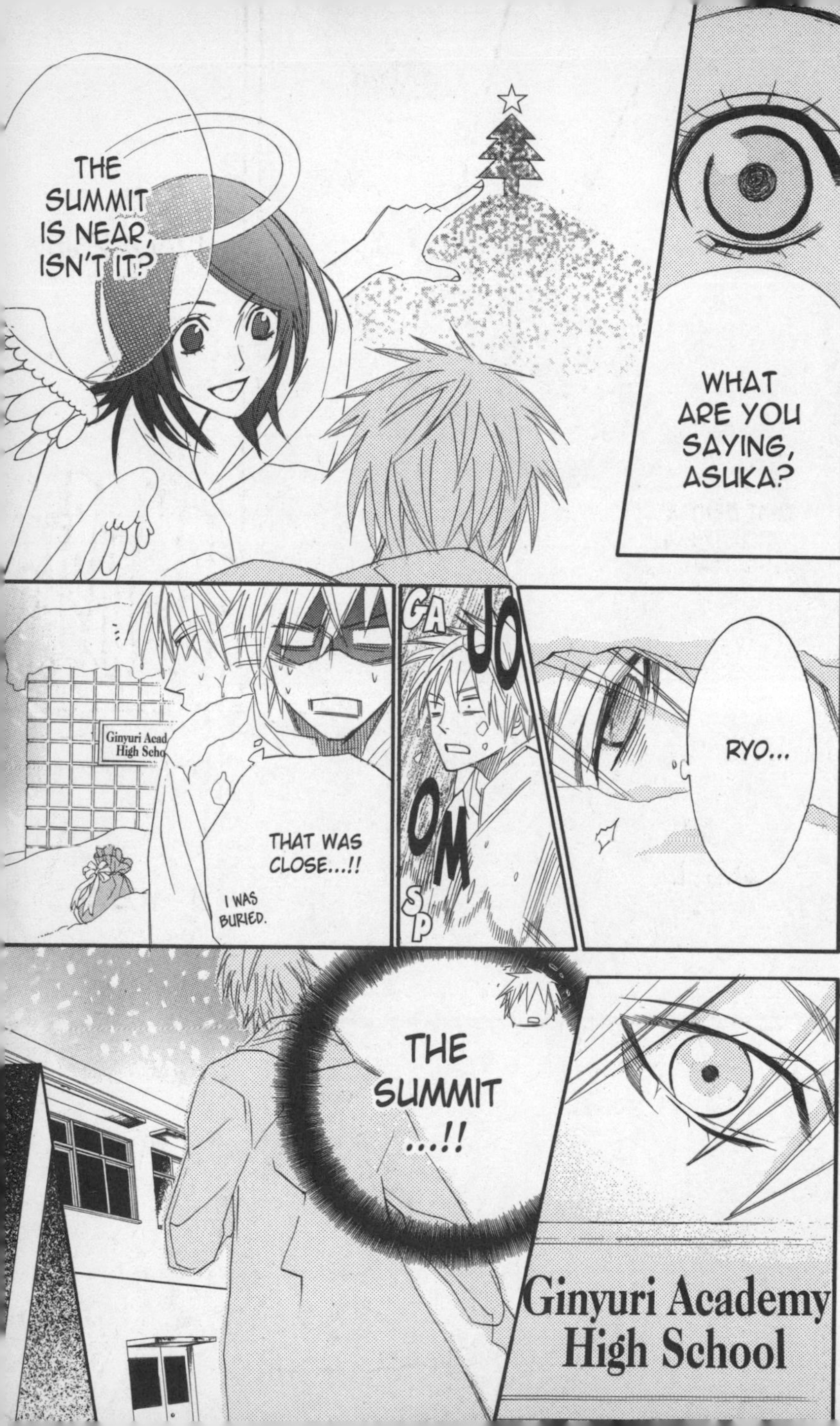
WHAT ARE YOU SAYING, ASUKA?
THE SUMMIT IS NEAR, ISN'T IT?
RYO...
GA
JO
OM
SP
THAT WAS CLOSE...!!
I WAS BURIED.
Ginyuri Acad
High Scho
Ginyuri Academy High School
THE SUMMIT ...!!

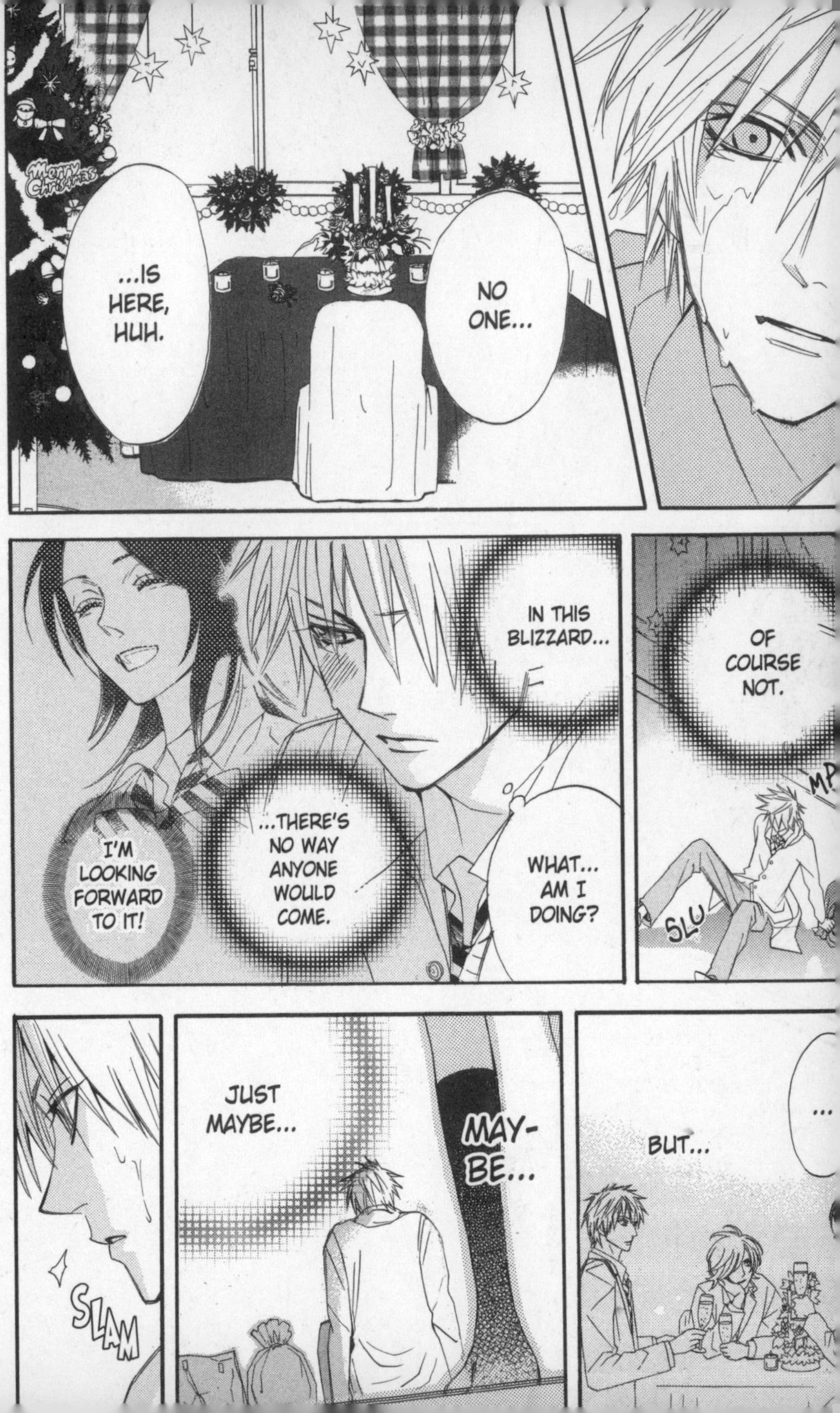
NO ONE...
...IS HERE, HUH.
Merry Christmas
OF COURSE NOT.
MP
SLU
IN THIS BLIZZARD...
...THERE'S NO WAY ANYONE WOULD COME.
WHAT... AM I DOING?
I'M LOOKING FORWARD TO IT!
...
BUT...
JUST MAYBE...
MAY-BE...
SLAM

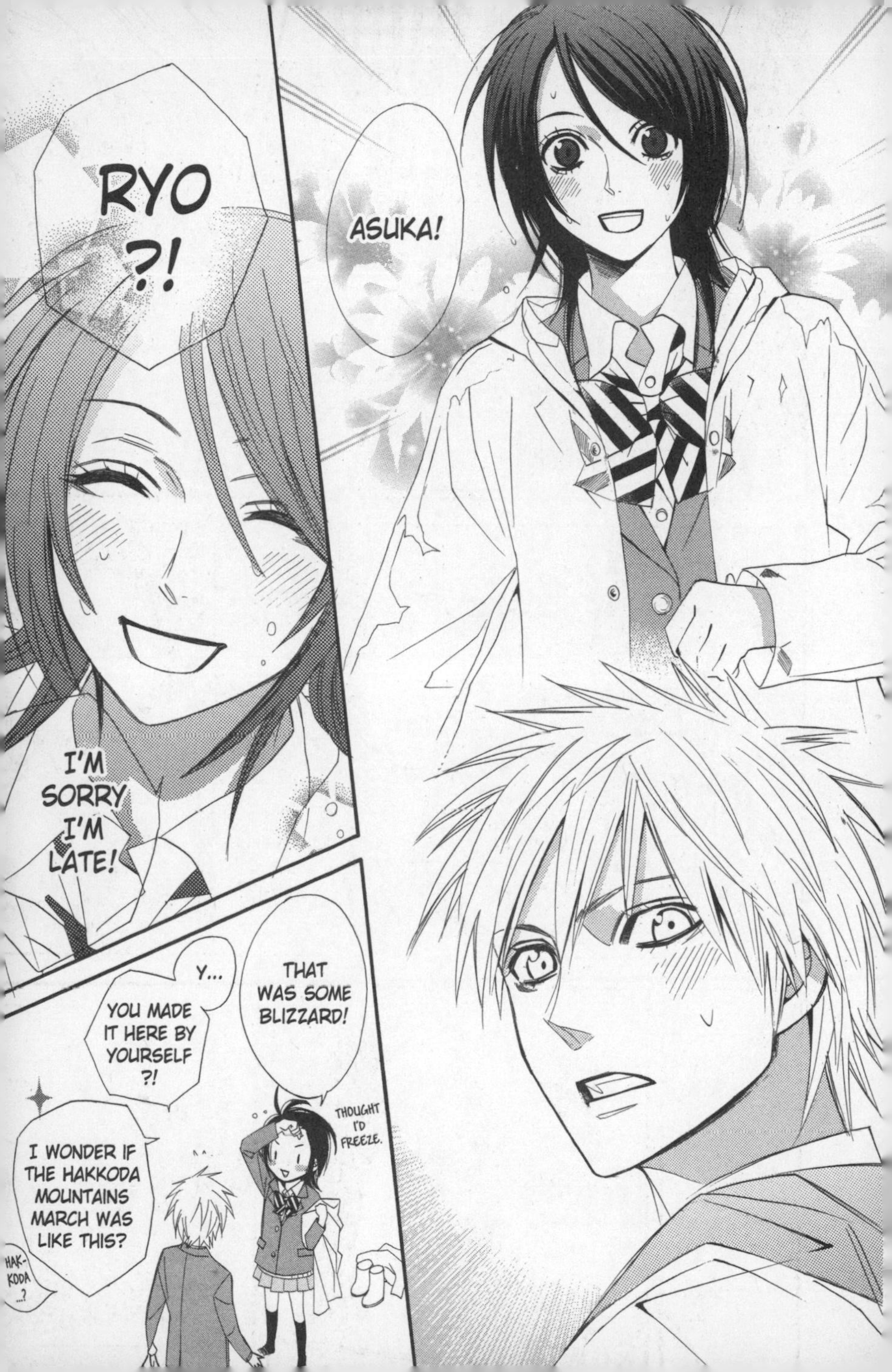
ASUKA!
RYO ?!
I'M SORRY I'M LATE!
THAT WAS SOME BLIZZARD!
Y...
YOU MADE IT HERE BY YOURSELF ?!
THOUGHT I'D FREEZE.
I WONDER IF THE HAKKODA MOUNTAINS MARCH WAS LIKE THIS?
HAK-KODA ...?

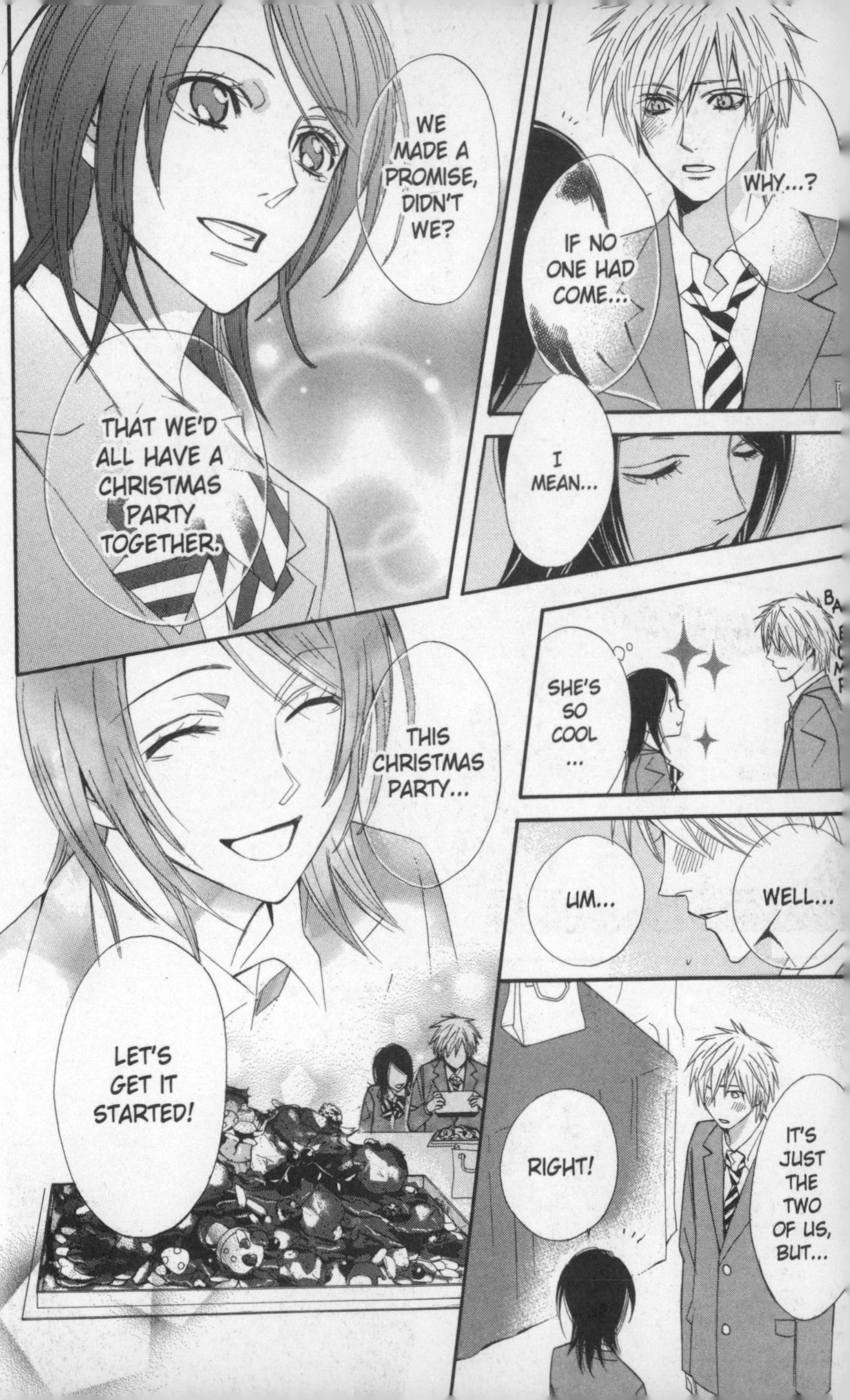
WHY...?
IF NO ONE HAD COME...
I MEAN...
SHE'S SO COOL ...
WELL...
UM...
IT'S JUST THE TWO OF US, BUT...
RIGHT!
WE MADE A PROMISE, DIDN'T WE?
THAT WE'D ALL HAVE A CHRISTMAS PARTY TOGETHER.
THIS CHRISTMAS PARTY...
LET'S GET IT STARTED!

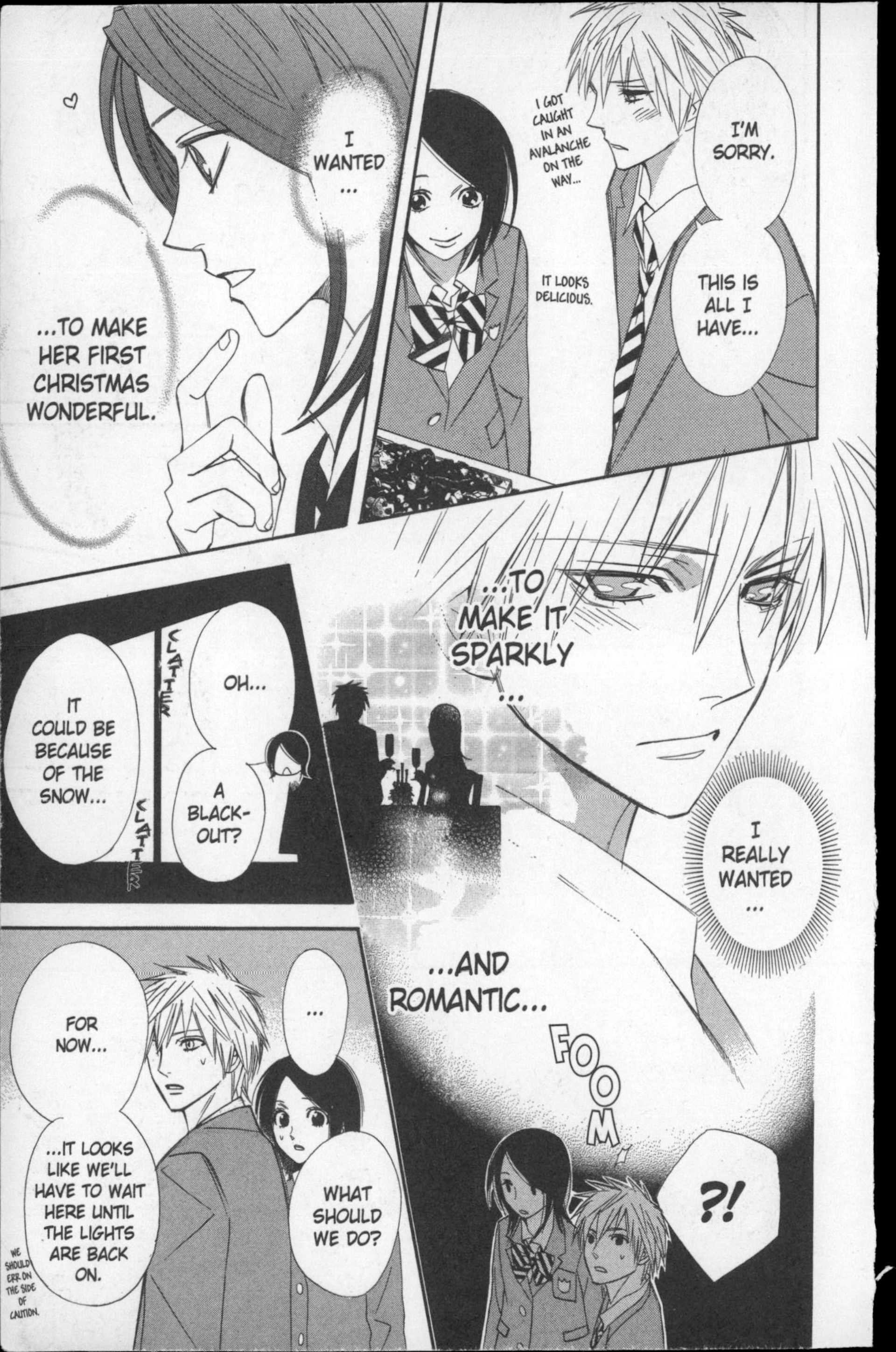
I'M SORRY.
I GOT CAUGHT IN AN AVALANCHE ON THE WAY...
THIS IS ALL I HAVE...
IT LOOKS DELICIOUS.
I WANTED ...
...TO MAKE HER FIRST CHRISTMAS WONDERFUL.
I REALLY WANTED ...
...TO MAKE IT SPARKLY ...
...AND ROMANTIC...
FOOM
?!
OH...
A BLACK-OUT?
CLATTER
IT COULD BE BECAUSE OF THE SNOW...
CLATTER
...
FOR NOW...
...IT LOOKS LIKE WE'LL HAVE TO WAIT HERE UNTIL THE LIGHTS ARE BACK ON.
WHAT SHOULD WE DO?
WE SHOULD ERR ON THE SIDE OF CAUTION.

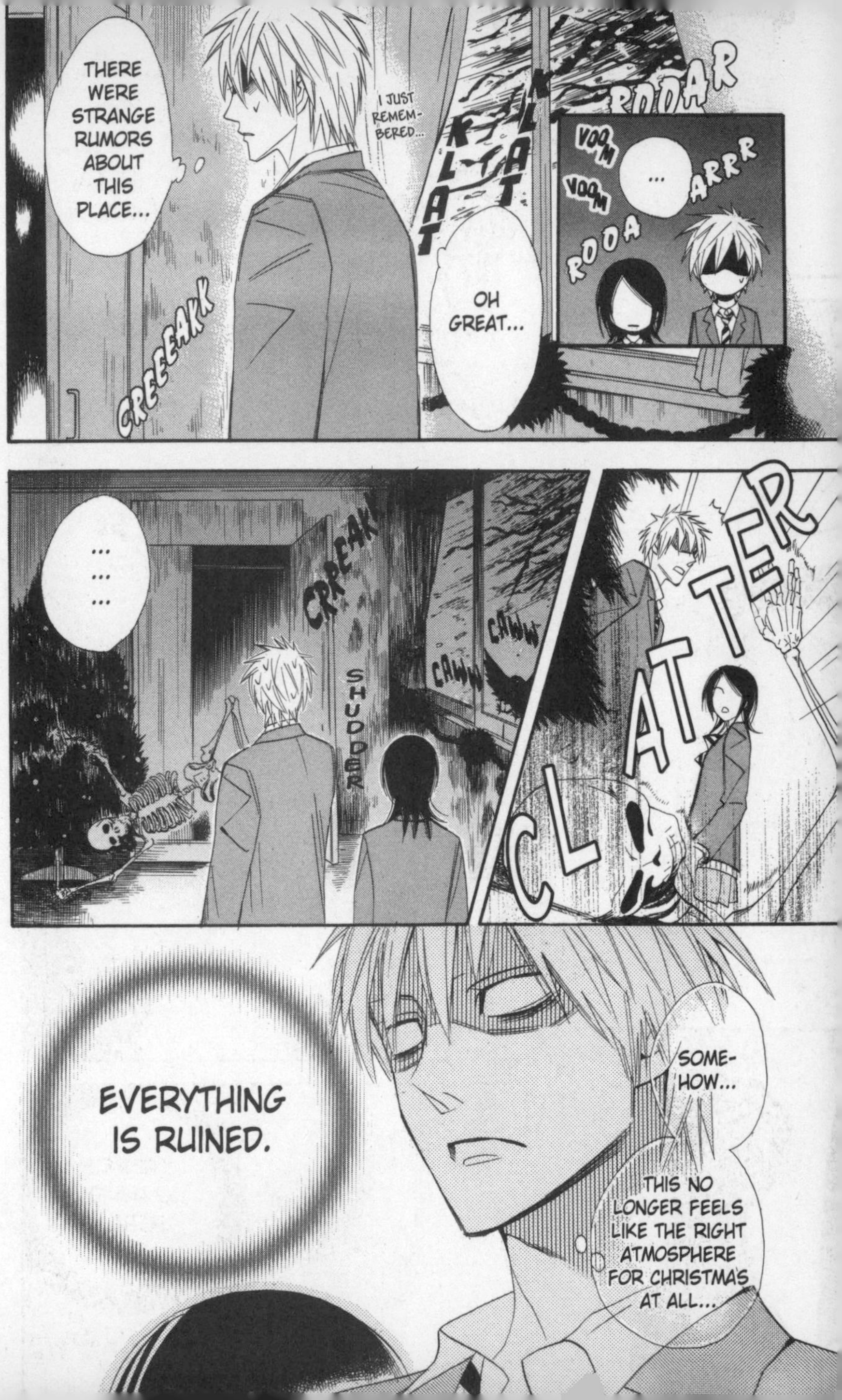
ROOAR
VOOM
VOOM
...
ARRR
ROOA
KLAT
KLAT
I JUST REMEMBERED...
OH GREAT...
THERE WERE STRANGE RUMORS ABOUT THIS PLACE...
CREEEAKK
CLATTER
CRREAK
CAWW
CAWW
SHUDDER
...
...
...
SOME-HOW...
THIS NO LONGER FEELS LIKE THE RIGHT ATMOSPHERE FOR CHRISTMAS AT ALL...
EVERYTHING IS RUINED.

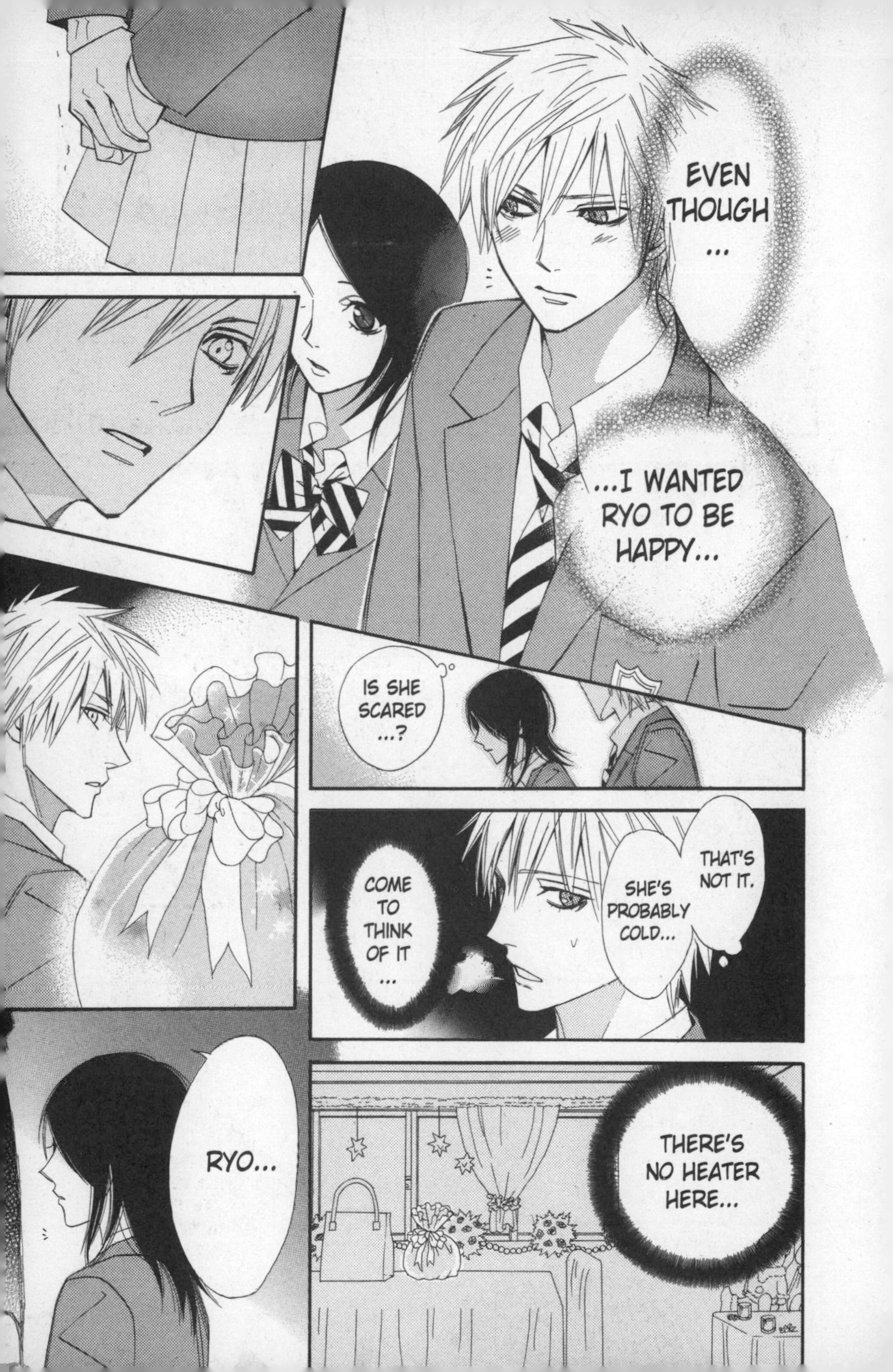
EVEN THOUGH ...
...I WANTED RYO TO BE HAPPY...
IS SHE SCARED ...?
THAT'S NOT IT.
SHE'S PROBABLY COLD...
COME TO THINK OF IT ...
THERE'S NO HEATER HERE...
RYO...

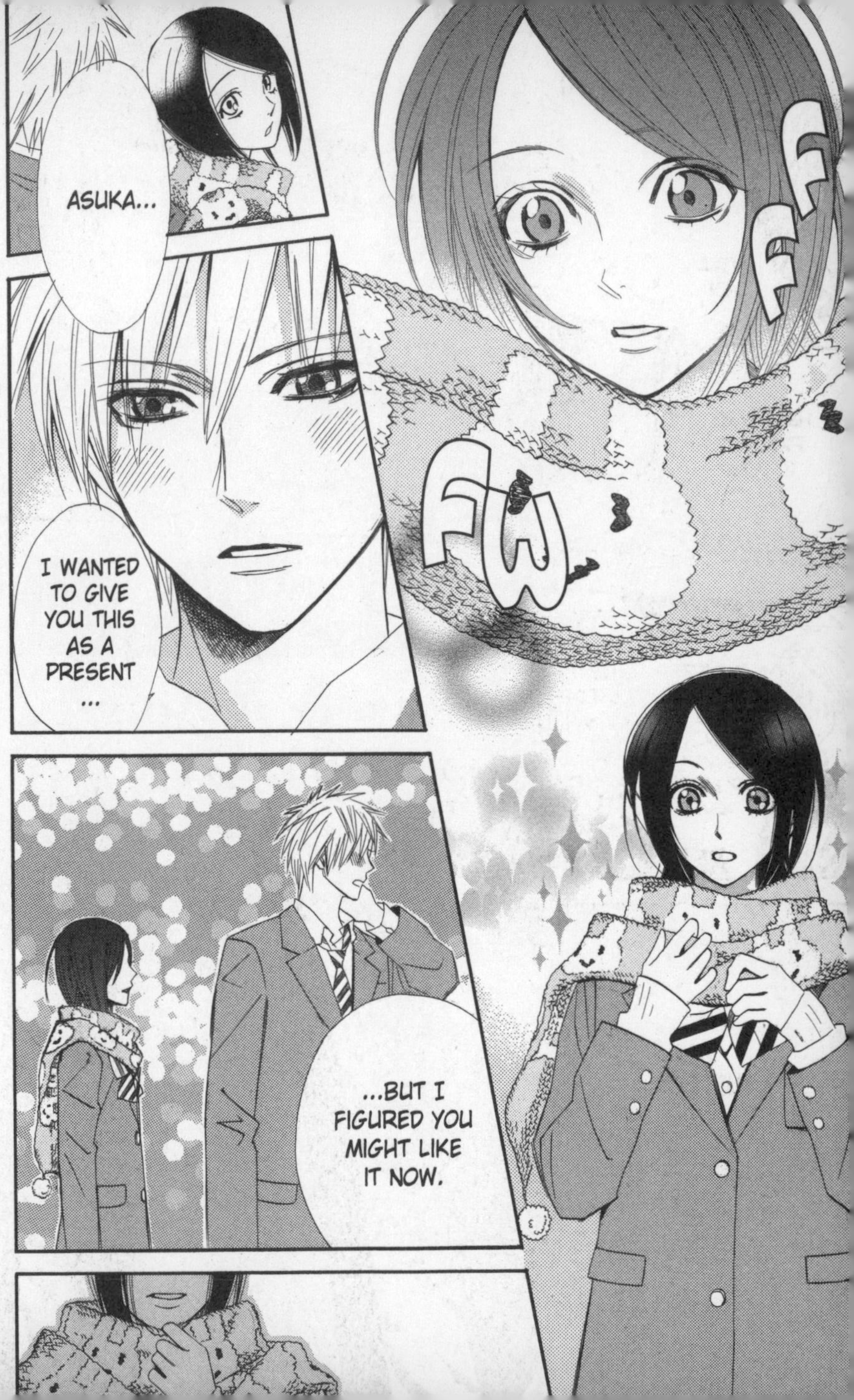
FF
FW
ASUKA...
I WANTED TO GIVE YOU THIS AS A PRESENT ...
...BUT I FIGURED YOU MIGHT LIKE IT NOW.

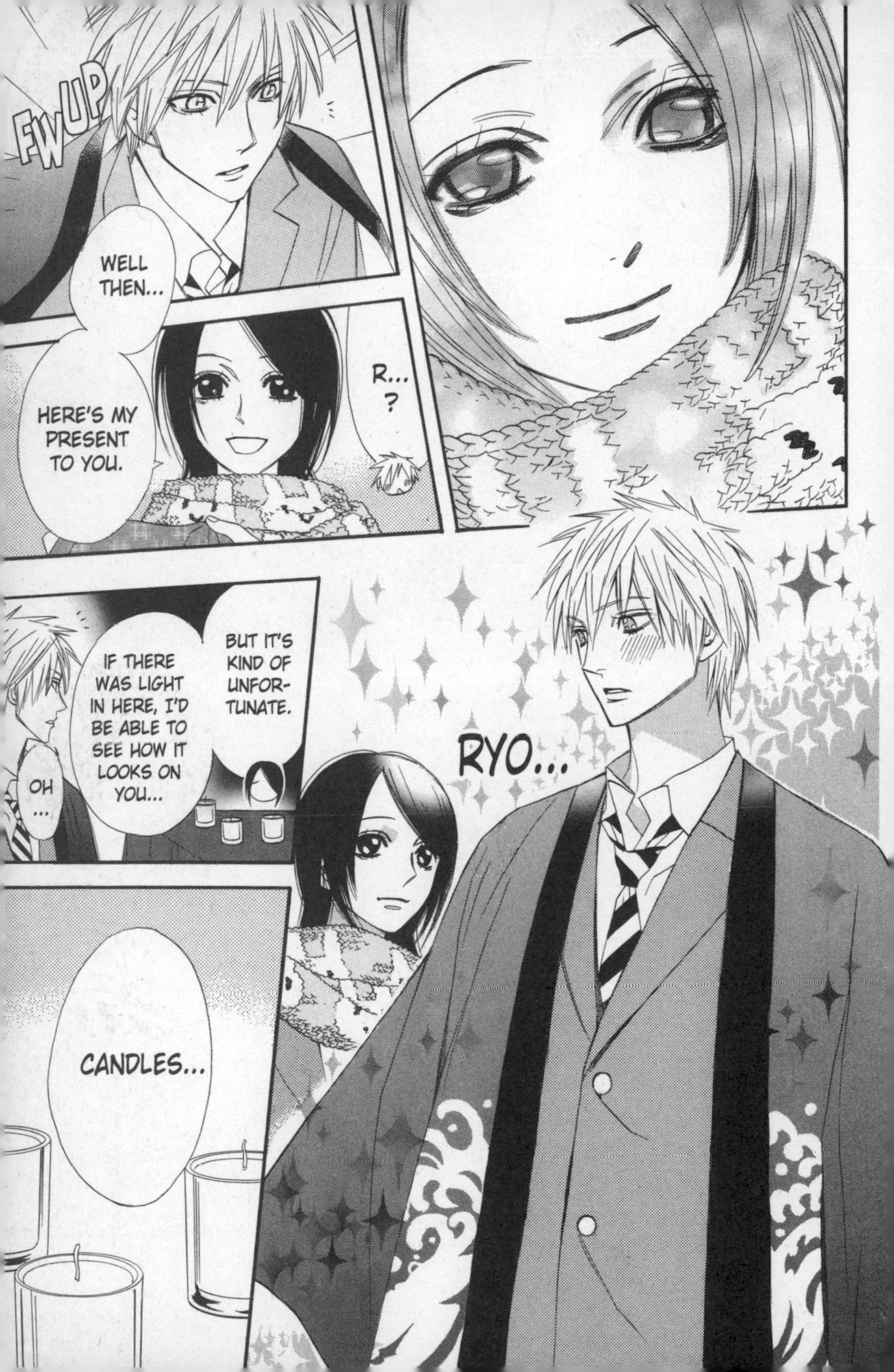
FWUP
WELL THEN...
R...?
HERE'S MY PRESENT TO YOU.
RYO...
BUT IT'S KIND OF UNFOR-TUNATE.
IF THERE WAS LIGHT IN HERE, I'D BE ABLE TO SEE HOW IT LOOKS ON YOU...
OH...
CANDLES...

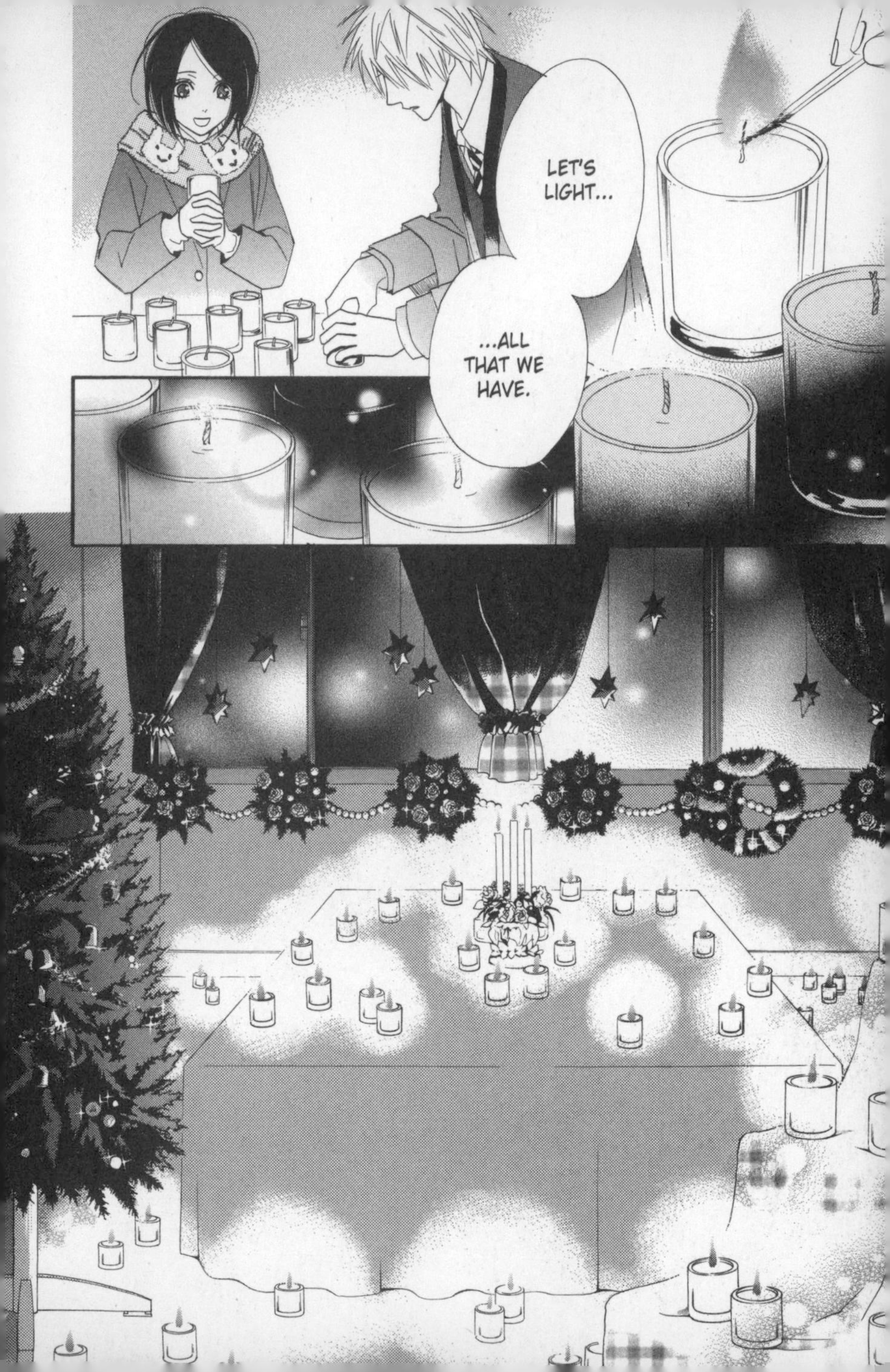
LET'S LIGHT...
...ALL THAT WE HAVE.

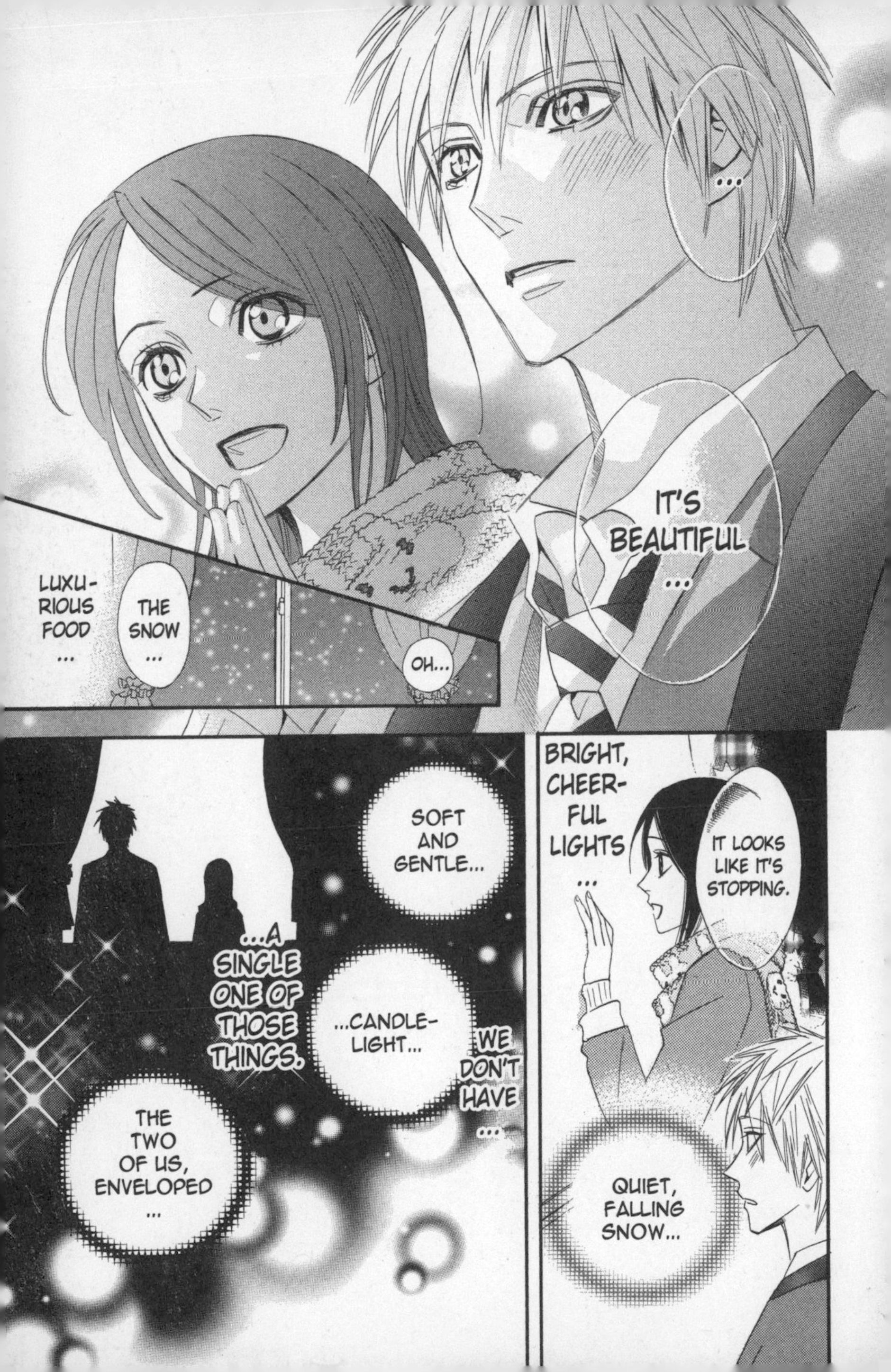
...
IT'S BEAUTIFUL ...
OH...
THE SNOW ...
LUXU-RIOUS FOOD ...
IT LOOKS LIKE IT'S STOPPING.
BRIGHT, CHEER-FUL LIGHTS ...
QUIET, FALLING SNOW...
SOFT AND GENTLE...
...CANDLE-LIGHT...
THE TWO OF US, ENVELOPED ...
WE DON'T HAVE ...
...A SINGLE ONE OF THOSE THINGS.

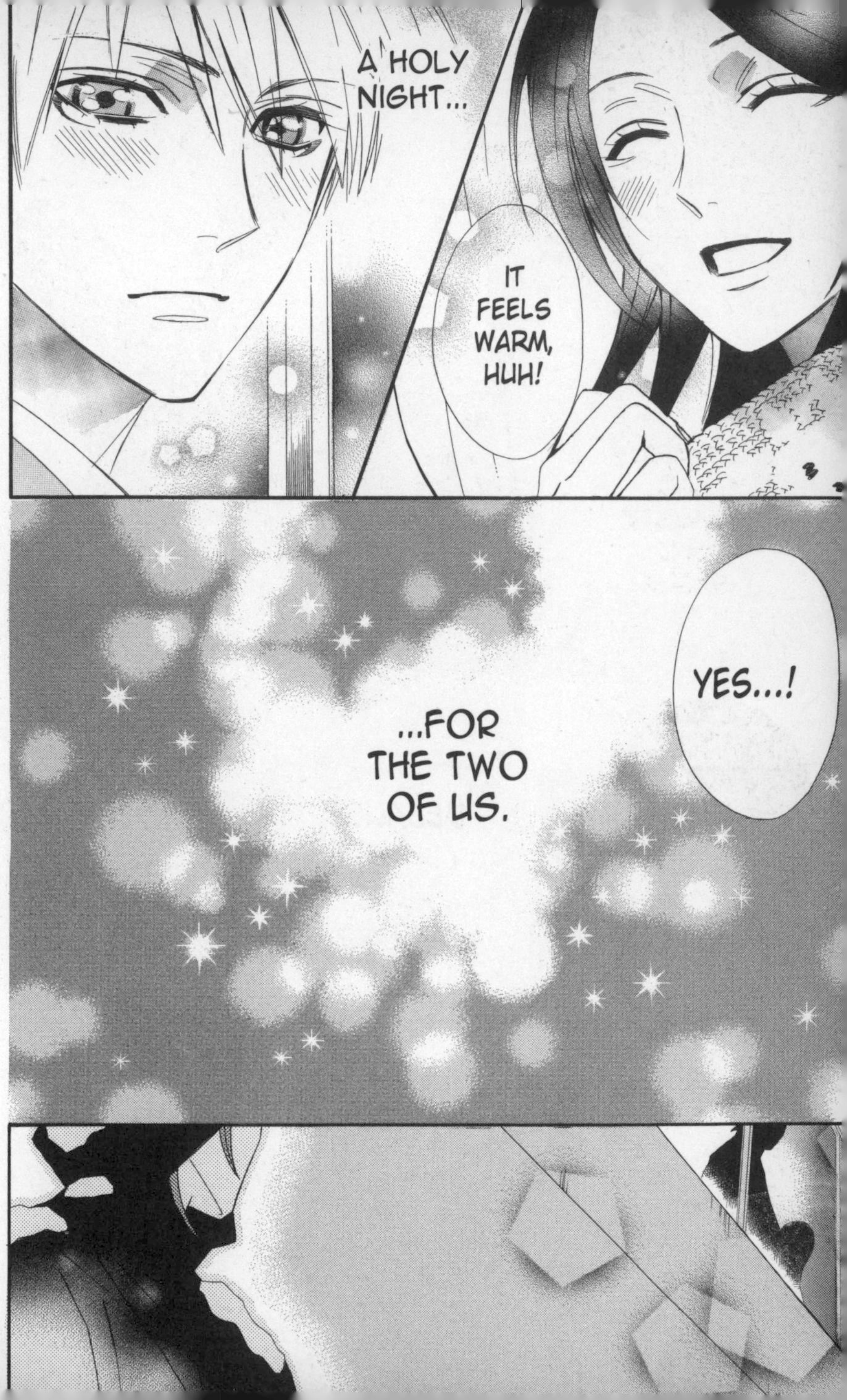
IT FEELS WARM, HUH!
A HOLY NIGHT...
YES...!
...FOR THE TWO OF US.

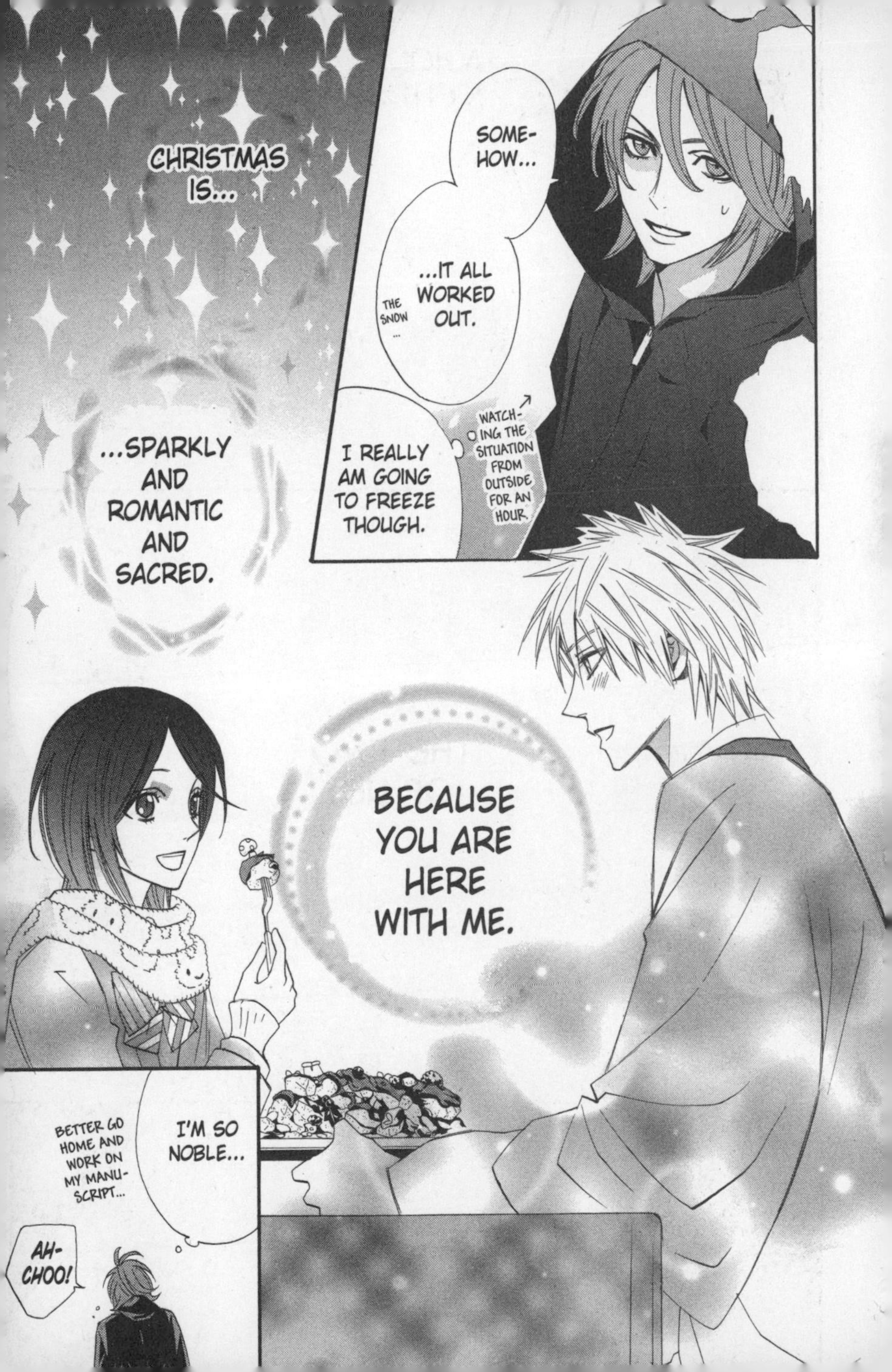
SOME-HOW...
...IT ALL WORKED OUT.
THE SNOW ...
WATCH-ING THE SITUATION FROM OUTSIDE FOR AN HOUR.
I REALLY AM GOING TO FREEZE THOUGH.
CHRISTMAS IS...
...SPARKLY AND ROMANTIC AND SACRED.
BECAUSE YOU ARE HERE WITH ME.
I'M SO NOBLE...
BETTER GO HOME AND WORK ON MY MANU-SCRIPT...
AH-CHOO!

OTOMEN

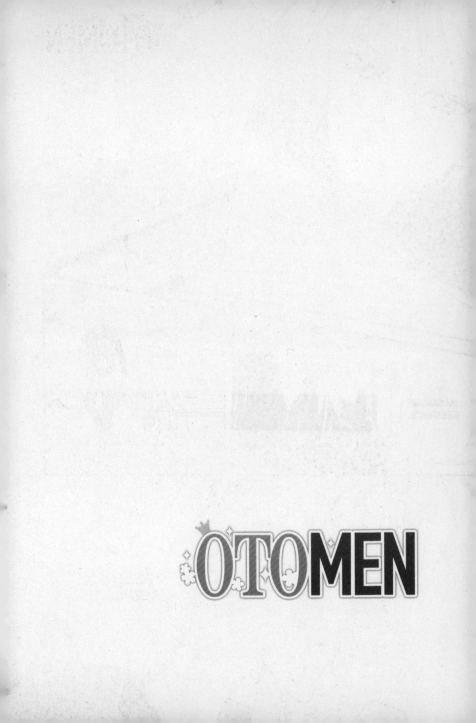

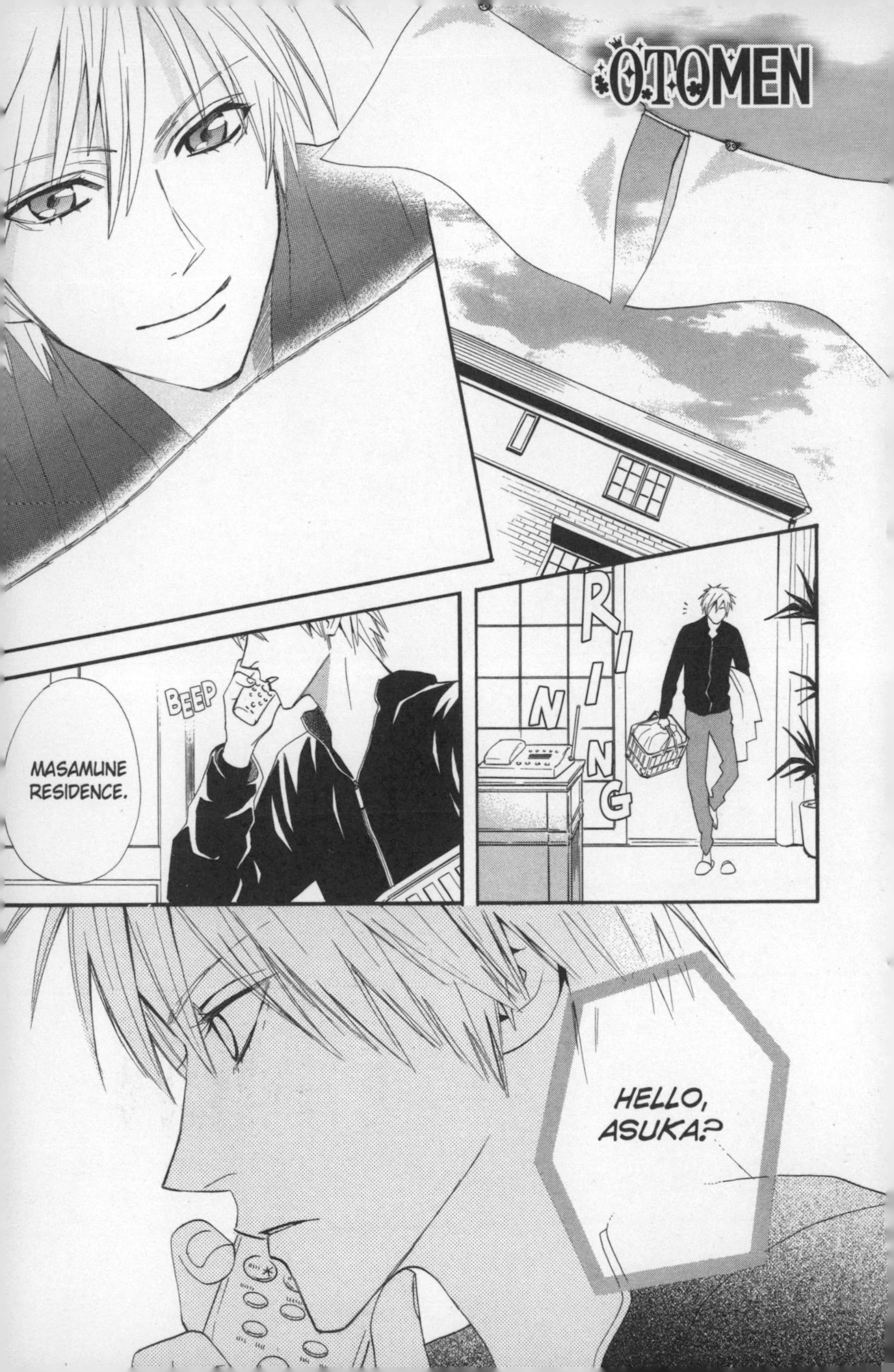
OTOMEN
RIIING
BEEP
MASAMUNE RESIDENCE.
HELLO, ASUKA?

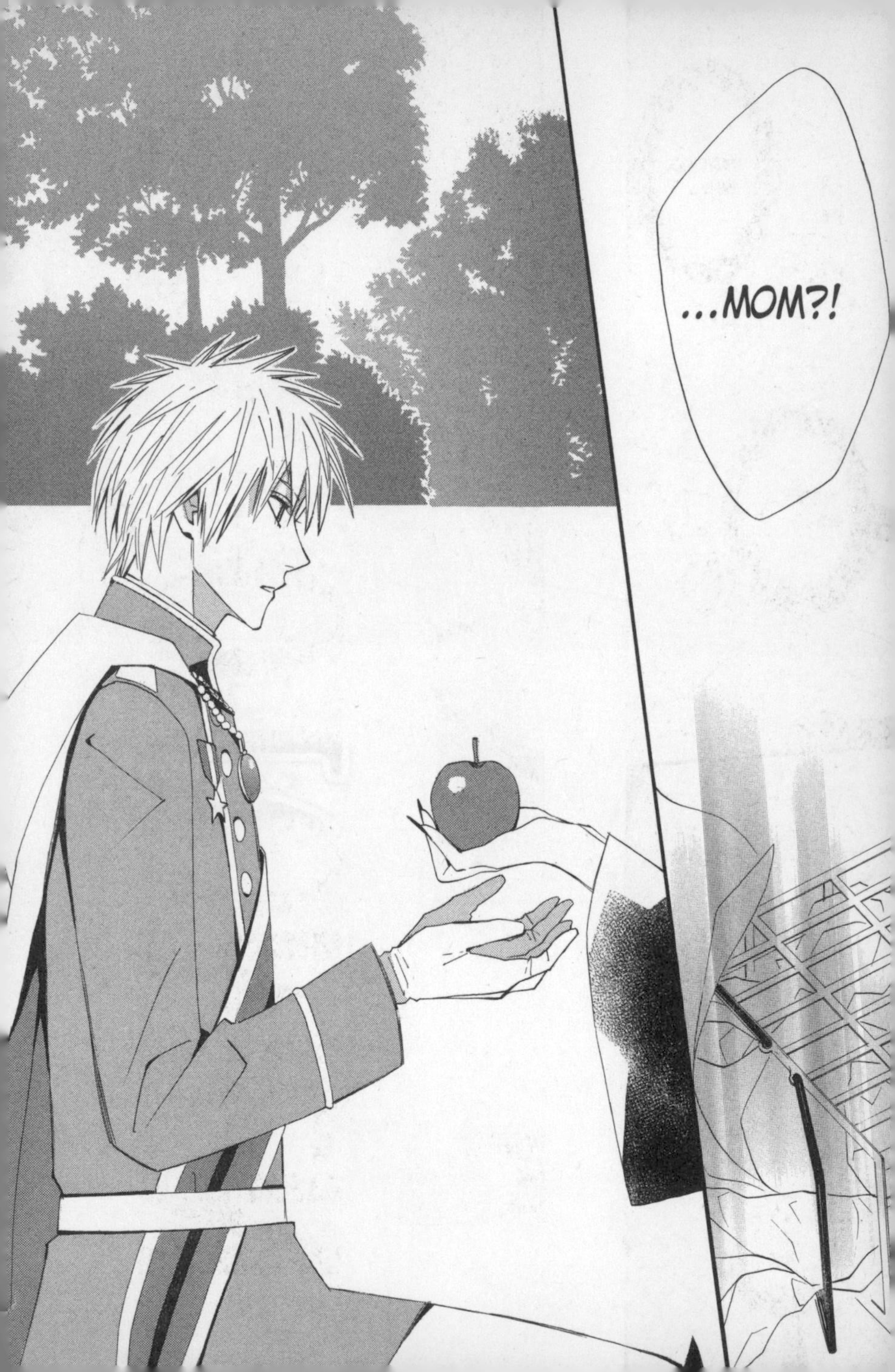
...MOM?!

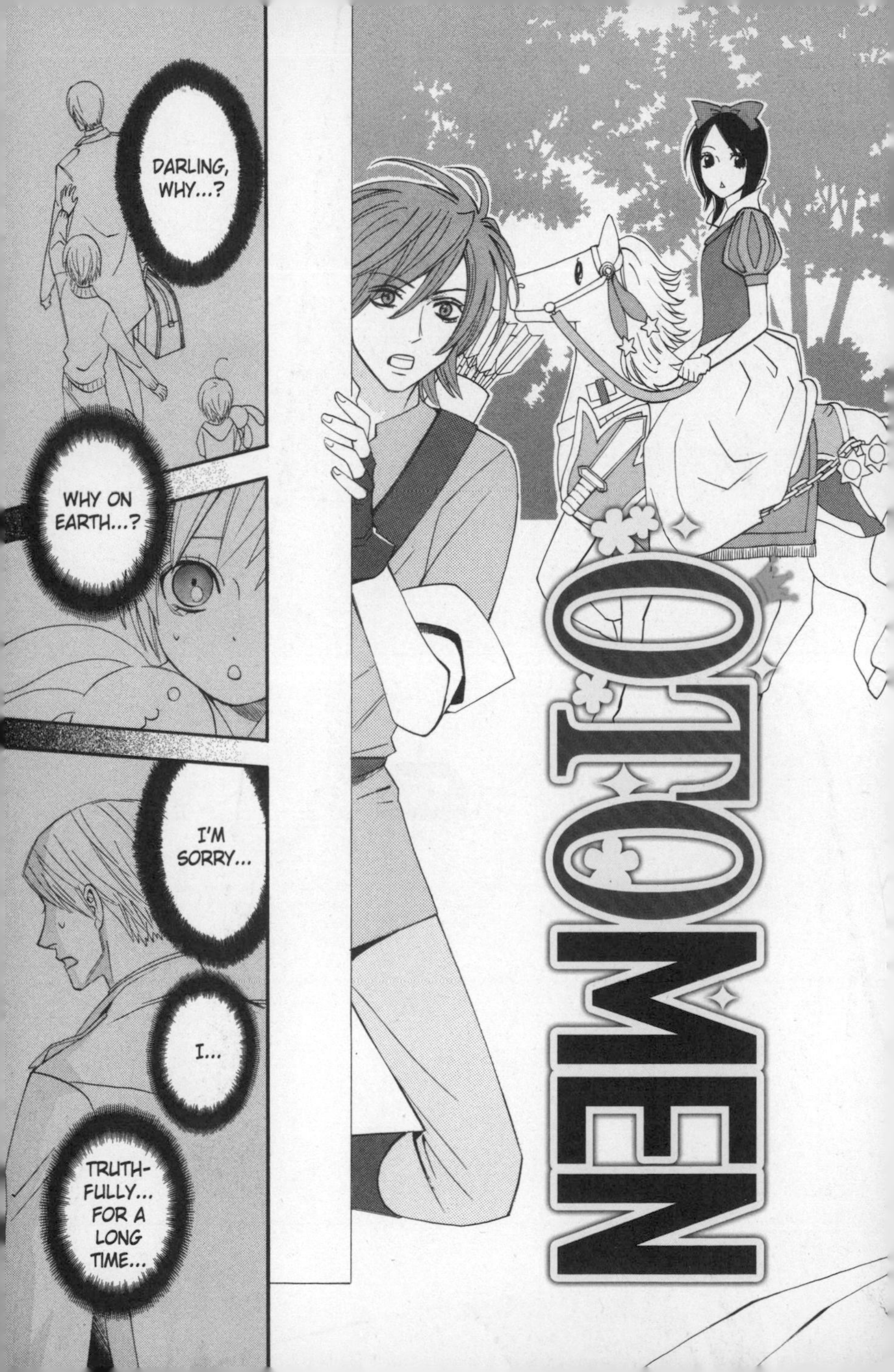
OTOMEN
DARLING, WHY...?
WHY ON EARTH...?
I'M SORRY...
I...
TRUTH-FULLY... FOR A LONG TIME...

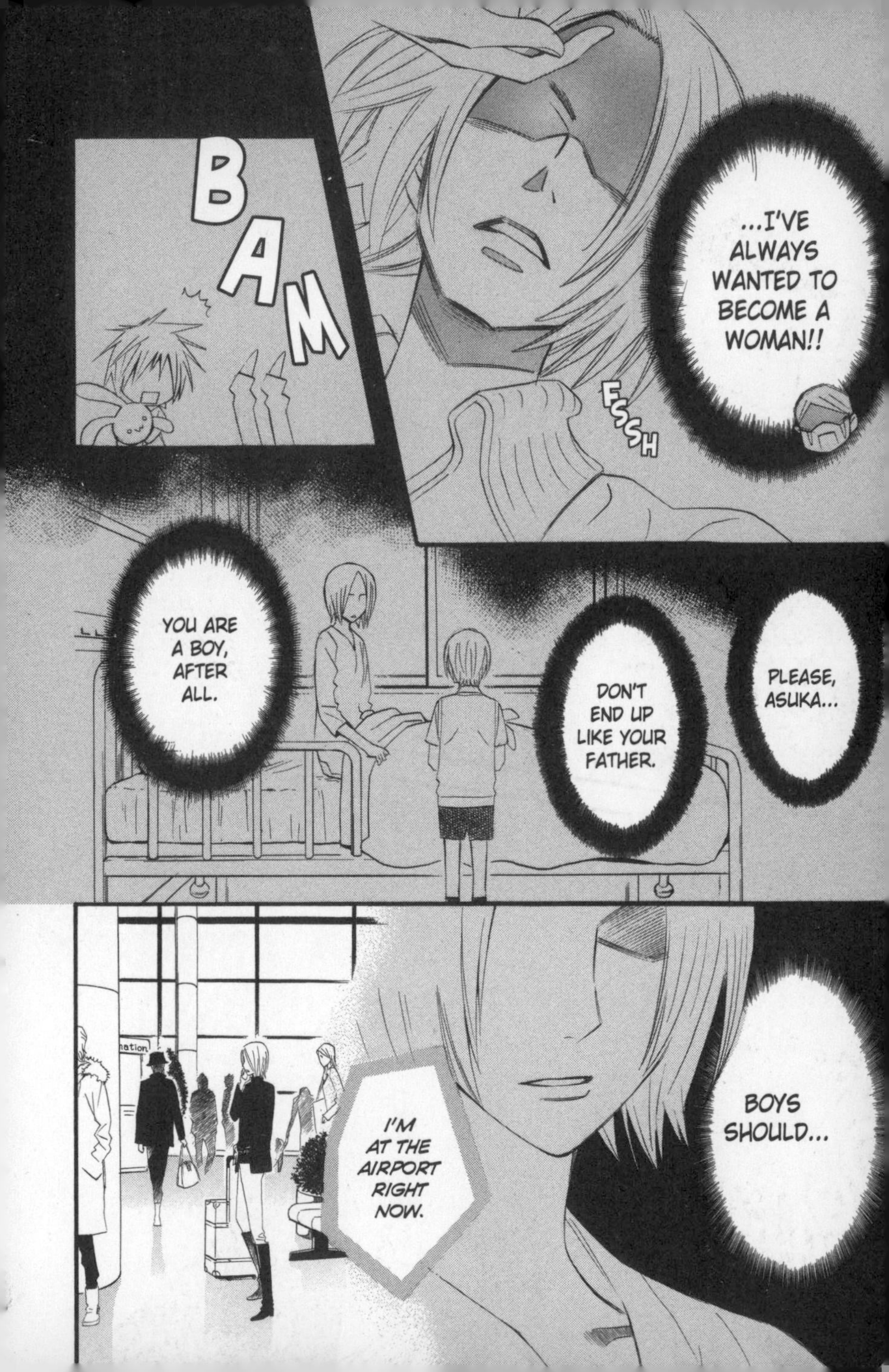
...I'VE ALWAYS WANTED TO BECOME A WOMAN!!
FSSH
BAM
PLEASE, ASUKA...
DON'T END UP LIKE YOUR FATHER.
YOU ARE A BOY, AFTER ALL.
BOYS SHOULD...
I'M AT THE AIRPORT RIGHT NOW.

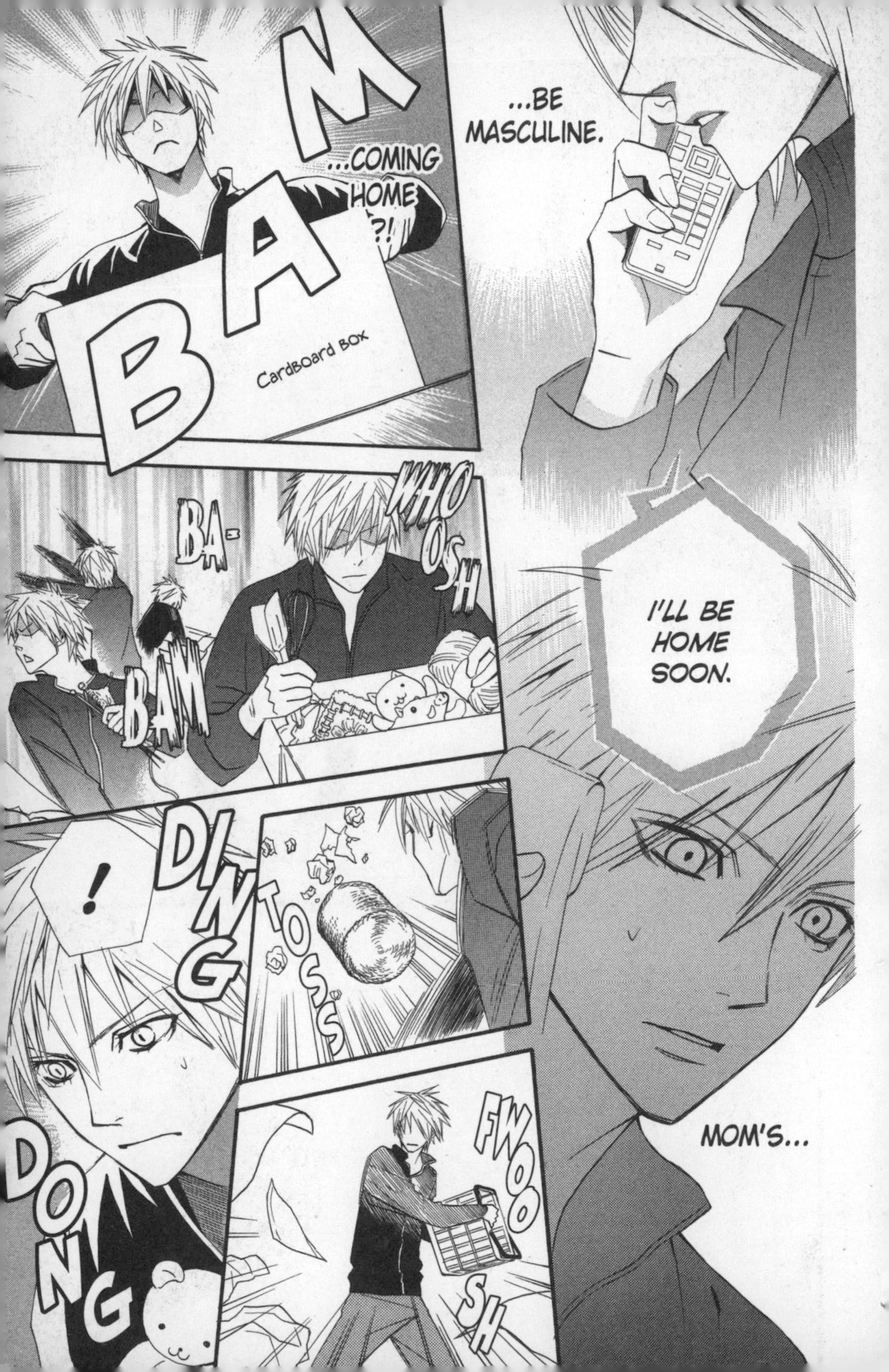

...BE MASCULINE.
I'LL BE HOME SOON.
MOM'S...
...COMING HOME ?!
BAM
Cardboard Box
WHOOSH
BA-BAM
TOSS
FWOOSH
DING DONG
!

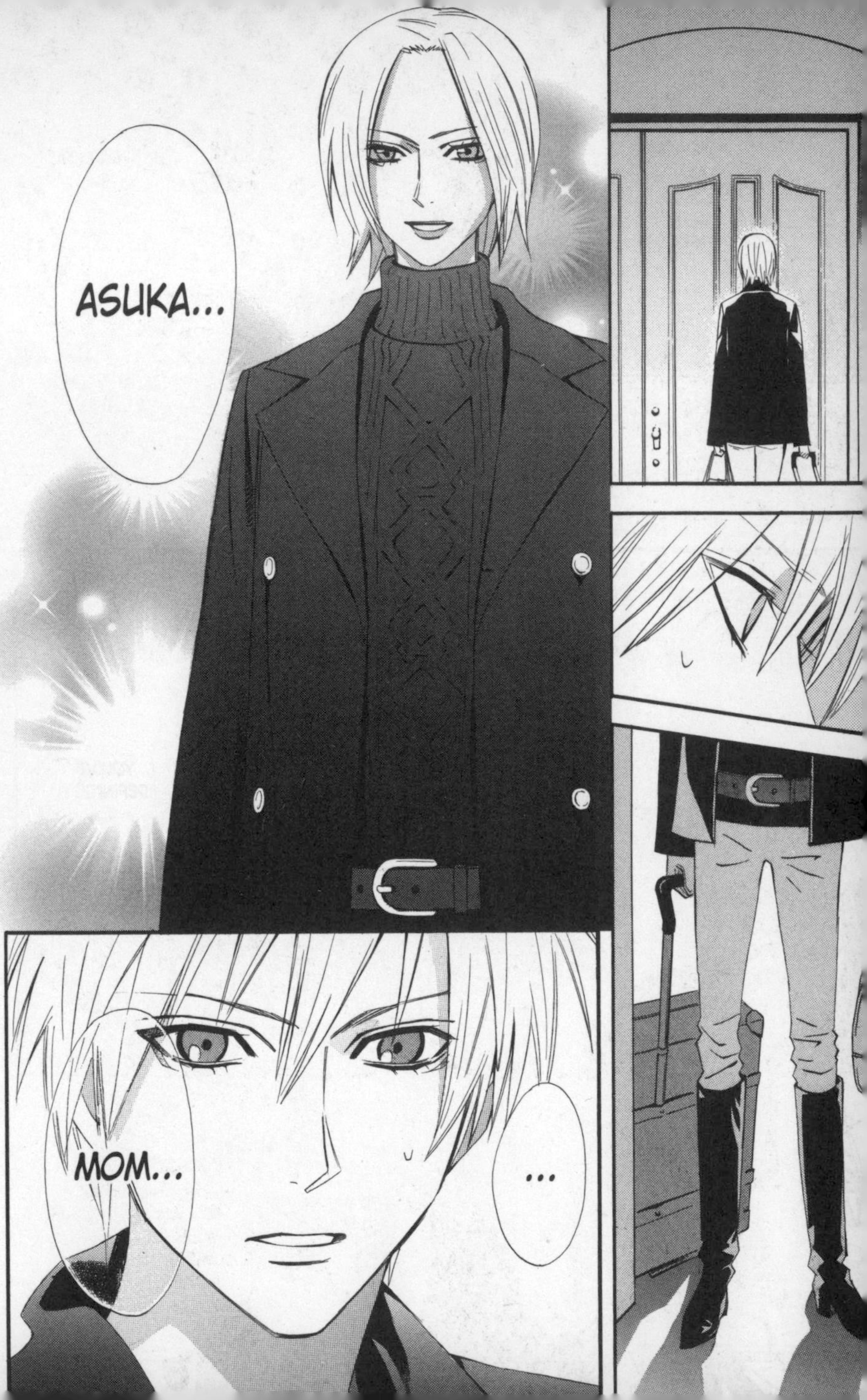
ASUKA...
...
MOM...

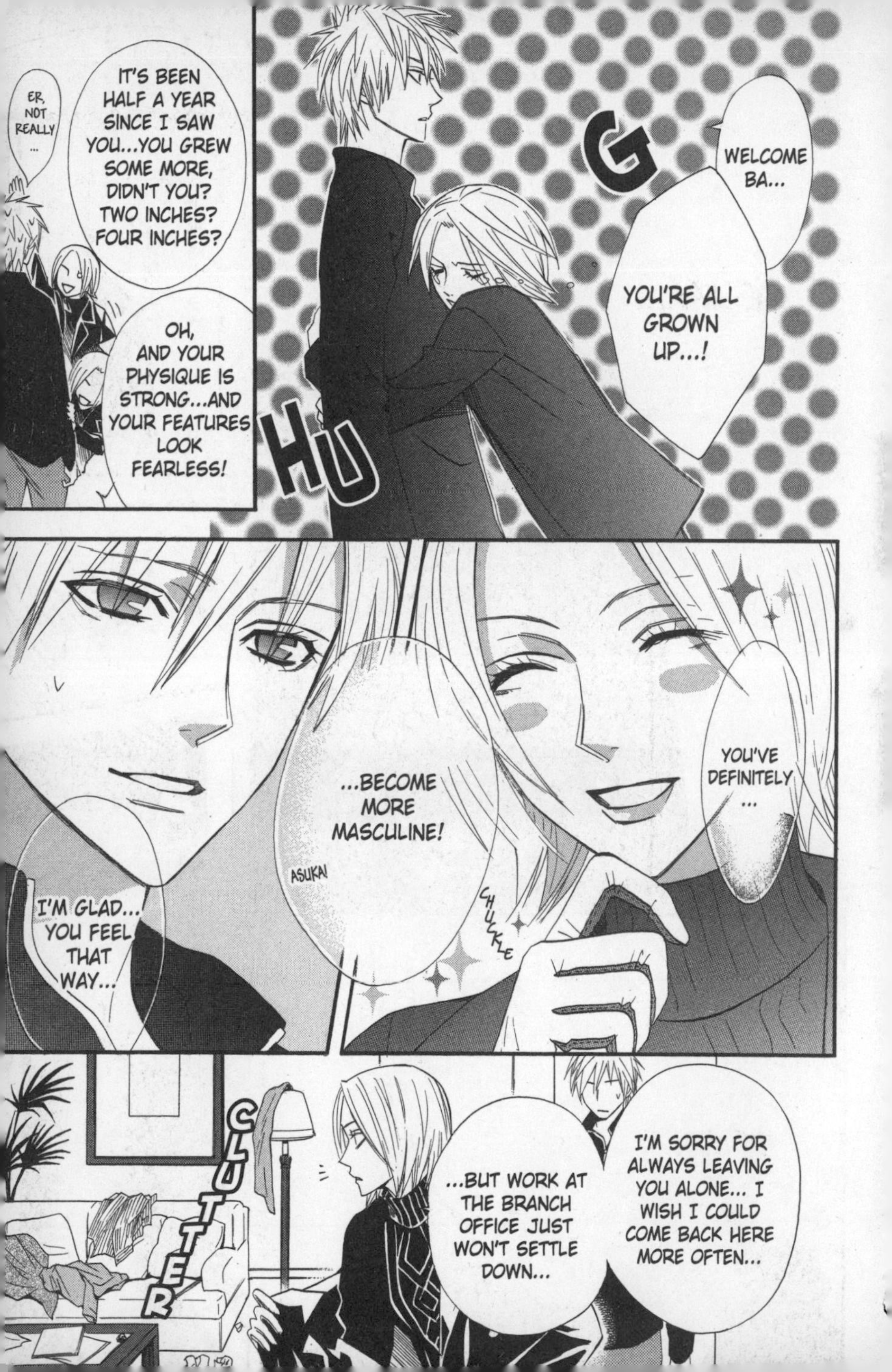
WELCOME BA...
HUG
YOU'RE ALL GROWN UP...!
IT'S BEEN HALF A YEAR SINCE I SAW YOU...YOU GREW SOME MORE, DIDN'T YOU? TWO INCHES? FOUR INCHES?
ER, NOT REALLY...
OH, AND YOUR PHYSIQUE IS STRONG...AND YOUR FEATURES LOOK FEARLESS!
YOU'VE DEFINITELY...
...BECOME MORE MASCULINE!
ASUKA!
CHUCKLE
I'M GLAD... YOU FEEL THAT WAY...
I'M SORRY FOR ALWAYS LEAVING YOU ALONE... I WISH I COULD COME BACK HERE MORE OFTEN...
...BUT WORK AT THE BRANCH OFFICE JUST WON'T SETTLE DOWN...
CLUTTER

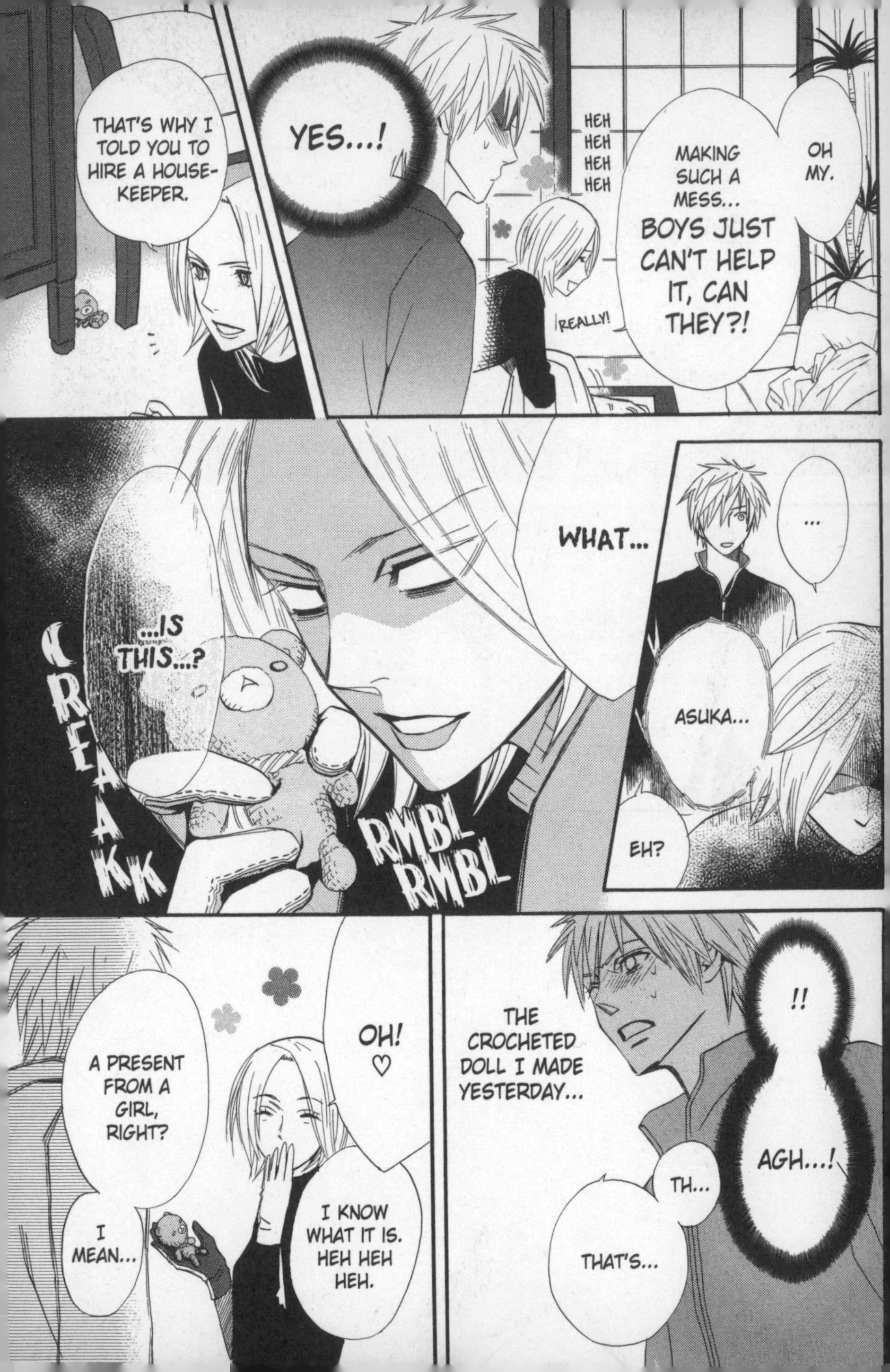
OH MY.
MAKING SUCH A MESS... BOYS JUST CAN'T HELP IT, CAN THEY?!
HEH HEH HEH HEH
REALLY!
YES...!
THAT'S WHY I TOLD YOU TO HIRE A HOUSE-KEEPER.
...
ASUKA...
EH?
WHAT...
...IS THIS...?
CREAAKK
RMBL RMBL
!!
THE CROCHETED DOLL I MADE YESTERDAY...
AGH...!
TH...
THAT'S...
OH! ♡
A PRESENT FROM A GIRL, RIGHT?
I KNOW WHAT IT IS. HEH HEH HEH.
I MEAN...

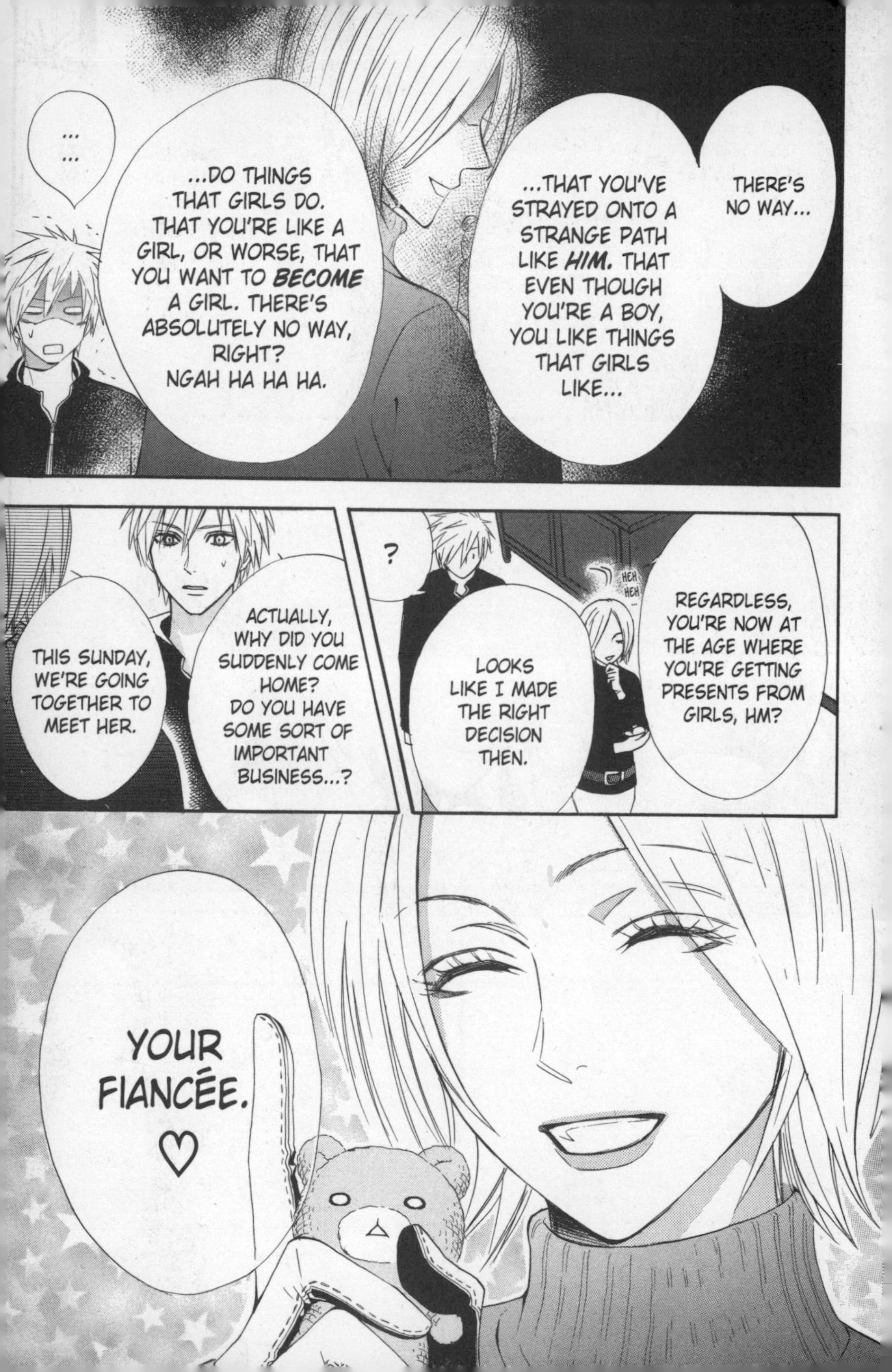
THERE'S NO WAY...
...THAT YOU'VE STRAYED ONTO A STRANGE PATH LIKE ***HIM.*** THAT EVEN THOUGH YOU'RE A BOY, YOU LIKE THINGS THAT GIRLS LIKE...
...DO THINGS THAT GIRLS DO. THAT YOU'RE LIKE A GIRL, OR WORSE, THAT YOU WANT TO ***BECOME*** A GIRL. THERE'S ABSOLUTELY NO WAY, RIGHT? NGAH HA HA HA.
... ...
REGARDLESS, YOU'RE NOW AT THE AGE WHERE YOU'RE GETTING PRESENTS FROM GIRLS, HM?
HEH HEH ...
LOOKS LIKE I MADE THE RIGHT DECISION THEN.
?
ACTUALLY, WHY DID YOU SUDDENLY COME HOME? DO YOU HAVE SOME SORT OF IMPORTANT BUSINESS...?
THIS SUNDAY, WE'RE GOING TOGETHER TO MEET HER.
YOUR FIANCÉE. ♡

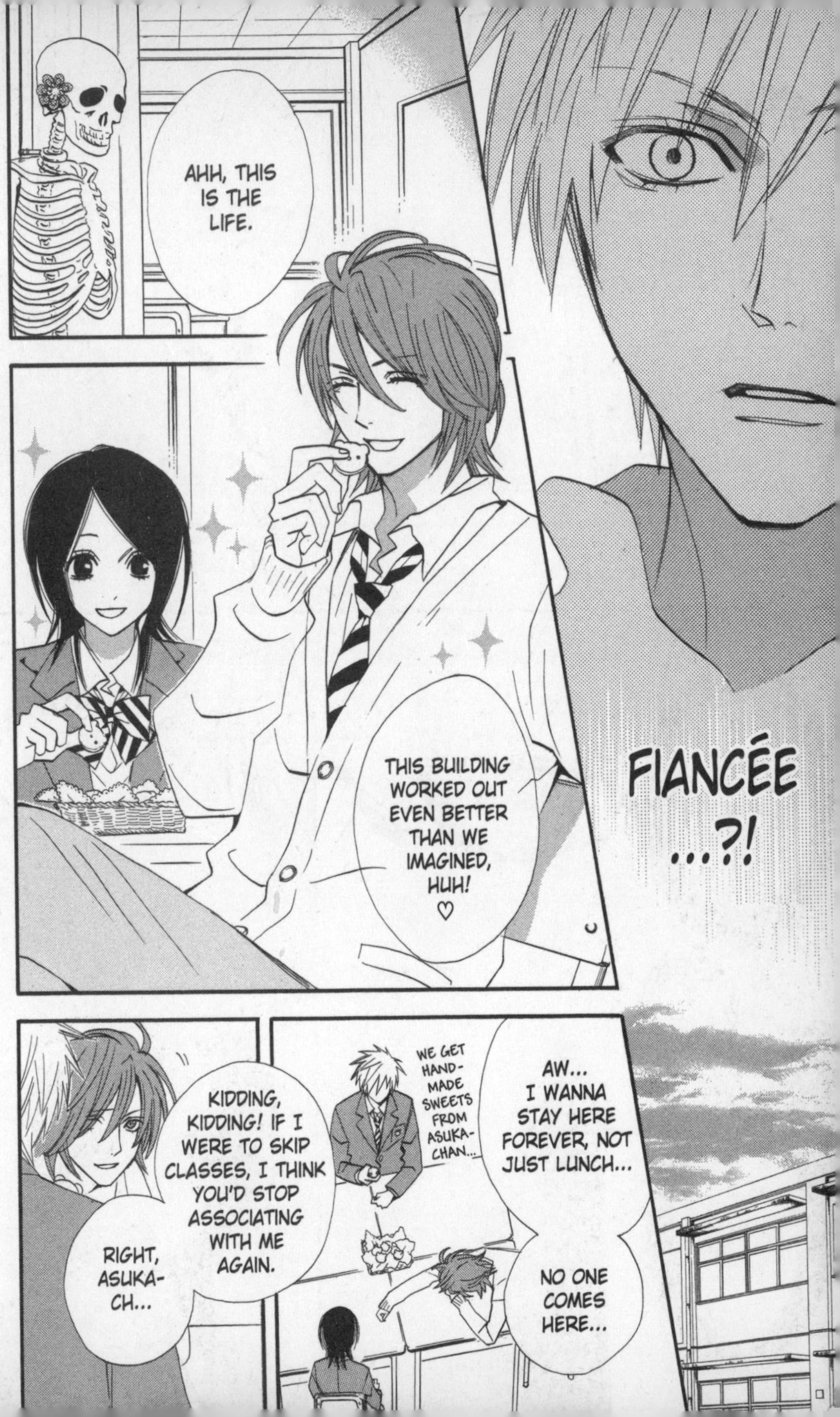
FIANCÉE ...?!
AHH, THIS IS THE LIFE.
THIS BUILDING WORKED OUT EVEN BETTER THAN WE IMAGINED, HUH! ♡
AW... I WANNA STAY HERE FOREVER, NOT JUST LUNCH...
WE GET HAND-MADE SWEETS FROM ASUKA-CHAN...
NO ONE COMES HERE...
KIDDING, KIDDING! IF I WERE TO SKIP CLASSES, I THINK YOU'D STOP ASSOCIATING WITH ME AGAIN.
RIGHT, ASUKA-CH...

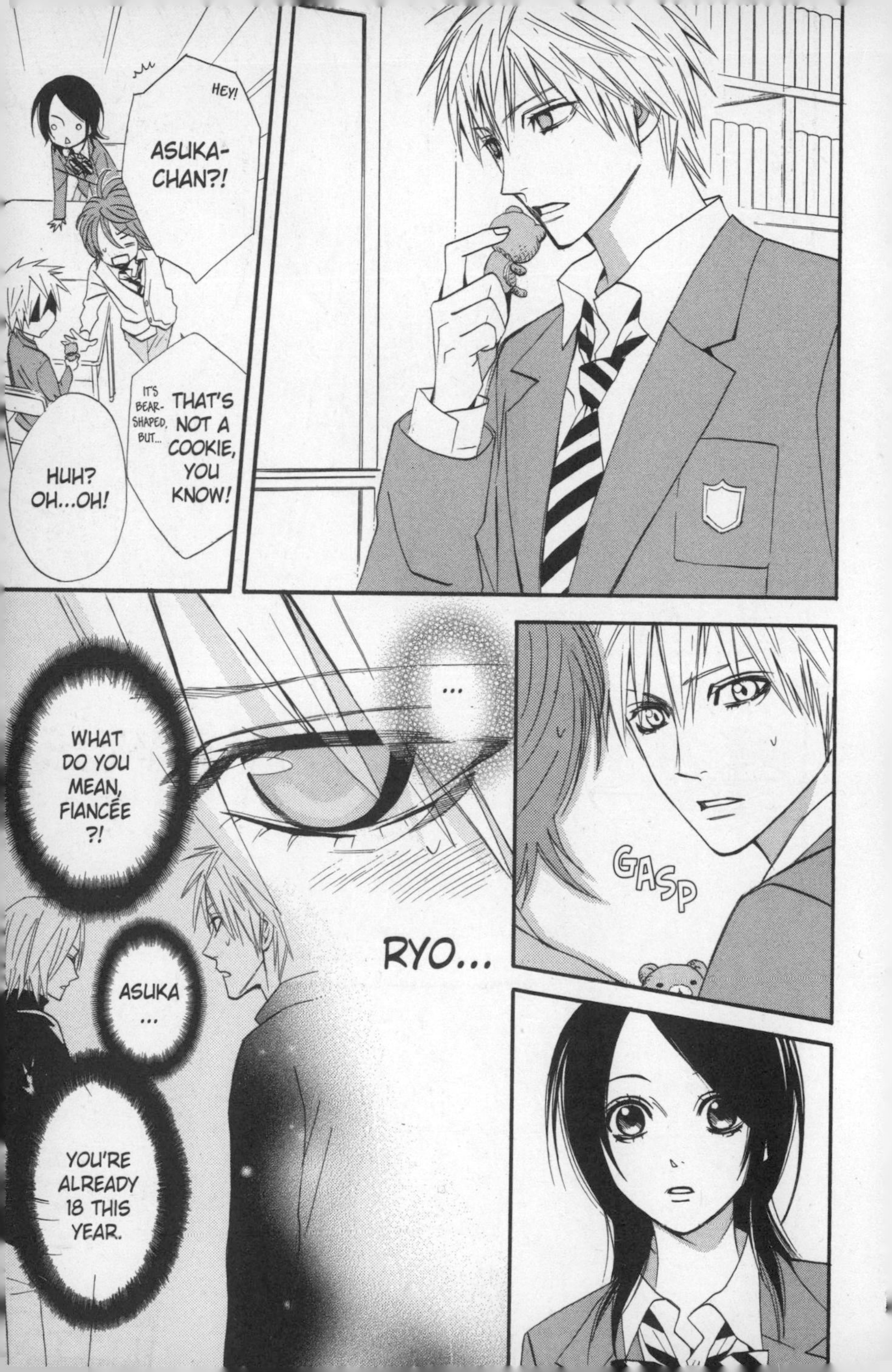
HEY!
ASUKA-CHAN?!
THAT'S NOT A COOKIE, YOU KNOW!
IT'S BEAR-SHAPED, BUT...
HUH? OH...OH!
GASP
RYO...
...
WHAT DO YOU MEAN, FIANCÉE?!
ASUKA...
YOU'RE ALREADY 18 THIS YEAR.

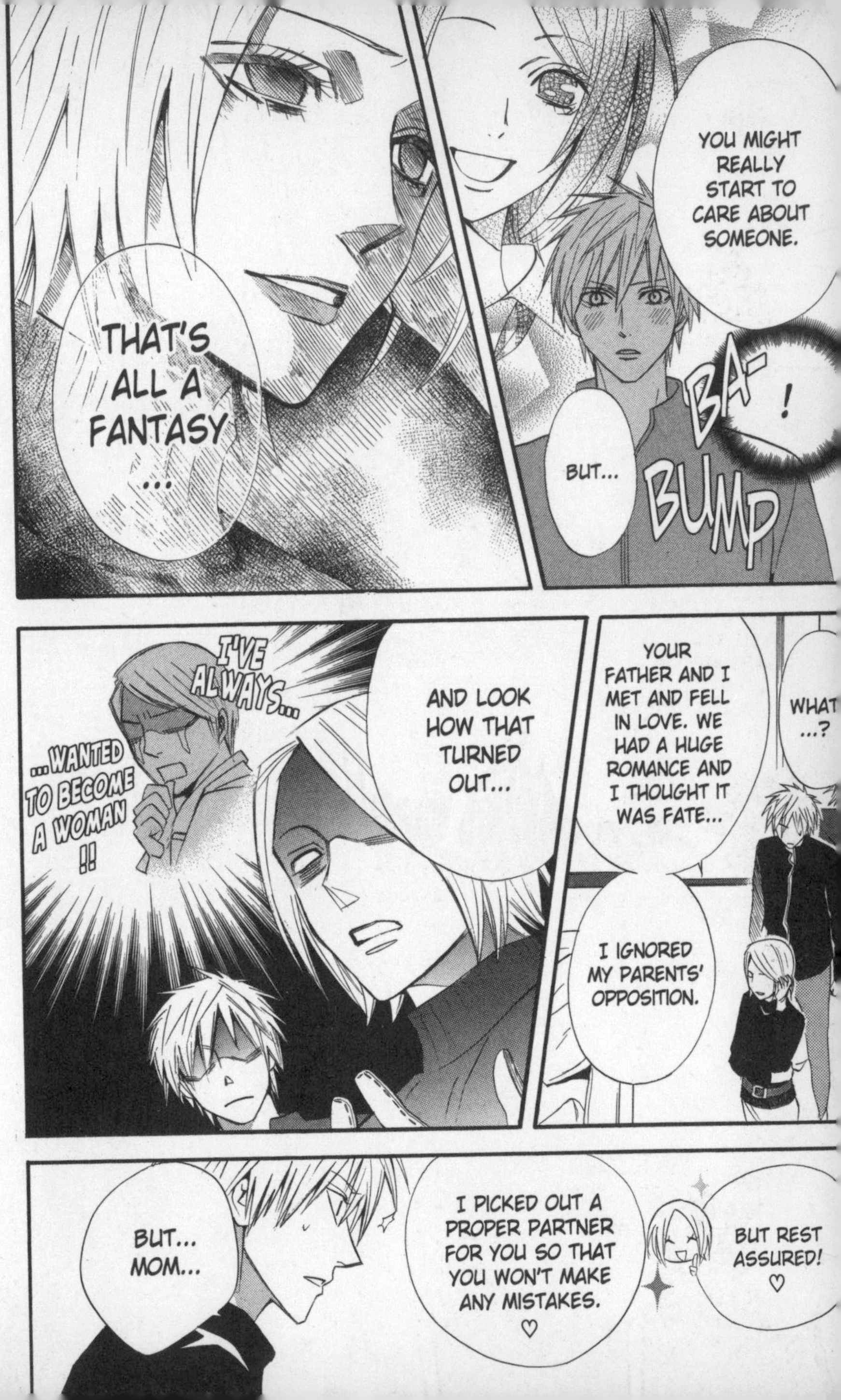
YOU MIGHT REALLY START TO CARE ABOUT SOMEONE.
BA-BUMP
!
BUT...
THAT'S ALL A FANTASY ...
WHAT ...?
YOUR FATHER AND I MET AND FELL IN LOVE. WE HAD A HUGE ROMANCE AND I THOUGHT IT WAS FATE...
I IGNORED MY PARENTS' OPPOSITION.
AND LOOK HOW THAT TURNED OUT...
I'VE ALWAYS...
...WANTED TO BECOME A WOMAN !!
BUT REST ASSURED! ♡
I PICKED OUT A PROPER PARTNER FOR YOU SO THAT YOU WON'T MAKE ANY MISTAKES. ♡
BUT... MOM...

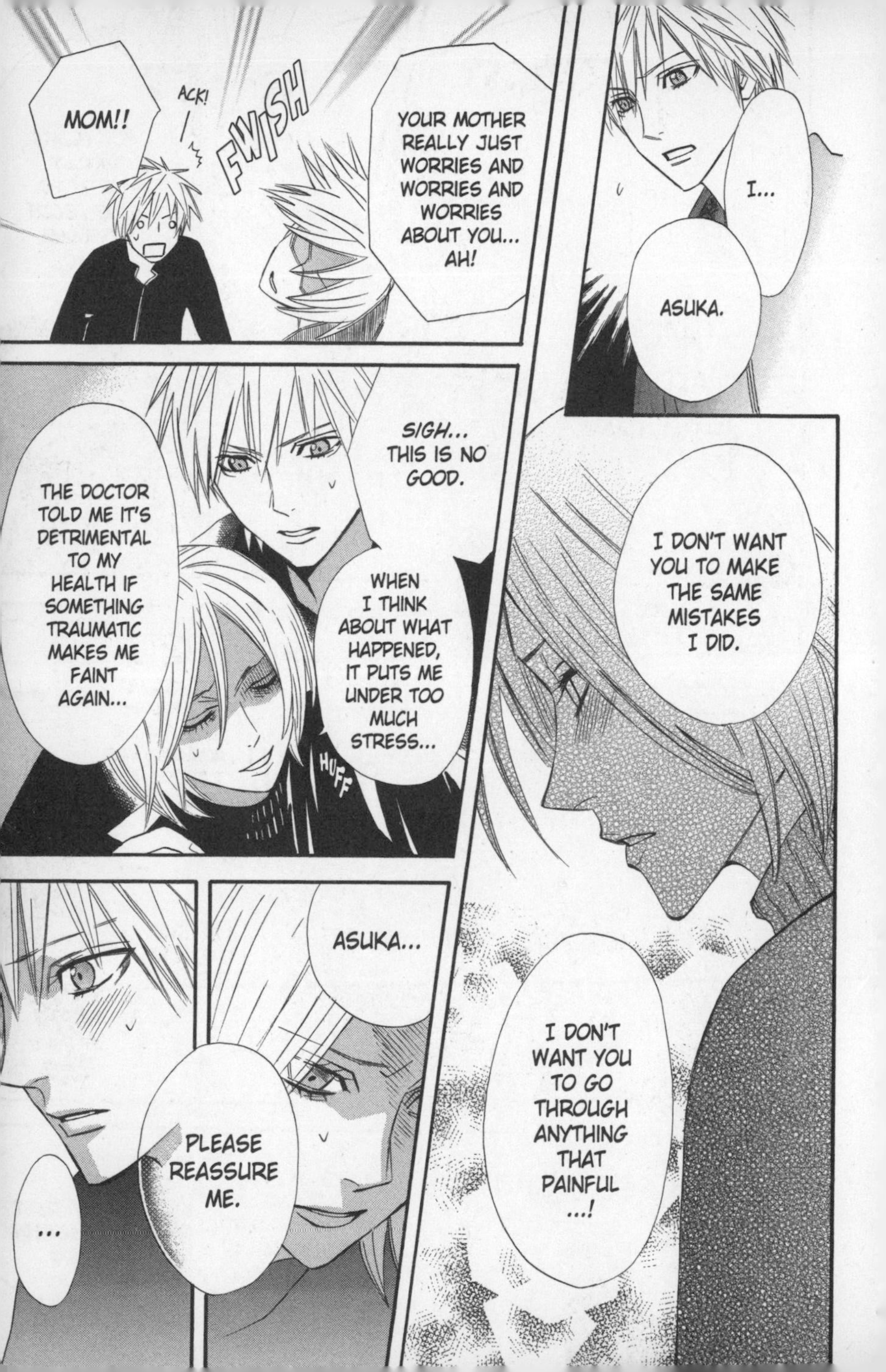
I...
ASUKA.
I DON'T WANT YOU TO MAKE THE SAME MISTAKES I DID.
I DON'T WANT YOU TO GO THROUGH ANYTHING THAT PAINFUL ...!
YOUR MOTHER REALLY JUST WORRIES AND WORRIES AND WORRIES ABOUT YOU... AH!
FWISH
ACK!
MOM!!
SIGH... THIS IS NO GOOD.
WHEN I THINK ABOUT WHAT HAPPENED, IT PUTS ME UNDER TOO MUCH STRESS...
HUFF
THE DOCTOR TOLD ME IT'S DETRIMENTAL TO MY HEALTH IF SOMETHING TRAUMATIC MAKES ME FAINT AGAIN...
ASUKA...
PLEASE REASSURE ME.
...

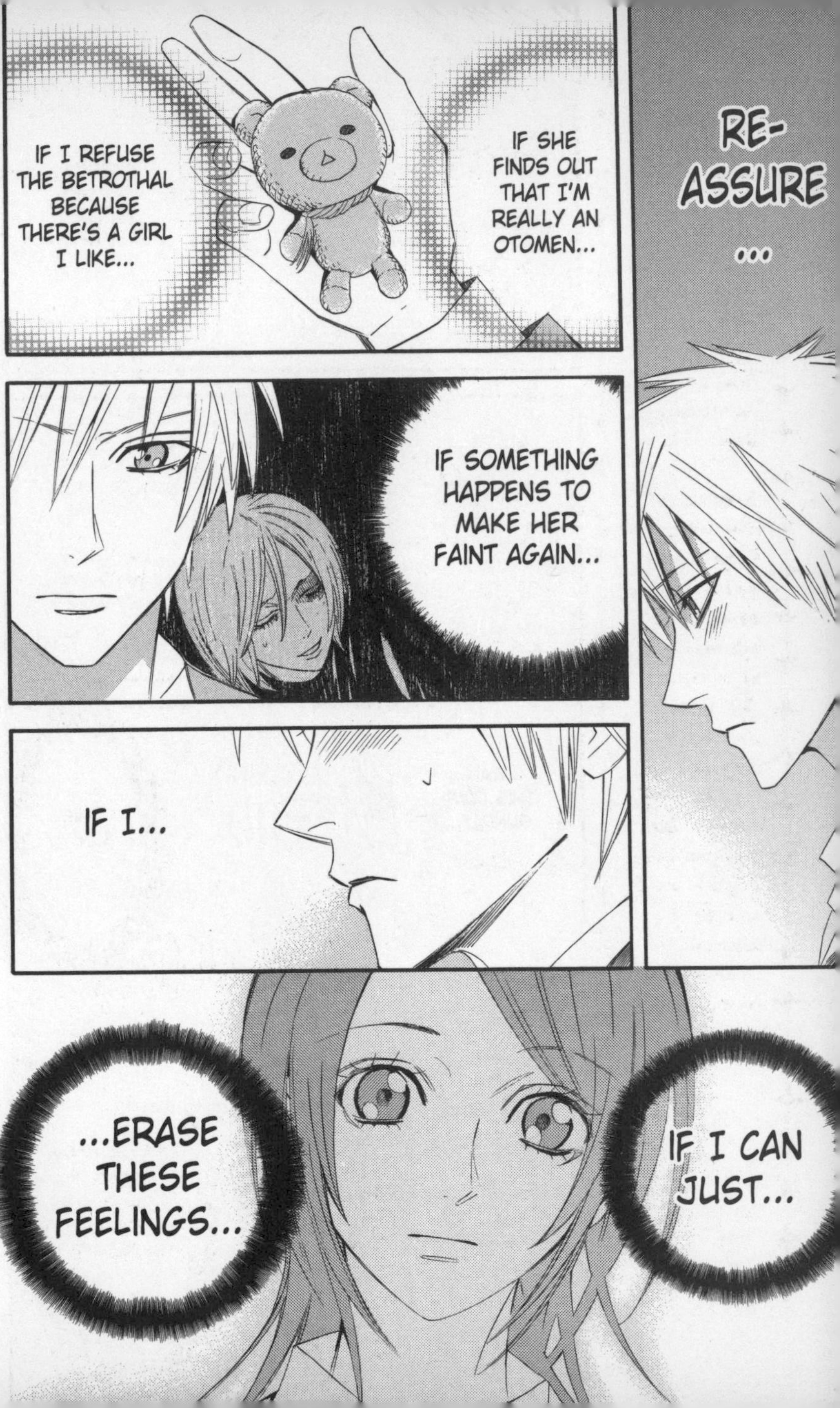
RE-ASSURE...
IF SHE FINDS OUT THAT I'M REALLY AN OTOMEN...
IF I REFUSE THE BETROTHAL BECAUSE THERE'S A GIRL I LIKE...
IF SOMETHING HAPPENS TO MAKE HER FAINT AGAIN...
IF I...
IF I CAN JUST...
...ERASE THESE FEELINGS...

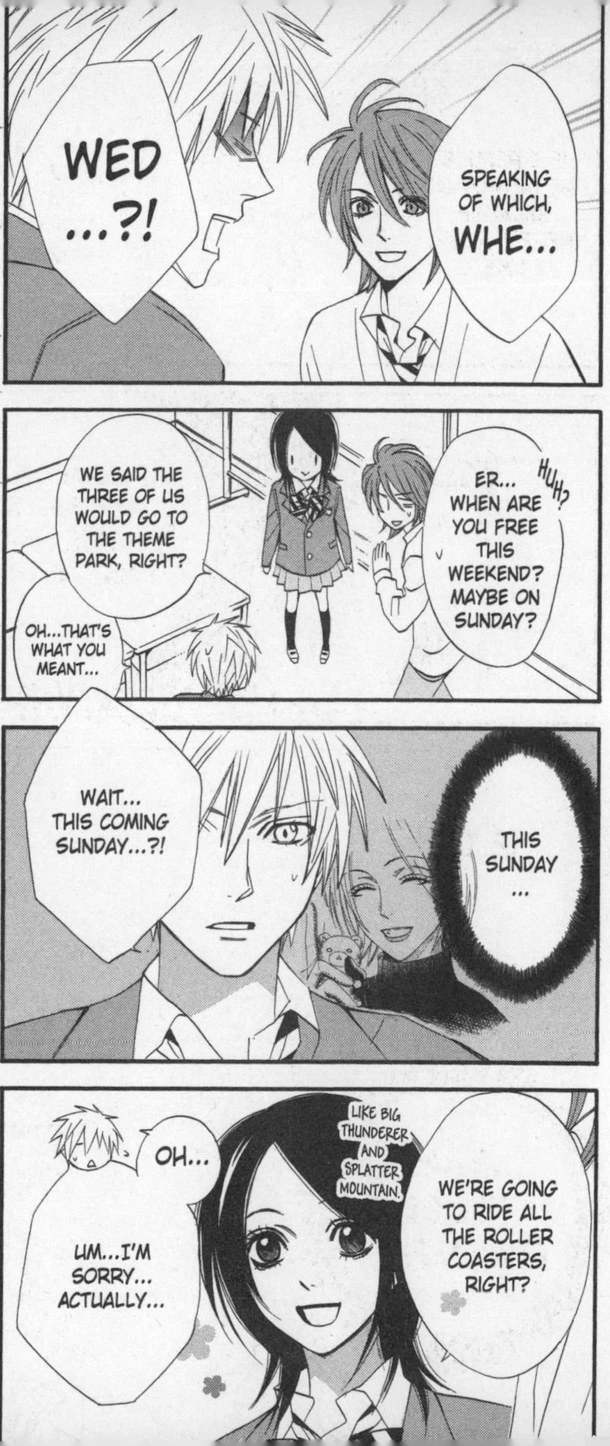
SPEAKING OF WHICH, WHE...
WED ...?!
ER... WHEN ARE YOU FREE THIS WEEKEND? MAYBE ON SUNDAY?
HUH?
WE SAID THE THREE OF US WOULD GO TO THE THEME PARK, RIGHT?
OH...THAT'S WHAT YOU MEANT...
THIS SUNDAY ...
WAIT... THIS COMING SUNDAY...?!
WE'RE GOING TO RIDE ALL THE ROLLER COASTERS, RIGHT?
LIKE BIG THUNDERER AND SPLATTER MOUNTAIN.
OH...
UM...I'M SORRY... ACTUALLY...

This is the first time I've written a two-part story. Asuka's mom finally appears. Asuka looks just like his mother.

It was a lot of fun drawing the Sakiyama parents, but I got caught up drawing in that style and it made my lines thick. This happens in *Love Chick* too. Every time I draw in a different style, that style affects my original style! I try to be careful not to get too influenced... It's actually quite fun to go against your old habits.

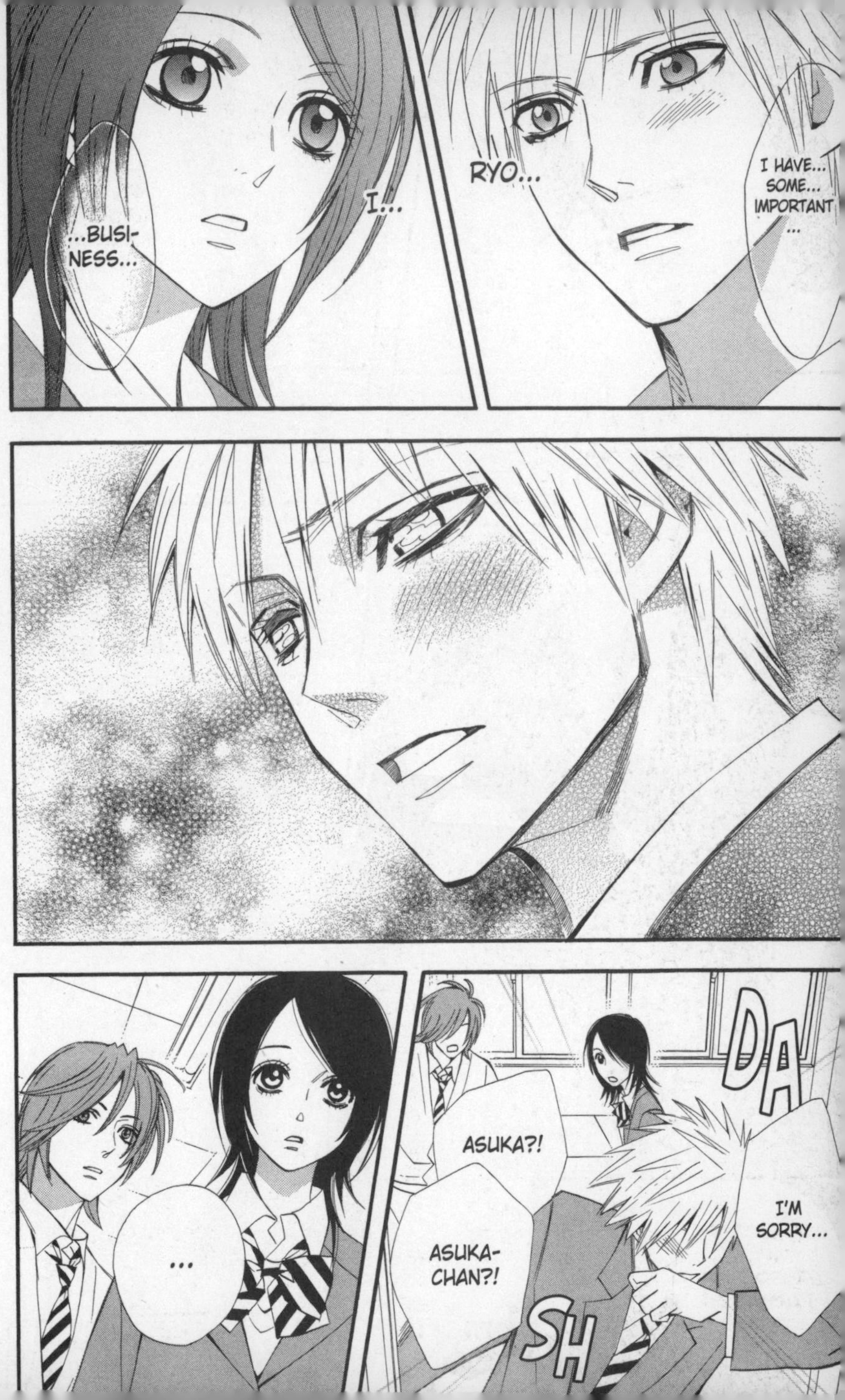
RYO...
I HAVE... SOME... IMPORTANT ...
I...
...BUSI-NESS...
DA
I'M SORRY...
ASUKA?!
ASUKA-CHAN?!
SH
...

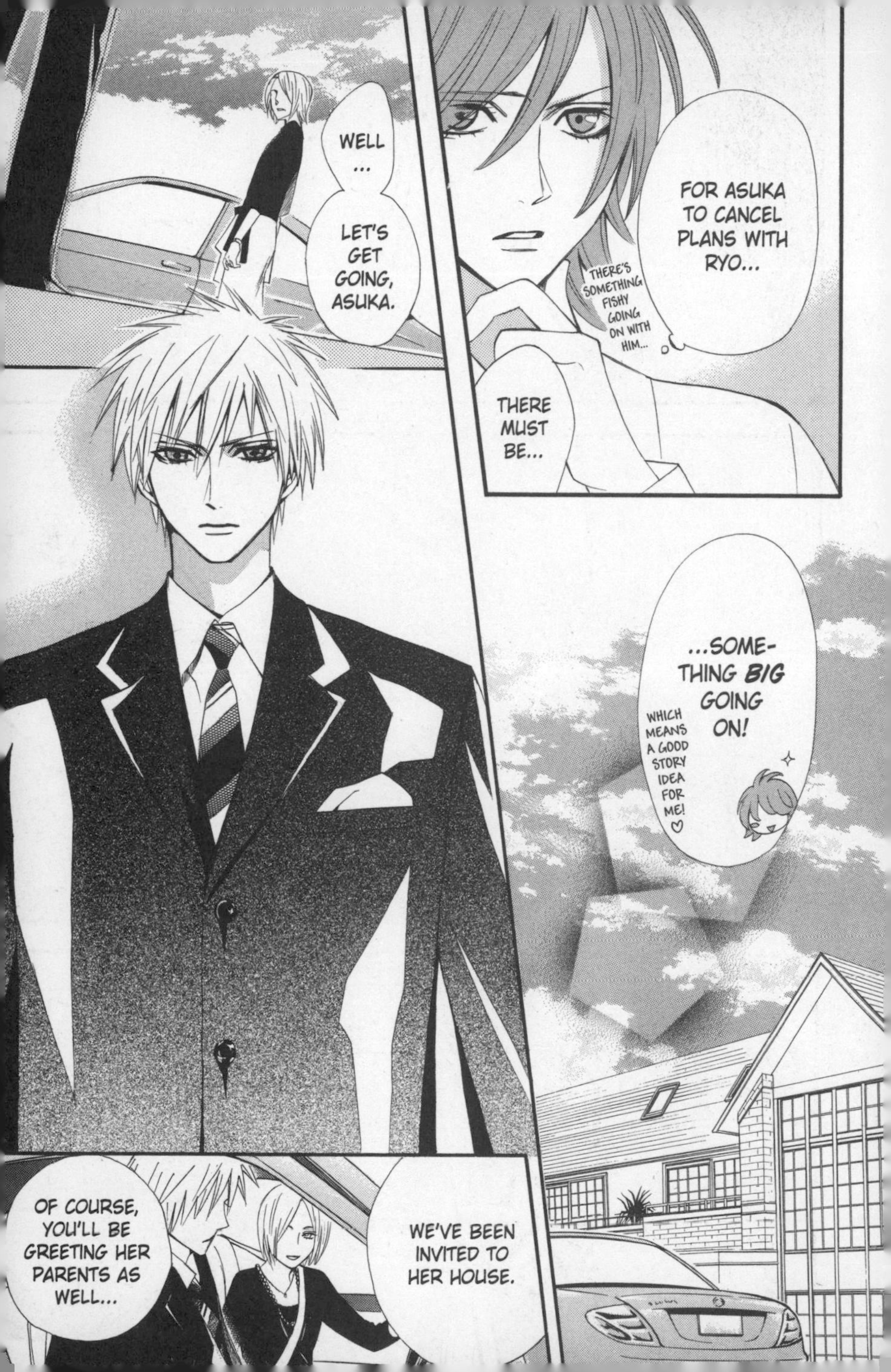
FOR ASUKA TO CANCEL PLANS WITH RYO...
THERE'S SOMETHING FISHY GOING ON WITH HIM...
THERE MUST BE...
WELL ...
LET'S GET GOING, ASUKA.
...SOME-THING BIG GOING ON!
WHICH MEANS A GOOD STORY IDEA FOR ME! ♡
WE'VE BEEN INVITED TO HER HOUSE.
OF COURSE, YOU'LL BE GREETING HER PARENTS AS WELL...

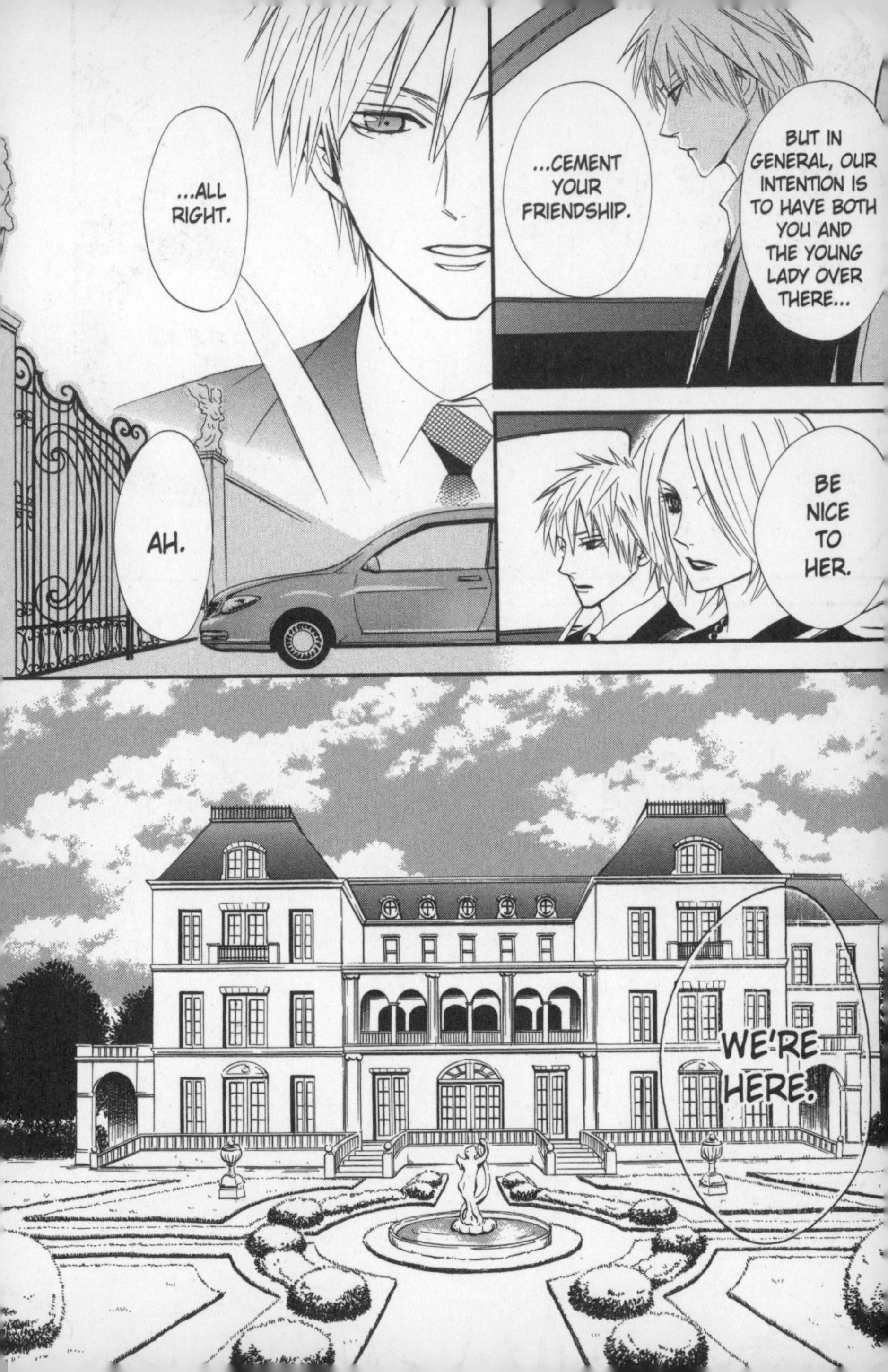
BUT IN GENERAL, OUR INTENTION IS TO HAVE BOTH YOU AND THE YOUNG LADY OVER THERE...
...CEMENT YOUR FRIENDSHIP.
BE NICE TO HER.
...ALL RIGHT.
AH.
WE'RE HERE.

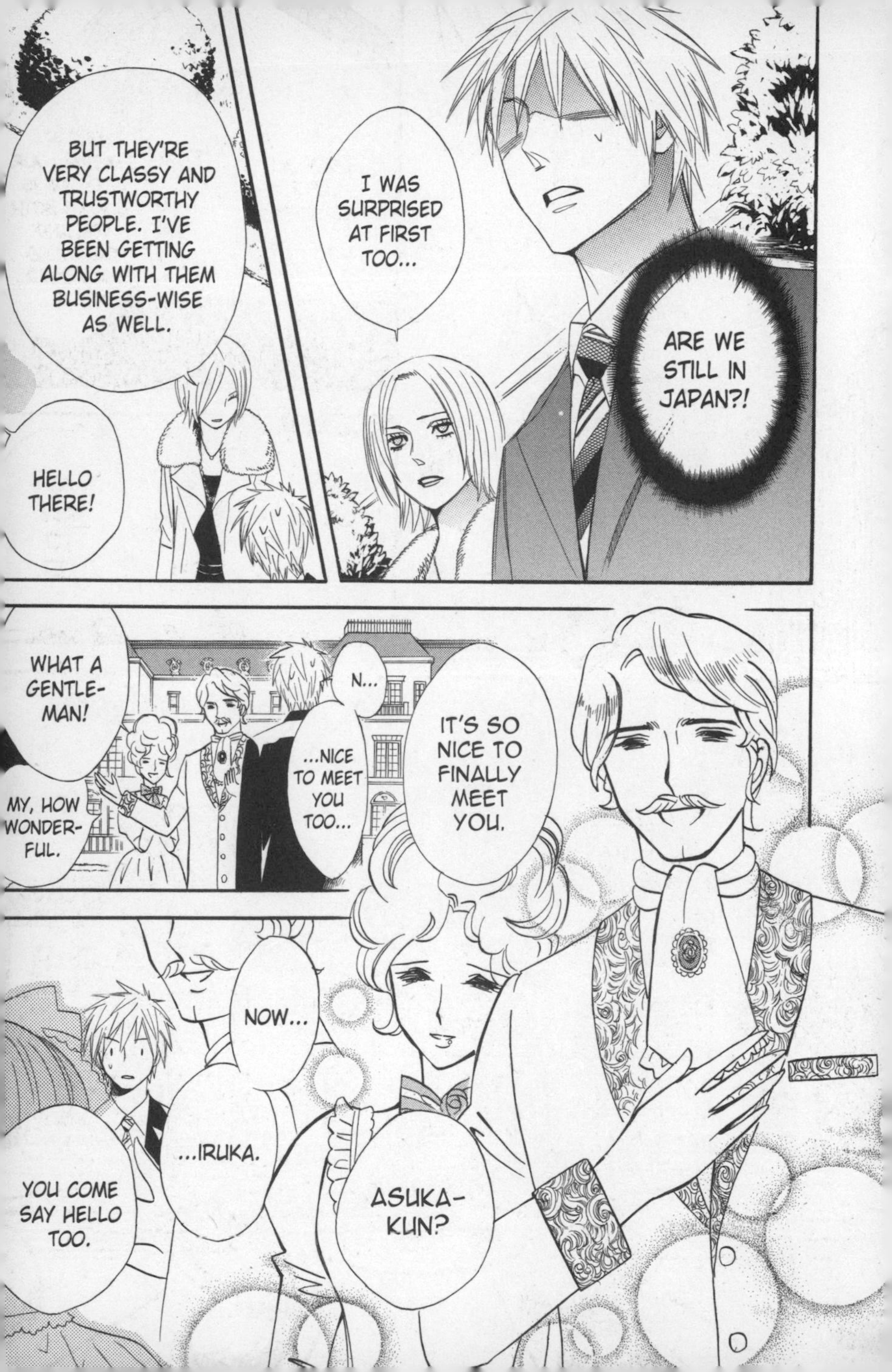
I WAS SURPRISED AT FIRST TOO...
ARE WE STILL IN JAPAN?!
BUT THEY'RE VERY CLASSY AND TRUSTWORTHY PEOPLE. I'VE BEEN GETTING ALONG WITH THEM BUSINESS-WISE AS WELL.
HELLO THERE!
IT'S SO NICE TO FINALLY MEET YOU.
N...
...NICE TO MEET YOU TOO...
WHAT A GENTLE-MAN!
MY, HOW WONDER-FUL.
NOW...
ASUKA-KUN?
...IRUKA.
YOU COME SAY HELLO TOO.

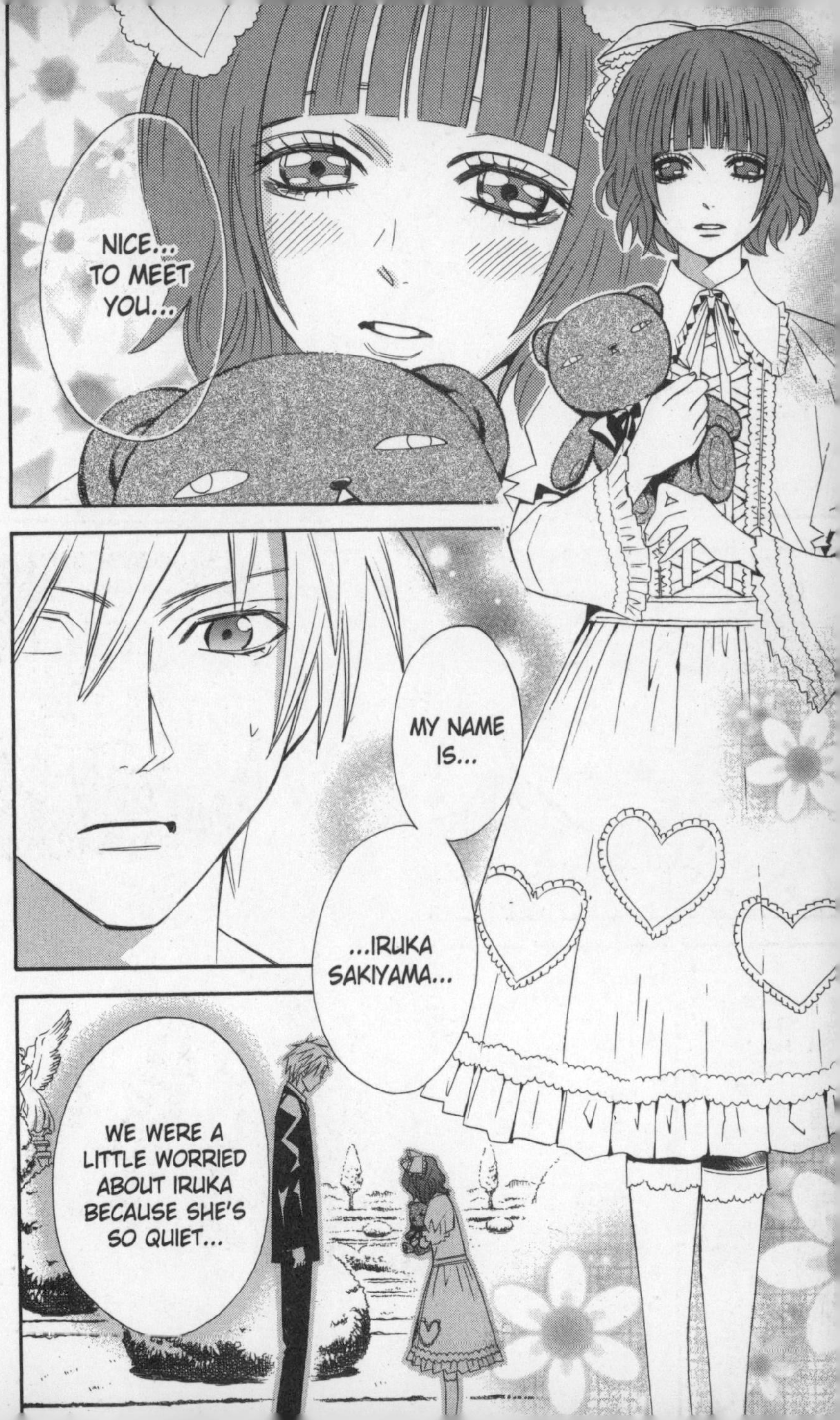
NICE... TO MEET YOU...
MY NAME IS...
...IRUKA SAKIYAMA...
WE WERE A LITTLE WORRIED ABOUT IRUKA BECAUSE SHE'S SO QUIET...

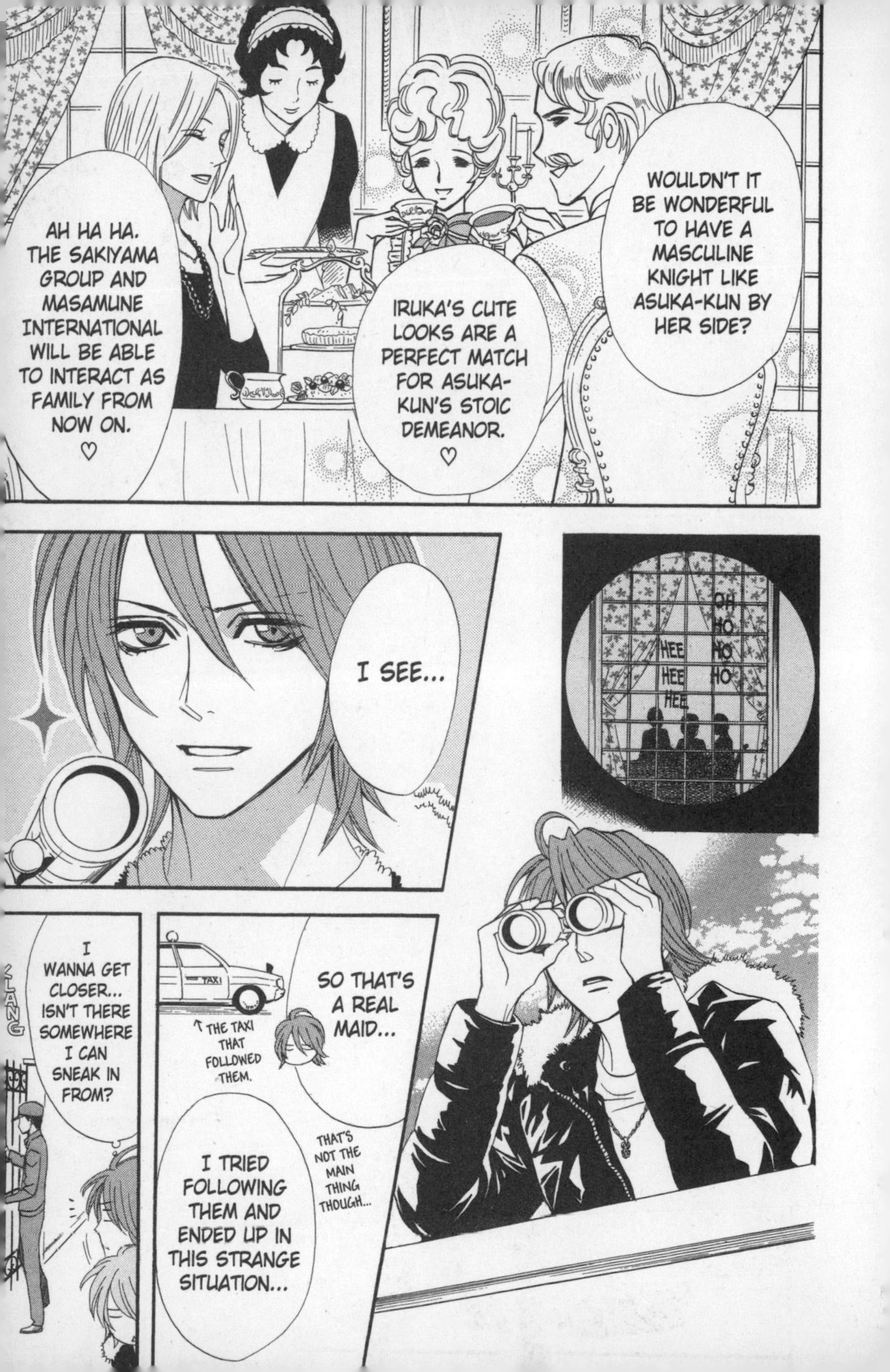
WOULDN'T IT BE WONDERFUL TO HAVE A MASCULINE KNIGHT LIKE ASUKA-KUN BY HER SIDE?
IRUKA'S CUTE LOOKS ARE A PERFECT MATCH FOR ASUKA-KUN'S STOIC DEMEANOR. ♡
AH HA HA. THE SAKIYAMA GROUP AND MASAMUNE INTERNATIONAL WILL BE ABLE TO INTERACT AS FAMILY FROM NOW ON. ♡
OH HO HO HO
HEE HEE HEE
I SEE...
SO THAT'S A REAL MAID...
↑THE TAXI THAT FOLLOWED THEM.
I TRIED FOLLOWING THEM AND ENDED UP IN THIS STRANGE SITUATION...
THAT'S NOT THE MAIN THING THOUGH...
I WANNA GET CLOSER... ISN'T THERE SOMEWHERE I CAN SNEAK IN FROM?
CLANG
TAXI

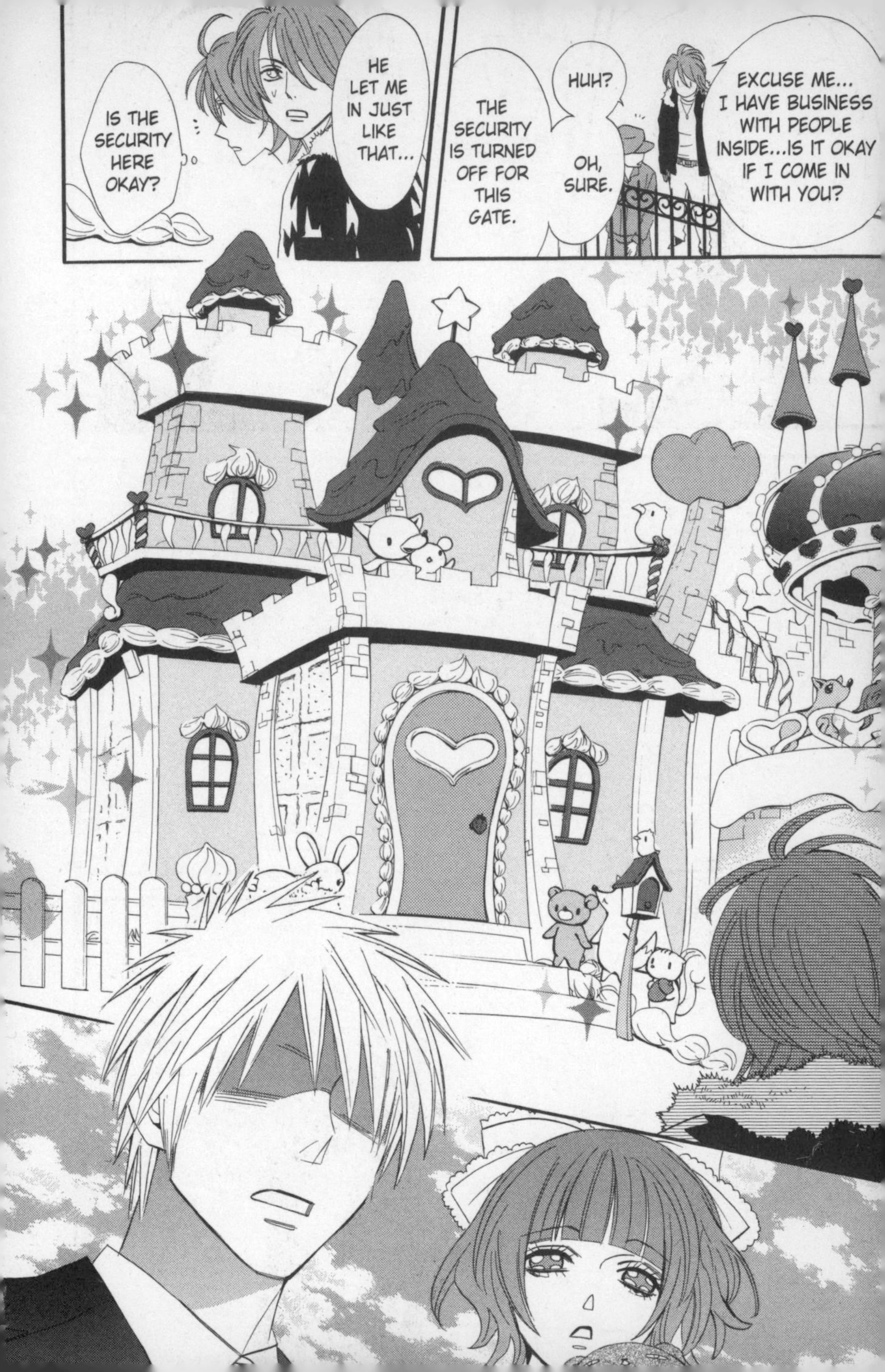
EXCUSE ME... I HAVE BUSINESS WITH PEOPLE INSIDE...IS IT OKAY IF I COME IN WITH YOU?
HUH?
OH, SURE.
THE SECURITY IS TURNED OFF FOR THIS GATE.
HE LET ME IN JUST LIKE THAT...
IS THE SECURITY HERE OKAY?

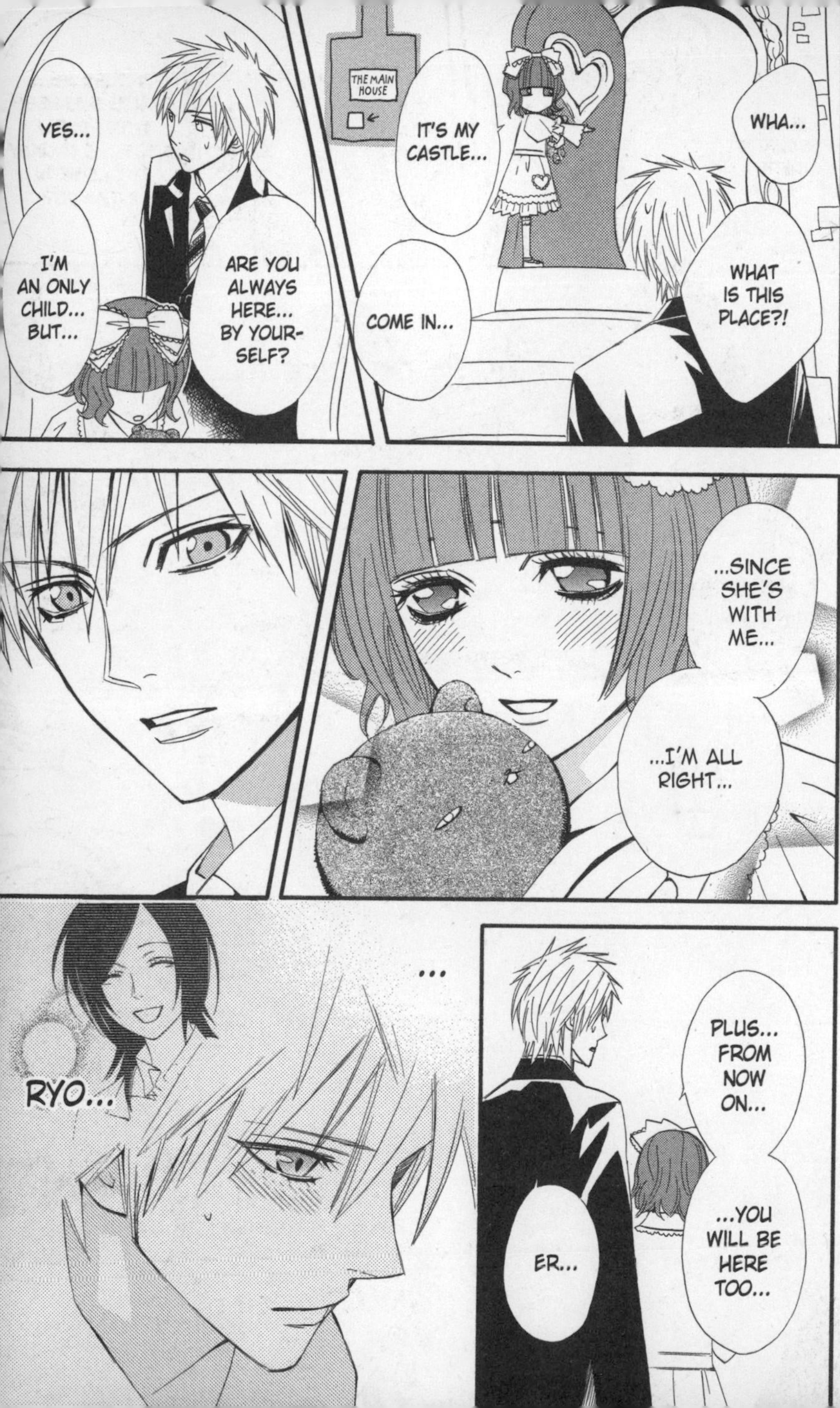
WHA...
WHAT IS THIS PLACE?!
THE MAIN HOUSE
IT'S MY CASTLE...
COME IN...
ARE YOU ALWAYS HERE... BY YOURSELF?
YES...
I'M AN ONLY CHILD... BUT...
...SINCE SHE'S WITH ME...
...I'M ALL RIGHT...
PLUS... FROM NOW ON...
...YOU WILL BE HERE TOO...
ER...
...
RYO...

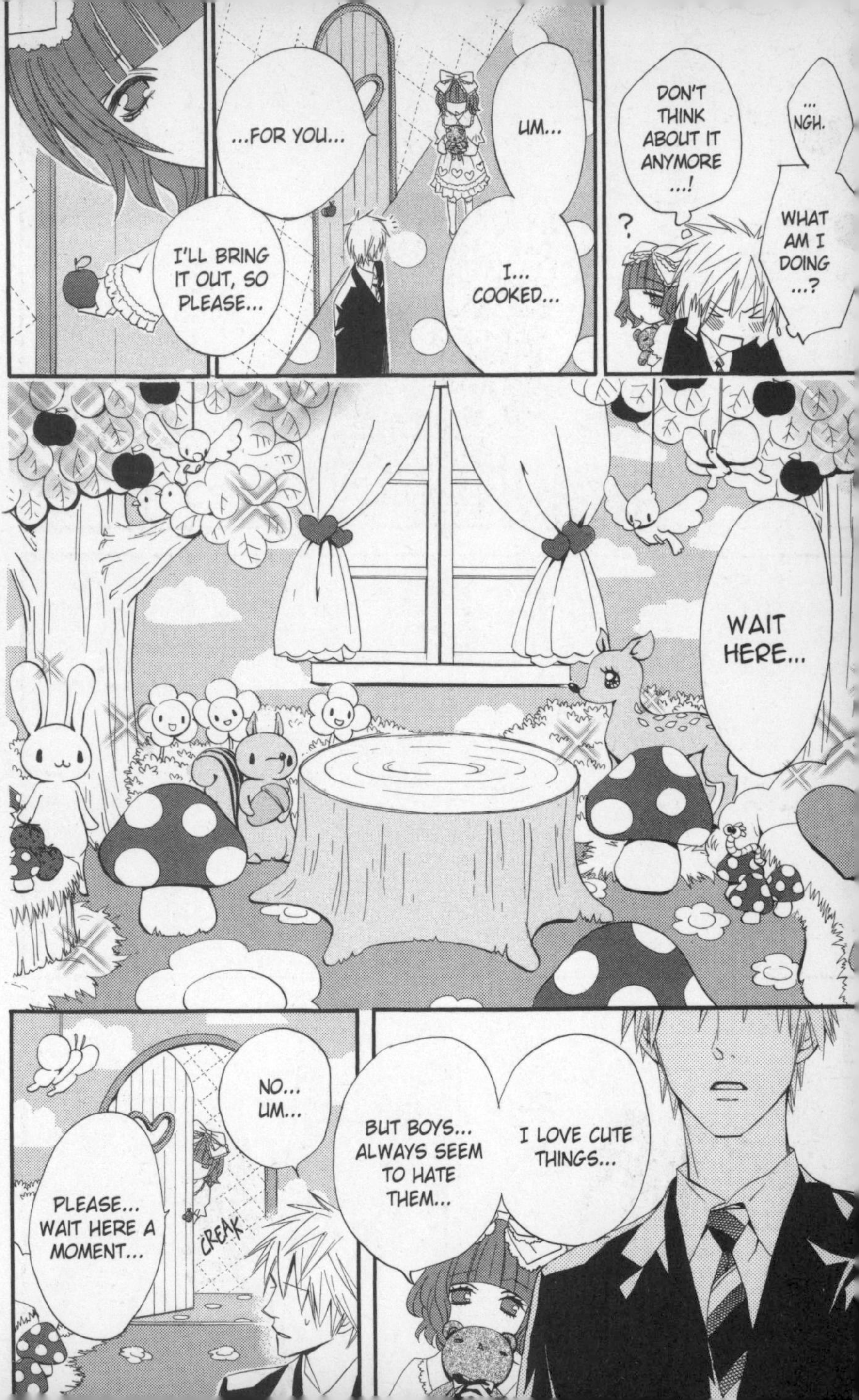
... NGH.
DON'T THINK ABOUT IT ANYMORE ...!
WHAT AM I DOING ...?
?
UM...
I... COOKED...
...FOR YOU...
I'LL BRING IT OUT, SO PLEASE...
WAIT HERE...
I LOVE CUTE THINGS...
BUT BOYS... ALWAYS SEEM TO HATE THEM...
NO... UM...
PLEASE... WAIT HERE A MOMENT...
CREAK

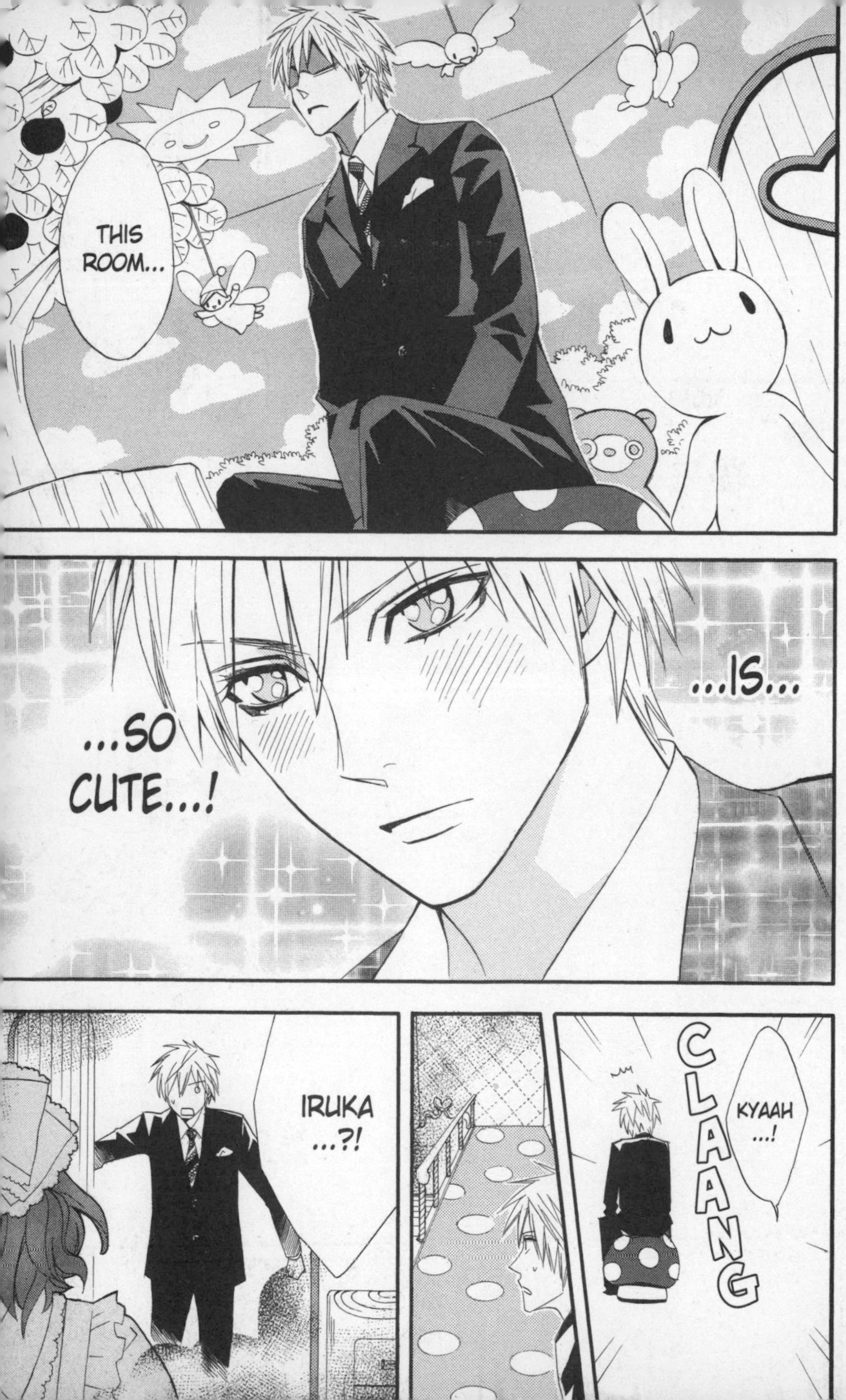
THIS ROOM...
...IS...
...SO CUTE...!
KYAAH ...!
CLAANG
IRUKA ...?!

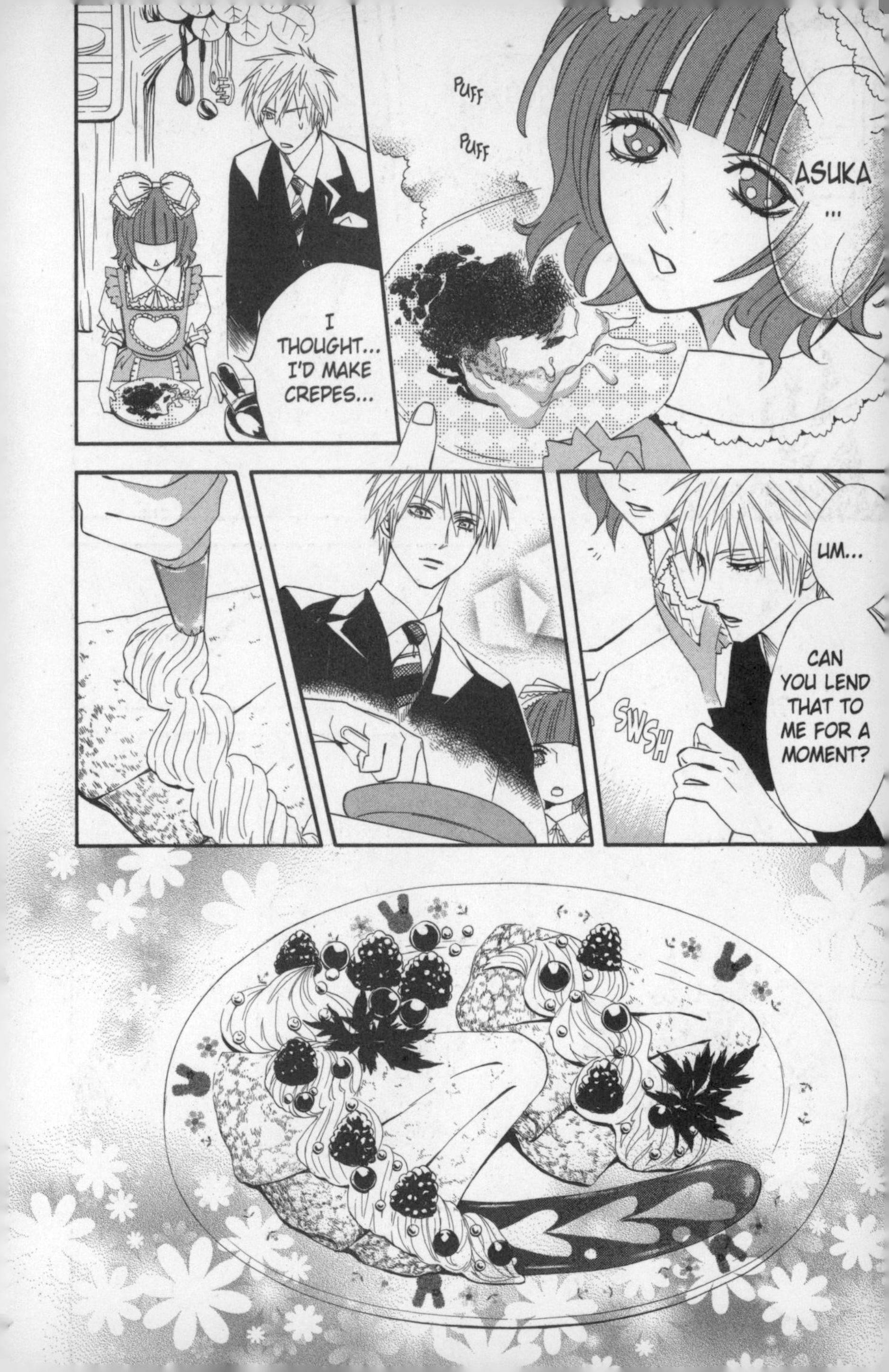
ASUKA ...
PUFF
PUFF
I THOUGHT... I'D MAKE CREPES...
UM...
CAN YOU LEND THAT TO ME FOR A MOMENT?
SWSH

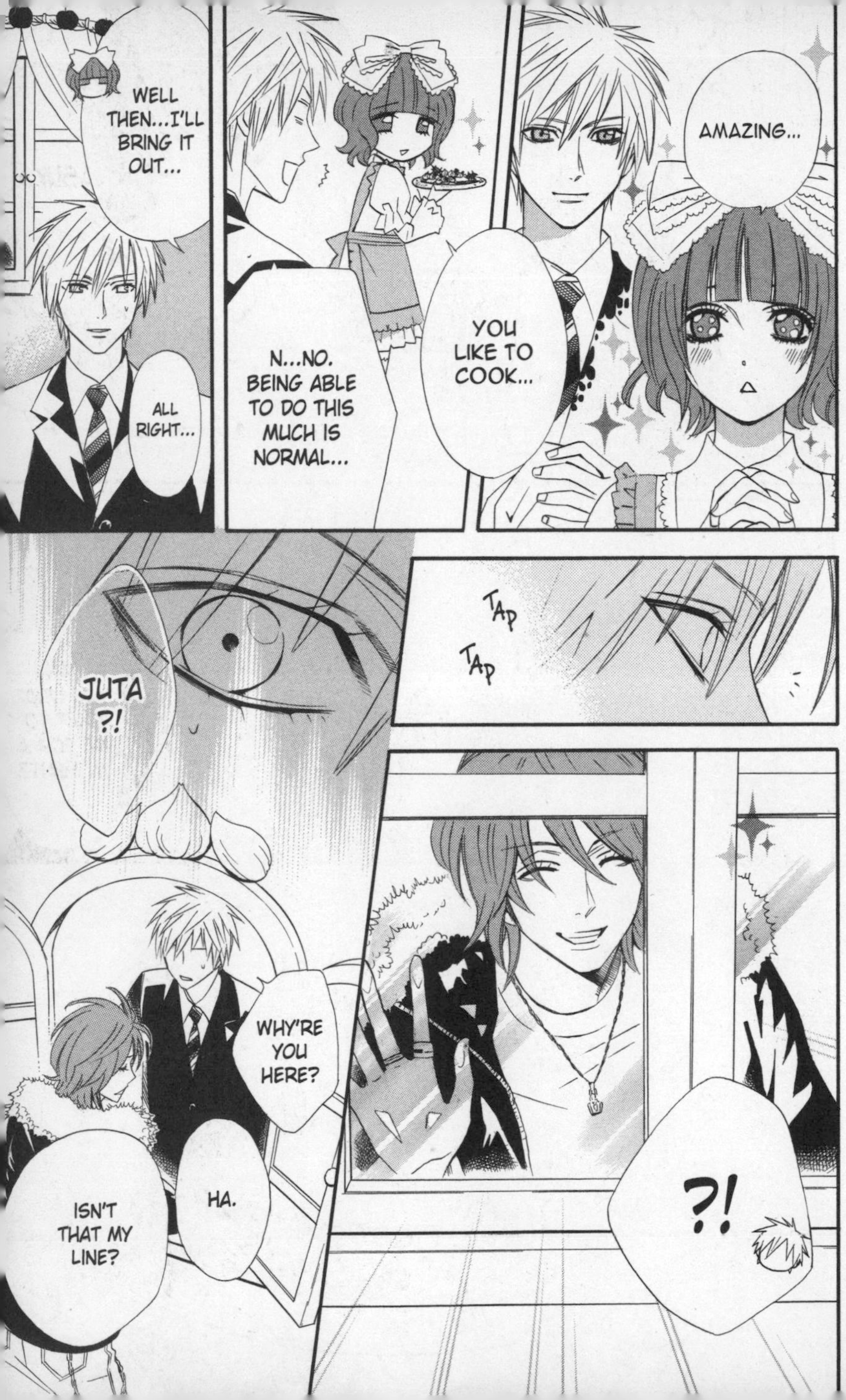
AMAZING...
YOU LIKE TO COOK...
N...NO. BEING ABLE TO DO THIS MUCH IS NORMAL...
WELL THEN...I'LL BRING IT OUT...
ALL RIGHT...
TAP
TAP
?!
JUTA ?!
WHY'RE YOU HERE?
HA.
ISN'T THAT MY LINE?

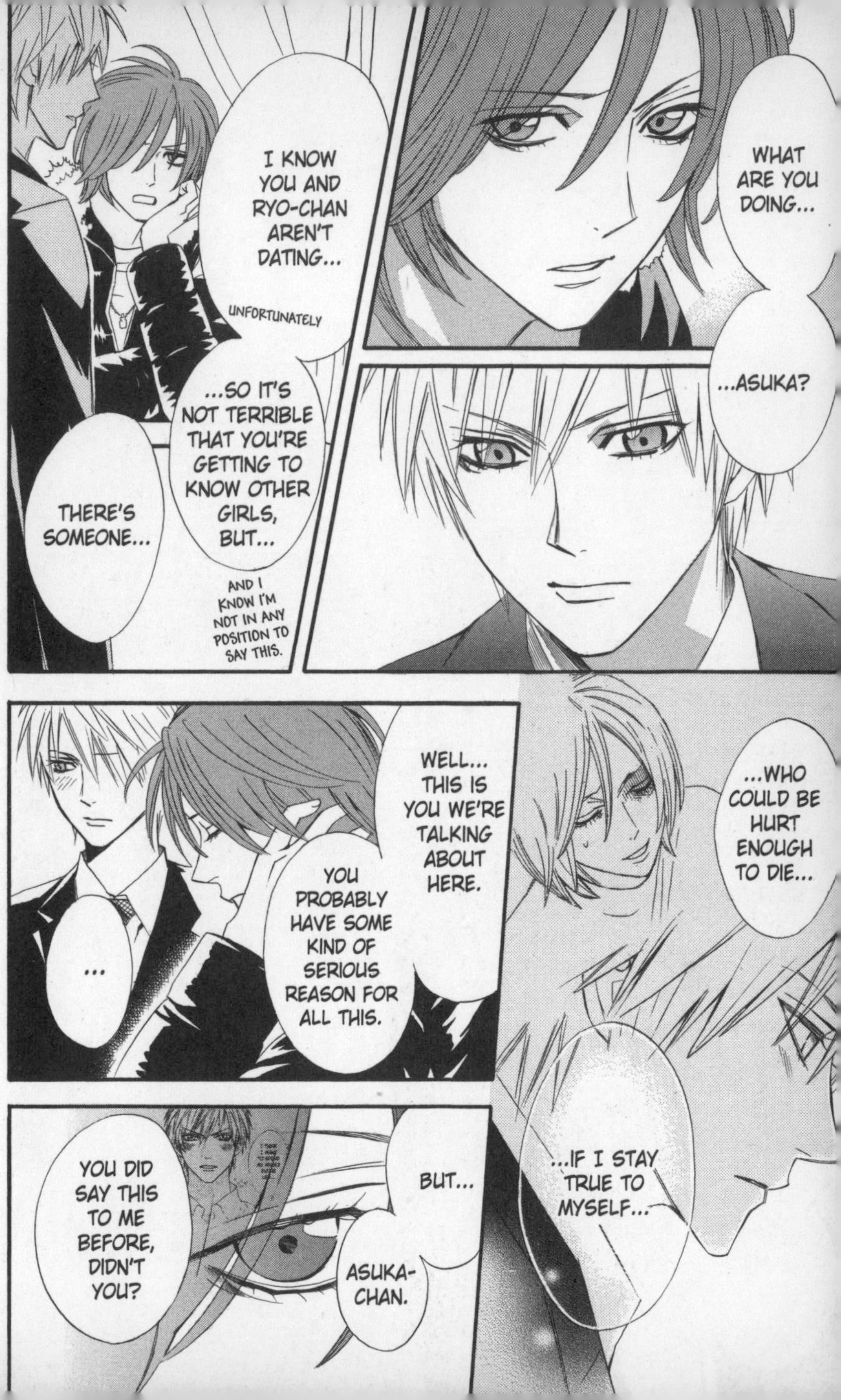
WHAT ARE YOU DOING...
...ASUKA?
I KNOW YOU AND RYO-CHAN AREN'T DATING...
UNFORTUNATELY
...SO IT'S NOT TERRIBLE THAT YOU'RE GETTING TO KNOW OTHER GIRLS, BUT...
AND I KNOW I'M NOT IN ANY POSITION TO SAY THIS.
THERE'S SOMEONE...
...WHO COULD BE HURT ENOUGH TO DIE...
...IF I STAY TRUE TO MYSELF...
WELL... THIS IS YOU WE'RE TALKING ABOUT HERE.
YOU PROBABLY HAVE SOME KIND OF SERIOUS REASON FOR ALL THIS.
...
BUT...
ASUKA-CHAN.
YOU DID SAY THIS TO ME BEFORE, DIDN'T YOU?

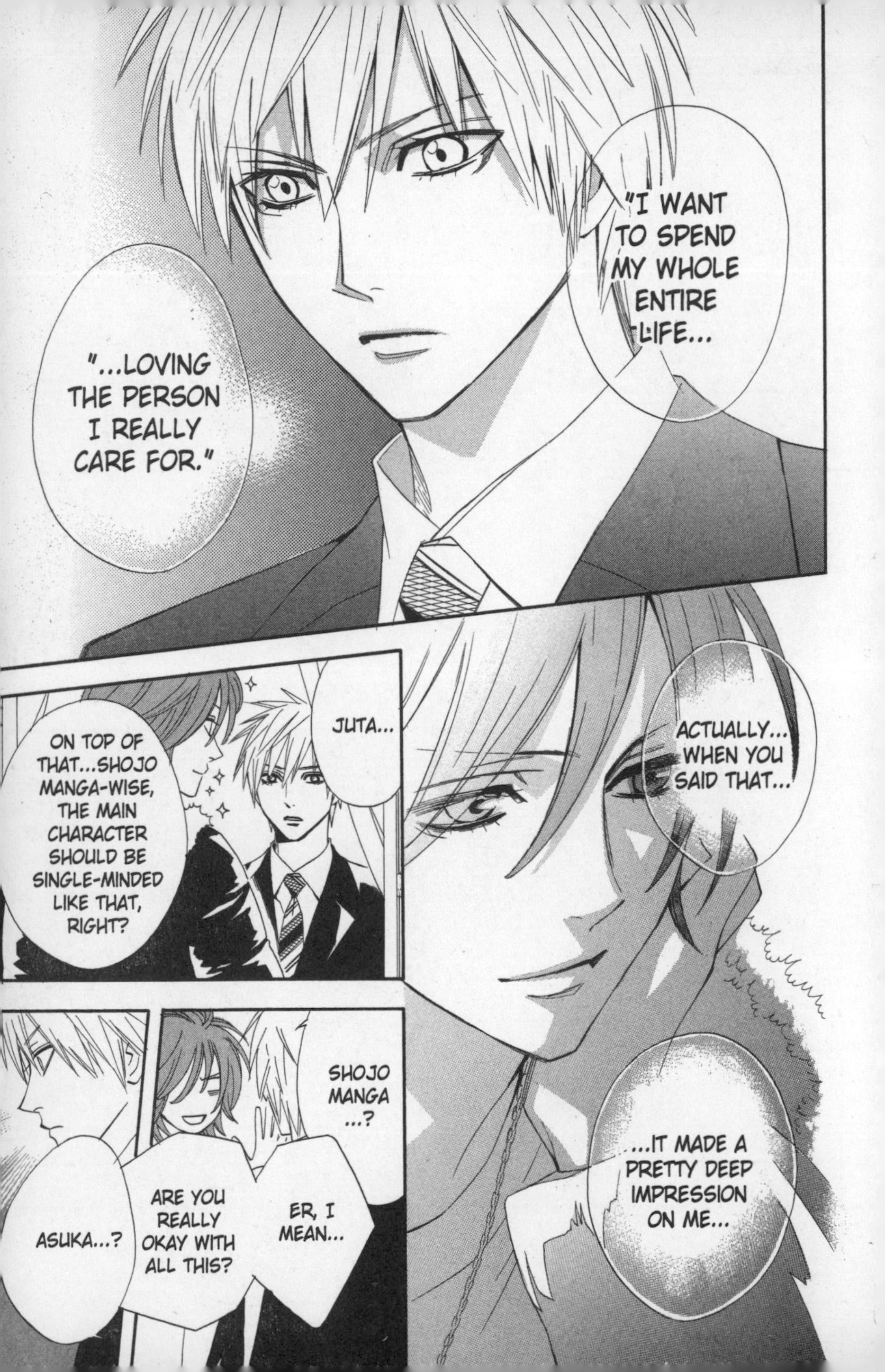
"I WANT TO SPEND MY WHOLE ENTIRE LIFE...
"...LOVING THE PERSON I REALLY CARE FOR."
ACTUALLY... WHEN YOU SAID THAT...
...IT MADE A PRETTY DEEP IMPRESSION ON ME...
JUTA...
ON TOP OF THAT...SHOJO MANGA-WISE, THE MAIN CHARACTER SHOULD BE SINGLE-MINDED LIKE THAT, RIGHT?
SHOJO MANGA ...?
ER, I MEAN...
ARE YOU REALLY OKAY WITH ALL THIS?
ASUKA...?

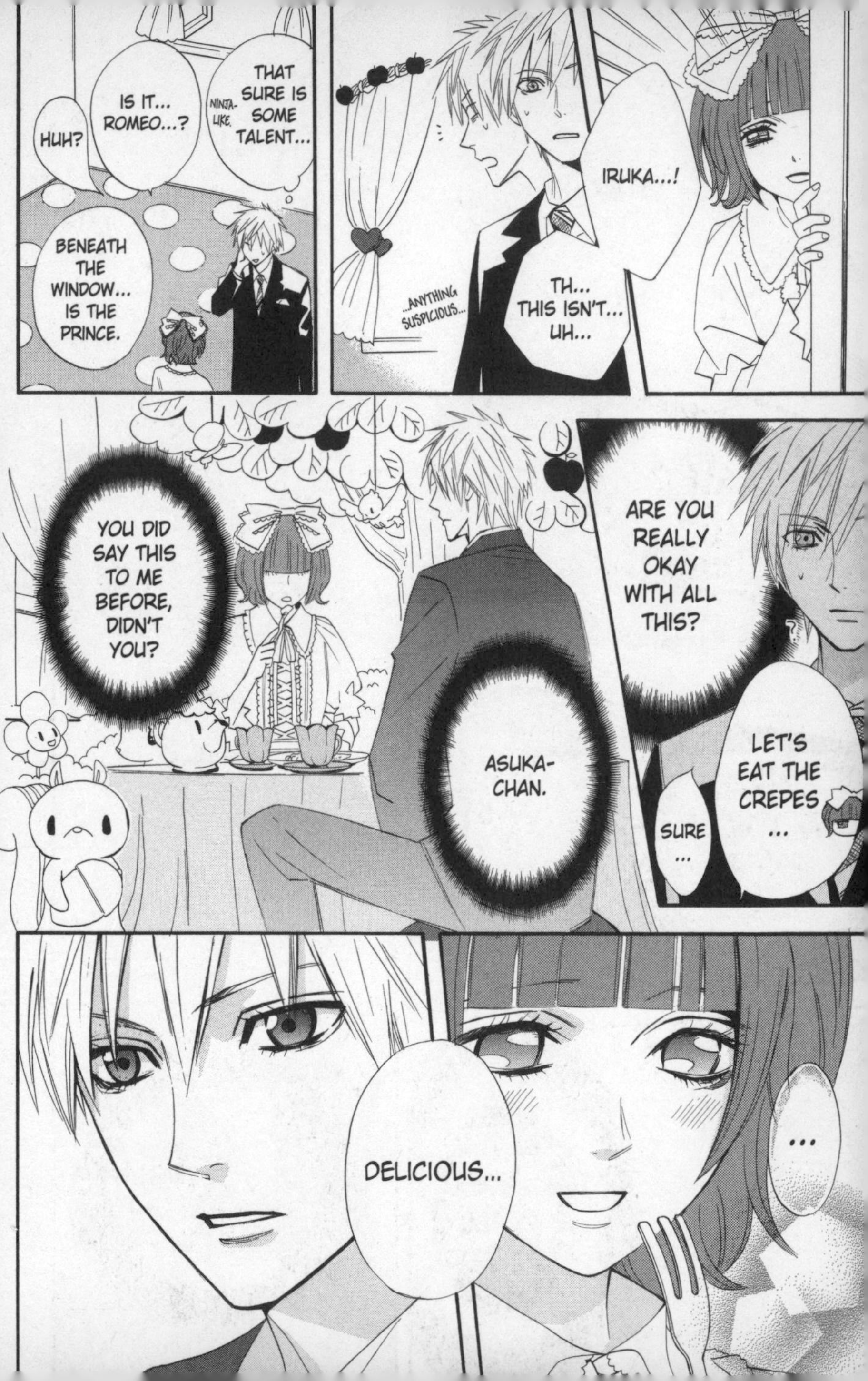
IRUKA...!
TH... THIS ISN'T... UH...
...ANYTHING SUSPICIOUS...
THAT SURE IS SOME TALENT...
NINJA-LIKE.
IS IT... ROMEO...?
HUH?
BENEATH THE WINDOW... IS THE PRINCE.
ARE YOU REALLY OKAY WITH ALL THIS?
LET'S EAT THE CREPES ...
SURE ...
YOU DID SAY THIS TO ME BEFORE, DIDN'T YOU?
ASUKA-CHAN.
...
DELICIOUS...

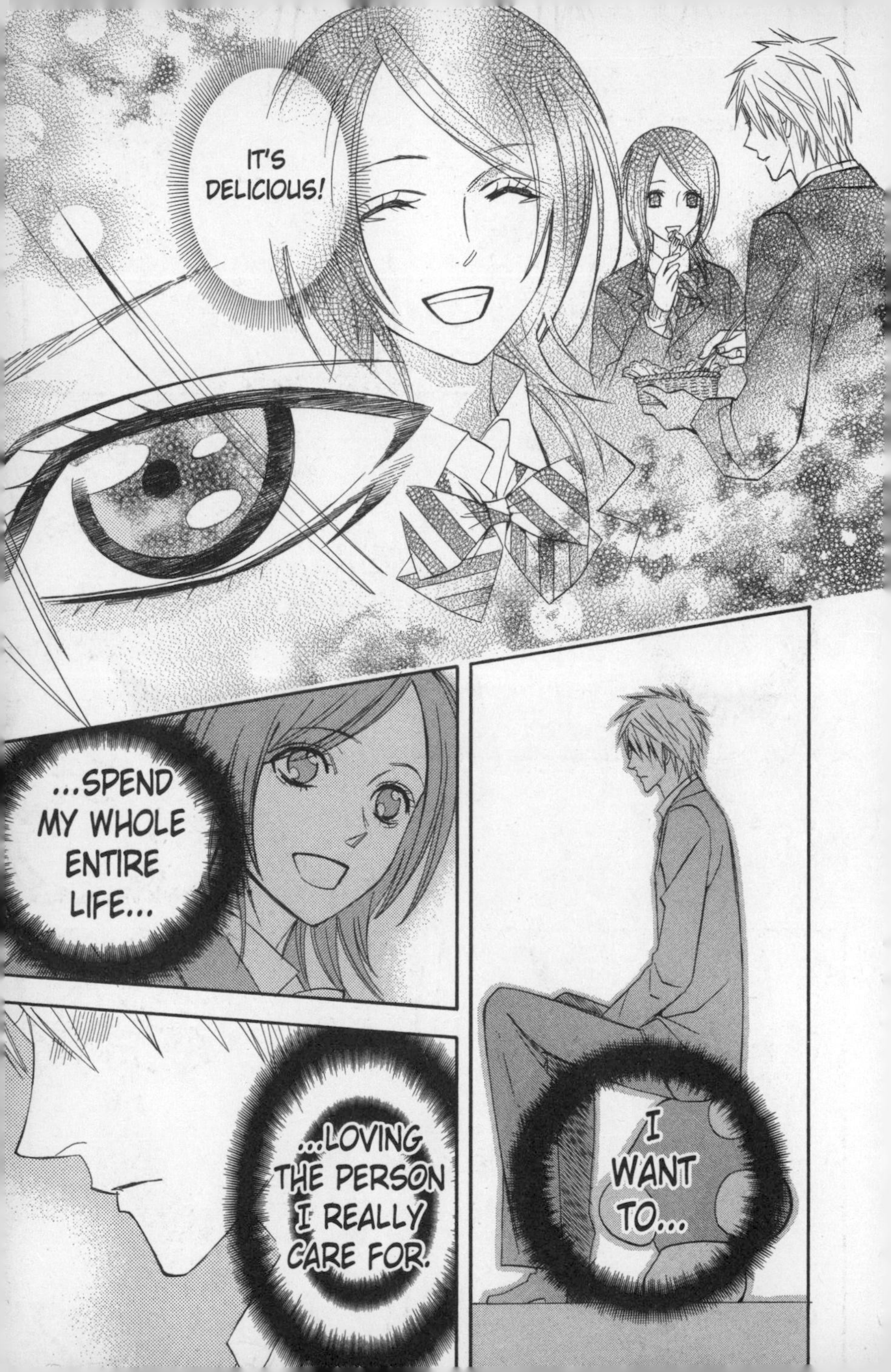
IT'S DELICIOUS!
I WANT TO...
...SPEND MY WHOLE ENTIRE LIFE...
...LOVING THE PERSON I REALLY CARE FOR.

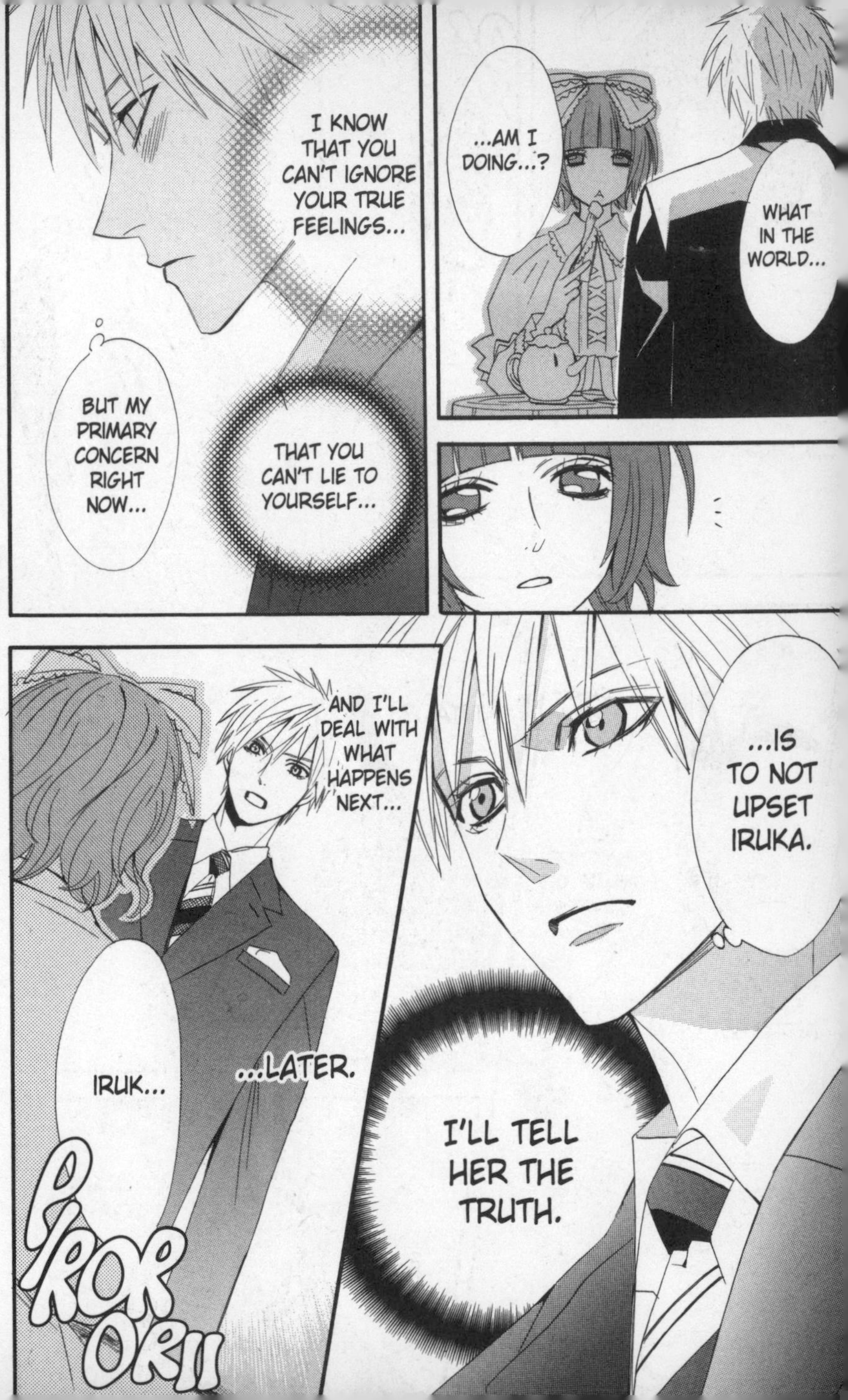
WHAT IN THE WORLD...
...AM I DOING...?
I KNOW THAT YOU CAN'T IGNORE YOUR TRUE FEELINGS...
THAT YOU CAN'T LIE TO YOURSELF...
BUT MY PRIMARY CONCERN RIGHT NOW...
...IS TO NOT UPSET IRUKA.
I'LL TELL HER THE TRUTH.
AND I'LL DEAL WITH WHAT HAPPENS NEXT...
...LATER.
IRUK...
PIROR
ORII

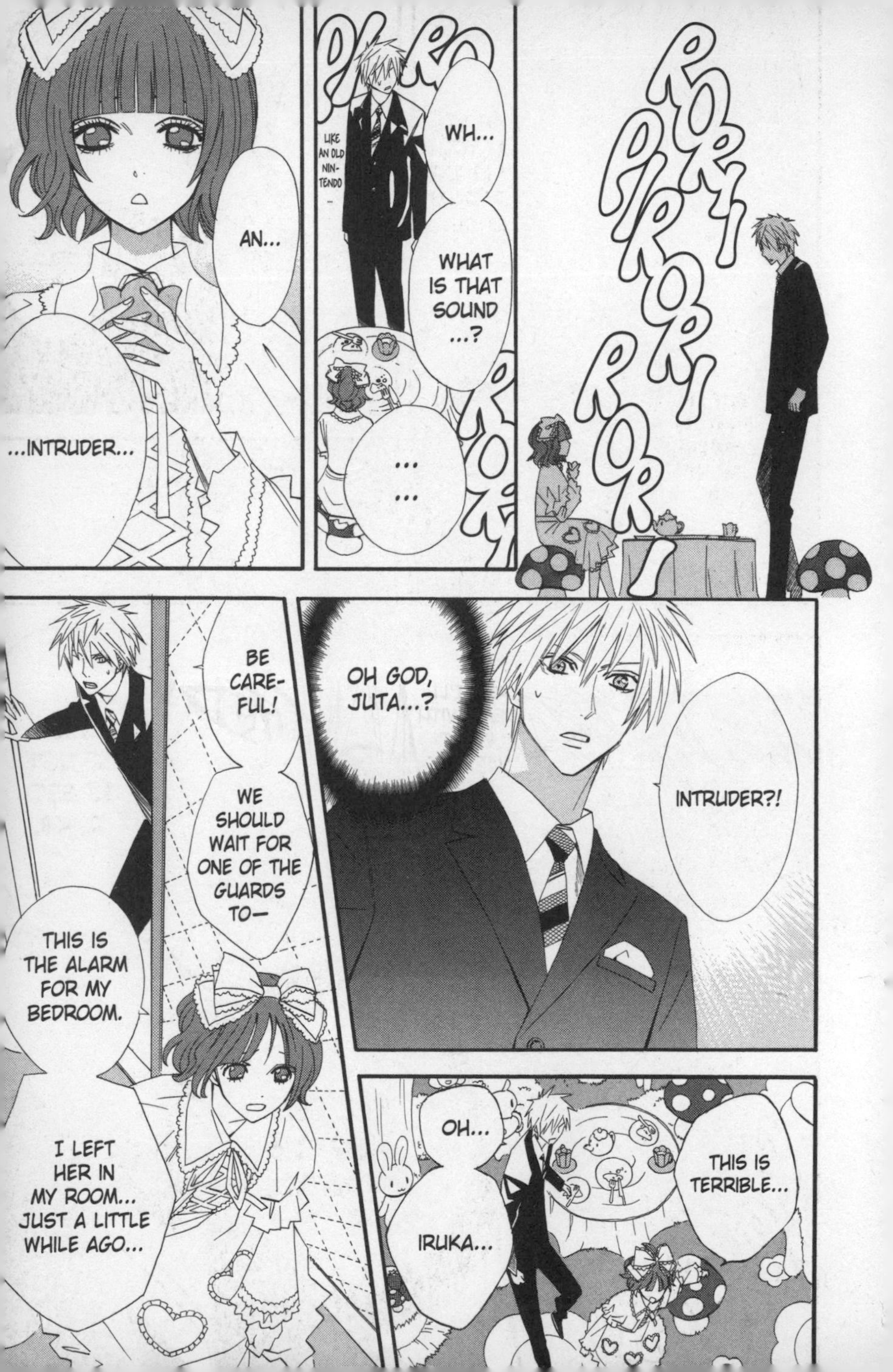
PIRIRORI
WH...
WHAT IS THAT SOUND ...?
LIKE AN OLD NIN-TENDO ...
... ...
AN...
...INTRUDER...
INTRUDER?!
OH GOD, JUTA...?
THIS IS TERRIBLE...
OH...
IRUKA...
BE CARE-FUL!
WE SHOULD WAIT FOR ONE OF THE GUARDS TO—
THIS IS THE ALARM FOR MY BEDROOM.
I LEFT HER IN MY ROOM... JUST A LITTLE WHILE AGO...

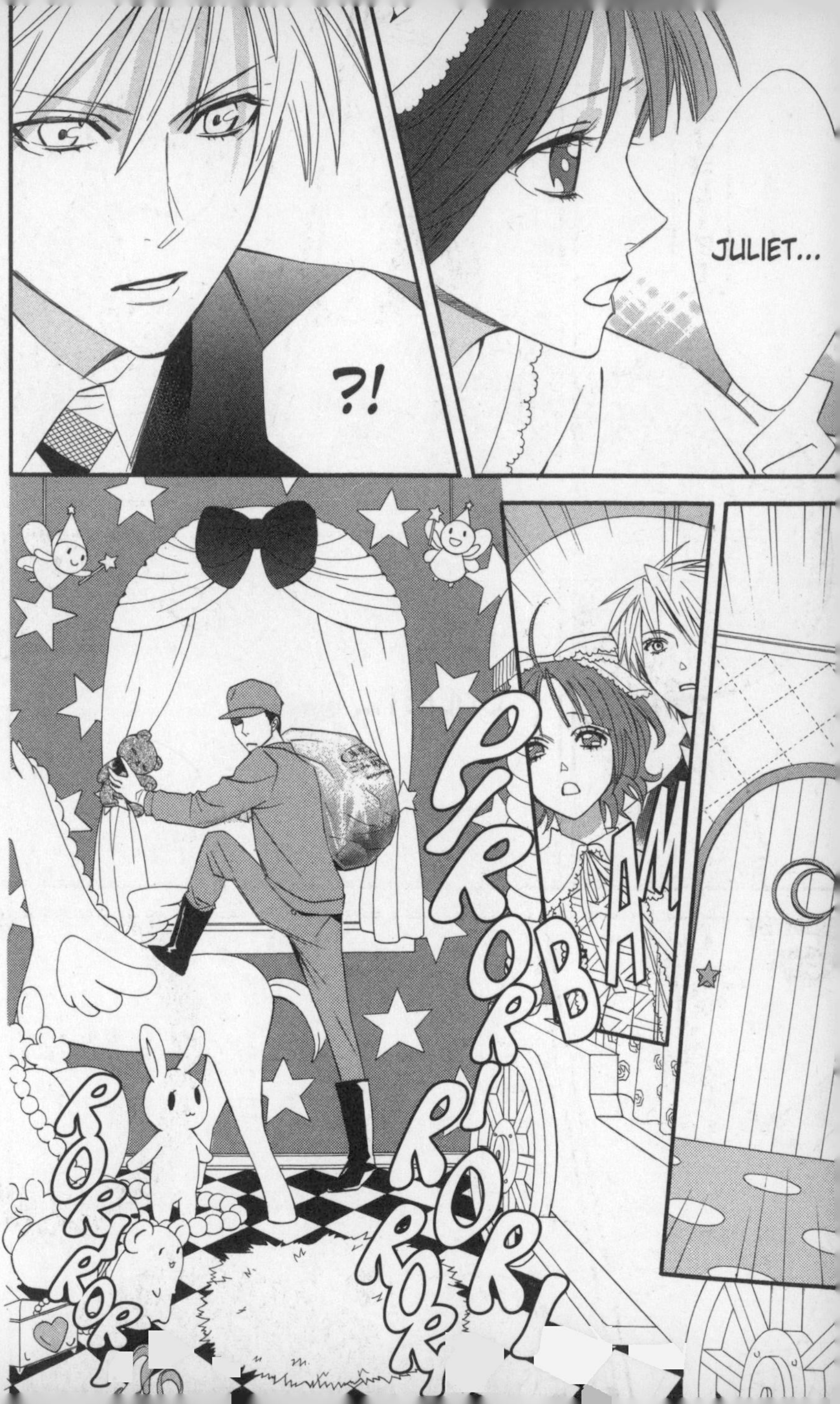
JULIET...
?!
BAM
PIRORI
RORI
RORORI
RORIROR

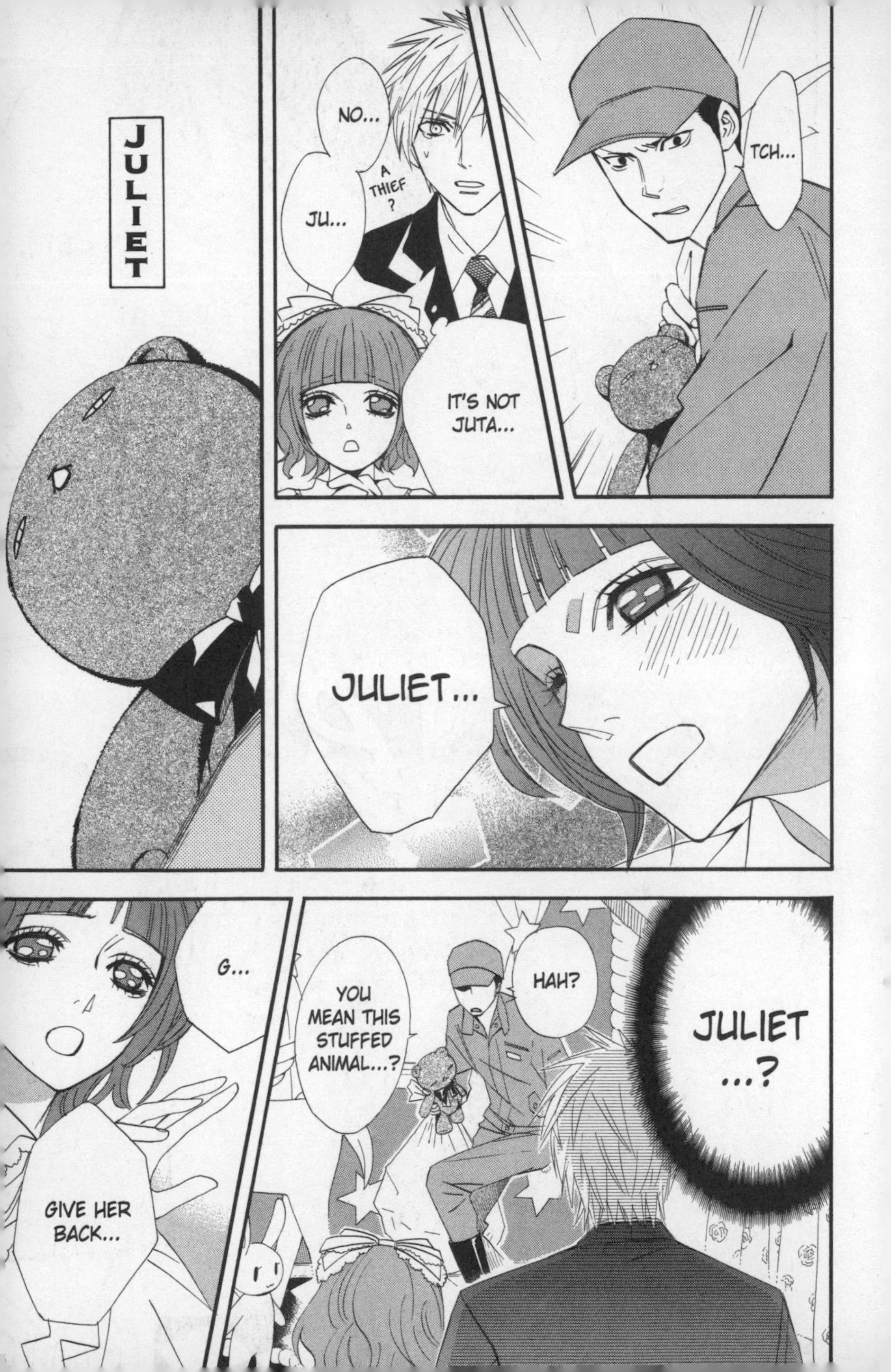
TCH...
NO...
A THIEF ?
JU...
IT'S NOT JUTA...
JULIET...
JULIET
JULIET ...?
HAH?
YOU MEAN THIS STUFFED ANIMAL...?
G...
GIVE HER BACK...

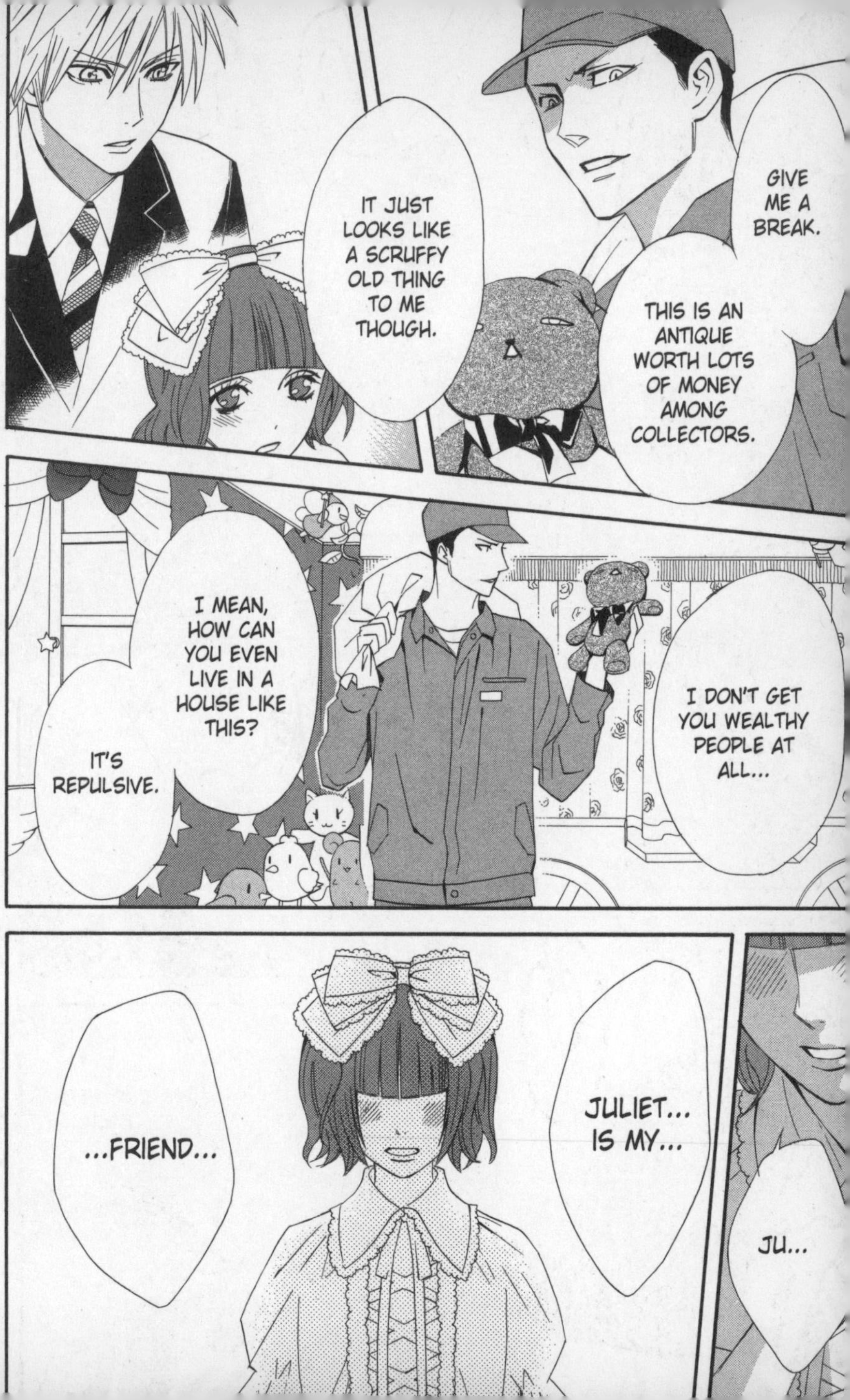
GIVE ME A BREAK.
THIS IS AN ANTIQUE WORTH LOTS OF MONEY AMONG COLLECTORS.
IT JUST LOOKS LIKE A SCRUFFY OLD THING TO ME THOUGH.
I DON'T GET YOU WEALTHY PEOPLE AT ALL...
I MEAN, HOW CAN YOU EVEN LIVE IN A HOUSE LIKE THIS?
IT'S REPULSIVE.
JU...
JULIET... IS MY...
...FRIEND...

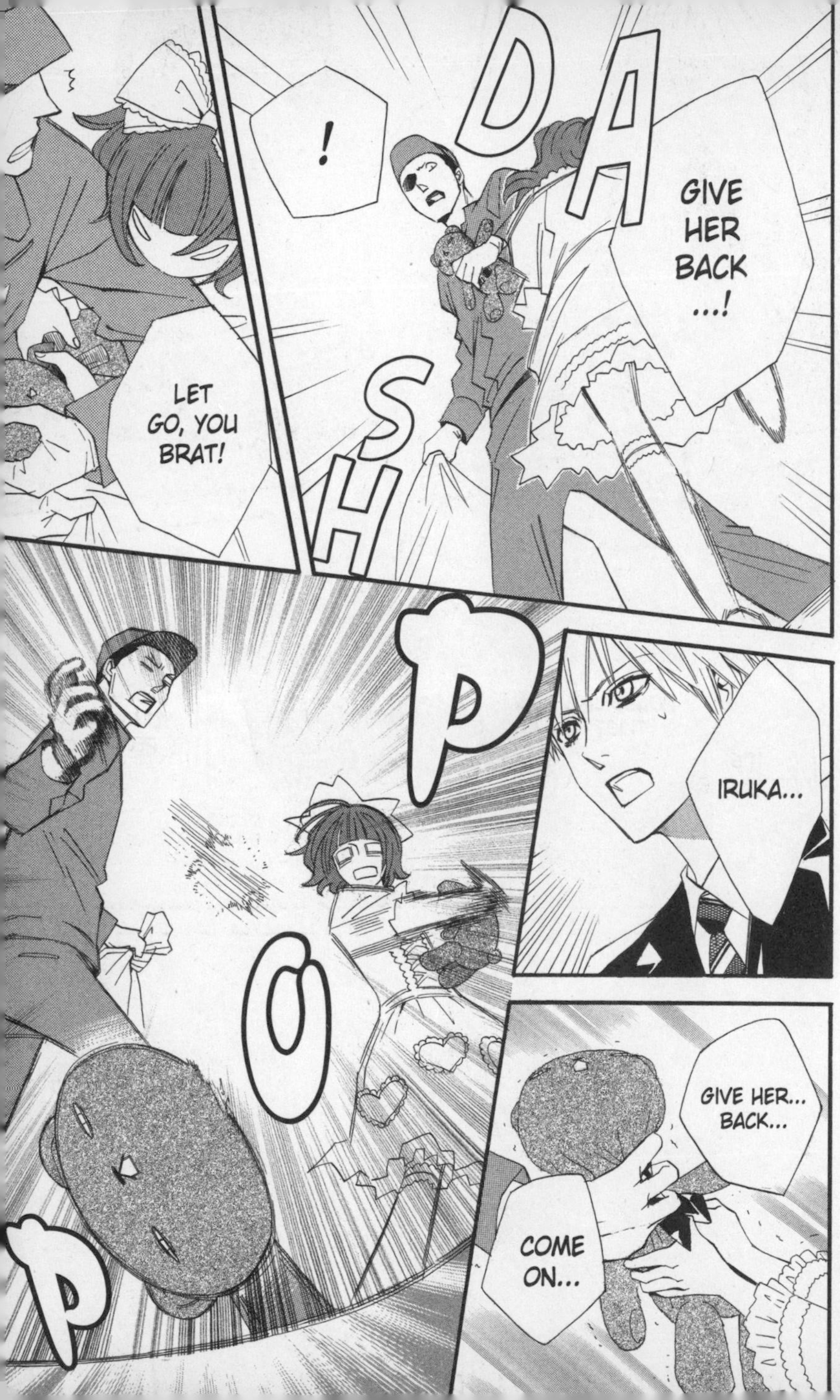
DA
GIVE HER BACK ...!
!
SH
LET GO, YOU BRAT!
IRUKA...
GIVE HER... BACK...
COME ON...
P
O
P

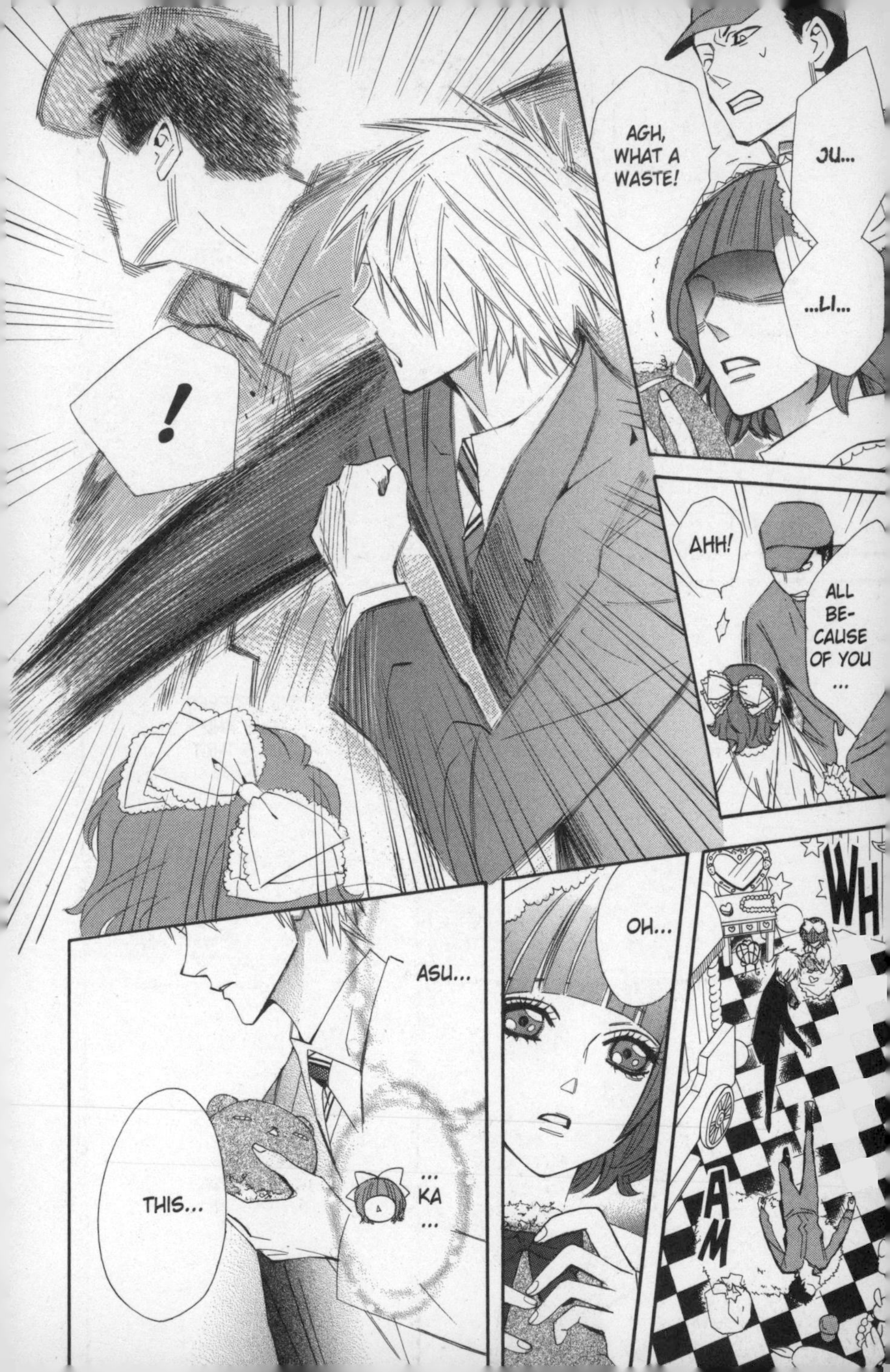

JU...
AGH, WHAT A WASTE!
...LI...
ALL BE-CAUSE OF YOU ...
AHH!
!
WHAM
OH...
ASU...
...KA...
THIS...

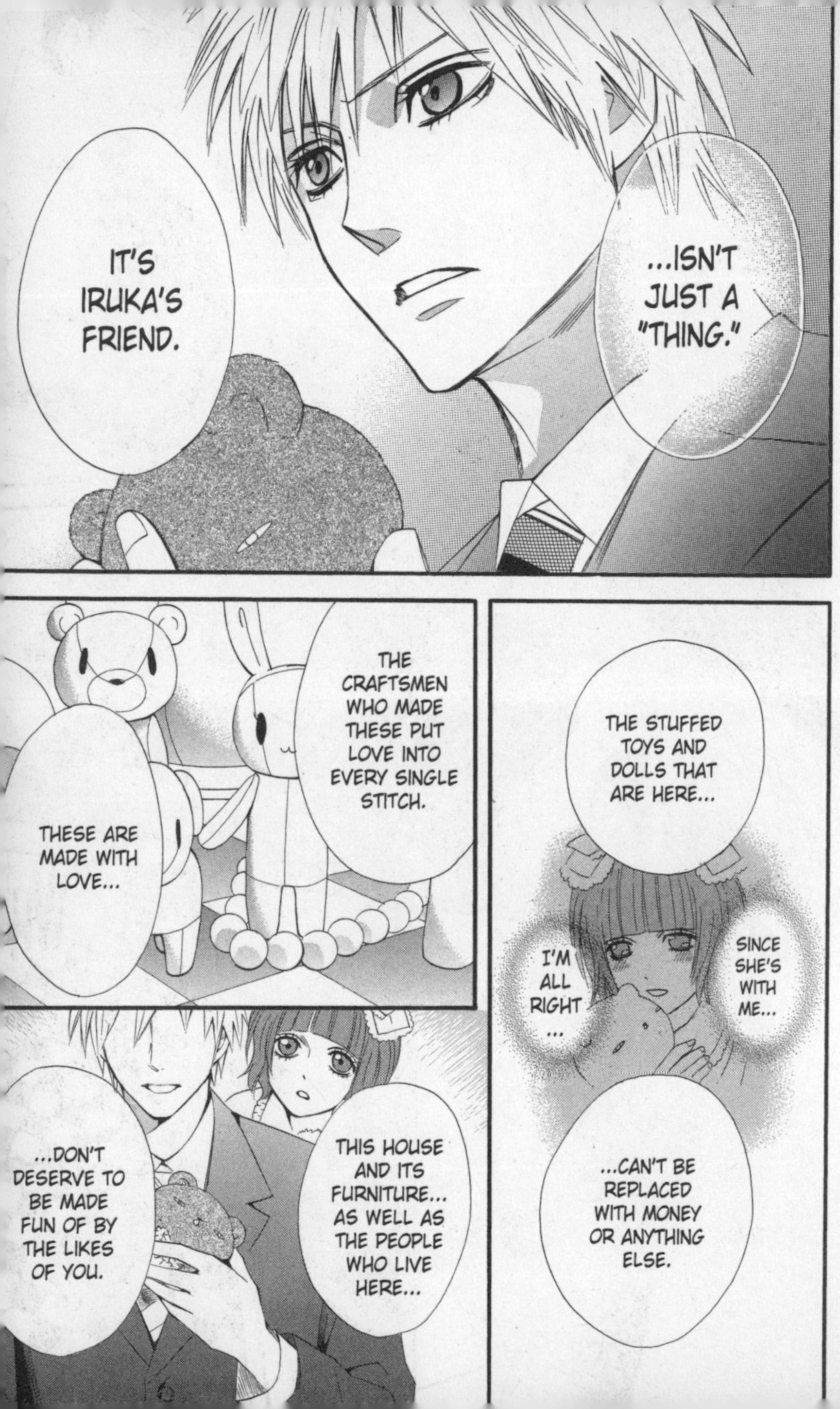

...ISN'T JUST A "THING."
IT'S IRUKA'S FRIEND.
THE STUFFED TOYS AND DOLLS THAT ARE HERE...
SINCE SHE'S WITH ME...
I'M ALL RIGHT...
...CAN'T BE REPLACED WITH MONEY OR ANYTHING ELSE.
THE CRAFTSMEN WHO MADE THESE PUT LOVE INTO EVERY SINGLE STITCH.
THESE ARE MADE WITH LOVE...
THIS HOUSE AND ITS FURNITURE... AS WELL AS THE PEOPLE WHO LIVE HERE...
...DON'T DESERVE TO BE MADE FUN OF BY THE LIKES OF YOU.

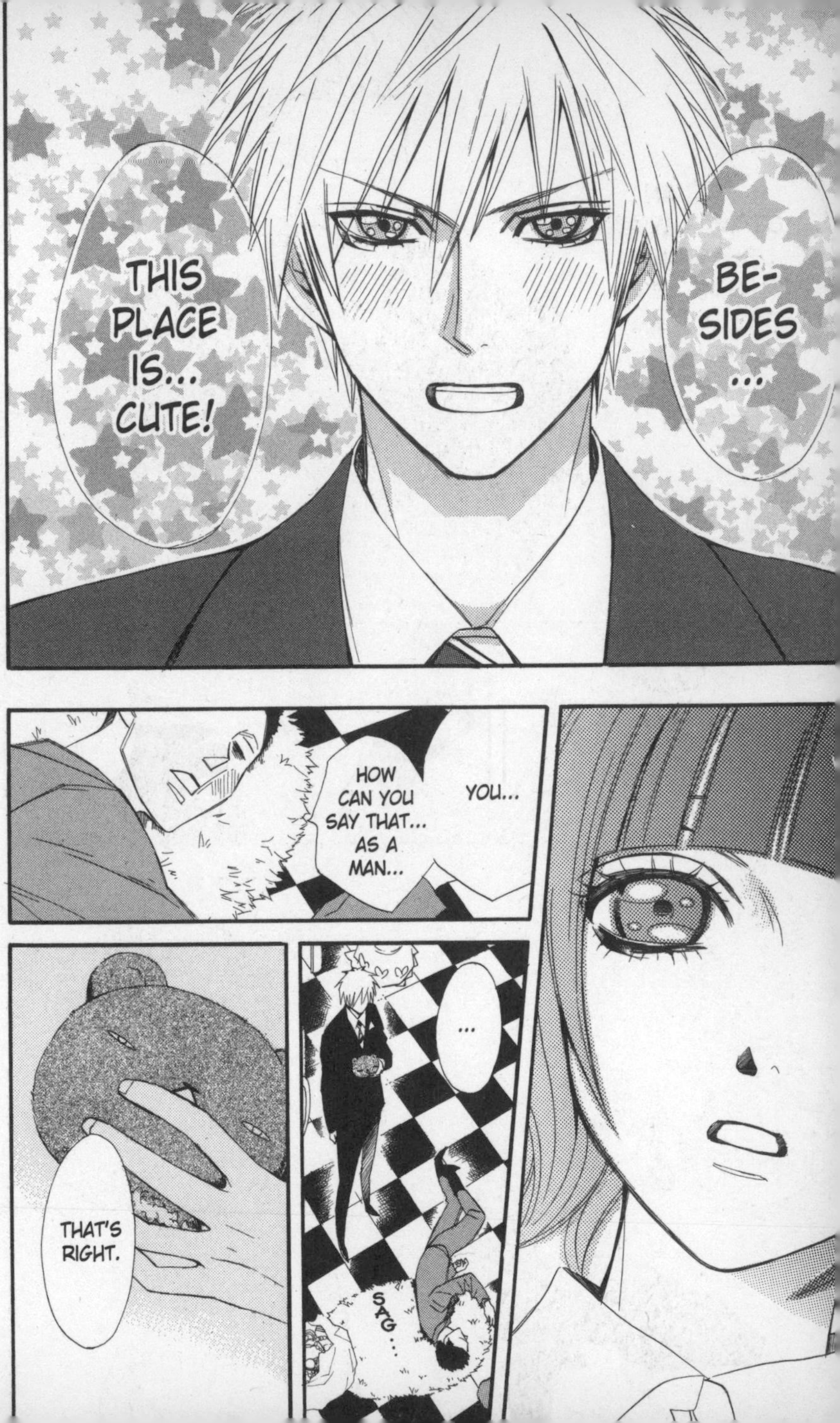
THIS PLACE IS... CUTE!
BE-SIDES...
YOU...
HOW CAN YOU SAY THAT... AS A MAN...
...
SAG...
THAT'S RIGHT.

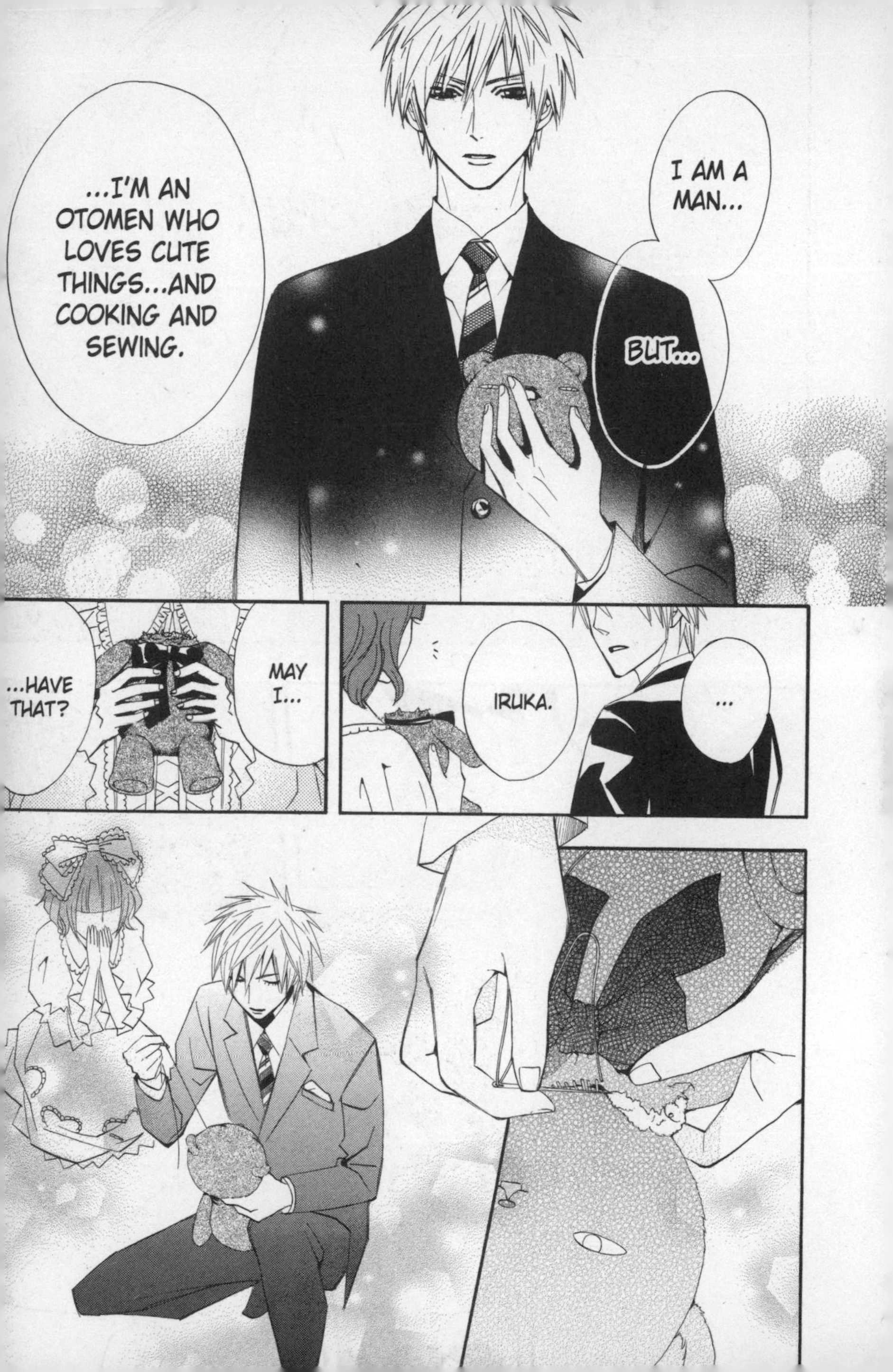
I AM A MAN...
BUT...
...I'M AN OTOMEN WHO LOVES CUTE THINGS...AND COOKING AND SEWING.
...
IRUKA.
MAY I...
...HAVE THAT?

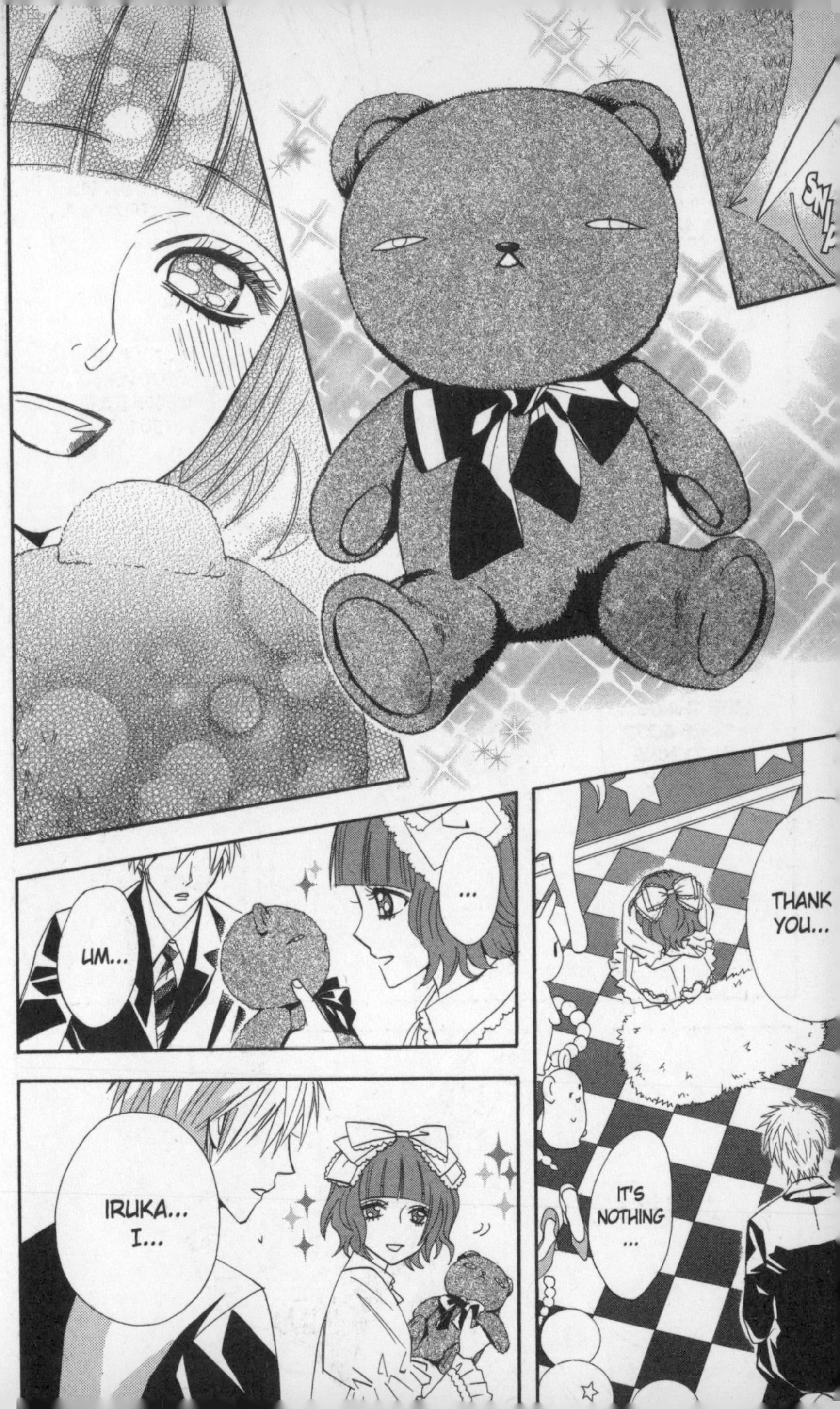
SNIP
THANK YOU...
IT'S NOTHING...
...
UM...
IRUKA... I...

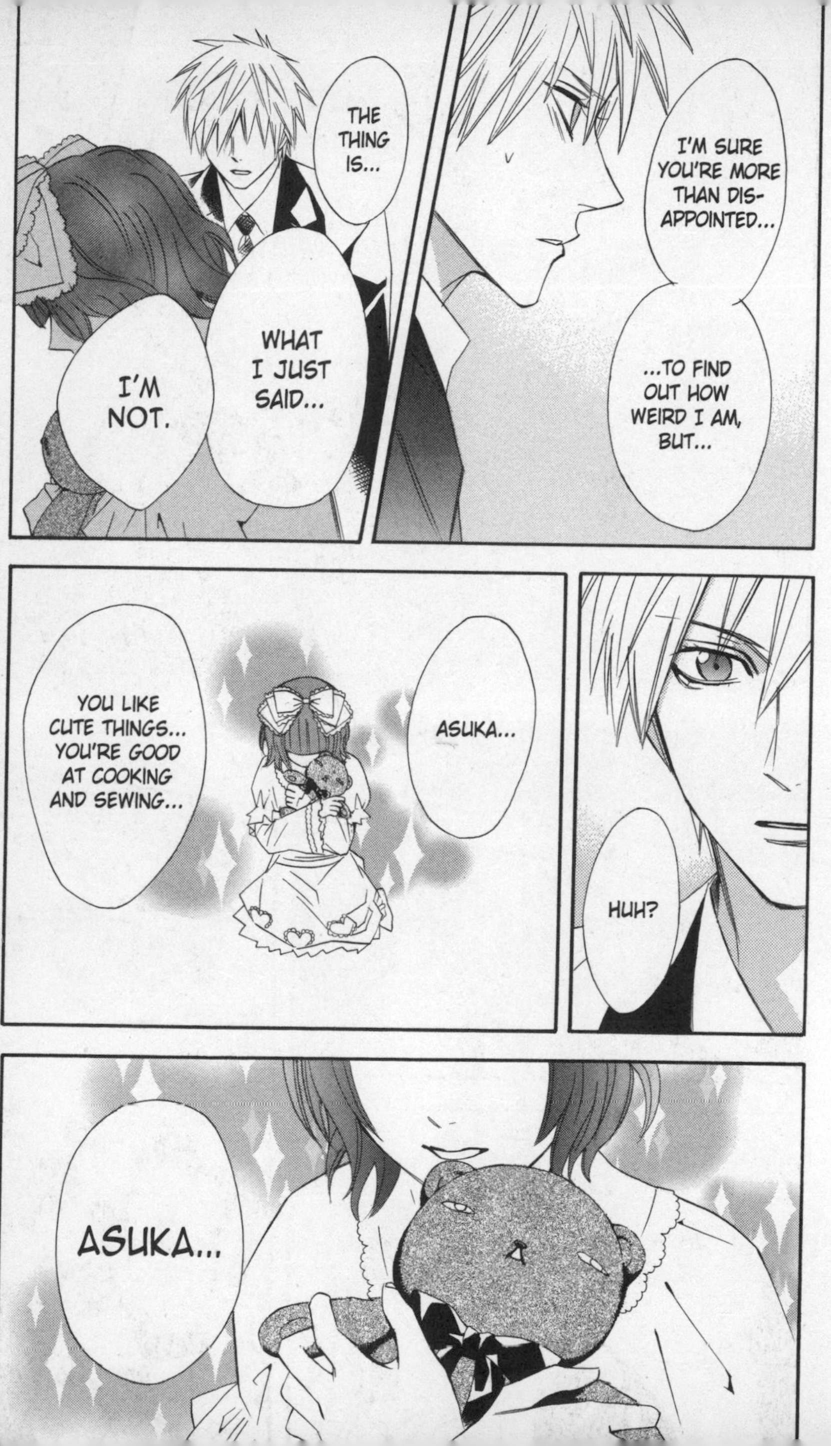
I'M SURE YOU'RE MORE THAN DIS-APPOINTED...
...TO FIND OUT HOW WEIRD I AM, BUT...
THE THING IS...
WHAT I JUST SAID...
I'M NOT.
HUH?
ASUKA...
YOU LIKE CUTE THINGS... YOU'RE GOOD AT COOKING AND SEWING...
ASUKA...

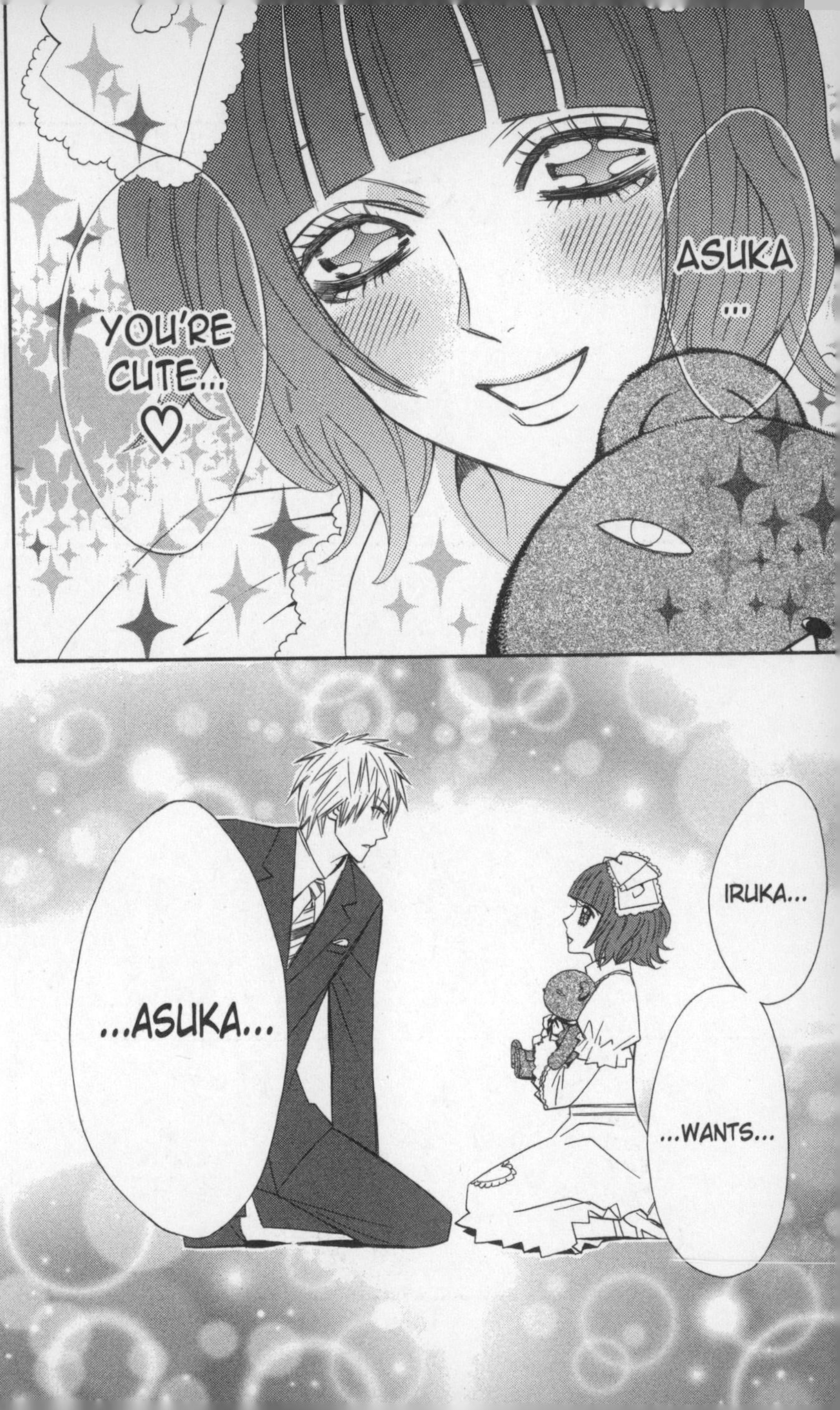
ASUKA ...
YOU'RE CUTE... ♡
IRUKA...
...WANTS...
...ASUKA...

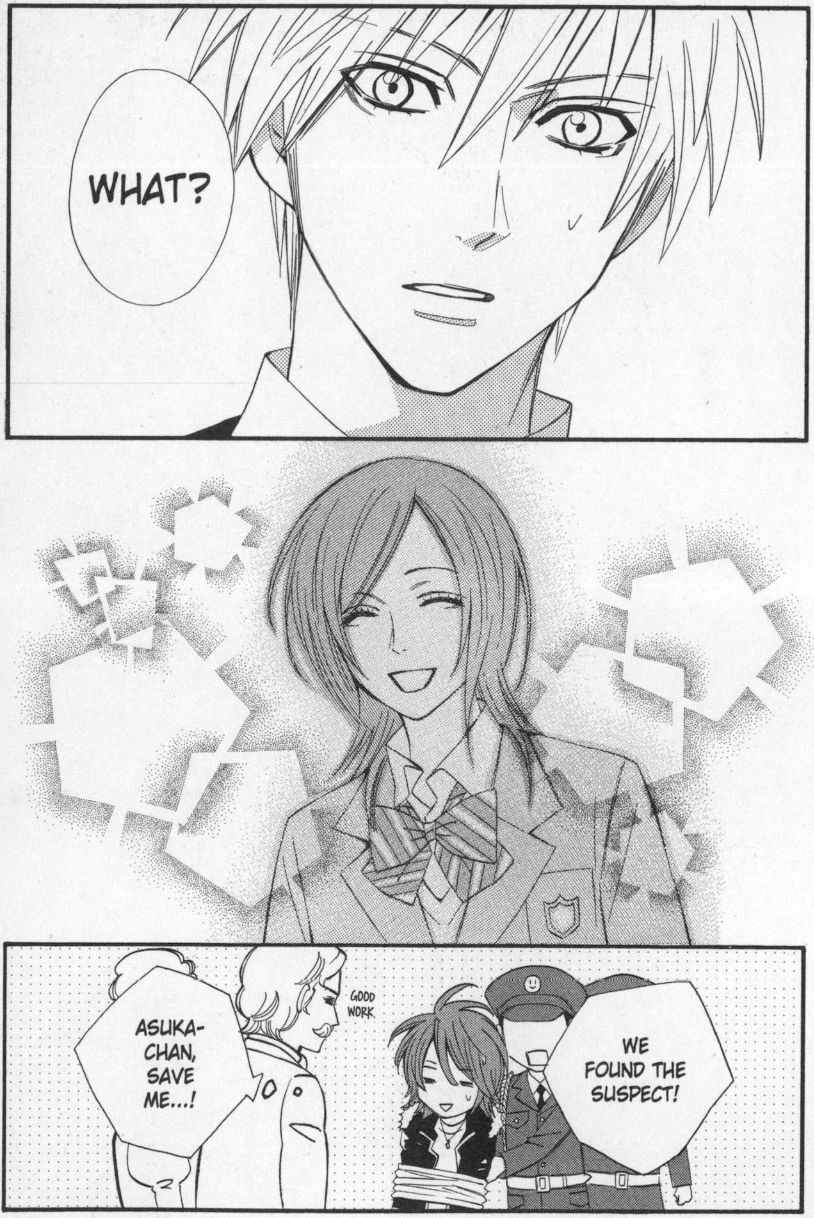
WHAT?
WE FOUND THE SUSPECT!
GOOD WORK.
ASUKA-CHAN, SAVE ME...!

OTOMEN

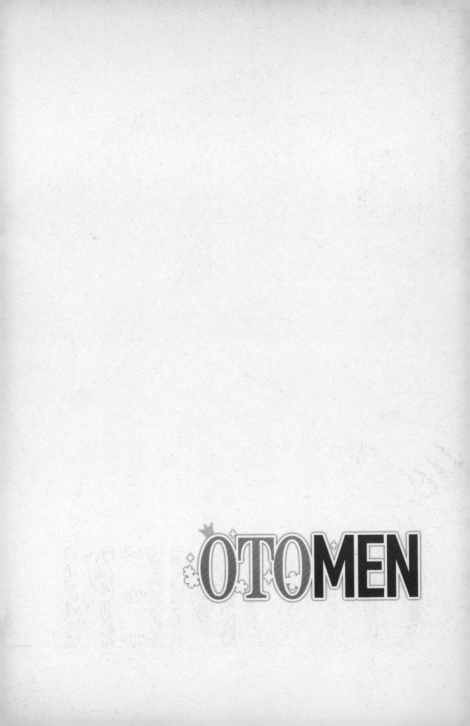

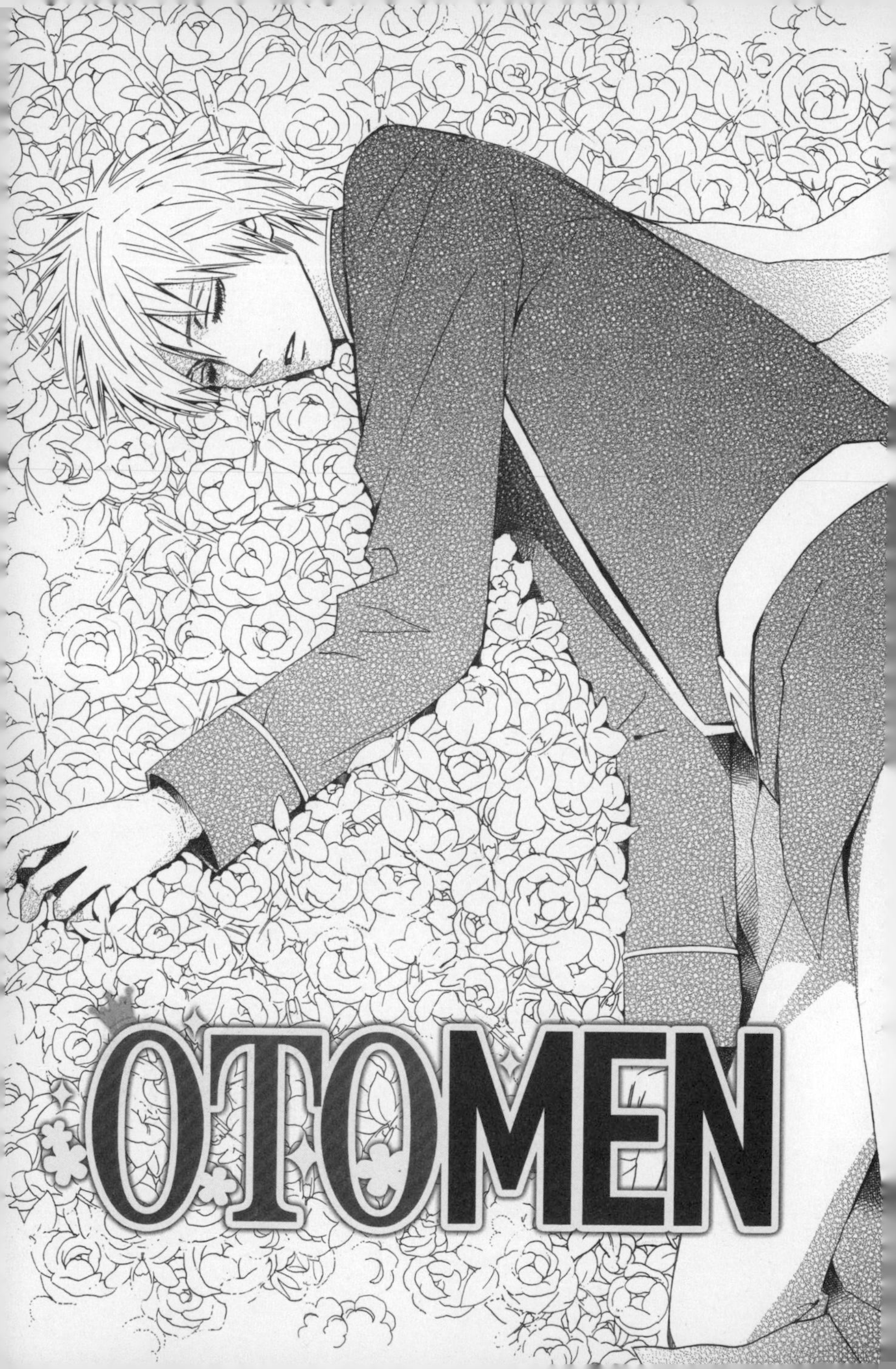
OTOMEN

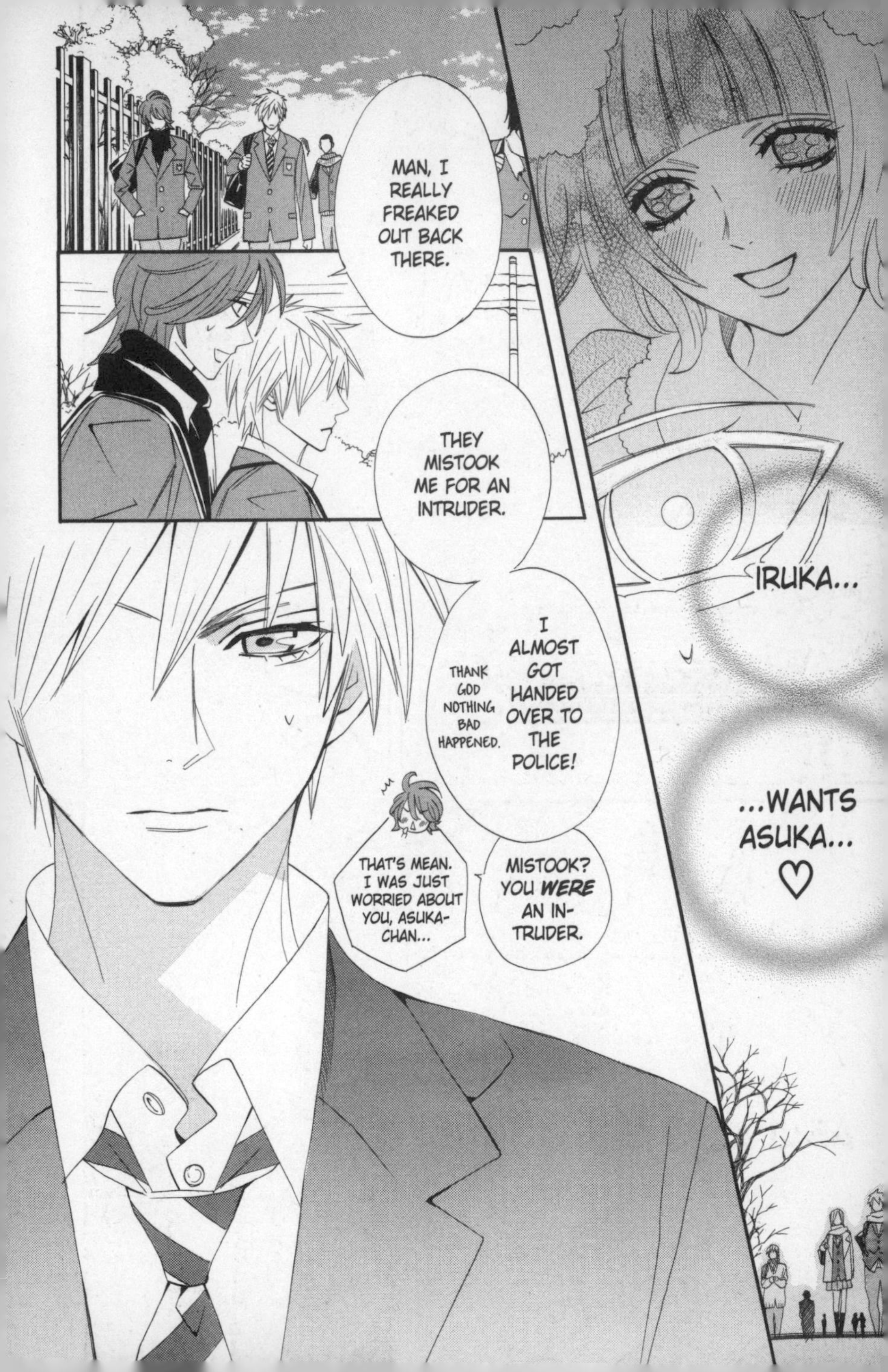
IRUKA...
...WANTS ASUKA... ♡
MAN, I REALLY FREAKED OUT BACK THERE.
THEY MISTOOK ME FOR AN INTRUDER.
I ALMOST GOT HANDED OVER TO THE POLICE!
THANK GOD NOTHING BAD HAPPENED.
MISTOOK? YOU *WERE* AN IN-TRUDER.
THAT'S MEAN. I WAS JUST WORRIED ABOUT YOU, ASUKA-CHAN...

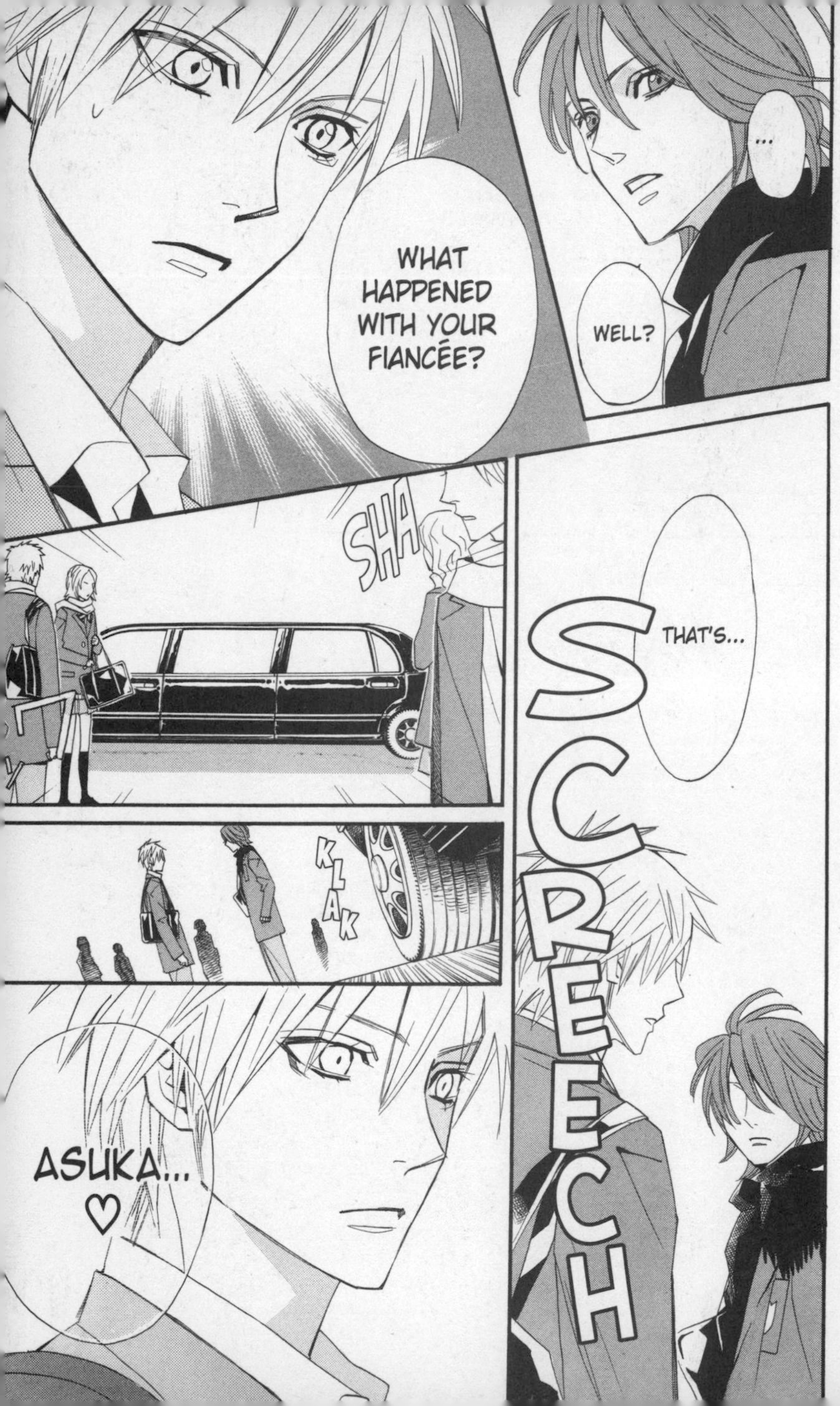
...
WELL?
WHAT HAPPENED WITH YOUR FIANCÉE?
THAT'S...
SCREECH
SHA
KLAK
ASUKA... ♡

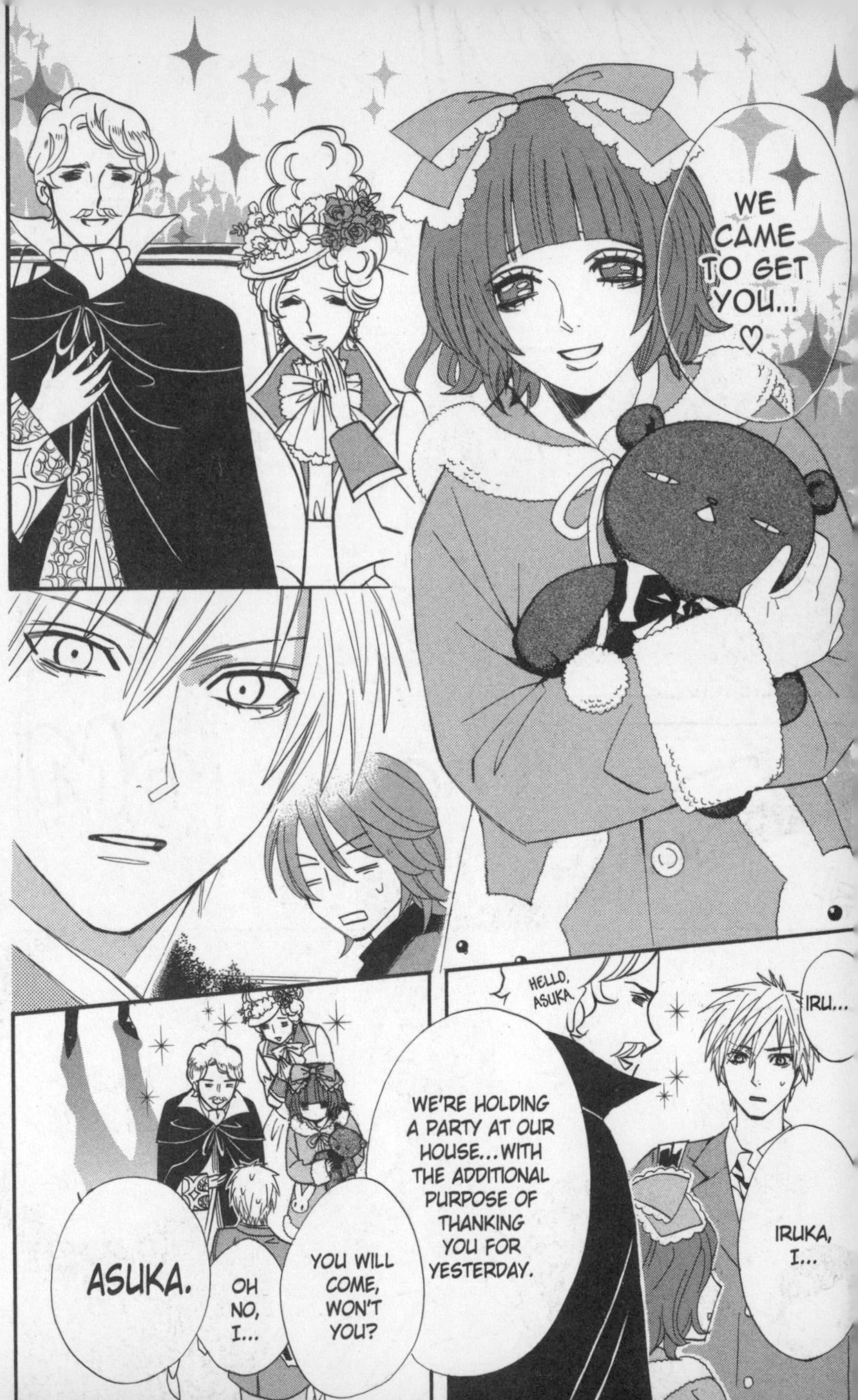
WE CAME TO GET YOU... ♡
HELLO, ASUKA.
IRU...
IRUKA, I...
WE'RE HOLDING A PARTY AT OUR HOUSE...WITH THE ADDITIONAL PURPOSE OF THANKING YOU FOR YESTERDAY.
YOU WILL COME, WON'T YOU?
OH NO, I...
ASUKA.

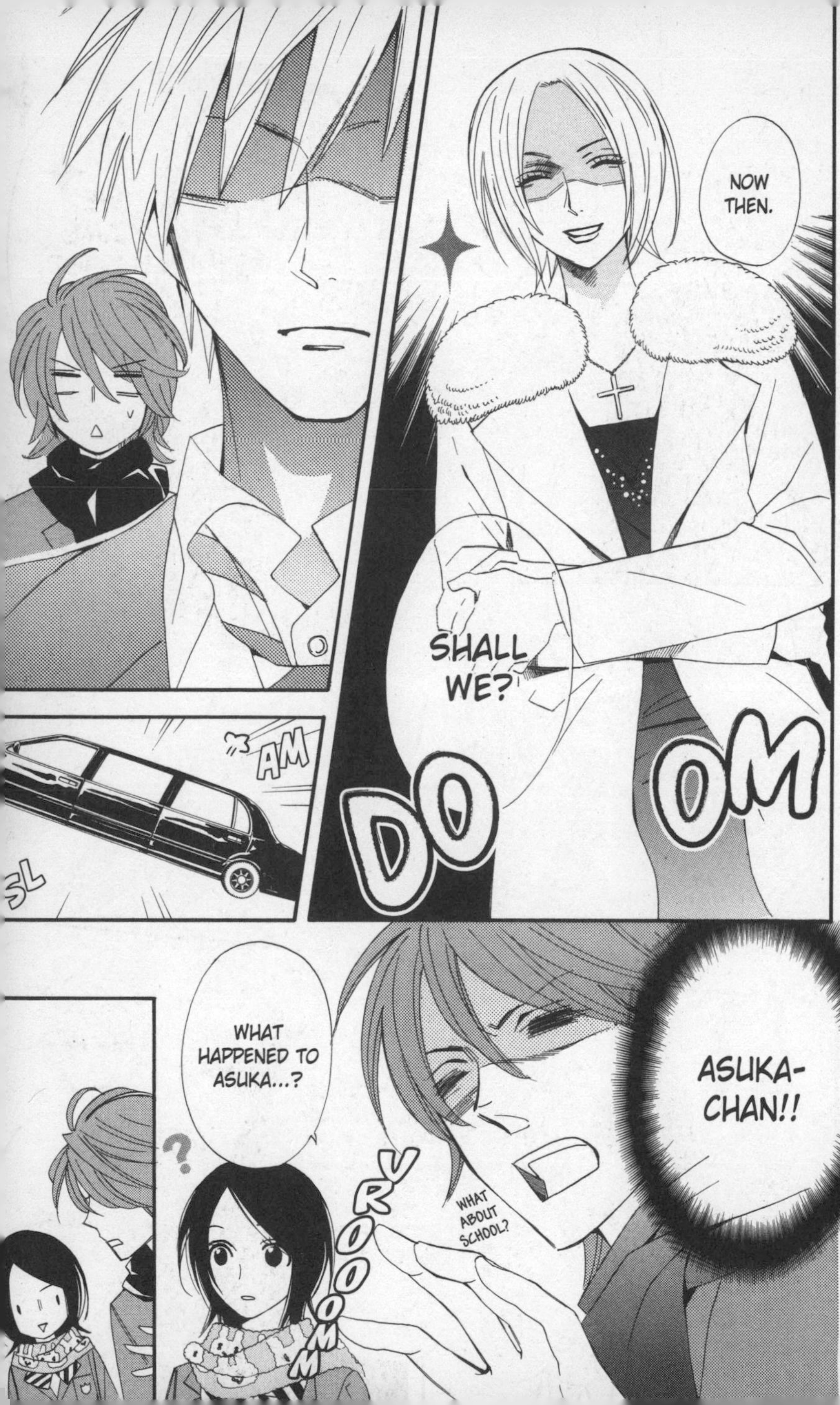
NOW THEN.
SHALL WE?
DO
OM
AM
SL
ASUKA-CHAN!!
WHAT ABOUT SCHOOL?
VROOOOMM
WHAT HAPPENED TO ASUKA...?
?

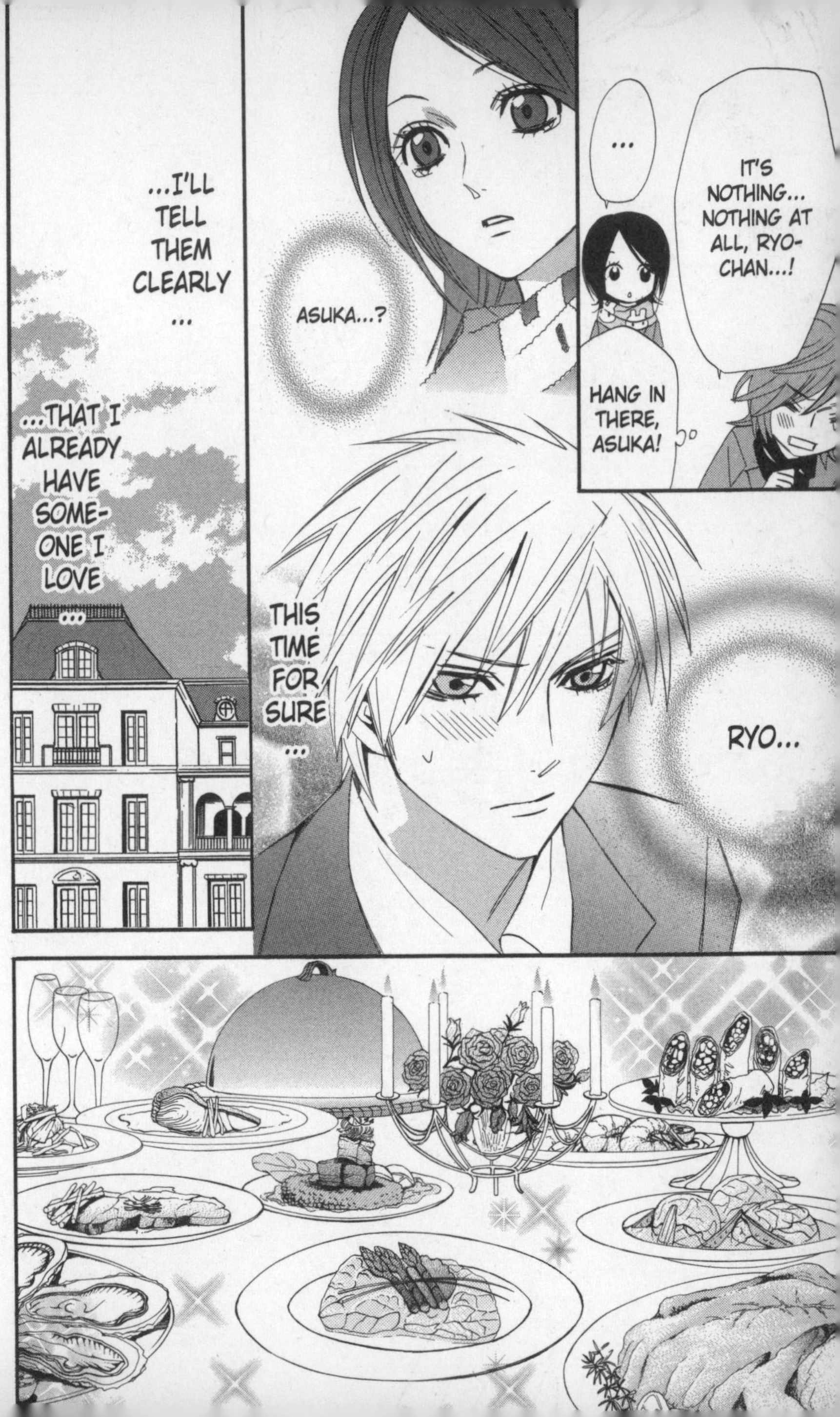
IT'S NOTHING... NOTHING AT ALL, RYO-CHAN...!
...
HANG IN THERE, ASUKA!
ASUKA...?
RYO...
THIS TIME FOR SURE...
...I'LL TELL THEM CLEARLY...
...THAT I ALREADY HAVE SOME-ONE I LOVE...

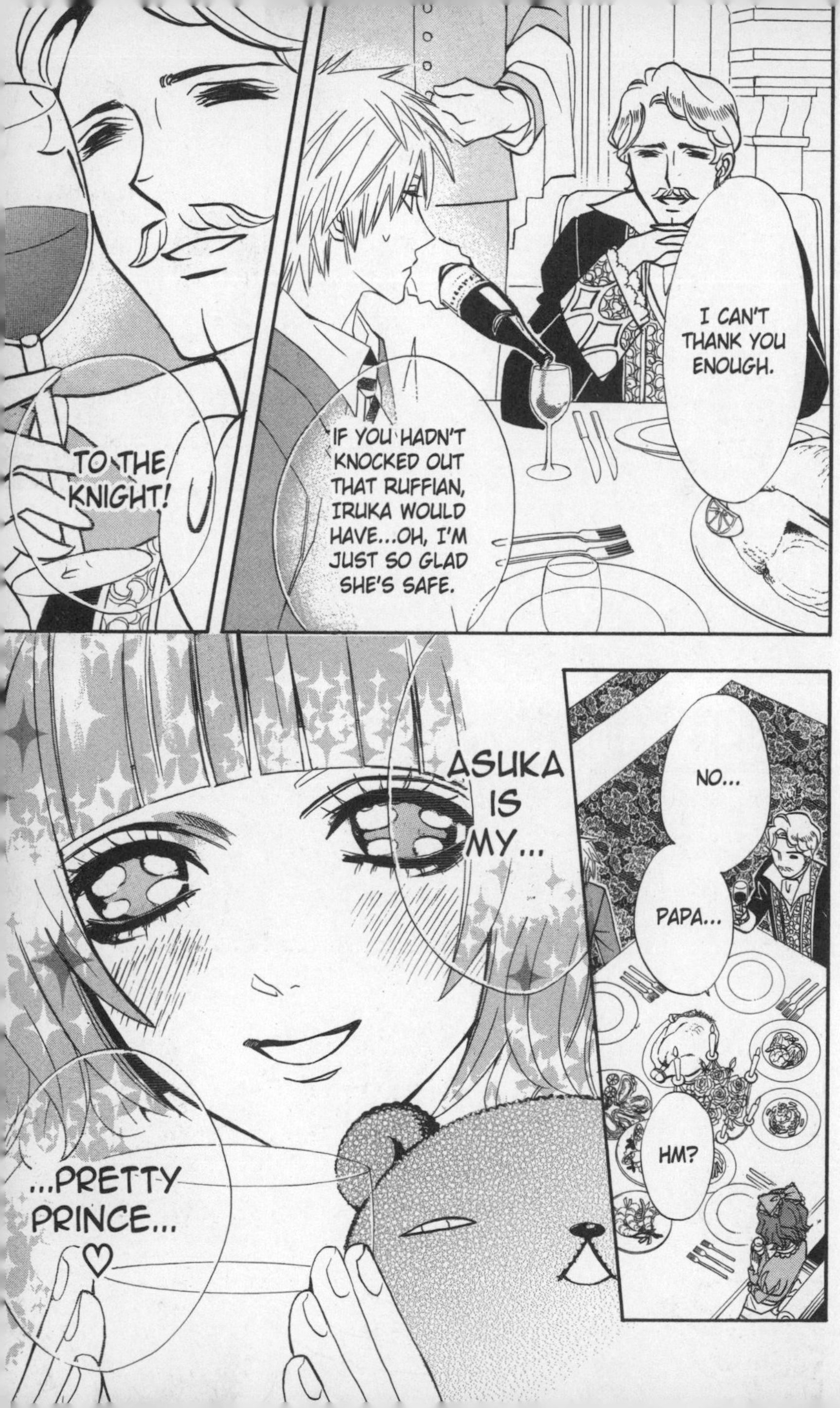
I CAN'T THANK YOU ENOUGH.
IF YOU HADN'T KNOCKED OUT THAT RUFFIAN, IRUKA WOULD HAVE...OH, I'M JUST SO GLAD SHE'S SAFE.
TO THE KNIGHT!
NO...
PAPA...
HM?
ASUKA IS MY...
...PRETTY PRINCE... ♡

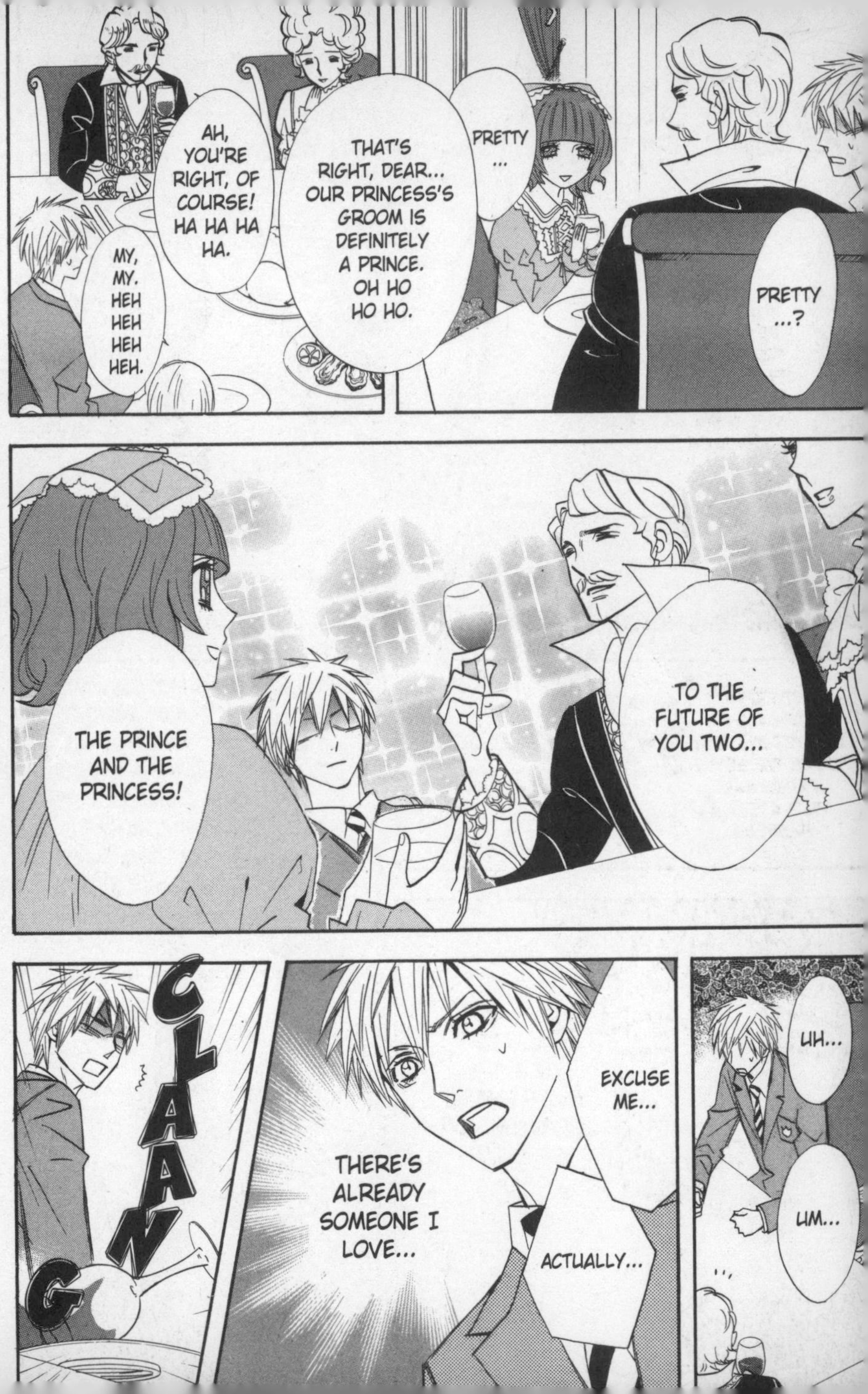
PRETTY ...
PRETTY ...?
THAT'S RIGHT, DEAR... OUR PRINCESS'S GROOM IS DEFINITELY A PRINCE. OH HO HO HO.
AH, YOU'RE RIGHT, OF COURSE! HA HA HA HA.
MY, MY. HEH HEH HEH HEH.
TO THE FUTURE OF YOU TWO...
THE PRINCE AND THE PRINCESS!
UH...
UM...
EXCUSE ME...
ACTUALLY...
THERE'S ALREADY SOMEONE I LOVE...
CLAAANG

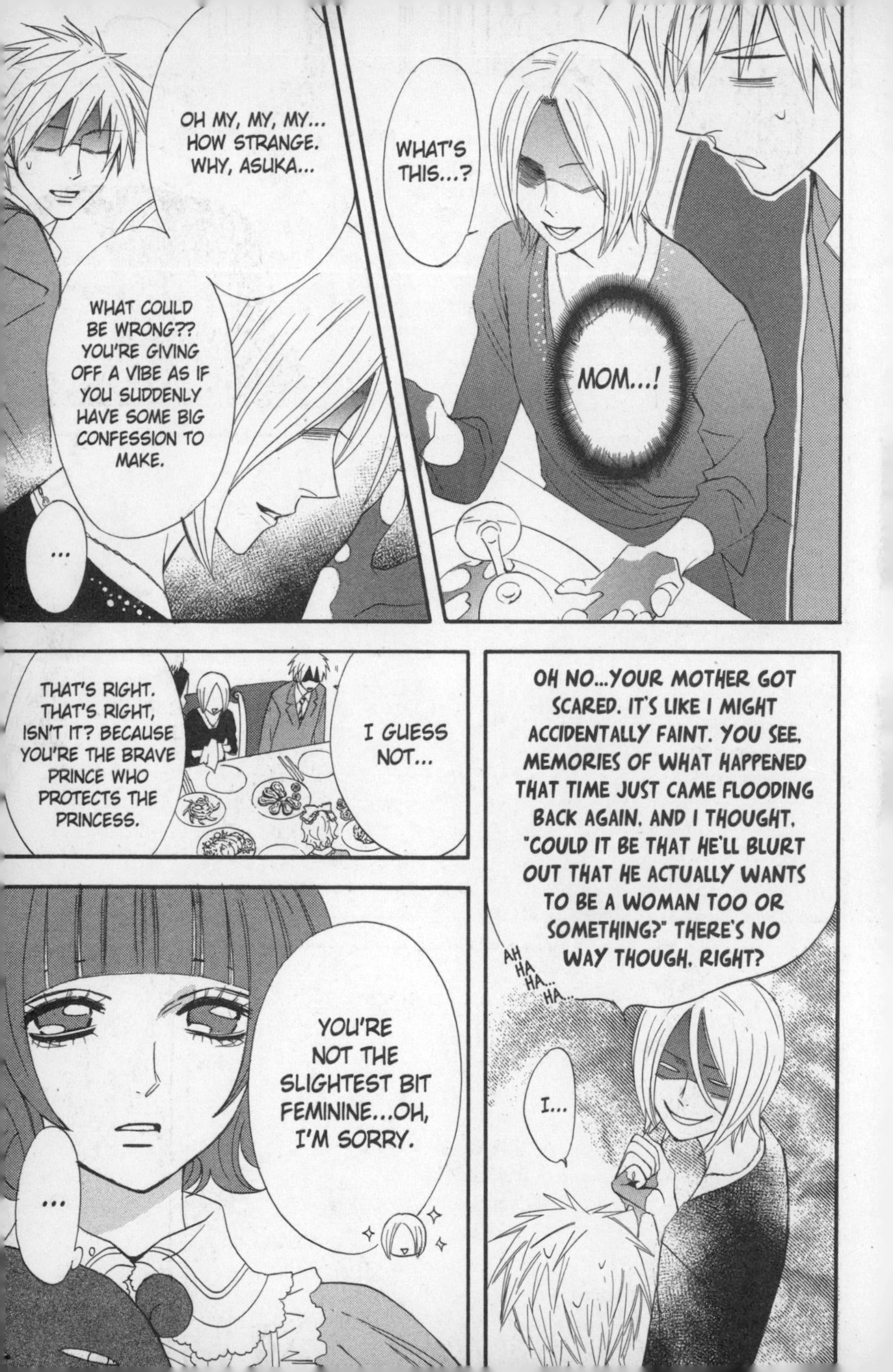
WHAT'S THIS...?
MOM...!
OH MY, MY, MY... HOW STRANGE. WHY, ASUKA...
WHAT COULD BE WRONG?? YOU'RE GIVING OFF A VIBE AS IF YOU SUDDENLY HAVE SOME BIG CONFESSION TO MAKE.
...
OH NO...YOUR MOTHER GOT SCARED. IT'S LIKE I MIGHT ACCIDENTALLY FAINT. YOU SEE, MEMORIES OF WHAT HAPPENED THAT TIME JUST CAME FLOODING BACK AGAIN, AND I THOUGHT, "COULD IT BE THAT HE'LL BLURT OUT THAT HE ACTUALLY WANTS TO BE A WOMAN TOO OR SOMETHING?" THERE'S NO WAY THOUGH, RIGHT?
AH HA HA... HA...
I...
I GUESS NOT...
THAT'S RIGHT. THAT'S RIGHT, ISN'T IT? BECAUSE YOU'RE THE BRAVE PRINCE WHO PROTECTS THE PRINCESS.
YOU'RE NOT THE SLIGHTEST BIT FEMININE...OH, I'M SORRY.
...

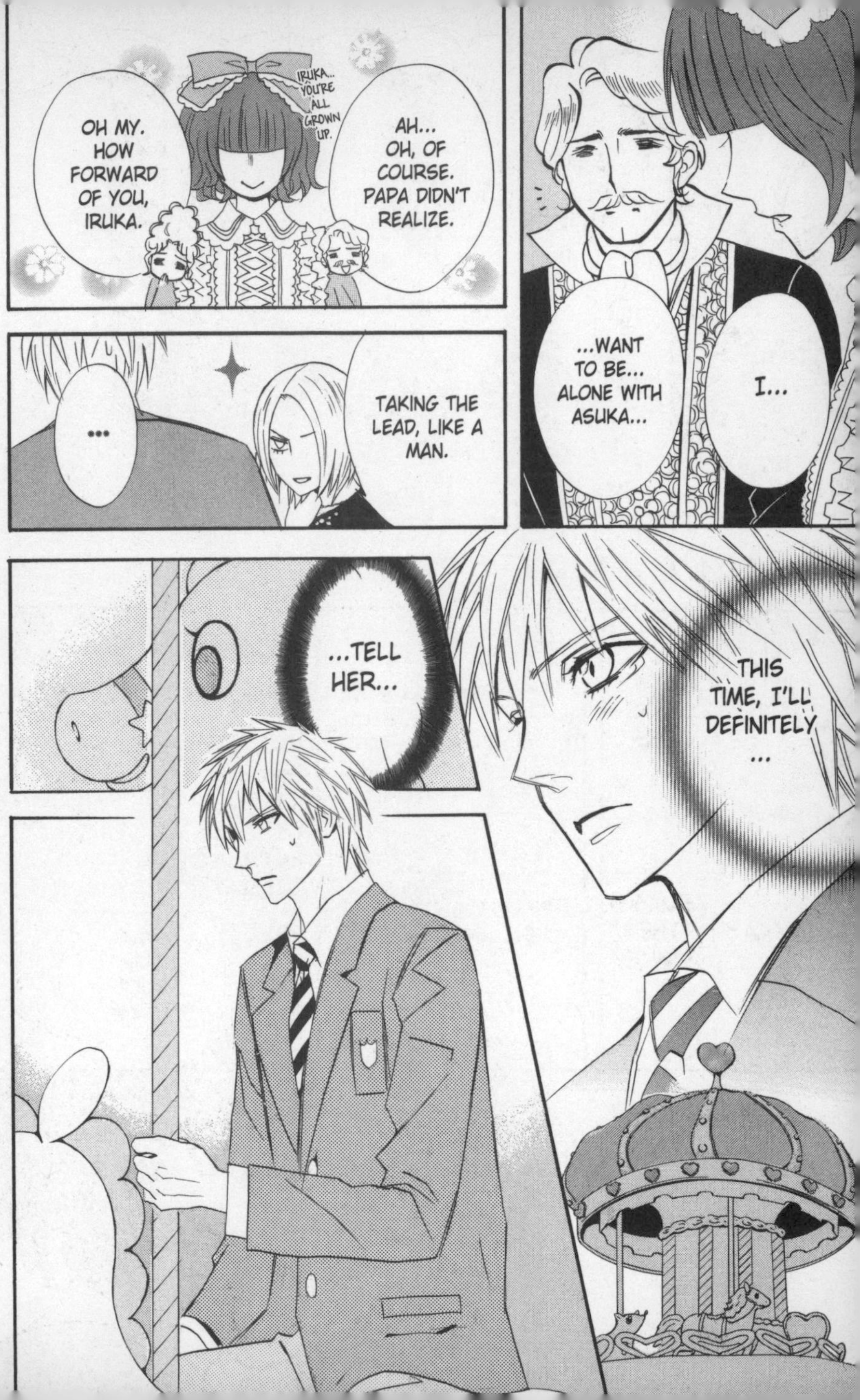
I...
...WANT TO BE... ALONE WITH ASUKA...
AH... OH, OF COURSE. PAPA DIDN'T REALIZE.
IRUKA.. YOU'RE ALL GROWN UP.
OH MY. HOW FORWARD OF YOU, IRUKA.
TAKING THE LEAD, LIKE A MAN.
...
THIS TIME, I'LL DEFINITELY ...
...TELL HER...

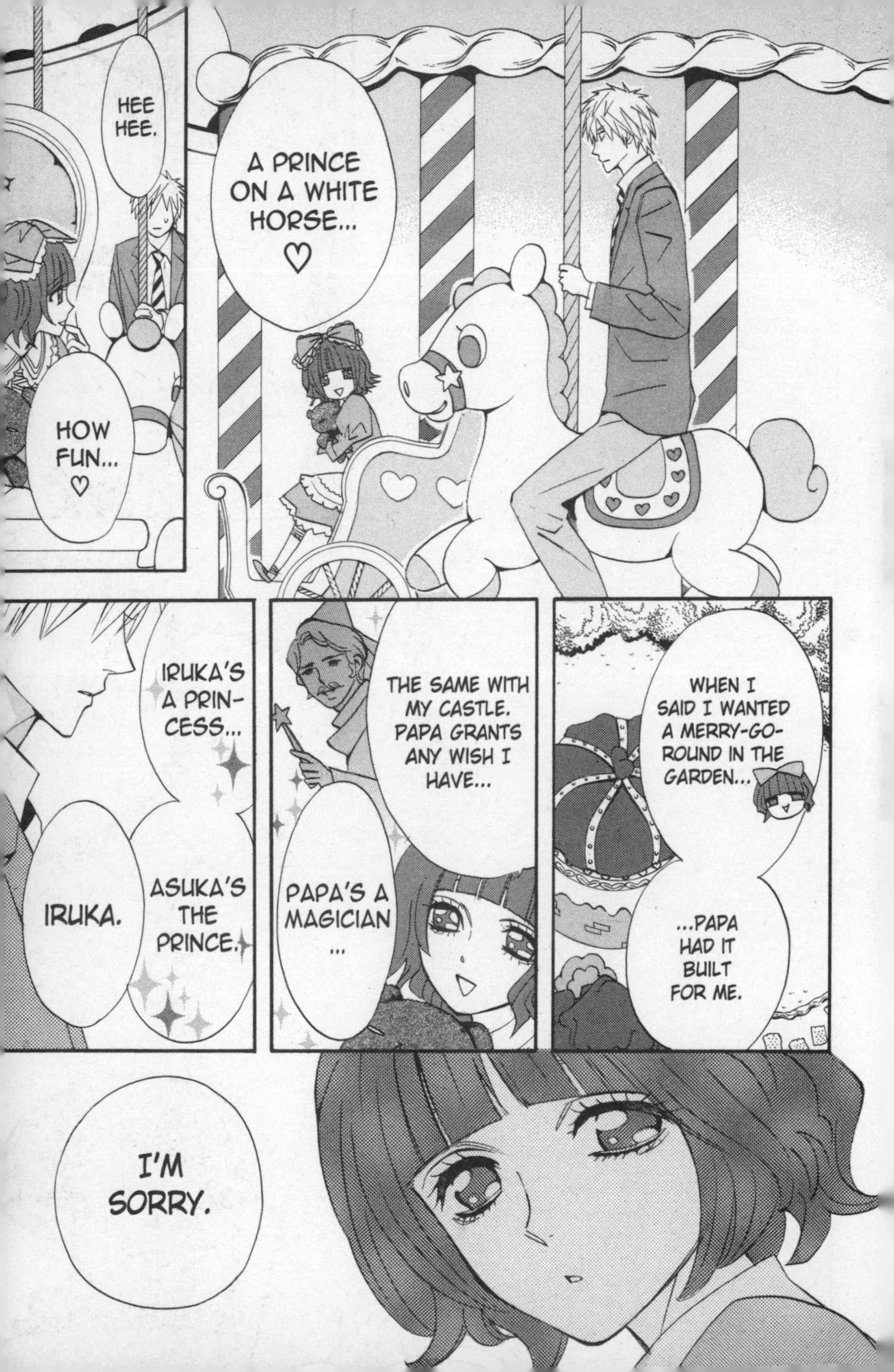
A PRINCE ON A WHITE HORSE... ♡
HEE HEE.
HOW FUN... ♡
WHEN I SAID I WANTED A MERRY-GO-ROUND IN THE GARDEN...
...PAPA HAD IT BUILT FOR ME.
THE SAME WITH MY CASTLE. PAPA GRANTS ANY WISH I HAVE...
PAPA'S A MAGICIAN ...
IRUKA'S A PRINCESS...
ASUKA'S THE PRINCE.
IRUKA.
I'M SORRY.

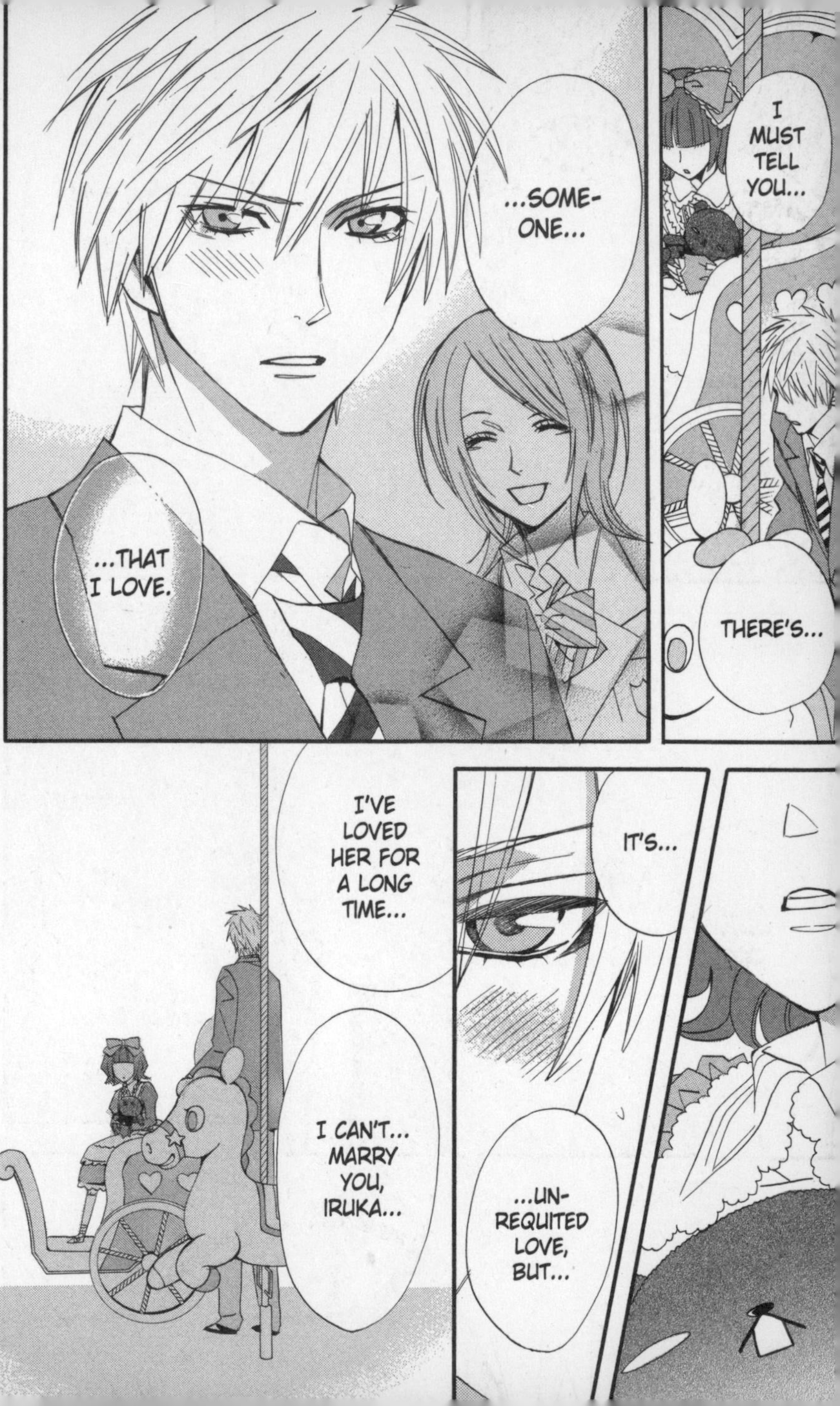
I MUST TELL YOU...
THERE'S...
...SOME-ONE...
...THAT I LOVE.
IT'S...
...UN-REQUITED LOVE, BUT...
I'VE LOVED HER FOR A LONG TIME...
I CAN'T... MARRY YOU, IRUKA...

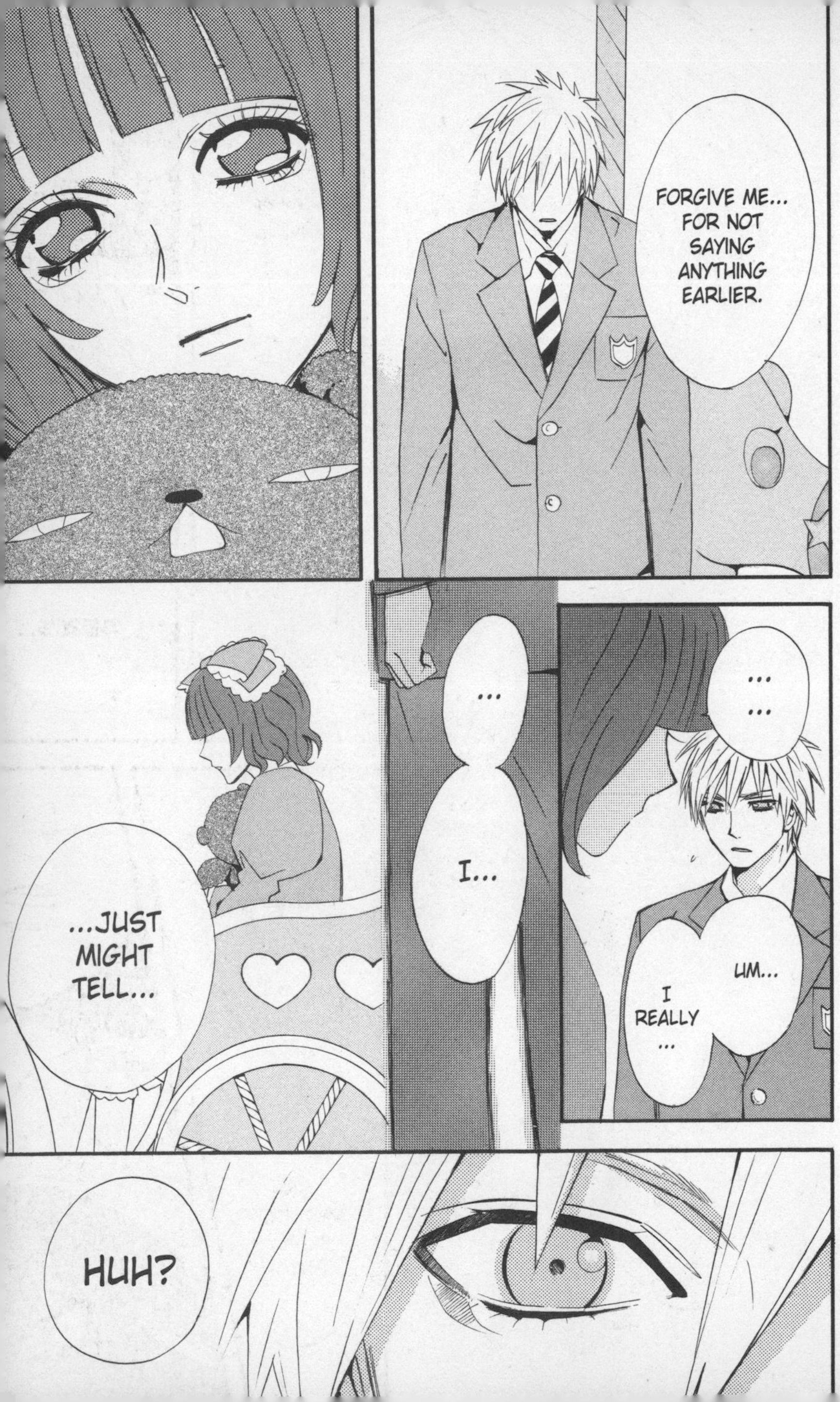
FORGIVE ME... FOR NOT SAYING ANYTHING EARLIER.
... ...
UM... I REALLY ...
...
I...
...JUST MIGHT TELL...
HUH?

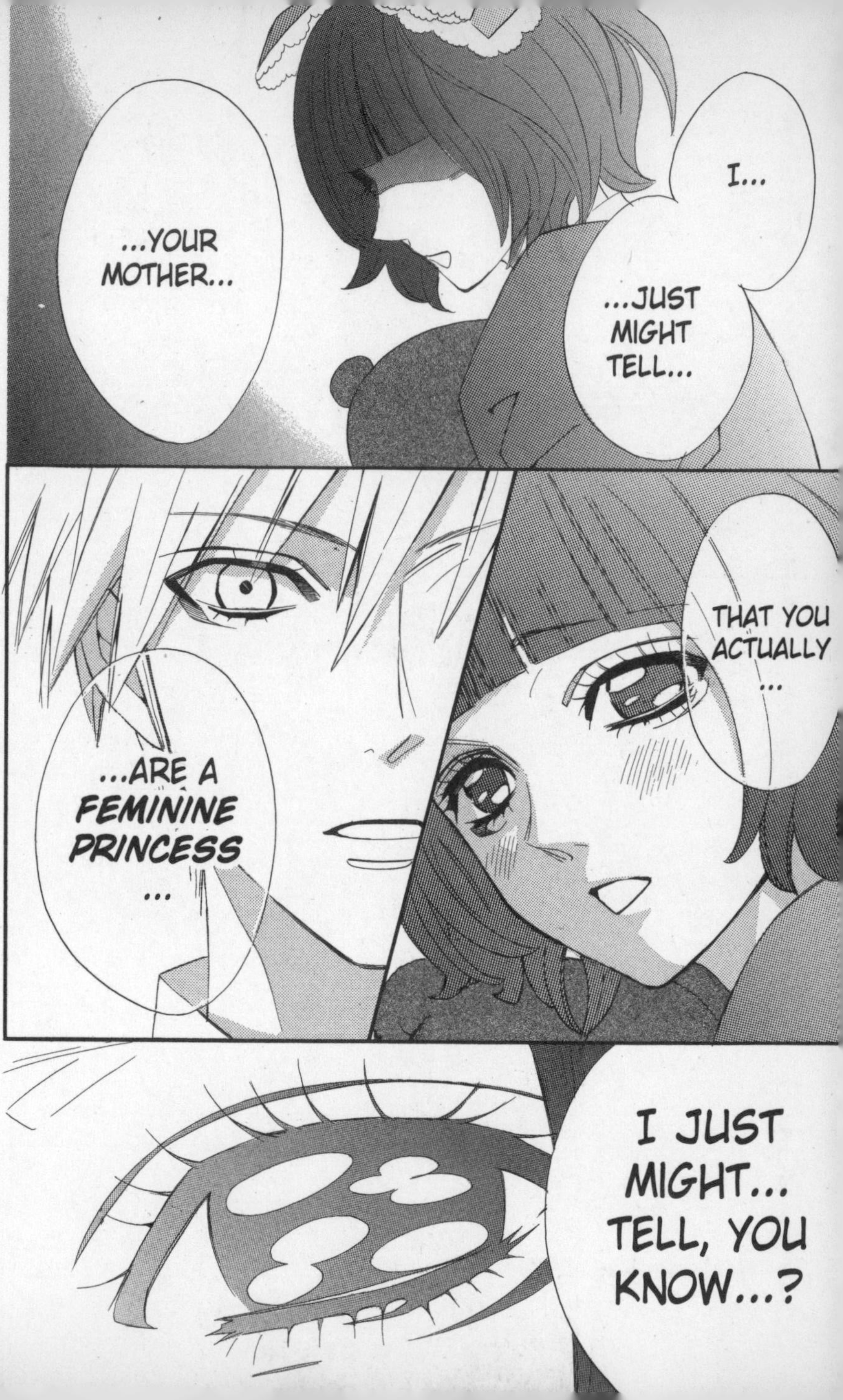
I...
...JUST MIGHT TELL...
...YOUR MOTHER...
THAT YOU ACTUALLY ...
...ARE A FEMININE PRINCESS ...
I JUST MIGHT... TELL, YOU KNOW...?

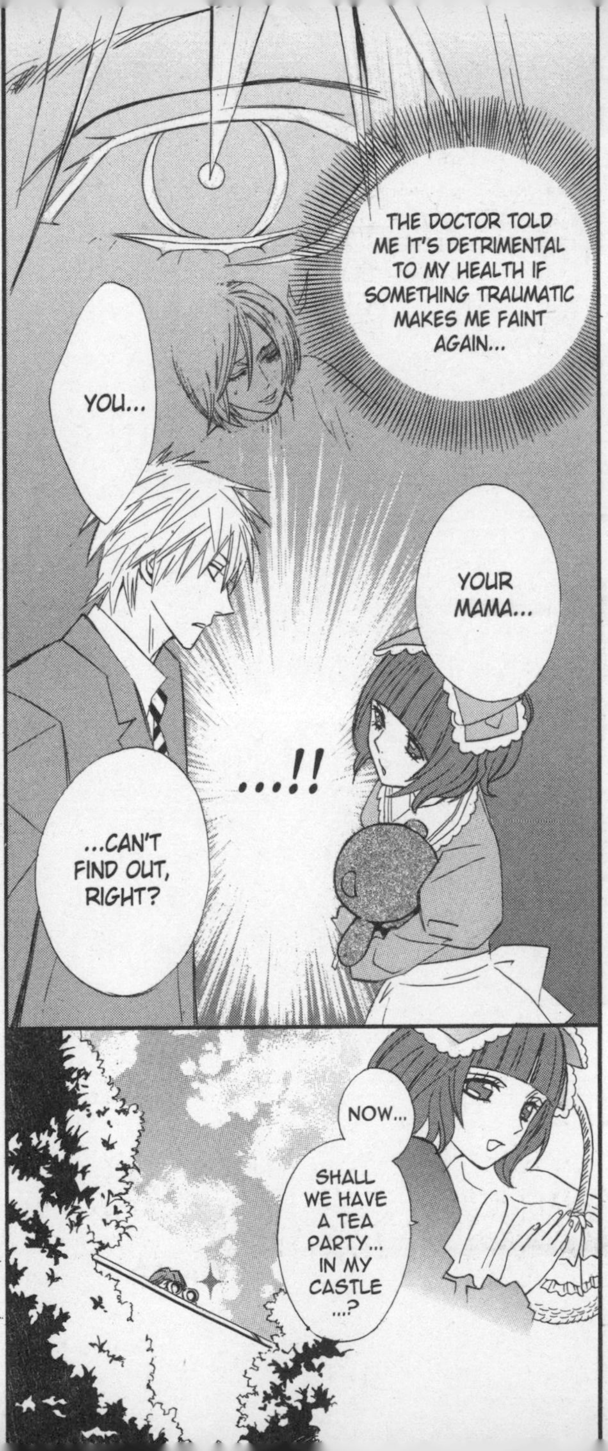
THE DOCTOR TOLD ME IT'S DETRIMENTAL TO MY HEALTH IF SOMETHING TRAUMATIC MAKES ME FAINT AGAIN...
YOU...
YOUR MAMA...
...!!
...CAN'T FIND OUT, RIGHT?
NOW...
SHALL WE HAVE A TEA PARTY... IN MY CASTLE ...?

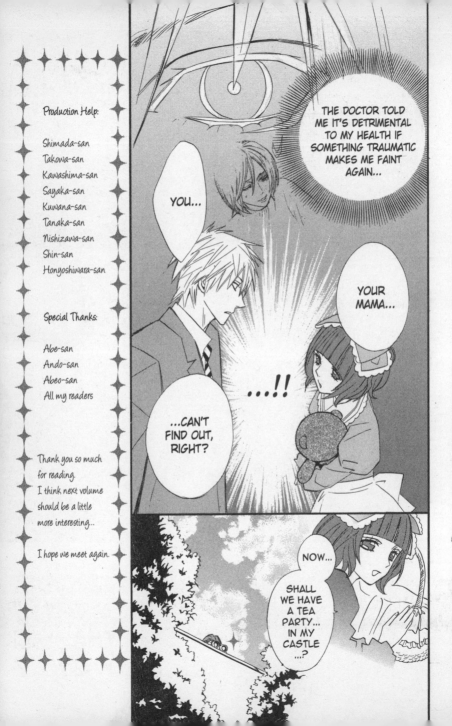

Production Help:

Shimada-san
Takowa-san
Kawashima-san
Sayaka-san
Kuwana-san
Tanaka-san
Nishizawa-san
Shin-san
Honyoshiwara-san

Special Thanks:

Abe-san
Ando-san
Abeo-san
All my readers

Thank you so much for reading. I think next volume should be a little more interesting...

I hope we meet again.

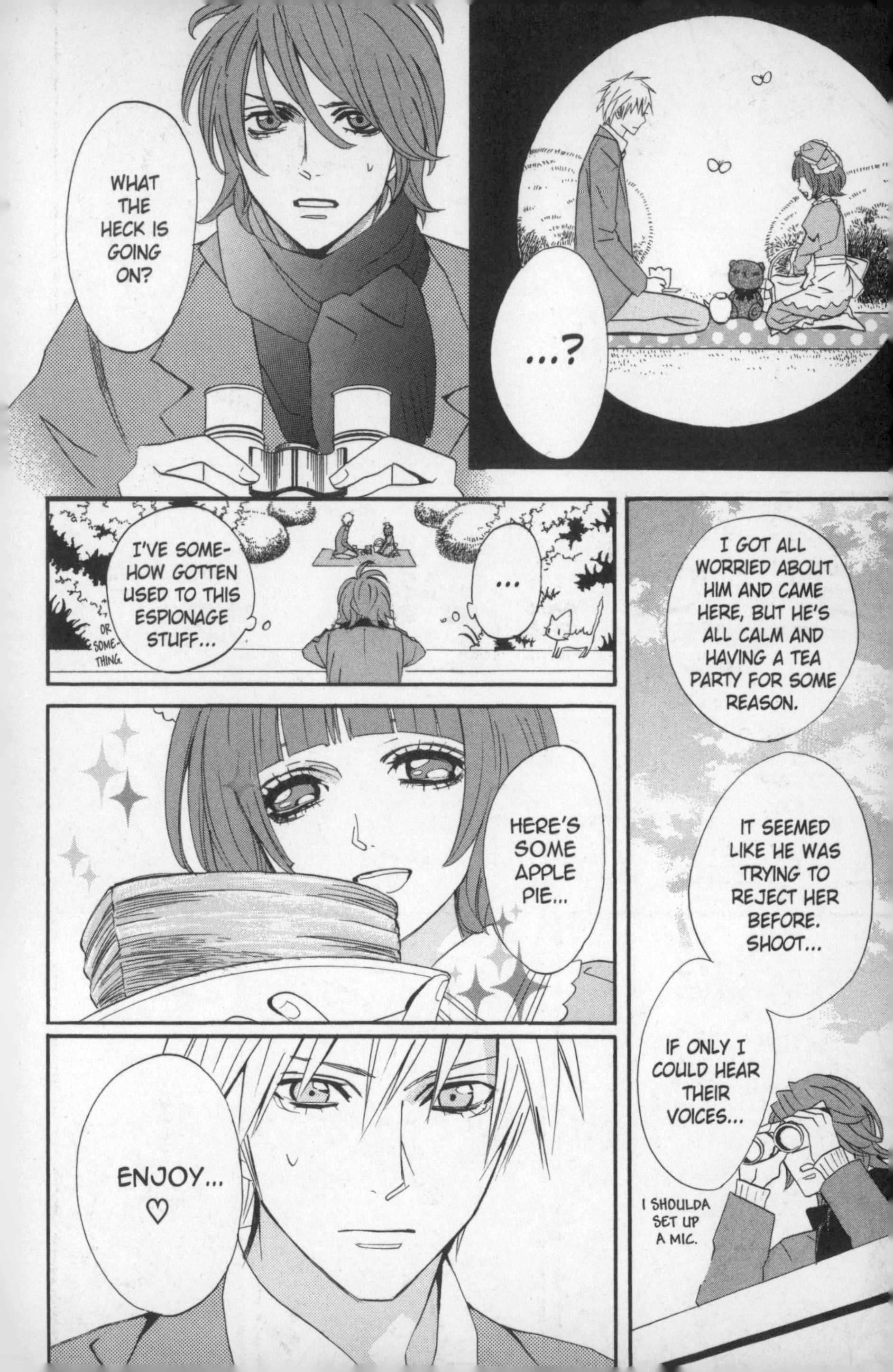
...?
WHAT THE HECK IS GOING ON?
I GOT ALL WORRIED ABOUT HIM AND CAME HERE, BUT HE'S ALL CALM AND HAVING A TEA PARTY FOR SOME REASON.
IT SEEMED LIKE HE WAS TRYING TO REJECT HER BEFORE. SHOOT...
IF ONLY I COULD HEAR THEIR VOICES...
I SHOULDA SET UP A MIC.
...
I'VE SOME-HOW GOTTEN USED TO THIS ESPIONAGE STUFF...
OR SOME-THING.
HERE'S SOME APPLE PIE...
ENJOY... ♡

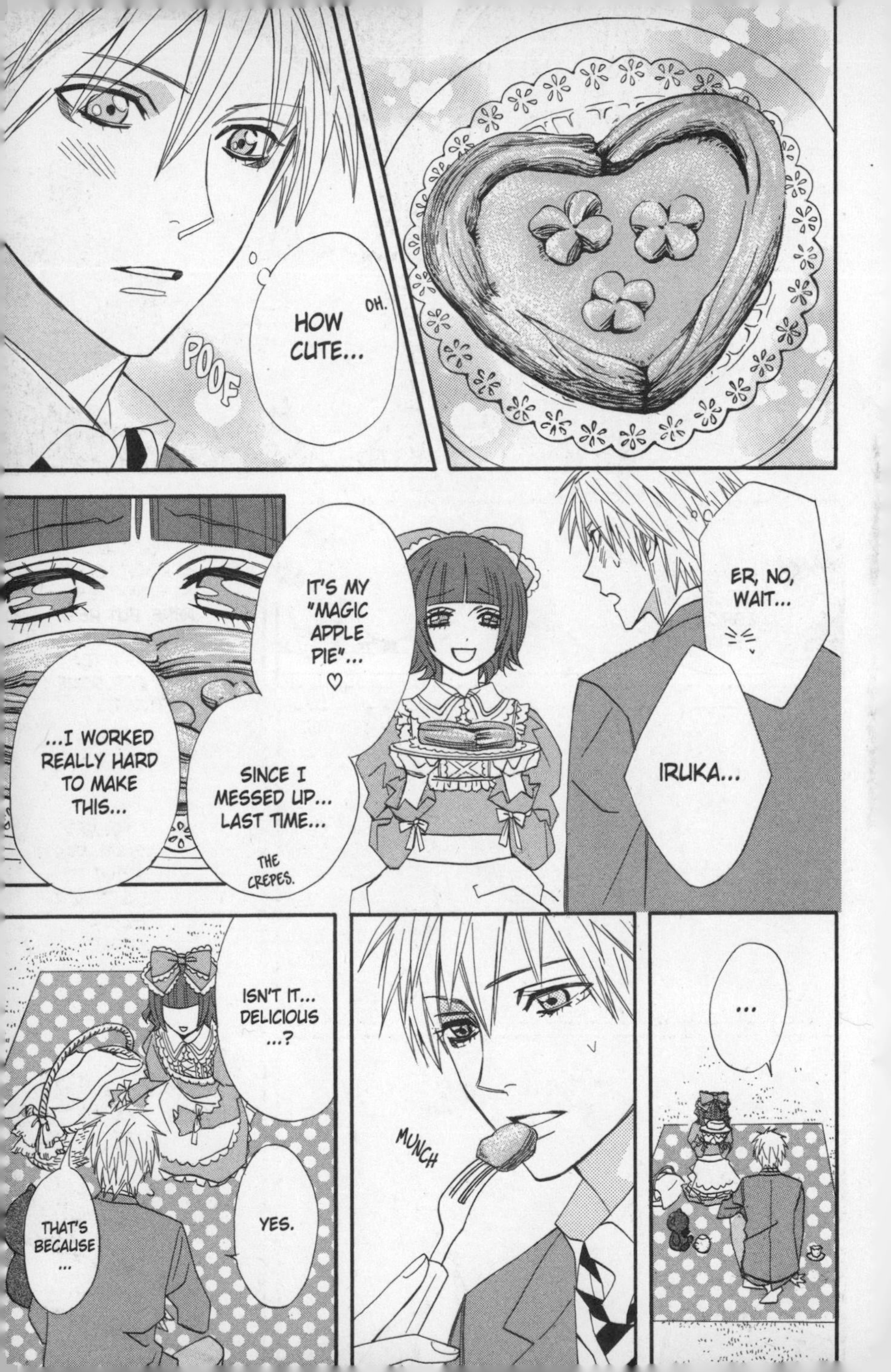
OH.
HOW CUTE...
POOF
ER, NO, WAIT...
IRUKA...
IT'S MY "MAGIC APPLE PIE"... ♡
SINCE I MESSED UP... LAST TIME...
THE CREPES.
...I WORKED REALLY HARD TO MAKE THIS...
...
MUNCH
ISN'T IT... DELICIOUS ...?
YES.
THAT'S BECAUSE ...

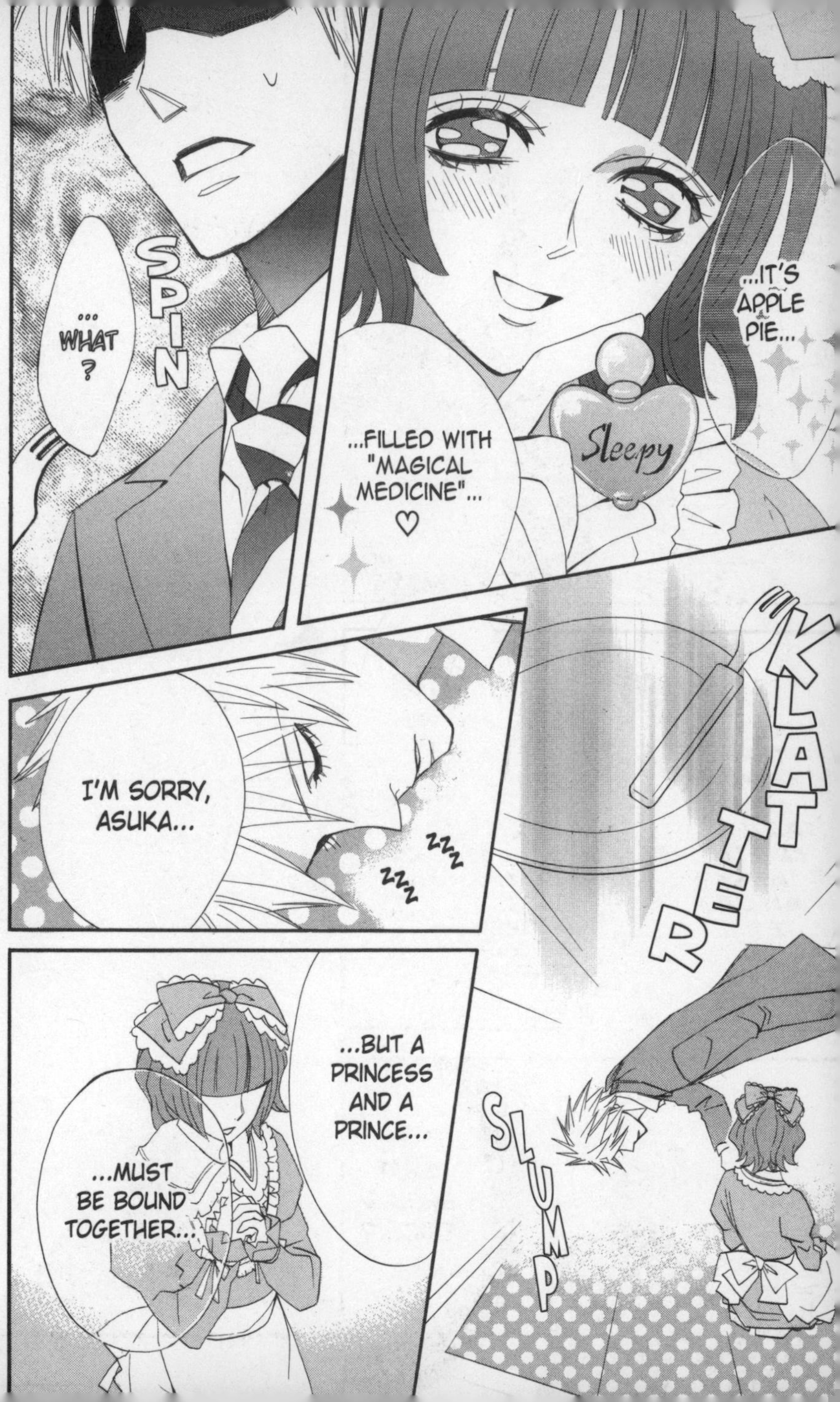
...IT'S APPLE PIE...
...FILLED WITH "MAGICAL MEDICINE"... ♡
Sleepy
SPIN
...WHAT?
KLATTER
SLUMP
I'M SORRY, ASUKA...
ZZZ ZZZ
...BUT A PRINCESS AND A PRINCE...
...MUST BE BOUND TOGETHER...

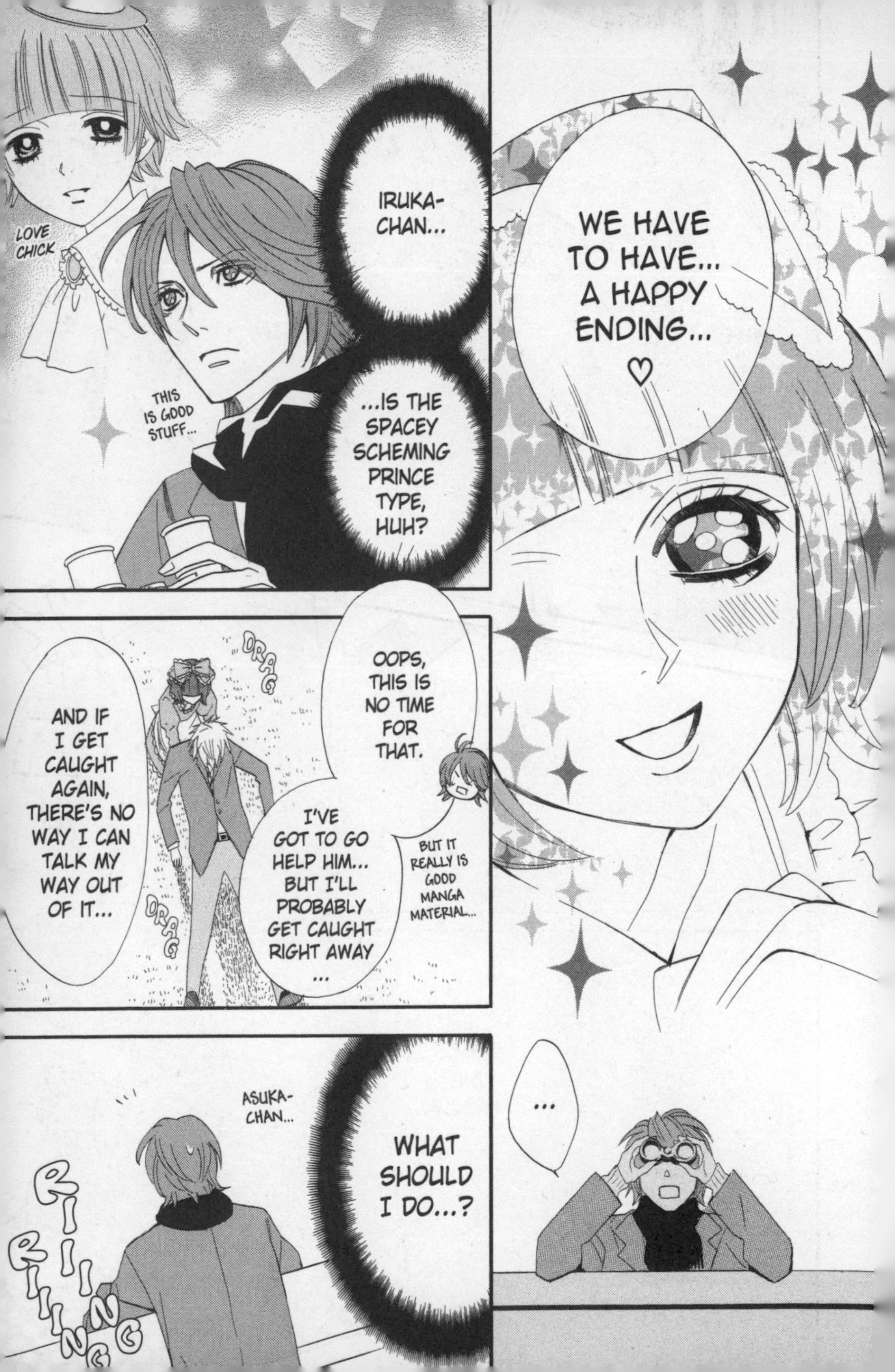
WE HAVE TO HAVE... A HAPPY ENDING... ♡
IRUKA-CHAN...
...IS THE SPACEY SCHEMING PRINCE TYPE, HUH?
LOVE CHICK
THIS IS GOOD STUFF...
OOPS, THIS IS NO TIME FOR THAT.
I'VE GOT TO GO HELP HIM... BUT I'LL PROBABLY GET CAUGHT RIGHT AWAY...
BUT IT REALLY IS GOOD MANGA MATERIAL...
DRAG
DRAG
AND IF I GET CAUGHT AGAIN, THERE'S NO WAY I CAN TALK MY WAY OUT OF IT...
...
WHAT SHOULD I DO...?
ASUKA-CHAN...
RIIING
RIIING

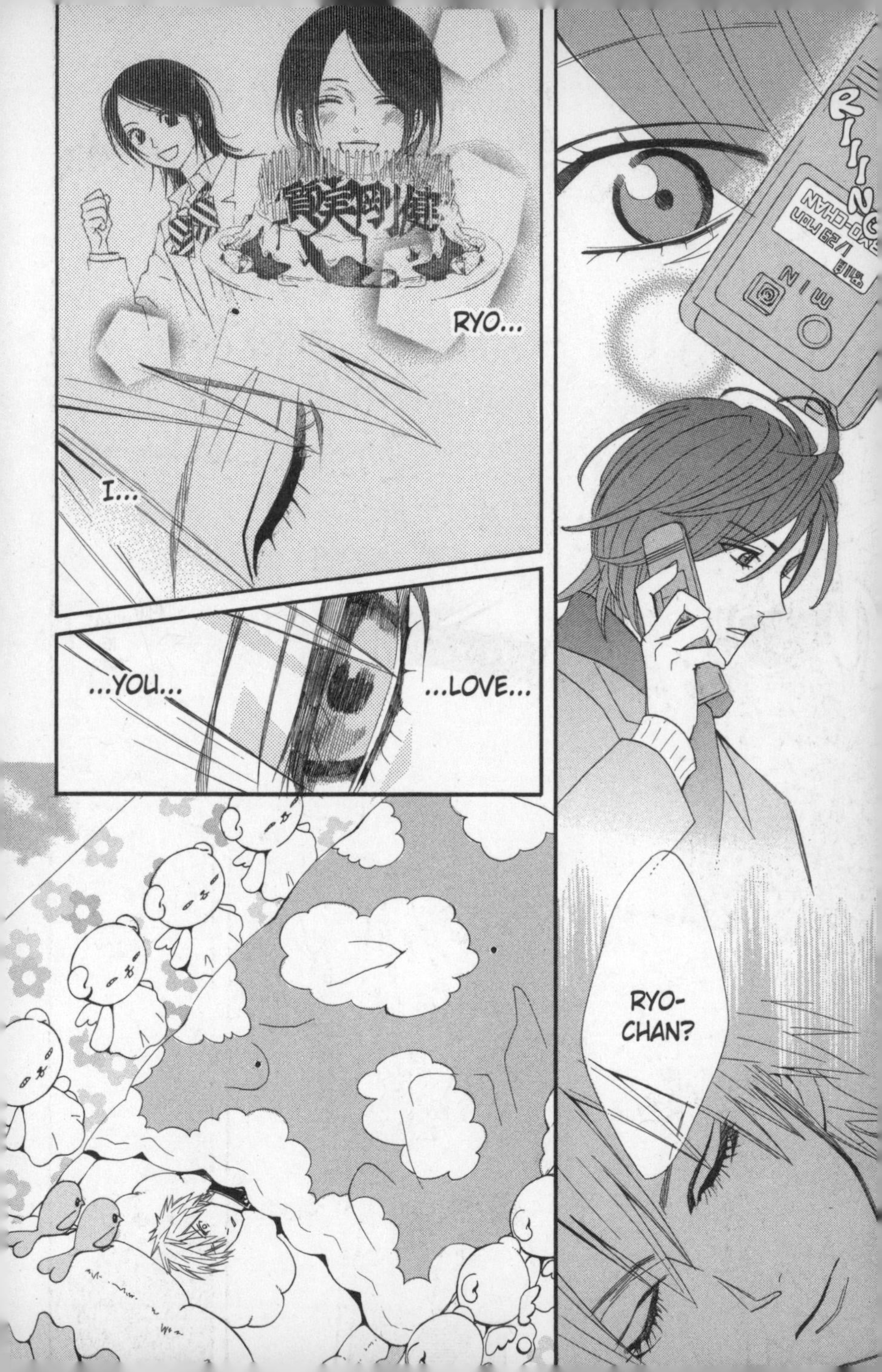
RIIING
RYO-
CHAN?
RYO...
I...
...LOVE...
...YOU...

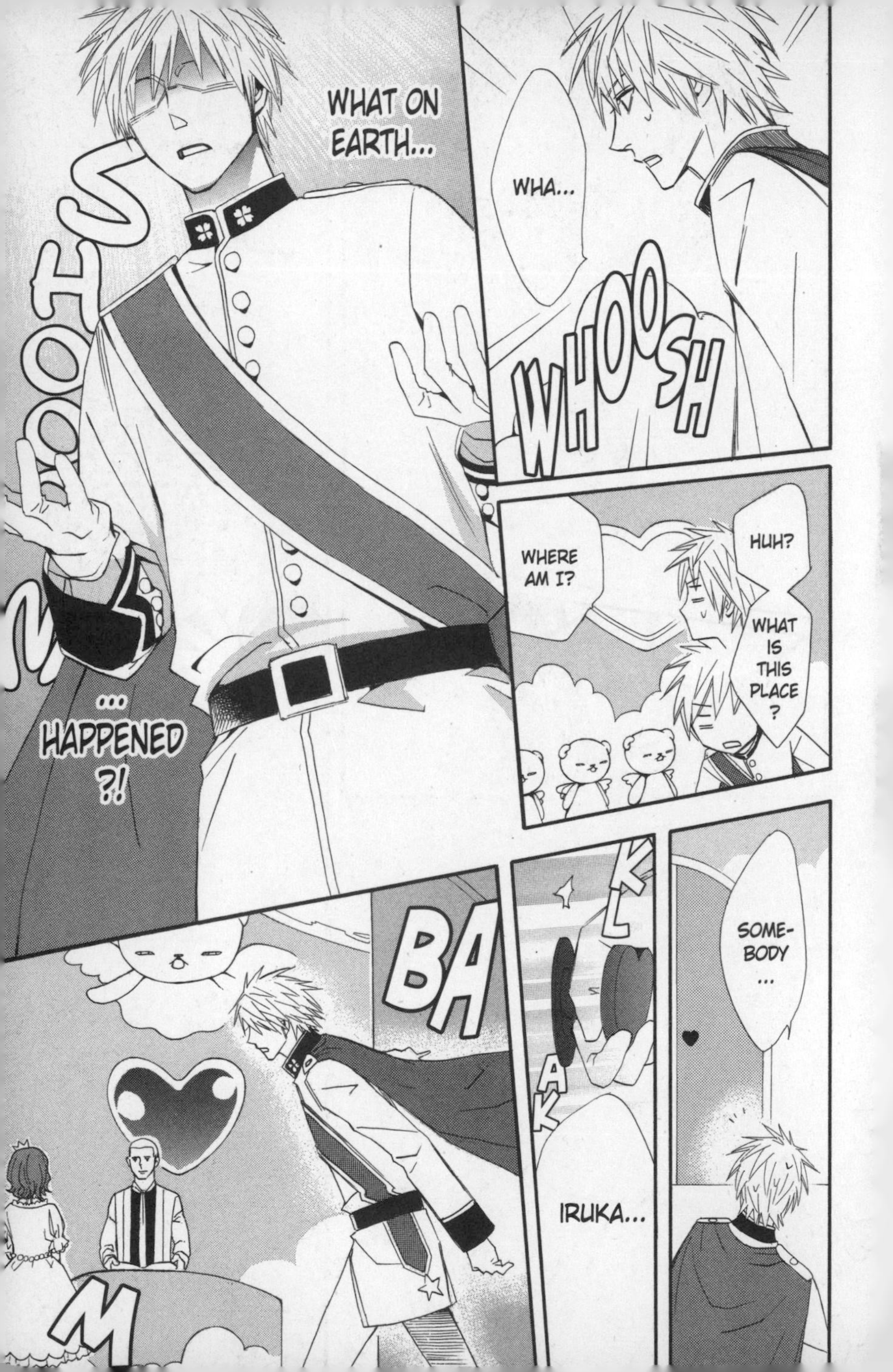
WHA...
WHOOSH
HUH?
WHERE AM I?
WHAT IS THIS PLACE?
WHAT ON EARTH...
...HAPPENED ?!
SHOOM
SOME-BODY...
IRUKA...
KLAK
BAM

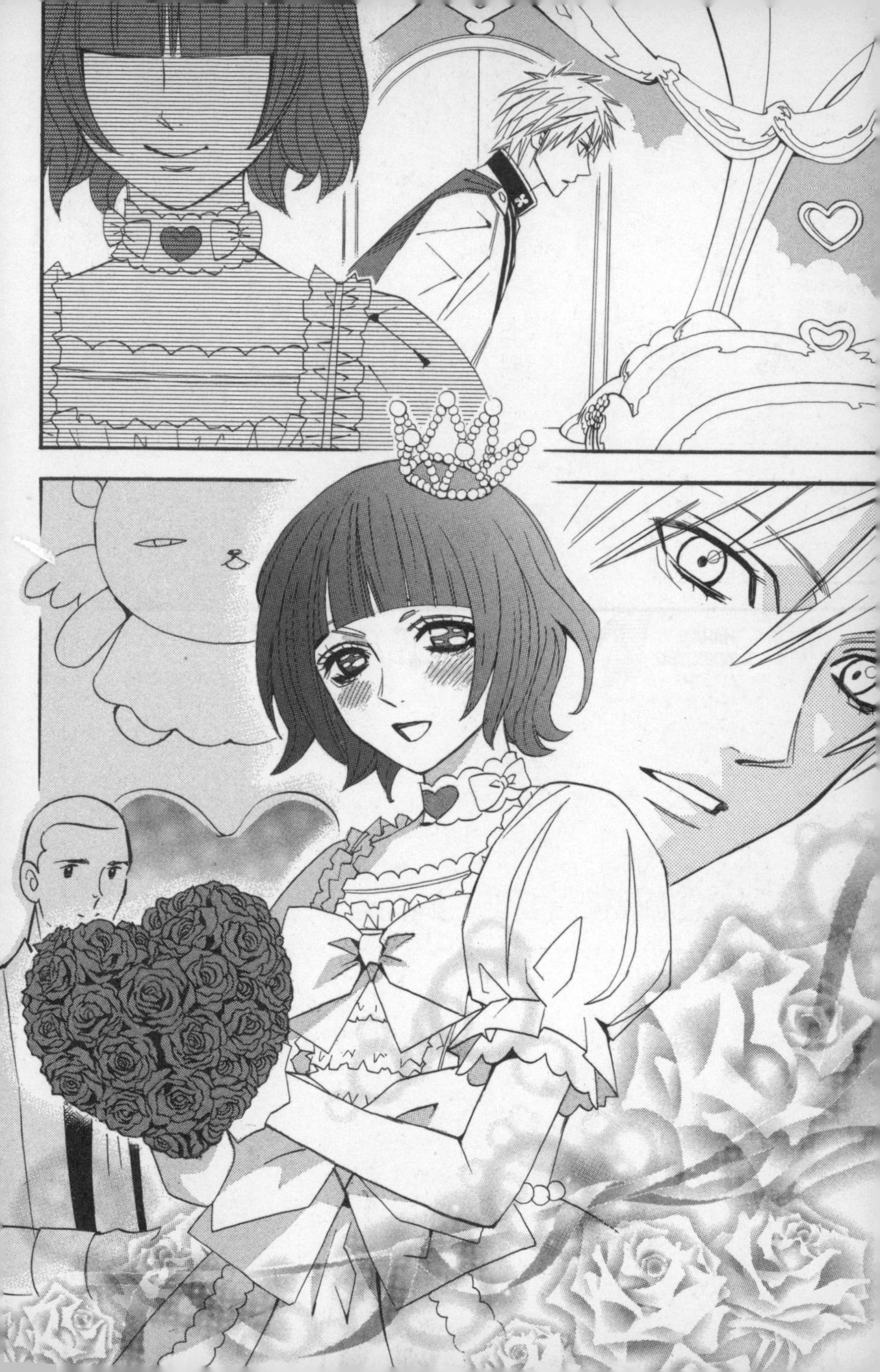

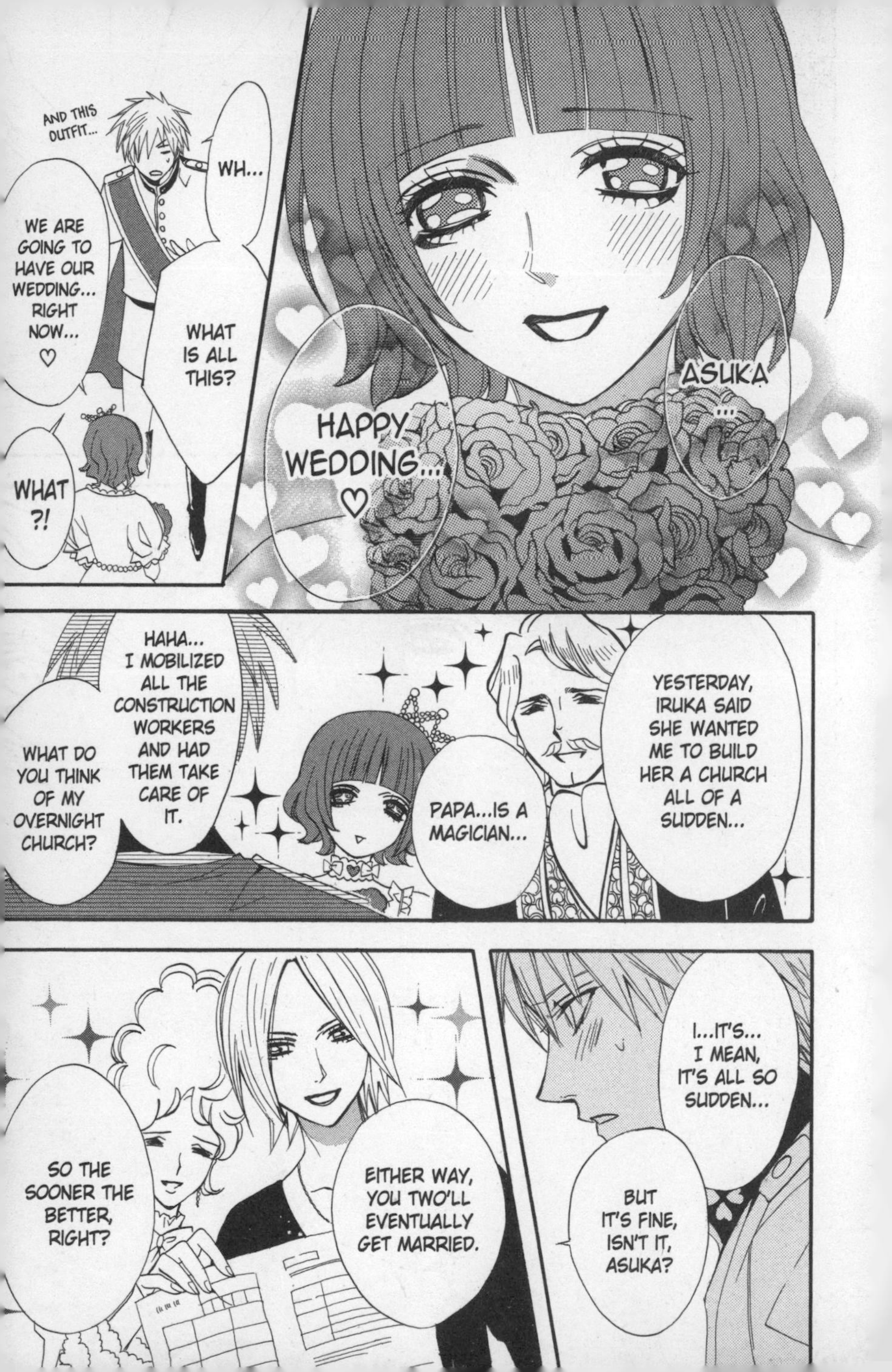

ASUKA...
HAPPY WEDDING... ♡
WH...
AND THIS OUTFIT...
WHAT IS ALL THIS?
WE ARE GOING TO HAVE OUR WEDDING... RIGHT NOW... ♡
WHAT ?!
YESTERDAY, IRUKA SAID SHE WANTED ME TO BUILD HER A CHURCH ALL OF A SUDDEN...
PAPA...IS A MAGICIAN...
HAHA... I MOBILIZED ALL THE CONSTRUCTION WORKERS AND HAD THEM TAKE CARE OF IT.
WHAT DO YOU THINK OF MY OVERNIGHT CHURCH?
I...IT'S... I MEAN, IT'S ALL SO SUDDEN...
BUT IT'S FINE, ISN'T IT, ASUKA?
EITHER WAY, YOU TWO'LL EVENTUALLY GET MARRIED.
SO THE SOONER THE BETTER, RIGHT?

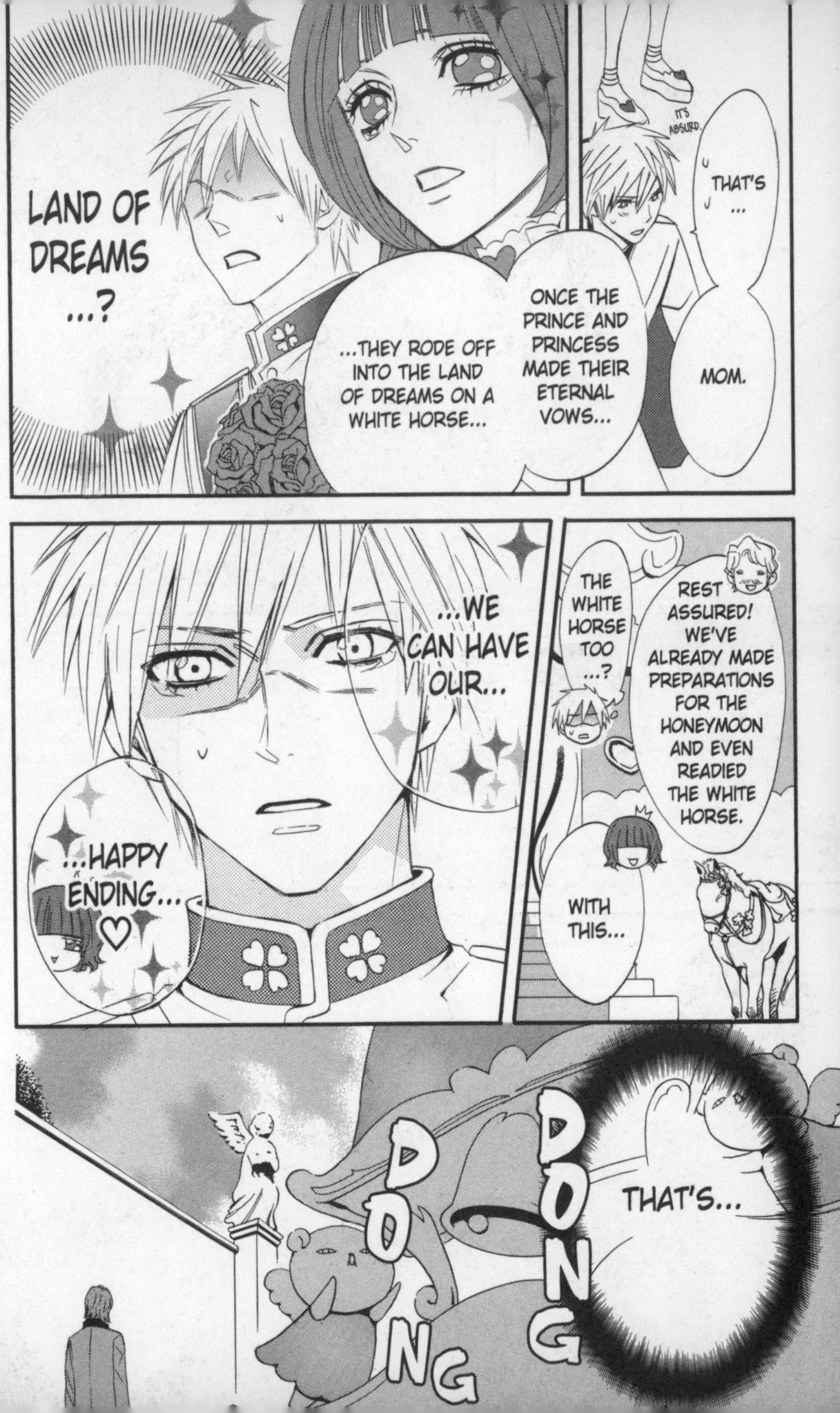
THAT'S ...
IT'S ABSURD.
MOM.
ONCE THE PRINCE AND PRINCESS MADE THEIR ETERNAL VOWS...
...THEY RODE OFF INTO THE LAND OF DREAMS ON A WHITE HORSE...
LAND OF DREAMS ...?
REST ASSURED! WE'VE ALREADY MADE PREPARATIONS FOR THE HONEYMOON AND EVEN READIED THE WHITE HORSE.
THE WHITE HORSE TOO ...?
WITH THIS...
...WE CAN HAVE OUR...
...HAPPY ENDING...♡
DONG
THAT'S...
DONG

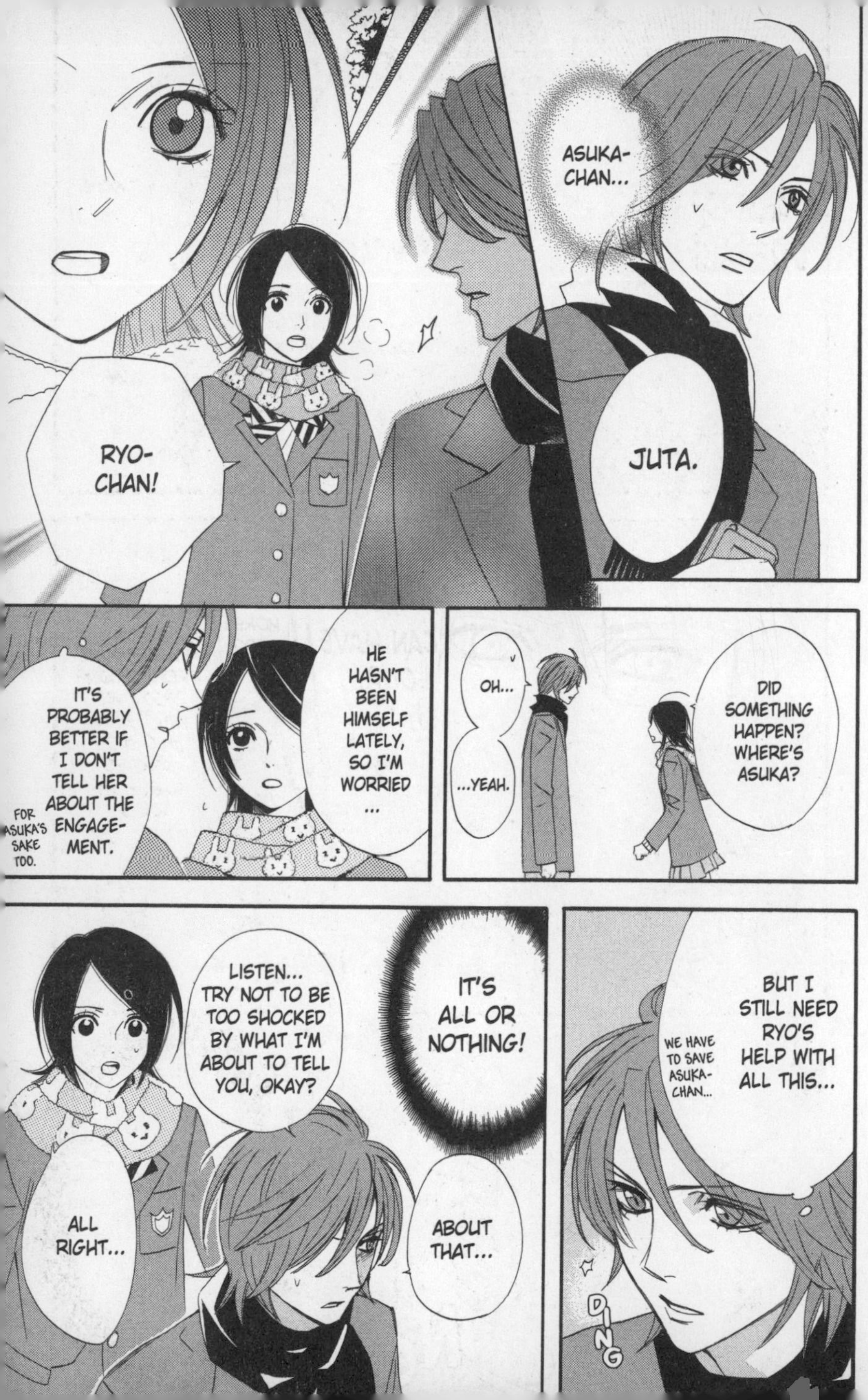

ASUKA-CHAN...
JUTA.
RYO-CHAN!
DID SOMETHING HAPPEN? WHERE'S ASUKA?
OH...
...YEAH.
HE HASN'T BEEN HIMSELF LATELY, SO I'M WORRIED...
IT'S PROBABLY BETTER IF I DON'T TELL HER ABOUT THE ENGAGE-MENT.
FOR ASUKA'S SAKE TOO.
BUT I STILL NEED RYO'S HELP WITH ALL THIS...
WE HAVE TO SAVE ASUKA-CHAN...
DING
IT'S ALL OR NOTHING!
LISTEN... TRY NOT TO BE TOO SHOCKED BY WHAT I'M ABOUT TO TELL YOU, OKAY?
ABOUT THAT...
ALL RIGHT...

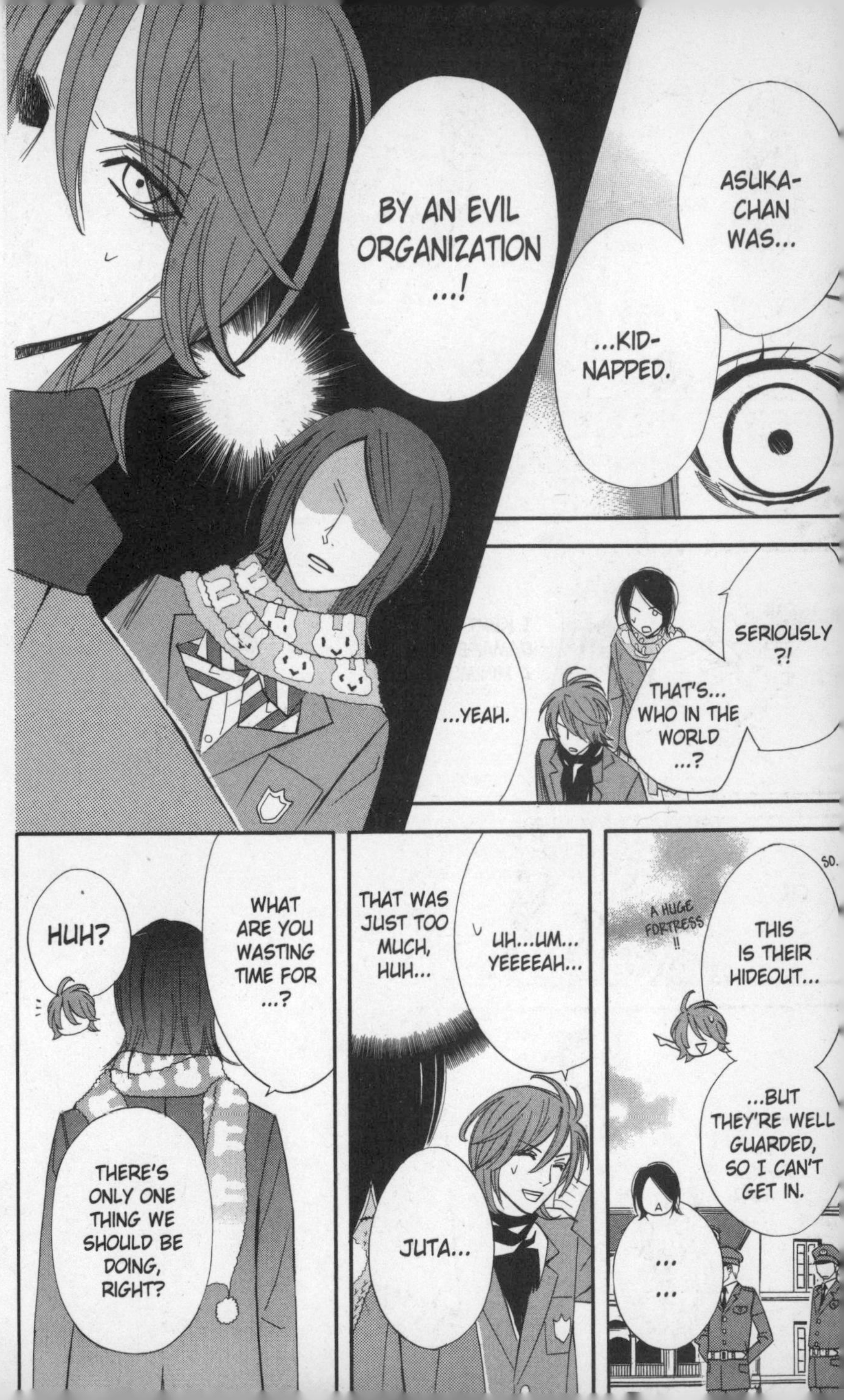
ASUKA-CHAN WAS...
...KID-NAPPED.
SERIOUSLY ?!
THAT'S... WHO IN THE WORLD ...?
...YEAH.
BY AN EVIL ORGANIZATION ...!
SO.
THIS IS THEIR HIDEOUT...
A HUGE FORTRESS !!
...BUT THEY'RE WELL GUARDED, SO I CAN'T GET IN.
... ...
UH...UM... YEEEEAH...
THAT WAS JUST TOO MUCH, HUH...
JUTA...
WHAT ARE YOU WASTING TIME FOR ...?
HUH?
THERE'S ONLY ONE THING WE SHOULD BE DOING, RIGHT?

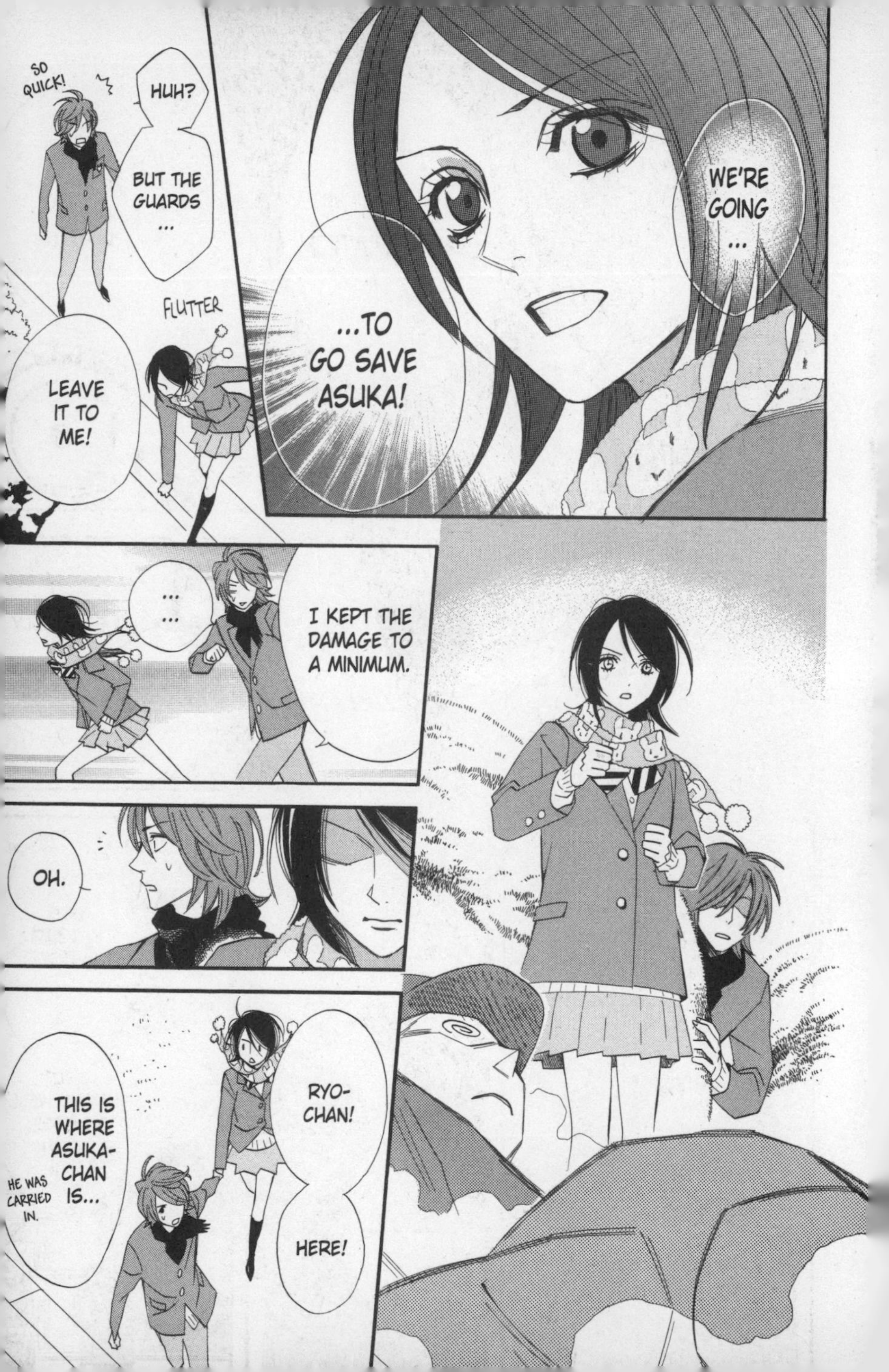
WE'RE GOING ...
...TO GO SAVE ASUKA!
HUH?
SO QUICK!
BUT THE GUARDS ...
FLUTTER
LEAVE IT TO ME!
I KEPT THE DAMAGE TO A MINIMUM.
... ...
OH.
RYO-CHAN!
HERE!
THIS IS WHERE ASUKA-CHAN IS...
HE WAS CARRIED IN.

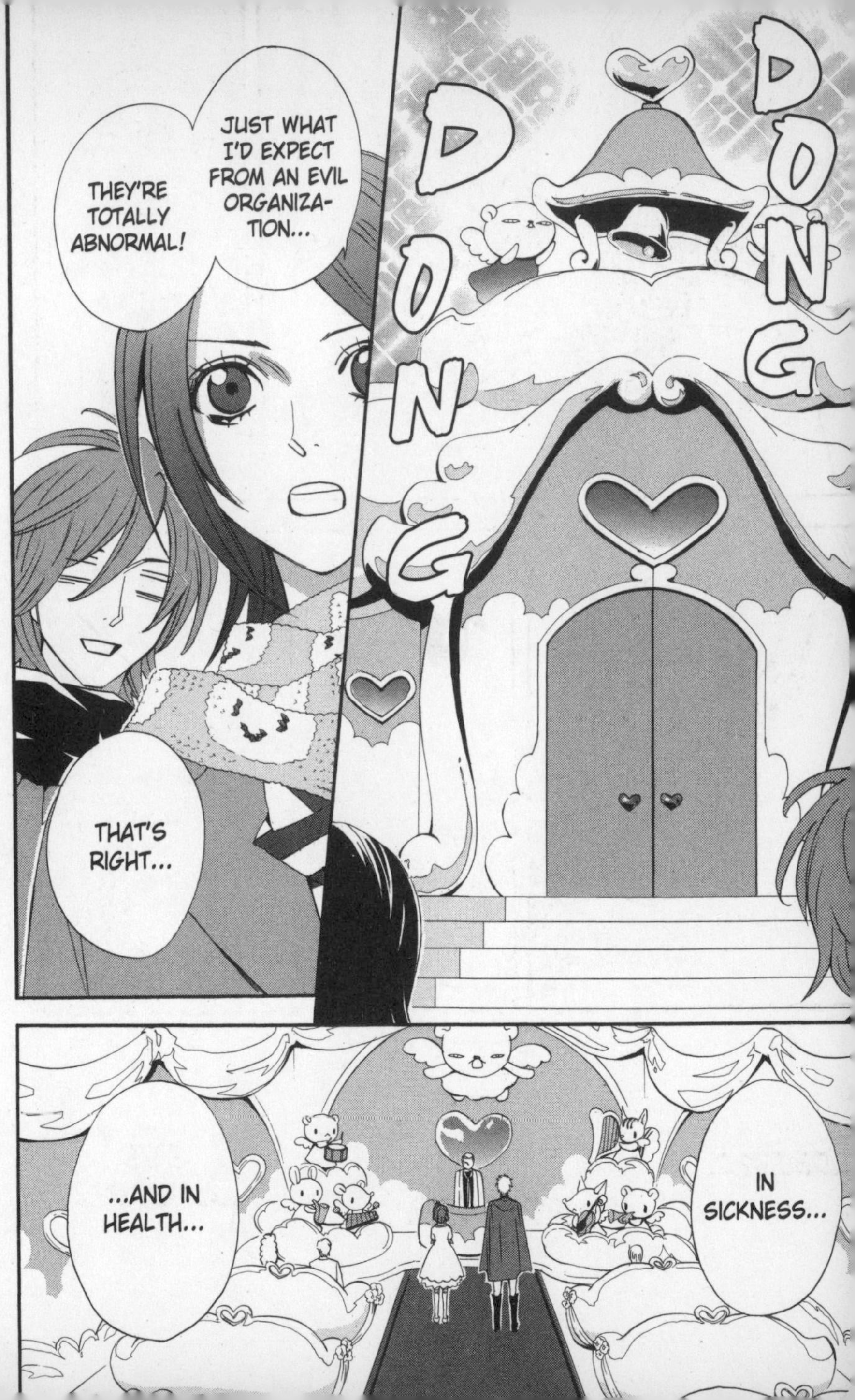
DONG
DONG
JUST WHAT I'D EXPECT FROM AN EVIL ORGANIZA-TION...
THEY'RE TOTALLY ABNORMAL!
THAT'S RIGHT...
IN SICKNESS...
...AND IN HEALTH...

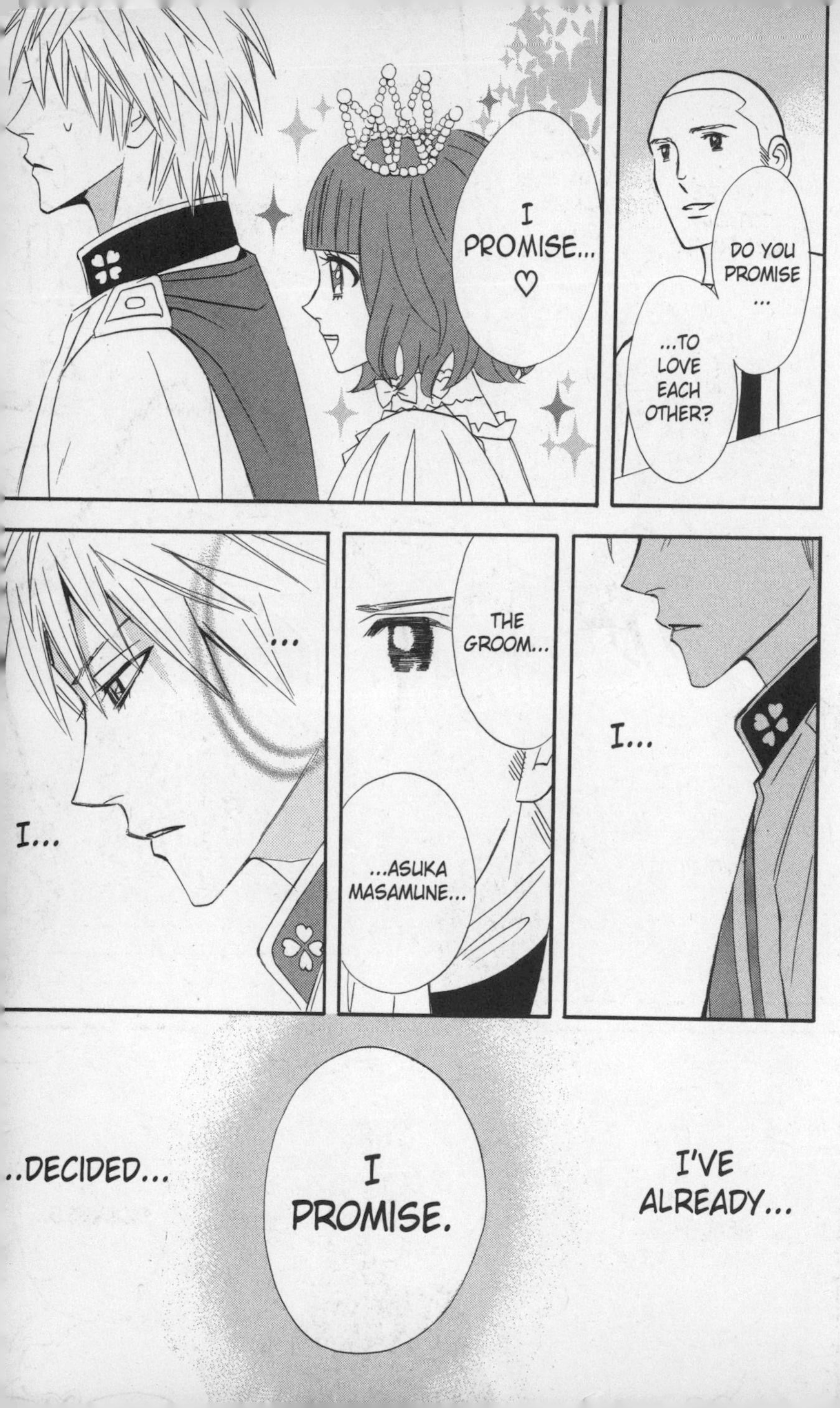
DO YOU PROMISE ...
...TO LOVE EACH OTHER?
I PROMISE... ♡
I...
THE GROOM...
...ASUKA MASAMUNE...
...
I...
I'VE ALREADY...
I PROMISE.
..DECIDED...

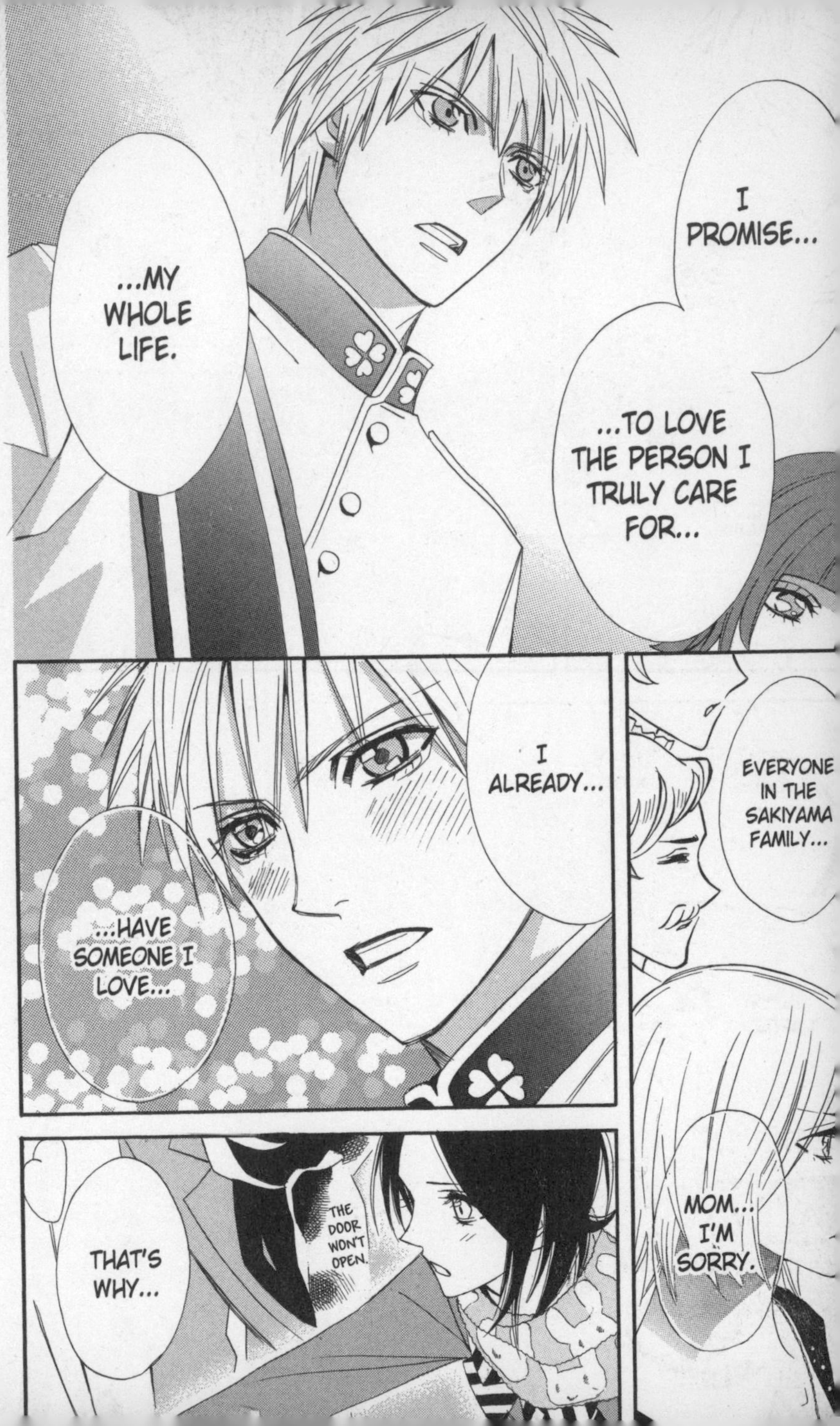
I PROMISE...
...TO LOVE THE PERSON I TRULY CARE FOR...
...MY WHOLE LIFE.
EVERYONE IN THE SAKIYAMA FAMILY...
MOM... I'M SORRY.
I ALREADY...
...HAVE SOMEONE I LOVE...
THE DOOR WON'T OPEN.
THAT'S WHY...

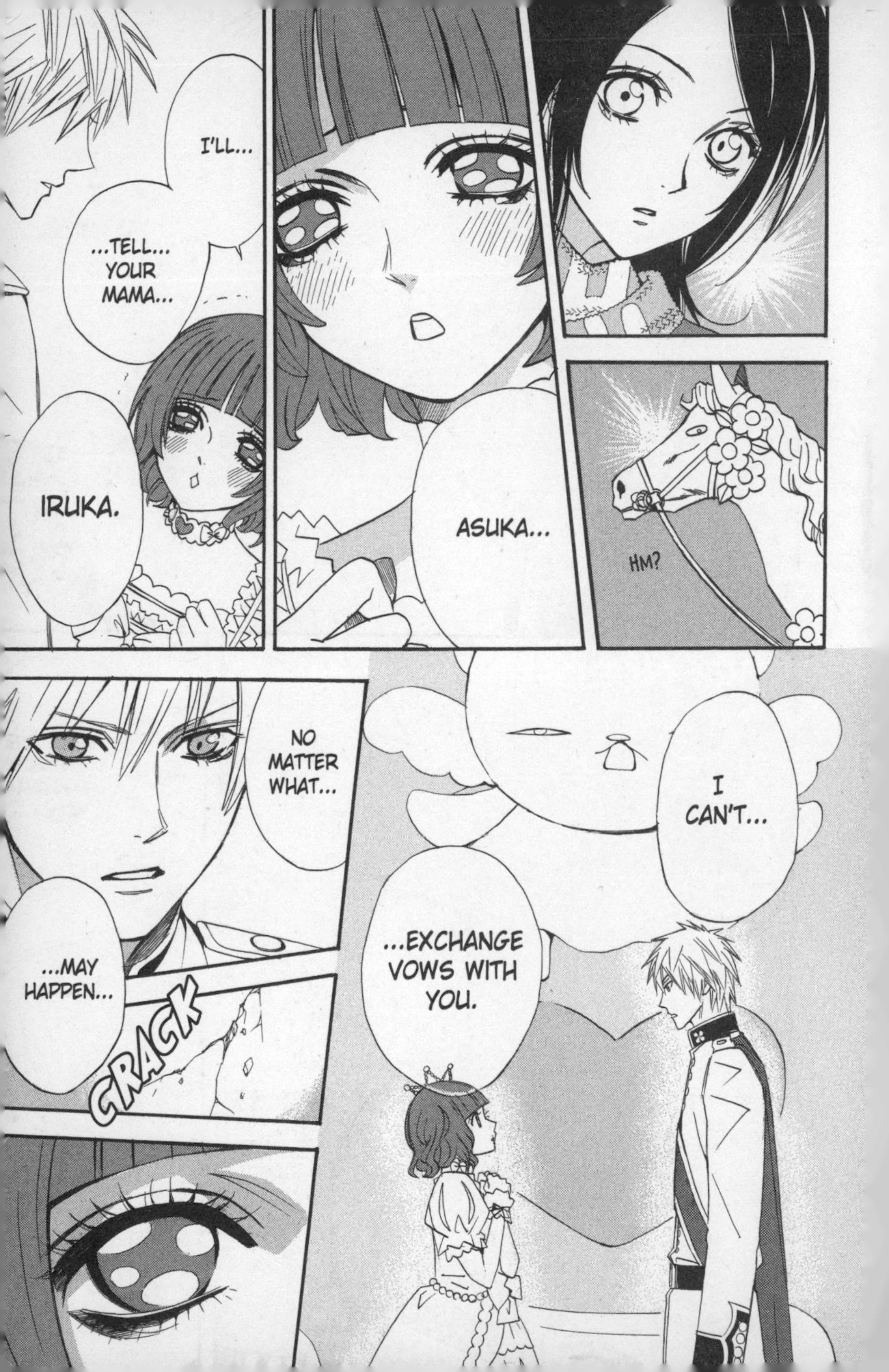
HM?
ASUKA...
I'LL...
...TELL... YOUR MAMA...
IRUKA.
I CAN'T...
...EXCHANGE VOWS WITH YOU.
NO MATTER WHAT...
...MAY HAPPEN...
CRACK

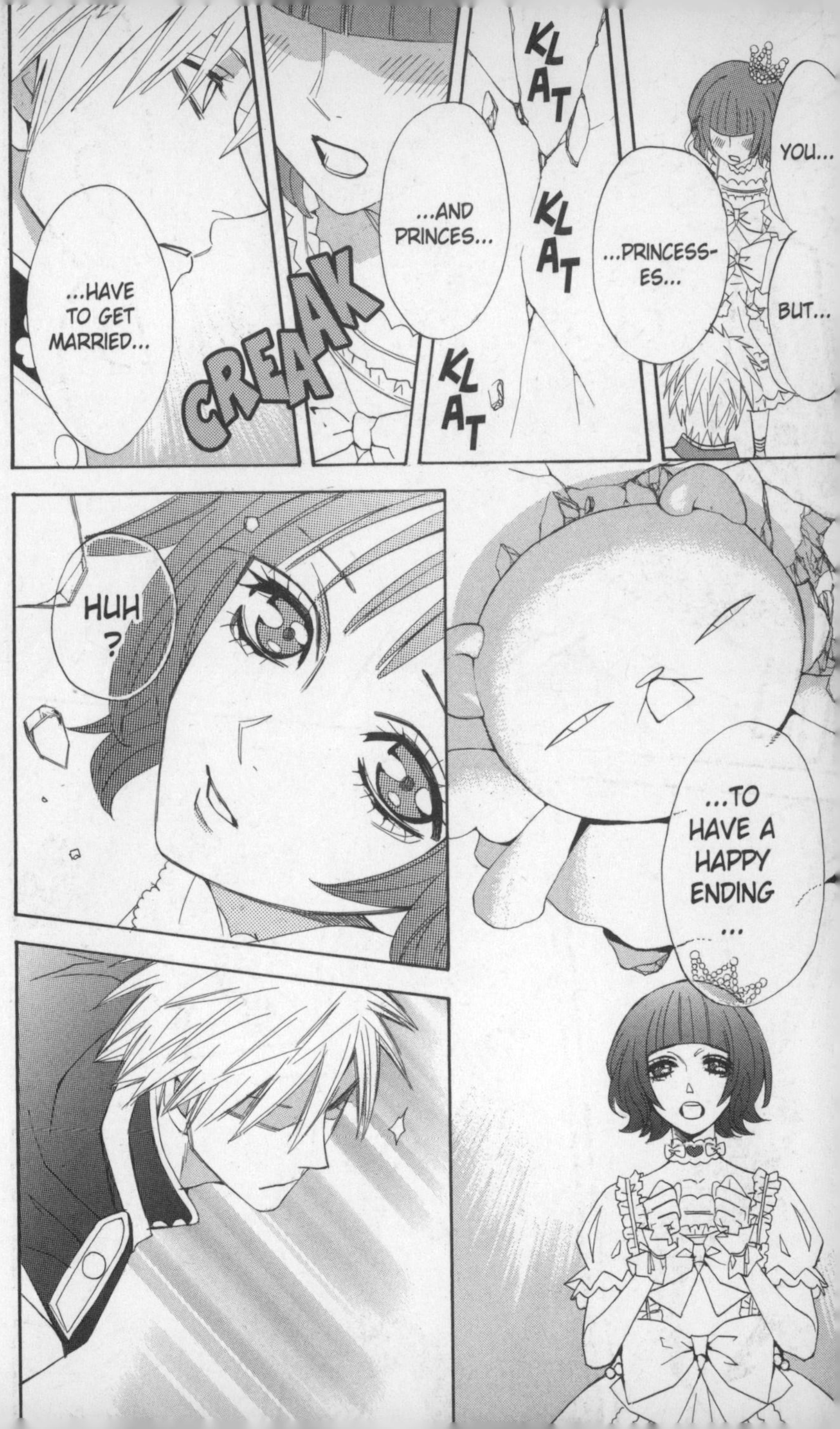
YOU...
BUT...
...PRINCESS-ES...
KLAT
KLAT
KLAT
...AND PRINCES...
CREAAK
...HAVE TO GET MARRIED...
...TO HAVE A HAPPY ENDING ...
HUH ?

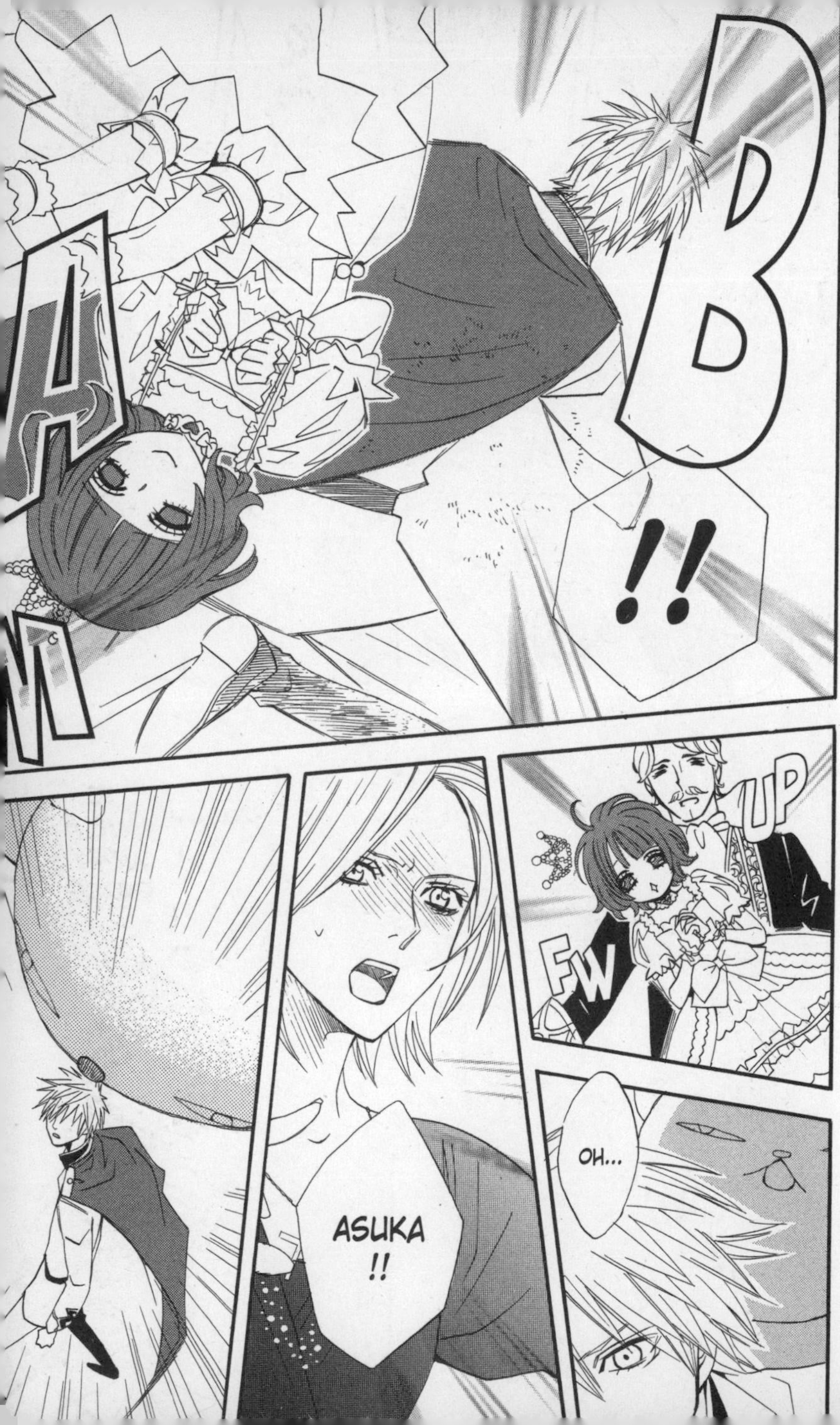
BAM
!!
FW UP
OH...
ASUKA !!

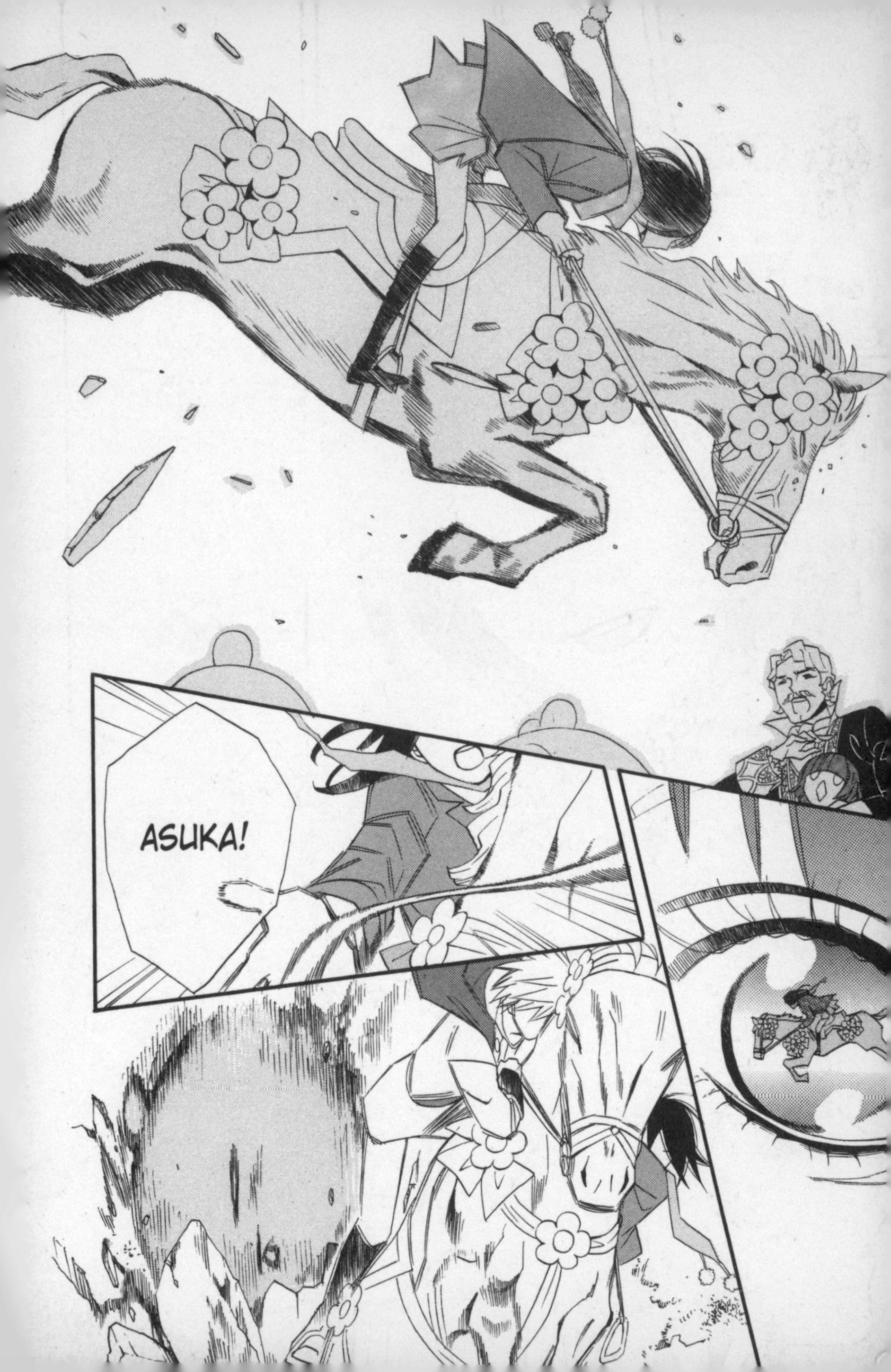
ASUKA!

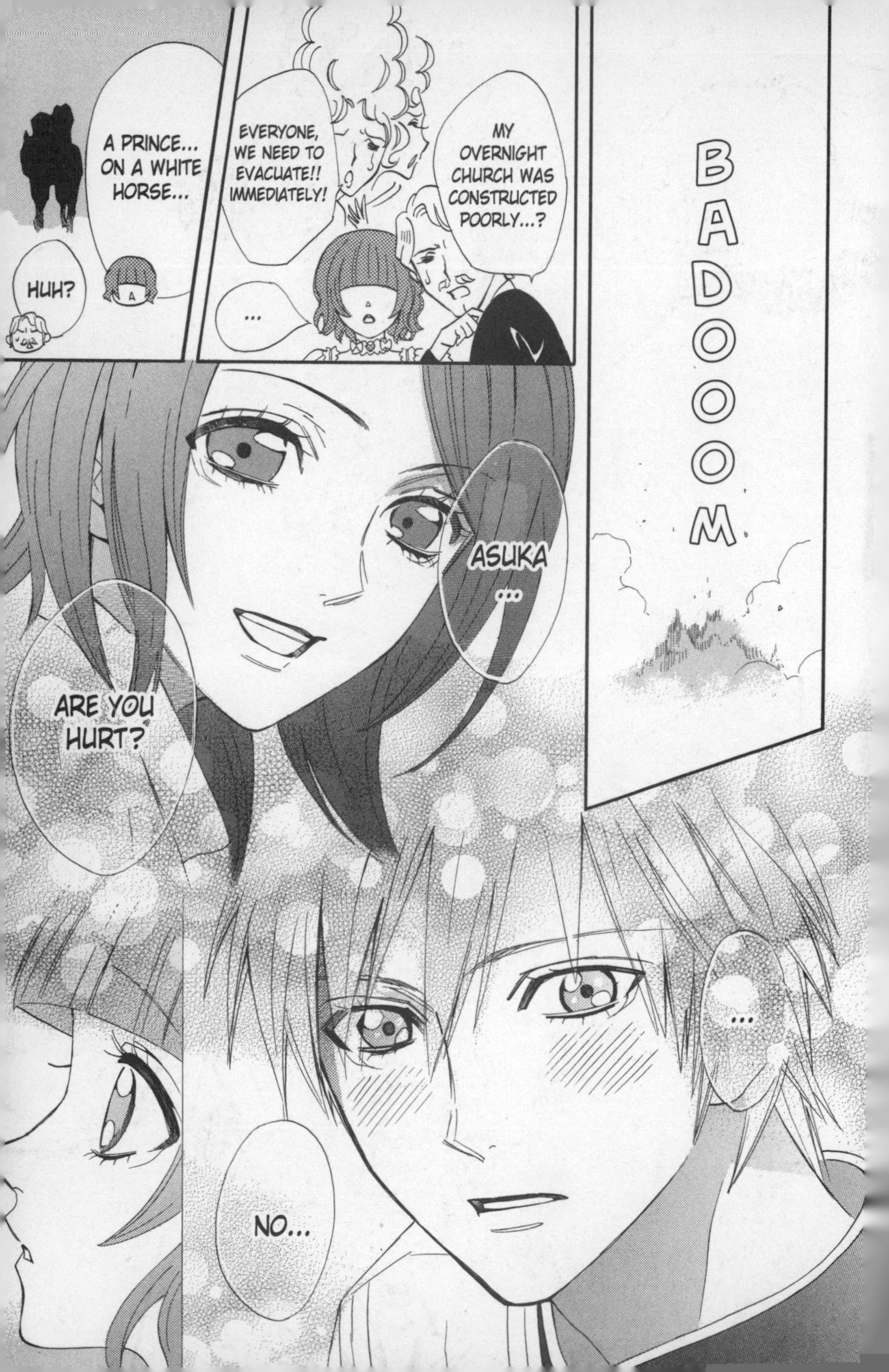

BADOOOOM
MY OVERNIGHT CHURCH WAS CONSTRUCTED POORLY...?
EVERYONE, WE NEED TO EVACUATE!! IMMEDIATELY!
...
A PRINCE... ON A WHITE HORSE...
HUH?
ASUKA ...
ARE YOU HURT?
...
NO...

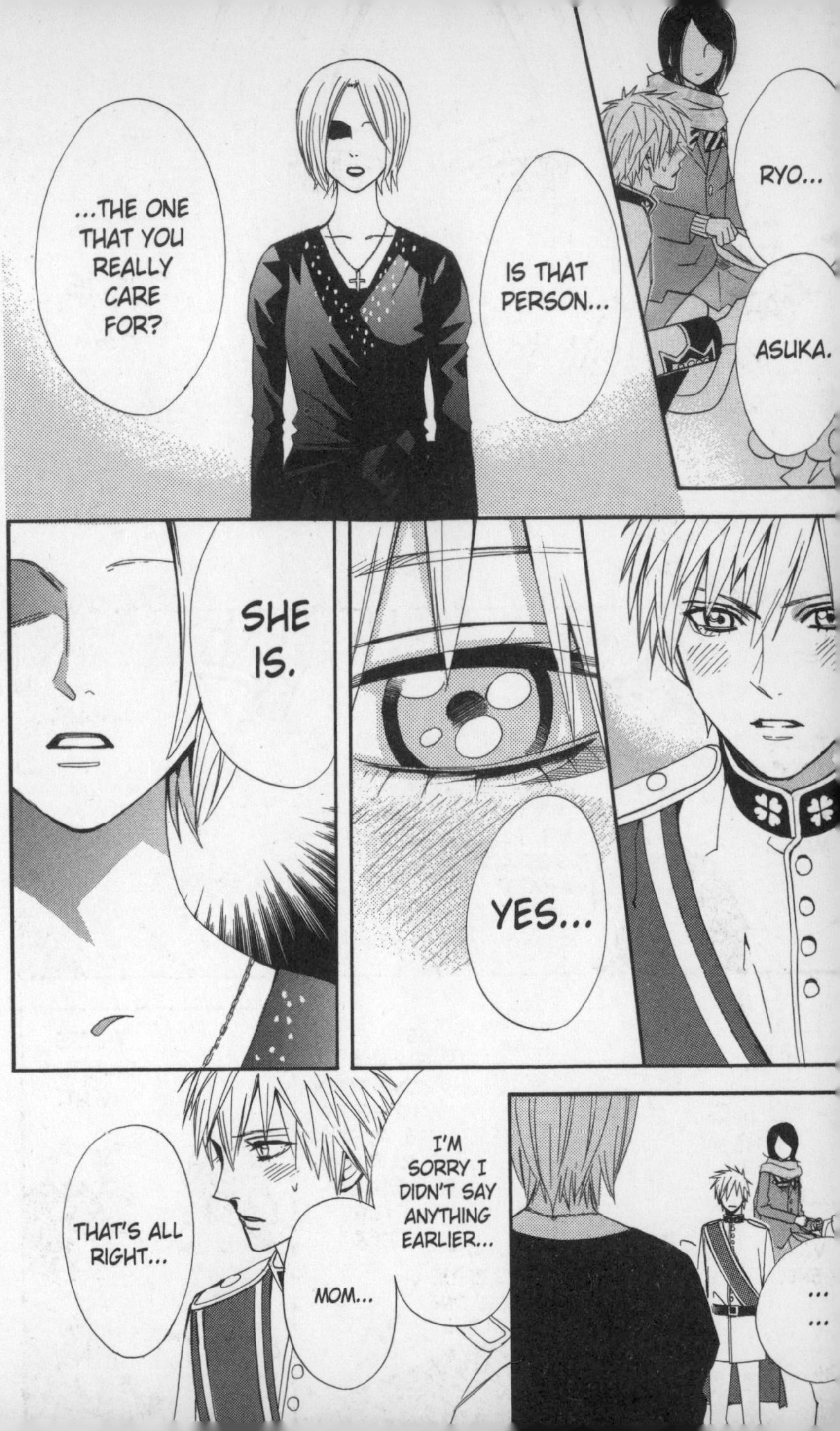
RYO...
ASUKA.
IS THAT PERSON...
...THE ONE THAT YOU REALLY CARE FOR?
YES...
SHE IS.
... ...
I'M SORRY I DIDN'T SAY ANYTHING EARLIER...
MOM...
THAT'S ALL RIGHT...

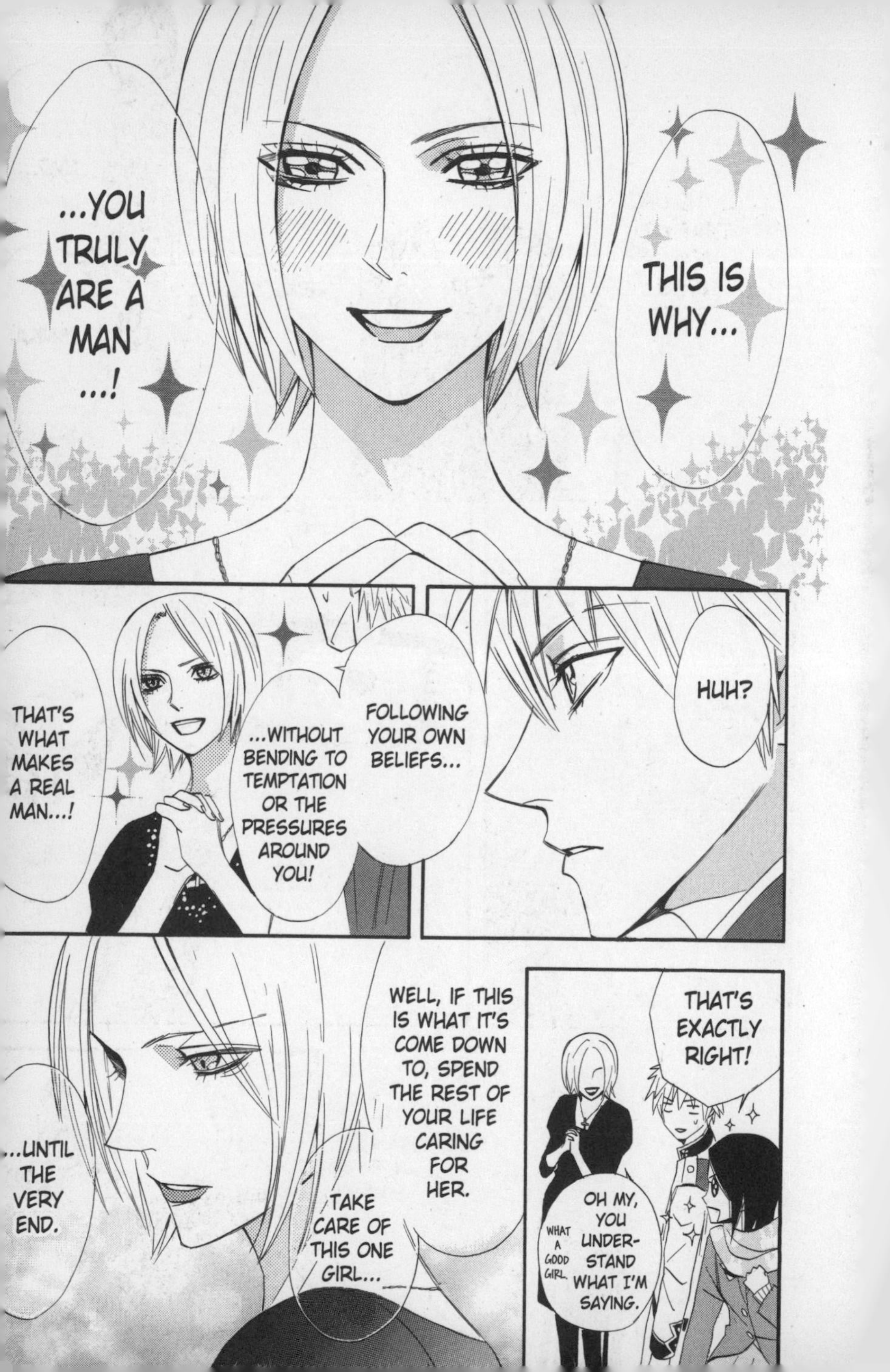
THIS IS WHY...
...YOU TRULY ARE A MAN ...!
HUH?
FOLLOWING YOUR OWN BELIEFS...
...WITHOUT BENDING TO TEMPTATION OR THE PRESSURES AROUND YOU!
THAT'S WHAT MAKES A REAL MAN...!
THAT'S EXACTLY RIGHT!
OH MY, YOU UNDERSTAND WHAT I'M SAYING.
WHAT A GOOD GIRL.
WELL, IF THIS IS WHAT IT'S COME DOWN TO, SPEND THE REST OF YOUR LIFE CARING FOR HER.
TAKE CARE OF THIS ONE GIRL...
...UNTIL THE VERY END.

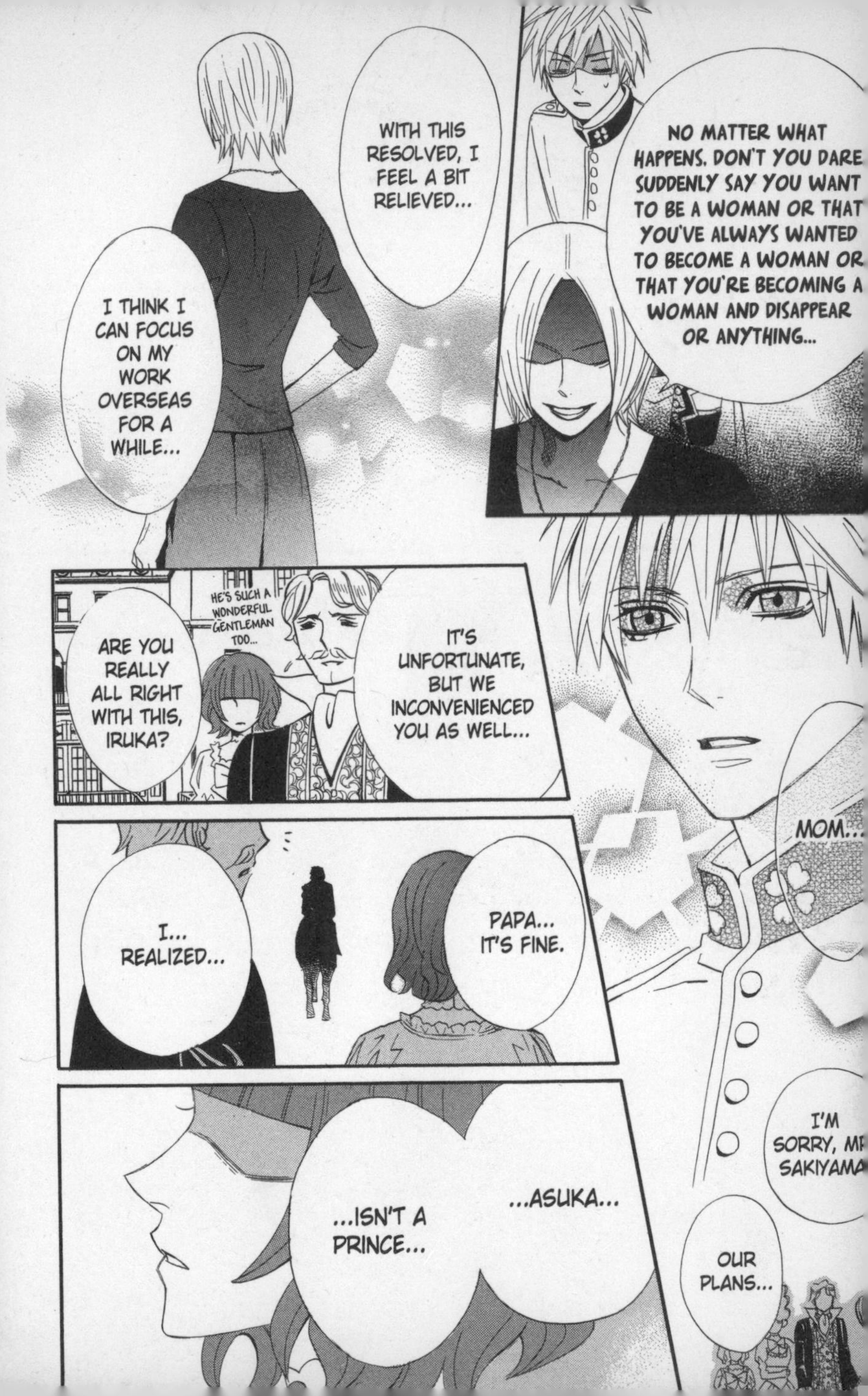
NO MATTER WHAT HAPPENS, DON'T YOU DARE SUDDENLY SAY YOU WANT TO BE A WOMAN OR THAT YOU'VE ALWAYS WANTED TO BECOME A WOMAN OR THAT YOU'RE BECOMING A WOMAN AND DISAPPEAR OR ANYTHING...
WITH THIS RESOLVED, I FEEL A BIT RELIEVED...
I THINK I CAN FOCUS ON MY WORK OVERSEAS FOR A WHILE...
MOM...
I'M SORRY, MR SAKIYAMA
OUR PLANS...
IT'S UNFORTUNATE, BUT WE INCONVENIENCED YOU AS WELL...
HE'S SUCH A WONDERFUL GENTLEMAN TOO...
ARE YOU REALLY ALL RIGHT WITH THIS, IRUKA?
PAPA... IT'S FINE.
I... REALIZED...
...ASUKA...
...ISN'T A PRINCE...

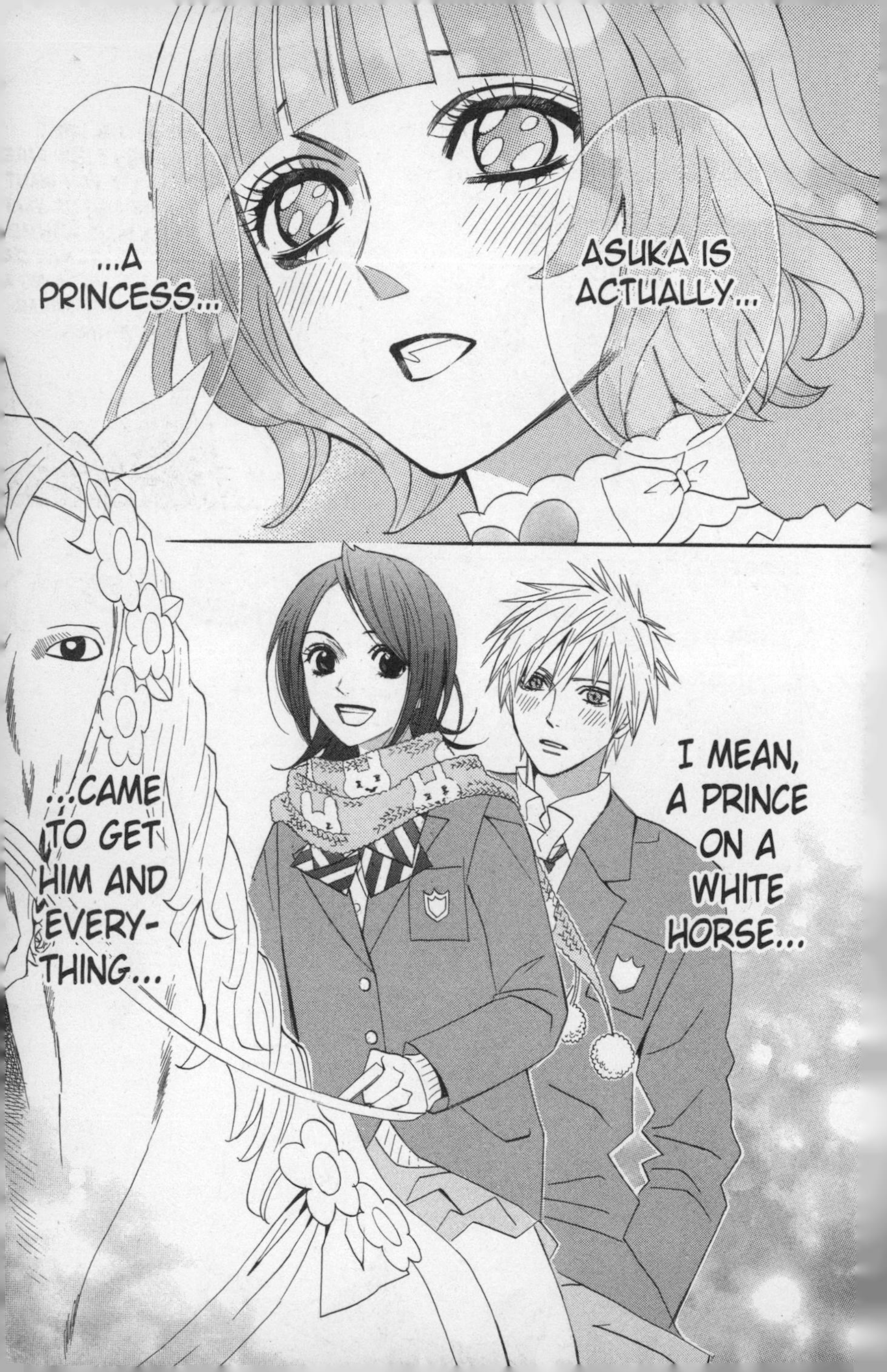
ASUKA IS ACTUALLY...
...A PRINCESS...
I MEAN, A PRINCE ON A WHITE HORSE...
...CAME TO GET HIM AND EVERY-THING...

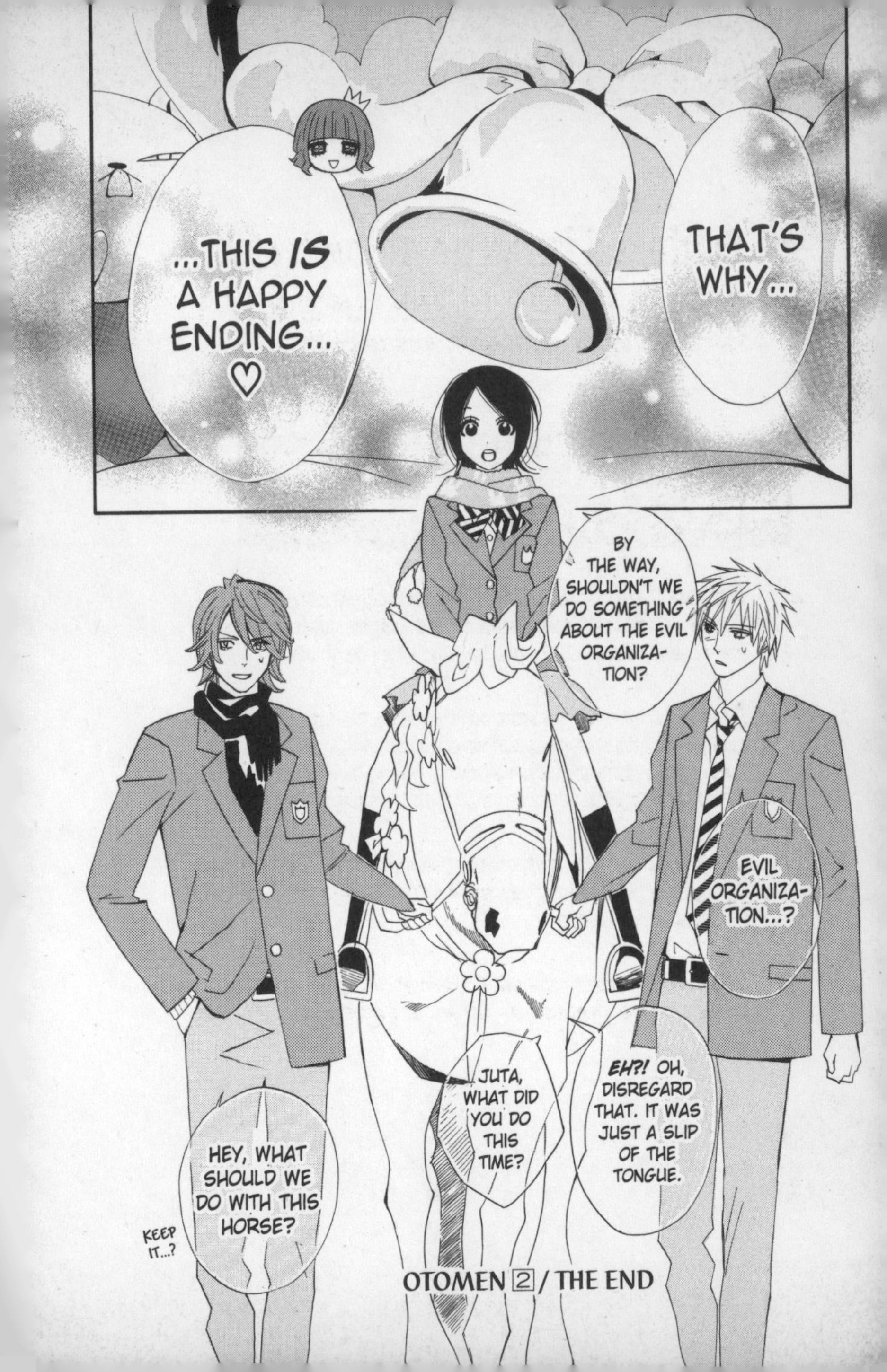
THAT'S WHY...
...THIS *IS* A HAPPY ENDING... ♡
BY THE WAY, SHOULDN'T WE DO SOMETHING ABOUT THE EVIL ORGANIZATION?
EVIL ORGANIZATION...?
*EH?!* OH, DISREGARD THAT. IT WAS JUST A SLIP OF THE TONGUE.
JUTA, WHAT DID YOU DO THIS TIME?
HEY, WHAT SHOULD WE DO WITH THIS HORSE?
KEEP IT...?

OTOMEN 2 / THE END

# Confused by some of the terms, but too MANLY to ask for help?

Here are some **cultural notes** to assist you!

# HONORIFICS

**Chan** – an informal honorific used to address children and females. *Chan* can also be used toward animals, lovers, intimate friends, and people whom one has known since childhood.

**Kun** – an informal honorific used primarily toward males. It can be used by people of more senior status addressing those junior to them or by anyone addressing boys or young men. Like *chan*, *kun* is often added to nicknames to emphasize friendship or intimacy.

**Senpai** – used to address one's senior colleagues or mentor figures. It is used when students refer to or address more senior students in their school.

**Sensei** – honorific title used to address teachers as well as professionals such as doctors, lawyers and artists.

### Page 16, panel 1 | **Hana to Mame**
The manga magazine that Asuka reads is called *Hana to Mame* (Flowers and Beans), a play on the *shojo manga* (girls' comics) magazine *Hana to Yume* (Flowers and Dreams) published by Hakusensha. The manga *Love Chick* that Asuka enjoys is serialized in *Hana to Mame*, and Juta is the secret author of that series.

### Page 19, panel 1 | **Bushido**
*Bushido* means "the way of the warrior" and is a code of conduct that emphasizes loyalty, bravery, sacrifice, faith, propriety, honor and simplicity. Yamato is specifically referring to the book *Bushido, the Soul of Japan* written by Inazo Nitobe.

### Page 22, panel 2 | **Men and Dou**
Two of the four strikes in kendo.

### Page 31, panel 3 | **Bento**
A lunch box that may contain rice, meat, pickles and an assortment of side dishes. Sometimes the food is arranged in such a way as to resemble objects like animals, flowers, leaves, and so forth.

### Page 89, panel 3 | **Hakkoda Mountains March**
In the winter of 1902, almost an entire infantry of soldiers died while crossing the Hakkoda Mountains for a military training exercise.

**Aya Kanno** was born in Tokyo, Japan.
She is the creator of *Soul Rescue* and *Blank Slate*
(originally published as *Akusaga* in Japan's
*BetsuHana* magazine). Her latest work, *Otomen*,
is currently being serialized in *BetsuHana*.

# OTOMEN

*Vol. 2*
The Shojo Beat Manga Edition

*Story and Art by* | **AYA KANNO**

*Translation & Adaptation* | **Lindsey Akashi**
*Touch-up Art & Lettering* | **Mark McMurray**
*Design* | **Fawn Lau**
*Editor* | **Amy Yu**

*Editor in Chief, Books* | **Alvin Lu**
*Editor in Chief, Magazines* | **Marc Weidenbaum**
*VP, Publishing Licensing* | **Rika Inouye**
*VP, Sales & Product Marketing* | **Gonzalo Ferreyra**
*VP, Creative* | **Linda Espinosa**
*Publisher* | **Hyoe Narita**

Otomen by Aya Kanno © Aya Kanno 2007
All rights reserved. First published in Japan in 2007 by HAKUSENSHA, Inc., Tokyo. English language
translation rights arranged with HAKUSENSHA, Inc., Tokyo. The stories, characters and incidents mentioned
in this publication are entirely fictional.

Printed in Canada

Published by VIZ Media, LLC
P.O. Box 77010
San Francisco, CA 94107

Shojo Beat Manga Edition
10 9 8 7 6 5 4 3 2 1
First printing, May 2009

www.viz.com

**PARENTAL ADVISORY**
OTOMEN is rated T for Teen and is recommended
for ages 13 and up. This volume contains
suggestive themes.
ratings.viz.com

store.viz.com